Planning, Scheduling, and Control Integration in the Process Industries

Other McGraw-Hill Engineering Books of Interest

Planning, Scheduling, and Control Integration in the Process Industries

C. Edward Bodington

McGraw-Hill, Inc.

New York   San Francisco   Washington, D.C.   Auckland   Bogotá
Caracas   Lisbon   London   Madrid   Mexico City   Milan
Montreal   New Delhi   San Juan   Singapore
Sydney   Tokyo   Toronto

Library of Congress Cataloging-in-Publication Data

Bodington, C. Edward.
   Planning, scheduling, and control integration in the process
   industries / C. Edward Bodington.
      p.   cm.
   ISBN 0-07-006413-X (alk. paper)
   1. Production planning.   2. Production control.   3. Scheduling
   (Management) I. Title.
   TS176.B62   1995
   658.5—dc20   95-3079
                                                     CIP

1 2 3 4 5 6 7 8 9 0 DOC/DOC 9 0 0 9 8 7 6 5

ISBN 0-07-006413-X

*The sponsoring editor for this book was Gail Nalven, the editing
supervisor was Bernard Onken, and the production supervisor was
Donald Schmidt. It was set in Century Schoolbook by Dina E. John
of McGraw-Hill's Professional Book Group composition unit.*

Printed and bound by R. R. Donnelley & Sons Company.

McGraw-Hill books are available at special quantity discounts to use
as premiums and sales promotions, or for use in corporate training programs. For more information, please write to the Director of Special
Sales, McGraw-Hill, Inc., 11 West 19th Street, New York, NY 10011.
Or contact your local bookstore.

This book is printed on recycled, acid-free paper containing a minimum
of 50% recycled de-inked paper.

Contents

Part 2   Implementation and Justification

Part 3   Examples of Integrated Systems

Preface

This book is for people who work in the process industries or who are preparing to do so. Almost everyone who works in the industry started out trained in some limited facet of its operations. We were trained in chemical engineering or control engineering or some other specialty, and we were given little preparation for something such as an integration project that will combine the skills and professions of many people. This book is designed to fill the need for an uncomplicated exposition of the elements that go into an integrated system and how the elements should work together.

Over the last few years, most companies have become aware that improvement in the performance of the supply chain from customer order to product delivery is essential to their continued success or even survival as a business. In many process industry businesses, there is an organizational and operational gap in the supply chain between planning for the business and control of processes to meet commitments. Filling the gap is a prerequisite to improving the supply chain, and that is the subject matter of this book. We are going to describe the use of computers and computer systems to integrate the production functions in the process industries. The main functions to be integrated are the *planning* of what is to be produced, *scheduling* of the operations and inventories over time, and *controlling* of the processes themselves to meet commitments.

By restricting the subject matter to just the main production functions, we clearly leave out numerous computer applications in other functional areas. Some of these other applications even may have the same names as the functions covered by this text. In some people's terminology, the terms *planning* and *scheduling* are used interchangeably and *controlling* means the functions of the accounting department.

Thus, we need to start out with clear definitions that we are going to write about:

Planning of process operations to meet product demands

Scheduling feeds, products, and inventories over time

Controlling processes to meet commitments

Integrating these functions via computer systems

We are not writing about planning for engineering and construction, scheduling of maintenance projects, or control of the budget. We grant that these areas are very important, but we also note that they are covered very well in the literature and in fact by many specific computer applications. For example, the design of process plants is one of the major development areas in the field of virtual reality, allowing a design engineer to "walk through" the planned process plant and "see" interferences and awkward equipment placement.

Our subject functions of planning, scheduling, and controlling are also the target of myriad computer applications, going back almost to the time of the invention of the computer. What is not commonplace is the integration of these functions so that they can work well together. Some companies are now working toward this integration as a goal. Articles are beginning to appear that discuss integration in general terms as a desirable objective. This text gives specific advice and recommendations on integration from people who are now working in industry, developing and implementing integrated systems. We want to help companies in the industry justify integration projects and implement them in less time and with greater confidence of a successful outcome.

In Part 1, each chapter will cover one of the elements or building blocks that an integrated system requires to function. Chapter 2, by Dr. J. P. Kennedy, is about process information systems and communications that are needed to collect, refine, and allow analysis of process data. Kennedy is the president of Oil Systems, Inc., of San Leandro, California. With his company, Dr. Kennedy has developed the PI system for data acquisition, storage, communication, and analysis. The PI system has been installed in more than 600 industrial sites worldwide.

Chapter 3, by Kirk Williams, is about database systems and information management needed to store and allow transfer of information between functions. Williams joined British Petroleum (BP) in Australia in 1977 and held positions in process engineering, process control, and planning before becoming project coordinator for the refinery information system at BP's Brisbane refinery. He was responsible for all aspects of their integrated planning, scheduling, control, and information project. In 1990, he was appointed to BP's European Systems Project as a project manager. He joined

Chesapeake Decision Sciences, Inc., in 1994 as their European projects manager.

Chapter 4 is on data reconciliation procedures that are needed to maintain the high quality of any data collected and to tune models of the processes so that they will make accurate predictions. Chap. 4 was written by C. E. Bodington and Gerard W. Cleaves. Cleaves is business development manager for Chesapeake Decision Sciences. Formerly, he worked for Exxon Corporation where, among several other assignments, he implemented data reconciliation projects in Exxon refineries.

Chapter 5 covers advanced process control systems. These systems represent the ultimate user of information provided by planning and scheduling. The authors of Chap. 5 are Carol R. Aronson and John A. Gudaz. Aronson is a director in the Hydrocarbon Processing Division at Setpoint, Inc., of Houston, Texas. She has participated in many advanced control system projects for Setpoint in North America, Europe, the United Kingdom, and Scandanavia. Her most recent assignment has been with Statoil in Norway. Prior to joining Setpoint, she helped develop and lead implementations of the first distributed batch control system at EMC Controls, Inc., and implemented polymer control systems at E. I. Du Pont de Nemours & Company. Gudaz is an independent consultant with extensive experience in the design and implementation of control systems in a wide range of process settings. He has been recently associated with Yokagowa Electric Corporation, where he was the chief architect of their Centum-CS distributed digital systems. Prior to working with Yokagowa, he was cofounder and vice president of CPRC and a vice president of EMC Controls, where he was the major developer of their EMCON D/3 distributed digital control system. He also implemented numerous projects while with Foxboro Company and previously with Taylor Instrument Company.

Chapter 6 covers scheduling technology and the interpretation of planning results into the schedule so that the plan and schedule are in agreement. Chap. 6 is authored by Dr. Donald E. Shobrys, manager of the Houston office of Chesapeake Decision Sciences, Inc. Shobrys has participated in the installation of scheduling systems in numerous refining, petrochemical, and manufacturing situations. Prior to joining Chesapeake, Shobrys worked for Exxon Corporation.

Chapter 7 on planning covers present-day practice in the petroleum industry, process modeling, linearization of models, and many other topics. Much of this material has never been presented in book form before. Chap. 7 was written by James N. Fisher and James W. Zellhart. Fisher is an independent consultant in the planning field, working for both industry and government. He has had a long career in process planning, working for Tidewater Oil Company, Bonner and Moore Associates, Bechtel, Inc., and most recently Chevron Corporation. He is also an associate of the Bechtel PIMS Group. Zellhart is presently a senior analyst working on planning systems development for Chevron Information Technology Company. He has applied linear and nonlinear programming to a wide variety of planning applications. Zellhart joined Chevron after its merger with Gulf Oil Corporation, where he was also involved in planning systems and process simulation.

Chapter 8 on expert systems is authored by Joseph F. Faccenda and Duncan A. Rowan, both of E. I. Du Pont de Nemours & Company. Faccenda is a consultant in the operations research group of Du Pont. He consults in the areas of business planning, supply chain analysis, operations analysis, and process optimization. Much of his work involves technologies of optimization, simulation, and expert systems. He has been with Du Pont for 15 years. Rowan is also an internal consultant and has worked in the area of advanced process control for 20 years with Du Pont. He performs process control studies using simulations, develops control strategies, and applies computer control systems. He has been actively applying on-line expert systems to processes for the last nine years. Applications include real-time diagnosis, process transition management, and production scheduling. He has also applied neural network technology to inferential process measurement and control, and he contributed a chapter to the Instrument Society of America's *Artificial Intelligence Handbook*.

Chapter 9 on detailed process modeling is written by C. E. Bodington. The chapter describes all facets of a model development project. Database generation, analysis, model form selection, and parameter estimation are all discussed. Bodington is an independent consultant specializing in process modeling and optimization for the process industries. He is also an associate of Chesapeake Decision Sciences. Prior to becoming a consultant, Bodington worked 32 years for Chevron Research Company, where he was the supervisor of the Optimization and Planning Systems Group and, more recently, of the Process Control Engineering Group.

Chapter 10 on management is a review by C. E. Bodington of current issues regarding the organizational structure that should be in place for a successful implementation of the integration project and the relationship of the project to employee training activities, safety, environmental issues, and quality management.

Part 2, composed of Chaps. 11 through 13, describes an emerging consensus about the way in which the elements of Part 1 should be connected in order to have a successful project. Part 2 establishes a way of thinking about or analyzing integration projects, and it includes a chapter on financial justification.

Part 3, composed of Chaps. 14 through 18, republishes papers from several different companies describing integration projects that they consider successful. Each paper was delivered at a meeting of either the American Institute of Chemical Engineers (AIChE) or the National Petroleum Refiners Association (NPRA). The source is given with each chapter. In some cases, the chapters have been updated by the authors to reflect the current status of the project. Each chapter is preceded by a discussion of the project, using the integration concepts presented in Part 2. Several additional papers about integration projects in the process industries are named in the references to Chap. 14 and are well worth study.

One of the great stumbling blocks inhibiting integration of these functions is *jargon*. Each field of endeavor communicates within itself much more efficiently by the use of field-specific jargon, well known to those in the field. Producing a jargonless text would help readers understand all the subject matter. However, one does not learn Chinese by studying translations. Consequently, the text includes all the jargon, but with precise definitions when terms are first presented. The Glossary defines jargon and other terms used in the text. This alone should help communication between members of the various fields who must work together in an integrated system. After all, communication is what it is all about.

Integration of planning, scheduling, and control could be thought of as a subset of *computer-integrated manufacturing* (CIM) applied to the process industries. However, use of the term *CIM* has not been very precise; it seems to have been applied to any project that uses information technology to integrate what would otherwise be islands of automation. The term has been replaced with the concept of *supply chain optimization* or integration of the business process from customer order through product manufacture and delivery. The integration of planning, scheduling, and control is then seen to be a stepping stone or prerequisite to supply chain optimization.

The purpose of this book is to provide insight into the various elements that comprise the integrated system and the considerations that are important in the integration. No one person is expert in all the technologies that these elements represent and that must be welded together to produce a successful integration, and therefore optimization, of a process industry business. The contributed chapters bring together the combined wisdom of people with years of experience in each of the elements needed in an integrated system—people who are now successfully implementing their parts of such systems in a wide variety of circumstances.

C. E. Bodington

ABOUT THE AUTHOR

C. Edward Bodington is an independent consultant who previously worked for 32 years at Chevron Research Company, where he was for many years the supervisor of the Optimization and Planning Systems Group, and also of the Process Control Engineering Group. At present, his consulting is in the field of computer integration of production functions for the process industries. He is also an associate of Chesapeake Decision Sciences, Inc., where he is a presenter of their seminars on functional integration. He holds chemical engineering degrees from Stanford University and the Massachusetts Institute of Technology. He resides in San Anselmo, California.

Acknowledgments

Working with the contributors and writing several chapters myself has been a stimulating and rewarding experience. To the contributors, who were introduced in the Preface, I give much praise for their excellent work. Carol Aronson, Dr. Pat Kennedy, Dr. Don Shobrys, and Kirk Williams deserve extra praise for their helpful reviews of several chapters. I also acknowledge the assistance and counsel of Dr. Tom Baker, president of Chesapeake Decision Sciences, and Gerry Cleaves and Jeff Howard, also of Chesapeake; Mrs. Benita Gray, who helped me understand how to put together a book based on contributions from several authors; Gail F. Nalven of McGraw-Hill, my editor, who really got this whole project started in the first place; and my wife, Helen, without whose help, encouragement, and careful proofreading I probably would not have persevered and to whom this book is dedicated.

The Elements

Introduction

C. Edward Bodington
Consultant

In the mid-1950s, computers were just beginning to be used for process calculations. It was clear immediately that personal productivity could be increased by computer use, which avoided many hours spent at desk calculators. Better solutions (i.e., more profitable or lower-cost ones) were obtained, more alternatives were explored, and more rigorous approaches were taken. As a result of the increased productivity and improved economic performance, the refining and petrochemical industries were attracted to computer use in almost every facet of the business.

Those who have been around long enough remember the monthly runs of the accounting and payroll systems on the only mainframe computer available in the company. These hours-long computer runs are remembered because those people not involved with accounting could not get near the machine until the runs were completed. The irritation was somewhat assuaged by the knowledge that the mainframe system was printing our paychecks.

In those days, computer use for financial data processing was quite advanced compared to the use for process calculations. However, by the end of the 1950s, there was significant use of computers for planning, process modeling, and design (Symonds, 1955; Garvin et al., 1957).

Several companies developed simulation programs that calculated plant performance and predicted the plant products, given a set of operating conditions and any other needed input. The companies developed their own mathematical models for the processes. The models were a computerization of the charts, tables, and correlations that had been developed over the years for use by hand, via the slide rule or desk calculator, in process design and engineering. These simulators would calculate from crude input through each process in turn, feeding results from process to process until the final plant products were estimated.

These programs were very useful for planning and for analytical uses. For example, an analytical study would determine the effect of a new feedstock or a new process on the existing plant. Companies developed these programs totally in-house; there were no commercial programs available. Some internal development concentrated on applications of the optimization technique of linear programming and used them for operations planning and gasoline blending (Bodington and Baker, 1990).

Figure 1.1 shows the hierarchy of computer applications from the customer and supplier level down to planning. Computer applications down to the planning level were already well advanced by the end of the 1950s. Improvement in the sophistication of these applications has been continuous. Every process industry business has computer applications for customer order handling and invoicing, accounting, payroll, personnel, planning, supply and distribution, maintenance, etc. Many of these applications work well together with the help of data communications and database technologies. In a plant, the planning tools may be able both to directly access inventory, supply, and demand quantities and economic parameters and to share results

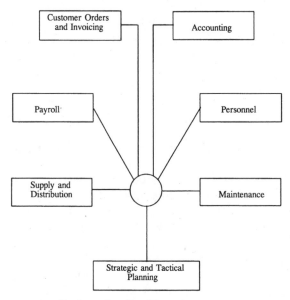

Figure 1.1 Business function hierarchy.

with other plants and the main office. However, many of these applications do not work well together. They are "islands of automation," each with its own distinct users, supporters, hardware, and software.

At the individual process level, computer use was later in getting started. Some hardware for data acquisition was developed in the 1950s. The first installations that performed process optimization were made in the late 1950s (Griffith and Stewart, 1961). Since those days, hardware and software for process control have undergone several reinventions, resulting in today's incredibly powerful *distributed control systems* (DCSs). These developments were parallel in time, but completely separate from developments in the business and planning area. The process control systems were produced by separate manufacturers, or divisions within a manufacturer, from those who produced computers for business and planning applications. Within user companies, separate groups of people worked with the two different kinds of hardware and software. These groups had different short- and long-term objectives and rarely talked to each other. Except for occasional conflicts over computer hardware purchases, each group hardly knew that the other existed.

By the 1980s it became apparent that there was a troublesome gap between the planning and controlling functions (Baker and Shobrys, 1985; Van Horn, 1985). The process control operators and the operations planners realized that they did not agree on the best way to run the processes. Control operators had a difficult time trying to relate planning results to their hour-by-hour situation. Planners had no good way to take advantage of the power of the advanced control systems on the processes, and they received no real feedback on the effects of their decisions. It was realized that optimization of the business could not truly be achieved unless planning, scheduling, and control could be brought into agreement.

In the 1990s, the gap is being bridged, and a consensus is emerging about how to get planning, scheduling, and control to work together successfully. Through the technologies of database management, data communications networks, and open-systems concepts, it is now possible for these functions to reliably communicate data and information. However, planning, scheduling, and control are fundamentally different in technology and in concept. Integrating these functions is a nontrivial task, involving both technical and organizational aspects. The demands for continuously improving productivity and economic performance require companies to close the gap. Integrated planning, scheduling, and control projects will be initiated at an accelerating rate over the next decade.

A description of the technologies needed to integrate the planning, scheduling, and control functions and of how they can be made to work together harmoniously is the subject matter of this book. The text will describe the integration of *planning* what is to be produced, *scheduling* the operations and inventories over time, and *controlling* the processes themselves, to meet commitments. To begin, let us define these terms in detail.

Planning is the forecasting of the average performance of a plant (a collection of interconnected processes) over some specified period, such as a month or a year. The plan specifies what inputs are needed and how they are to be used to produce the plant outputs. The plan usually includes forecasts of the values of individual process performance parameters such as yields, product qualities, flow rates, temperatures, and pressures. The modern plan also includes economic information about the impact of changes in parameters on plant profitability.

Scheduling is the specification of the inputs to and outputs from each process and inventory, plus the timing and sequencing of each production operation, whether batch or continuous, over some short scheduling period, such as a week or 10 days. Although the horizon is a week or 10 days, today's operation is the most important. Operations are not averaged over the scheduling period; rather, time and operations move continuously from the beginning of the period to the end. Ideally, the schedule is revised each day as needed so that it always starts from current actual performance.

Control is both the second-by-second regulation of each process in response to known and unknown disturbance patterns and the economic optimization of each process within the context of the plan and schedule. Regulatory control is the lowest level in the control hierarchy in which the objectives are usually stable operation and safety. *Advanced control* is a term that covers a multitude of higher-level techniques such as multivariable predictive model control, inferential control, and dynamic model control. The objective of these higher-level techniques is to move the process to some limits (constraints), maximize or minimize some variable such as conversion or feed rate, or do an economic optimization by using dollar values of inputs and outputs. Sophisticated advanced control systems may be doing all these simultaneously.

Integration means automating the transfer of information among the three functions so that they may be effectively coordinated. At any given time, all three functions must agree on the best way to run the business and must be able to achieve that state. The objective of integration is *optimization*—finding and achieving the most profitable or lowest-cost way to run the business.

Integration of planning, scheduling, and control could be thought of as a subset of *computer-integrated manufacturing* (CIM) applied to the process industries. However, use of the term *CIM* has not been very precise; it seems to have been applied to any project that uses information technology to integrate what would otherwise be islands of automation. The term has been replaced with the concept of *supply chain optimization* or integration of the business process from customer order through product manufacture and delivery. The integration of planning, scheduling, and control is then seen to be a stepping stone or prerequisite to supply chain optimization.

The purpose of this book is to provide insight into the various elements that comprise the integrated system and the considerations that are important in the integration. No one person is expert in all the technologies that these elements represent and that must be welded together to produce a successful integration and therefore optimization of a process industry business. The contributed chapters bring together the combined wisdom of people with years of experience in each of the elements needed in an integrated system—people who are now successfully implementing their parts of such systems in a wide variety of circumstances.

Within any company, an integration project will require a team of, in no particular order, control engineers, process engineers, planners, schedulers, computer scientists, operations research practitioners, managers, and process operators, all of whom need to have some understanding of the technologies basic to the profession of the other team members. Use of the information in this book should reduce the learning time for such a team, shorten the design time for a system, and help avoid mistakes. If by reading this book any of the above objectives are met, our purpose will have been served.

References

Baker, T. E., and D. E. Shobrys (1985): "The Integration of Planning, Scheduling and Control," Paper no. CC-85-97, presented at the National Petroleum Refiners Association Computer Conference, New Orleans, October 27–30.

Bodington, C. E., and T. E. Baker (1990): "A History of Mathematical Programming in the Petroleum Industry," *Interfaces,* vol. 20, no. 4, July-August, pp. 117–127.

Garvin, W. W., H. W. Crandall, J. B. John, and R. A. Spellmann (1957): "Applications of Linear Programming in the Oil Industry," *Management Sci.,* vol. 3, no. 4, pp. 407–430.

Griffith, R. E., and R. A. Stewart (1961): "A Nonlinear Programming Technique for the Optimization of Continuous Processes," *Management Sci.,* vol. 7, no. 2, pp. 379–392.

Symonds, G. H. (1955): *Linear Programming—The Solution of Refinery Problems,* Esso Standard Oil Company, New York.

Van Horn, L. D. (1985): "Integrating Process Control and Operating Target Decisions," presented at the Instrument Society of America Convention, Philadelphia, October.

2

Process Information Systems and Communications

Dr. J. P. Kennedy
Oil Systems, Inc.

Introduction

Process industry applications that depend on timely, accurate process data simply will not work unless the network and communications system can deliver what is needed.

Process information systems depend on both a configuration database that comprises the definition of the process, its products, and its equipment and an operations database that holds the history of operation. The historical data are unique, the volume is immense, and the data arrive as bursts of unsolicited input. The data quantity can change dramatically in a short time as a result of changes in feed character, operation, shift changes, or faults in the process. Over the last three decades, special techniques and systems have been built to handle these data. Process configuration data, though somewhat more stable, are also voluminous and subject to continuous change.

Companies have spent fortunes amassing data (perhaps encouraged by the misnamed information age), but these data cannot be considered an asset unless they are correctly presented, analyzed, and converted to information in a robust, maintainable system. Part of this data conversion process lies within the scope of data collection, validation, training, and analytical tools, but a major factor is also the reengineering of the business system to take advantage of timely data.

Most process data are discarded or put in unusable form (paper) at the end of each working day. Companies that utilize more than a few percent of their history in the decision process are rare.

In this chapter we discuss the information network to support planning, scheduling, and control integration. There are ten topics of discussion:

- Process information system
- Evolution of process computer systems
- Networks and communications requirements
- Interfaces
- Description of system users
- System applications
- Backbone for continuous improvement
- Data treatment and storage
- Metrics
- System support requirements

Manufacturing requires an open computing and networking architecture that creates an operations work group and provides real-time data and process information to electronic workstations for plant personnel and applications (performance monitoring, scheduling, planning, optimization, modeling). These workstations contain applications for those who set goals, those who formulate plans, those who implement strategies, and those who maintain and operate the plant and its systems. Each user has a different job; the work group applications are for decision support and operating decisions and will no longer be simple personal computers (PCs) with spreadsheets or word processors in a stand-alone environment. As more users work remote to the process, greater care is required to ensure that accurate data are received to prevent unprofitable and possibly hazardous incidents due to errors from bad data or lack of timely good data.

The system must contain both operation history information and process configuration databases that support rapid retrieval by the plant personnel through their applications. Process configuration data do not change often, but without a maintained database, they can be lost in the paper landfill of documents and therefore become inaccessible to applications. The alternative—to have each workstation application maintain its own history and configuration—would be impossible to maintain.

Although the required database servers can be constructed with today's technology, the applications that use these data will never operate properly without better information than is currently available. The security, reliability, and validity of the data brought into the database environment "untouched by human hands" must be improved. We could learn a lot from the methods used by instrumentation and other hardened systems to transfer data up the chain reliably while maintaining the data's utility and timeliness. Decision support requires continuously available, reliable, and accurate data.

The communications strategy and network are an equal partner with the databases that works toward the goal of robust, reliable data transmission. As data become integral to the operation rather than being used for after-the-fact accounting, they must be received reliably in a timely fashion for actions to be taken. This means that the network is a critical part of the system, much more important than the kind of computer, type of personal computer, or brand of instrumentation (the three emotional decisions in systems). Properly designed, the network and communications-layer software will render decisions on which computer or operating system moot.

Most plants have been unable to attain satisfactory performance from integrated plant information systems because past implementations have worked toward the wrong architecture. Most managements rank process control on the bottom and optimization on the top of a single hierarchical line of functions, much as they would have been performed in a host mainframe computer. This model, proposed 20 years ago by Ted Williams of Purdue, is likely wrong because:

1. It neglects the infrastructure (engineering, integration, training, and support).

2. Integrated applications were not a design requirement—each department had installed software for its own needs.

3. The scope of the applications was wrong, for they were designed to perform separate functions rather than to support business processes.

Host systems must now be reengineered. To do this, we need more than bits flowing down a wire (or fiber). We need an environment where applications flourish and routinely share data, objects, programs, rules, and routines.

Promoting change is the key. We should be working toward migration by attrition of legacy systems in such a way that the information system supports continuous improvement of business systems. The job of information system managers is not to change the company, but their departments, to enable operating divisions to reorganize.

Many early *manufacturing resource planning* (MRP) systems failed because they did not promote change but simply automated an existing, inefficient paper system, often not even eliminating the existing system. The infrastructure should support the organization that you wish to become, not the obsolete organization you have today! Instead of having a distinct set of modules (laboratory, maintenance, MRP II, safety, process data manager, environment, reconciliation, etc.) as was the old design, we need to create systems that can evolve as the applications learn. The technical task is not simply to redesign applications so that they run in a client/server mode (since the existing applications may be the wrong ones); it is to design an infrastructure of open-access, robust networks so that new developments—many of them unimagined at this time—can be quickly and professionally incorporated.

Process Information System

Two information servers are described in this section: the configuration information system and the operations information system. The *configuration information system* is the systematic storage of the physical configuration and the data attached to that configuration. The *operations information* is the history of plant performance.

At present, collecting the configuration data in a single database is not common. However, as processes become automated, separation of the configuration data to a single database is a good long-term strategy, because it makes the overall system more maintainable.

The operations information system, sometimes called the *process data manager,* is the process history. Existing older facilities are trying to compete with newer world-scale plants built with newer technology. Literally, the existing facilities' only advantage is the knowledge of how they run today. This is the asset that is discarded at the end of each working day by keeping only summary reports of operation on paper. The function of the operations information system is to store these data and provide them to the workstations of plant personnel, who will hopefully be running applications that use this knowledge to competitive advantage.

The basic historian is designed to store massive amounts of data. In a large site, there could be dozens of interfaces to data sources and hundreds of thousands of points. In addition to the interfaces, there are other basic services suitable for applications:

- Performance monitoring and models
- Graphics and trending
- Spreadsheet add-ins
- Statistical quality control

- Event and alarm logging

These applications assist the user in reporting and troubleshooting, but their main advantage lies in their role as a supplier of real-time data and services.

Evolution of Process Computer Systems

To understand the process information system designs, it is important to consider the history of process computing and its evolution from the single-host plant computer. The introduction of the *distributed control system* (DCS) in the early 1970s had a dramatic effect on data use in the plant environment. Initially, only the operator was afforded the improved accuracy and flexibility of digital technology, but soon others in the plant demanded better and more accurate data capture. Although there were several attempts to put control computers in the field from 1965 (IBM 1800) through the 1980s (SETCON,* HW 4500, AAI), the first systems for personnel other than the operator started to appear around 1983 (Oil Systems, Inc., PI system). In those days, the scope of the data available was usually a recently installed DCS plus some manual inputs and thermocouple multiplexors. Figure 2.1 shows schematically such a system.

These early computer systems were useful for the control engineers and those close to the process, but the networks were not sufficient to send data reliably around the plant or to exchange data with other systems. The head office generally had its own financial systems that relied on paper reports. The plant systems supported advanced controls and unit reports for the individual unit. The disadvantages of these systems were that data were missing for many of the high-value applications (e.g., models) which themselves were not mature and did not expect to see data from the field. Finally, the presentation was not very user-friendly and required extensive training.

As the use of the DCS expanded, however, a maintenance problem arose that has not really been solved today. Since the units are under the domain of a single engineer, the reports and functions on the computer were driven by that person's needs. What one engineer would call a unit report could be dramatically different from a unit report satisfactory to the engineer on another process. In addition, others associated with the plant wanted to use computers, particularly the PCs, in their own ways.

Each group developed its own system, and the result was the infamous "islands of automation" shown in Fig. 2.2. The effect on the maintainability and reliability of the systems left much to be desired. The point-to-

---

*See the "Trademarks" section at the end of the chapter.

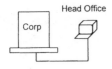

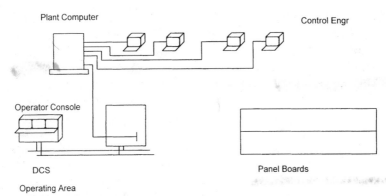

Figure 2.1 Systems linked to DCS circa 1983.

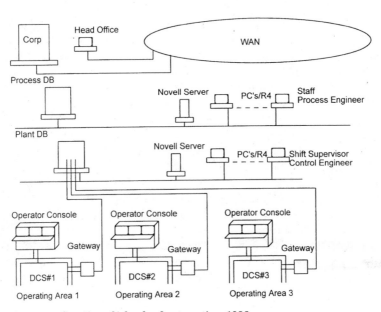

Figure 2.2 Creation of islands of automation, 1986.

point interfaces propagated, and particularly in Europe, the plantwide systems became electronic spaghetti as links ran everywhere, attempting to get the information needed. Networks, used more in the United States, were a solution, but not as installed at most plants at this time.

Elimination of the islands of automation was attempted over the next few years by simply connecting the disparate networks until users discovered that the same links that collected process data could write to the valves. Figure 2.3 shows a typical system that was built to integrate the different islands safely, including special software that buffered the control network from the information network.

The links to the head office and to outside were still not as professional as required, and the PC was used mostly as a terminal instead of as a participating client. Integration involved remote operation of a central computer rather than the sharing of computing resources.

In Fig. 2.4, the system is much more modern, even though the basic hardware has not changed. The database computers no longer drive any displays or applications; they serve data to applications. Modern applications are based on access to commercial databases such as Oracle or Sybase. The databases are accessible via standard tools such as the Microsoft ODBC (open data base connect) standard.

The information platform is now complete. The PCs are running applications in a distributed mode. Data may be coming from the real-time data server or from the process database. The next step is to

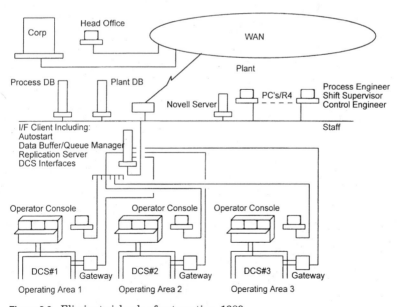

Figure 2.3 Eliminate islands of automation, 1989.

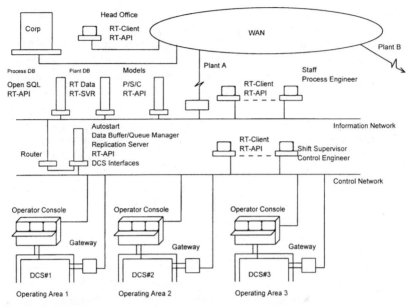

Figure 2.4   Client/server computing, 1993.

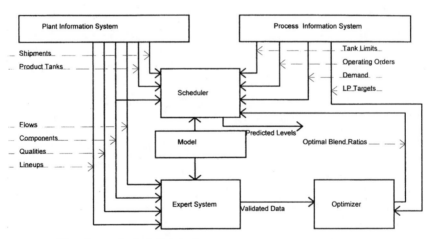

Figure 2.5   Planning and scheduling tool.

evolve the integrated applications so that they present a reasonable
interface to the people, but allow the system to remain maintainable.

Figures 2.5 and 2.6 are samples of how integrated applications will
soon dominate the process environment. Figure 2.5 is a simple planning and scheduling workstation. The expert system is a convenient
way to bring data into an application since there are often rules that

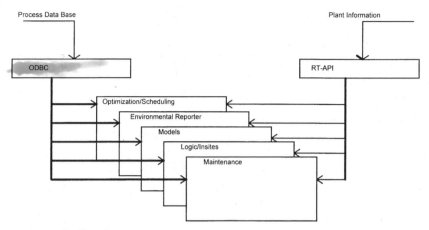

Figure 2.6 Staff workstation.

must be followed (e.g., if laboratory data have not been entered for x days, force manual review of data before they are used). Configuration data from the process database and real-time data from the history information system are combined with the process mathematical models (stored as process information) to provide insight on the planning of the plant.

The workstation shown in Fig. 2.6 is the simple evolution of the application shown in Fig. 2.5. A person rarely has a single job in a plant and would not want to go to a different application or different look and feel to do combined tasks, such as taking the results of the planning and scheduling session and generating a set of working orders for the operator and reports for managers. In Fig. 2.6, each application would have the same structure as the planning and scheduling task shown in Fig. 2.5. The next wave of object technology, OLE 2.0, will make it possible to design integrated applications rather than to connect data.

Networks and Communications

The networks and communications are the key part of an integrated system. In one process study of a large refinery, we found that some data (in this case a pipeline schedule for a refinery) were entered into various computer systems seven different times (twice into different applications on the same computer). This level of redundancy makes the systems impossible to understand and maintain. The only opportunity to make a distributed, nonredundant system design that supports the required applications is at the beginning. Retrofit of architecture is a very frustrating and unsatisfying experience owing to the incredible inertia of an existing organization; yet information system master plans are rare.

The network and communications architecture has four levels of information flow supplying many different users linked in logical work groups:

- *Local control network* (LCN)—usually redundant, supplied by the DCS vendor

- *Control network*—created by adding an interface client

- *Information network*—serves the needs of the plant

- *Wide-area network* (WAN)—corporate architecture above the plant architecture.

The purpose of these layers is to provide needed network services while isolating the highway that contains the connection of the operator console and instrumentation to the control network. The control network needs to be more secure than the information network, since faults could cause the operator to lose her or his view of the process or bad data to be output. Faults or no, it will be connected, however, if for no other reason than to show pictures (video) of the stacks and provide access to on-line manuals via the control console.

Without proper communications infrastructure, great ideas will not get to those who need them, information required for continuous improvement will die in the control room, and people will not use a system that is an unfriendly, lackluster performer. In addition to robustness, the network and communications infrastructure must be maintainable with built-in security.

Figure 2.7 shows a typical physical layout of a plant network. Each set of users has special requirements such as fully redundant hardware, automatic switchover, and no data loss. Proper location of the functions is a critical step. For example, the installation of a scheduling program (which requires flows, levels, laboratory values, and transactions) on the control network would fail for lack of appropriate data.

The local control network is the communications medium that is established and maintained by the control vendors. It is fully redundant so that the operator does not lose his or her window to the process. As a result, little foreign equipment will be found on this network. Often the control vendors will produce and support a gateway that attaches to the local control networks and communicates via RS232/IEEE 802.3 or other means, but data access is predefined by the control vendor.

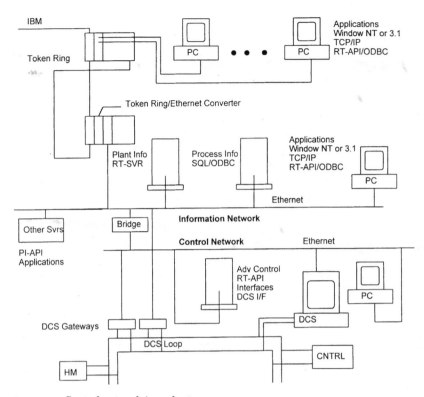

Figure 2.7   Control network in a plant.

Newer control systems support projection of an X-Window onto the operator console from an external computer on the network, but this is an error about to be rectified. An X-Window is not a program client in the operator console, but it represents the first attempt to open up the proprietary control console to external applications. Applications in this environment follow no standard, so this approach changes the presentation from different screens to different windows on the same screen, but there is still no common look and feel. The X-Window standard is not consistent with the Macintosh or Microsoft Windows or even other X-Window applications. The network that feeds this, however, is important because it has access to the operator console and because some potential faults could result in loss of the process window. The advantage is that it brings video, documents, and access to other external systems such as the plant information system to the operator on her or his screen. One application that uses this feature is advanced control since it must provide special displays to the operator.

The next level of communication—the information network—is not always separate, as would be dictated by good practice. This network serves engineers, managers, and other staff personnel who require the "near real-time" data but typically are responsible for the longer-term operation and economics of the plant. This is the level that typically needs *no data loss* as the form of redundancy rather than a hot switchover. For many applications (pharmaceutical batch tracking) the redundancy of data storage is the most important requirement. All laboratory systems, maintenance systems, and planning and scheduling software are heavy users of this network.

There are also conventional *local-area networks* (LANs) and WANs that support the enterprise computing in a company. The plant network often supplies either data (RJE, flat file) or data access (LU 6.2, SQL) to these systems. Many users are moving to full transmission control protocol/Internet protocol (TCP/IP) which gives managers on the upper network access to clients in system applications. Initially, management did not believe that they needed "near real-time" data, but aware management has made these plant data critical for operating information and decision support. Also, since this is the primary mechanism of information exchange between plants, several applications, such as a best-practices or process technical service application, require this network.

Distributed design ensures that the control network is totally isolated from the information network for communication between the DCS and the rest of the system. Control systems prefer to broadcast their data in the manner and at the time appropriate for them to a real-time data server, which then services any and all queries from the information network. It is this combination of broadcast and query that ensures the integrity of the control network.

The creation of the separate layer of communication satisfies the dual requirement for plant data collection and historicization. A specific master plan for the networks should be prepared for each installation with special attention given to the legacy applications that must be replaced.

The separation of the control data traffic from the information traffic requires a series of special considerations. Given that there could be several control systems on each information network, the design must consider the following topics:

- Open interfaces to other network levels
- Time synchronization
- Data translation
- Historicization

■ Interoperable data services

The open data server that provides data to all applications is labeled RT-SVR on the figures.

Open interface to other network levels

At one time it was thought that integrated systems would still consist of separate applications (maintenance, laboratory, operations, accounting); but when information structure is reengineered, these applications are composed of reusable clients that support business processes and the plant data services. For example, planning optimization and scheduling require access to both the plant information and the process information. It would be a mistake for each module to keep an independent copy of the history and plant configuration without proper replication techniques. The same is true for a predictive maintenance workstation, advanced control workstation, or training workstation. This open interface has three main parts:

■ Client/server

■ Support event operation

■ Embedded replication servers

Client/server design separates functions so that the workstations do not depend upon heavy data access across loaded networks. The bandpass of the network (like memory and disk) should be guarded as a critical resource for the information structure. One advantage of this design is that the client can be designed to run in any platform— UNIX, Windows, DOS, OS/2, Macintosh—so that developers can work in the environment most appropriate for them. Many, e.g., would contend that reporting should be under Windows by using tools like Access, whereas a mixed-integer optimization using the sophisticated algorithms developed by IBM should be in distributed AIX processors.

Time synchronization

As more systems are installed on the control network, time synchronization becomes important. Often the only way to order data properly from different plant areas or even different plants is by the time stamp of the data. In addition, non-real-time data (laboratory data, manual inputs) also depend on the time stamp to make them meaningful when combined with real-time data and to place them correctly in the historian. An interface client is time synchronized by the host, and most interfaces should support system master (time set by the system) or distributed control system master (time set by the DCS) time setting.

Data translation

Often it is desirable to have data sourced from the information network to the DCS. For example, a point from one DCS or a central calculation is translated via the interfaces to a point on another DCS. This is also true for points from manual inputs and laboratory data. Many advanced control programs require laboratory data (properly time-stamped) for operation.

Historicization

The historian should maintain the data in a compressed format so that all applications and users who need to can access these data without concern that they are getting averages or samples instead of the raw data. The historian must also be designed so that it cannot overload the DCS. The key is that the data are gathered from the DCSs via broadcast from the interface client which deals with DCS via subroutines supplied by the vendor. Data are then broadcast to the historian; therefore, queries to the information network cannot affect the loading of the DCS. A large historian can have up to 100,000 points and typically stores data on-line for 1 to 2 years before archiving to tape.

Interoperable data services

Inquiries can come from many different sources, and these could be in various environments. TCP/IP, LU6.2, Decnet, Token Ring, and Ethernet are all encountered. The data client—the *real-time applications program interface* (RT-API)—should run in all workstations (e.g., IBM RS6000, Sun Sparcstation, Digital Vax, Digital Decstation, HP-UX, OSF/1, MS-DOS, and NT) and support data communication with the historian.

Interfaces

The value of process computers tends to be proportional to the amount of data available and the amount of history on-line. Automatic data collection through a series of interfaces allows modern systems to access and store several orders of magnitude more data than typical mainframe systems that rely on manual data entry. Most applications can assume that needed data are available or can be added with straightforward methods.

Since interfaces are a link between programs from different vendors, interfaces are usually the hardest programs to design, maintain, and debug. On the device side, the system must recognize and handle the particular protocol and actions of the equipment while presenting these data to the plant information system in a standard format. This section addresses the following aspects of interfacing:

- Basic functionality
- Construction and test methods
- Distributed operation
- Failover and redundancy
- Maintainability

Although it is desirable to make the philosophy of the interface constant, each device can have individual requirements, and the field device may not support the commands necessary to implement all features. Having a published standard is very useful for comparing the available features of interfaces.

Basic functionality

An interface should have a number of basic features and advanced features if the field device will support them. These are basic features:

- Data collection for required points
- Time stamp and synchronization
- Staying functional in the presence of start-up, shutdown, communication failures
- Bad-data flags
- Error handling
- Attempt at database reconciliation between plant information system, instrumentation, and smart field devices
- Exceptions sent to the plant information systemization interruption and other predictable phenomena
- Output capability

The interface is designed for continuous use at its main task of collecting data. If allowed by the field devices, it should handle on-line configuration changes, addition and deletion of points, and checking of its status. The most efficient means of data collection (e.g., lists by exception) should be used.

The information system will time-synchronize the field devices, and the rest of the system uses time to keep track of the different signals and their interrelations. Most instrumentation does not send a time stamp with the variables, so the interface will time-stamp the data. For some types of data, this is the wrong time stamp. For example, if a laboratory system or manual input system sends data to the plant information system, the correct time stamp reflects when the sample was pulled or the reading taken. The interface must be responsible for ascertaining the correct time stamp and sending it along with the event. The information system is designed to handle non-real-time data properly. The same problem can exist with outputs where a time stamp must be added to the point before it is written out (e.g., laboratory data for an operator).

An interface must stay functional in the presence of start-up, shutdown, and communication failures. This is a feature that was missed in many early interfaces. If the system is designed for a person to reset the interface when these events occur, then the system manager will spend much time unnecessarily restarting interfaces and the interface will lose data. In some cases, the restart of an interface is a major transient for the instrumentation. The interface is designed to accommodate known failure modes, such as continuing to retry when the communication is lost.

The interface will have additional information about a point due to its intimate connection to and knowledge of the field device. Some of these status decisions could be bad input, I/O timeout, or system not responding. The interface should flag the data as bad and not send false data to the system. Certain procedures for handling bad data, such as data substitution, should be followed at the application level.

Error handling is important for an interface. Since in modern systems hardware errors seldom occur, when they do occur, the messages must be clear and the actions taken (error handling) should make sense.

Digital instrument systems and smart field devices often have database information that is redundant with a plant and process information system. If this configuration information is available, particularly a journal of changes, the interface should attempt to reconcile its database with the field. If this is not done, the normal changes that happen in a large facility (change range on transmitters, add/or delete points, change descriptors) can be quite troublesome. With some of the new legal requirements for management of change, better DCS gateways should be forthcoming from vendors that service the industries handling hazardous materials. Regardless of the errors, it is the responsibility of the interface to ensure that no bad or misleading data are sent to the plant information system.

All networks and systems will work better if the interface works by exception and does not send redundant information to the plant information system; i.e., the interface maintains the last value received and sends a new value to the plant information system only if there is a change.

Most interfaces to instrument systems have output capability. These are usually sent by exception. Checking (e.g., Is Mode = Computer?) should be done by the application program sending the data. Outputs should be handled with care due to the potential danger.

Construction and test methods

Interfaces are some of the more difficult programs to write. Ideally, the basic interface program is standard, and only the links to the instrumentation will need to be written. The first step, before a single line of code can be written, is to write the interface operations manual. It should contain sections on

- Description of operation
- Basic requirements
- Interface and hardware setup
- Start-up and shutdown
- Point configuration
- Loading calculations
- Error handling and messages

Once the manual is completed, a simulator should be designed to help in the testing process. The construction of the simulator based on the manuals of the instrument company will often clarify the commands and point to misconceptions that would result in errors. A simulator is an essential element of the testing procedures.

The coding is then completed, and the system is checked out against the simulator. Tests such as removing and reconnecting the interface cable should be completed and documented. The interface can then be stress-tested for a fixed configuration so that these data are available for the design of the final environment.

The support requirements for interfaces do not vary from those for other software. The proper maintenance tools (listed later) should be included for remote diagnosis and fixing. The biggest challenge is to keep the software updated and include new features as they are provided by the vendor. The library of simulators is useful for this, as it is impossible to keep the actual equipment around and maintained.

Distributed operation

For maintenance and security reasons, many users prefer to run the interfaces on a remote node via the RT-API. This has the distinct advantage of being able to support different environments for the interface and the plant information system. For example, some instrument vendors use specific hardware (e.g., Foxboro and Westinghouse use the Sun workstation), and this may be different from the desired hardware environment for the plant information system.

A remote interface or interface client has three parts:

- Replication server
- Queue manager
- Real-time applications program interface (RT-API)

The replication server is used to replicate the point attribute file on the remote interface and the plant information system. This allows applications (other than the interface) to run on the remote node. These applications would be those that needed direct access to the data coming in from the interface (advanced controls, expert alarm management system, on-line models). The queue manager accepts the events (e.g., tag, value, time-stamp) from the interface and puts them in a queue. If the communication links are down, the queue saves the events, thereby eliminating the data loss. The RT-API is the set of communication routines used by any application to read and write from a plant information system. The system should also be designed to restart without the home node up.

Failover and redundancy

There are two other data integrity features of interfaces, failover and redundancy. For reports that are critical (environmental, batch records), holes in the data can be a problem. For environmental reports, loss of data causes a company considerable paperwork to prove compliance during these periods and can even cause the Environmental Protection Agency (EPA) to increase the enforcement level.

The failover is handled by putting two copies of the interface into different nodes. The interface programs can be load-balanced (i.e., each takes one-half the load), and should one fail, the other reconfigures itself to pick up all critical variables, which may not be the total set of variables. When the other interface restarts, the balanced operation is resumed. A procedure to take over is usually implemented for maintenance purposes.

Redundancy is more difficult to design and build. In addition to the queue manager mentioned above, it is sometimes possible to interrogate the history module on the instrument system. This provides a highly secure method of tracking a limited number of points.

Maintainability

The maintainability of the interfaces is a key item. This will require

- Verify program
- I/O rates
- Simulator
- Data collection rate settable by the system manager to adjust the load on both the information system and the instrument system

Standards

The verify program can be run remotely and reports back what programs are running, version levels, central processing unit (CPU) load, and other important parameters in the system. Data from our support lines indicate that many of the calls are the result of one of the programs involved in the interface not running, which is detected by the verify program. It also picks up errors in installation and other problems that may be caused by human error.

Interfaces are installed with an I/O monitor to keep statistics on the interface. These data are stored in the plant information system as any other variable is. Typical I/O rates are the archiving rate, equation calculation rate, exception rate, compression rate, network error rate, and other variables. These variables, over time, tell the system manager when there are potential problems, and they can be used to help set the loadings.

The simulator created during the construction of the interface is a valuable maintenance tool for adding and testing upgrades to interfaces in the field before they are installed.

The interface must have the handles required to allow the system manager to set the loading of the system, gateway, and instrumentation. This usually requires tools for setting the polling time and the phasing of the data collection and a measurement of the I/O rates.

Description of System Users

The process information system is for plant personnel and is distributed across many boundaries. The system consists of servers that provide data reliably, clients that provide good operator interfaces, and other functions aimed directly at the individual users; e.g., an operator uses a maintenance system for different functions than the warehouse manager does. The client is composed of common services (e.g., planning tools) and programs specifically designed for a function and requires careful study of the needs of the user. Each workstation will be unique and suited to the job of its users.

Typical users in a plant operations work group are operators, shift supervisors, staff, and senior management. Each of these has different needs, and their jobs must be defined to engineer the proper software system. Most legacy systems were designed around departments (laboratories, maintenance, accounting) instead of business processes. The new users must be considered part of an operations work group composed primarily of plant personnel, but which could include customers and management. The objective of the work group is to reliably produce high-quality products for customers at competitive prices.

The communication required to perform operations tasks today is beyond the capabilities of a paper-based system and will become increasingly so as more organizations eliminate jobs and add procedures such as ISO 9000. Documents must be easily accessible and maintainable so all get a consistent view. Plant data must be available reliably to all who may need them—operation history information, configuration data, and documents. This will likely require different servers in every plant for documents (e.g., Lotus Notes), operations information (e.g., Oil Systems PI system), and configuration information (e.g., MK Furgeson plant database).

Careful analysis of these tasks early on can save an immense rework of the information architecture. One example of the wrong approach is the interviewers who ask production personnel if, say, 5-minute averages are sufficient for their job. Most will answer in the affirmative because this is sufficient for their current job as they perceive it. However, storing averages almost precludes any maintenance troubleshooting and many of the environmental reports; but worse, it prevents the evolution of new applications and operating techniques based on the added information. The approach must be to define the applications and then look at the data needs, or store everything in a compressed format (my particular choice), which actually takes less storage than the 5-minutes averages.

Operators

The operator's job was once defined as sheer terror—staying alert in a hazardous area with little to do until there is a failure. Anticipation and problem avoidance are now the objectives. The DCS console is the operator's prime interface to the plant. New consoles are workstations and can support clients and X-Windows to allow the operator a single window. This is intended to simplify the interface to the process and applications such as advanced controls, what-if analysis, video/voice, and other features.

The way a process operator interacts with the process has changed radically over the last decade. In the new Occupational Safety and Health Administration (OSHA) Personnel Safety Management (PSM) laws governing the management of process safety and rules for human factors when hazardous material is involved, the operator interface is critical. It is no longer simply unwise to build the engineers' dream and give the displays to the operator without consideration of how she or he will operate in all conditions—it is illegal. The new rules (and common sense) dictate that the operators be provided a constant, maintainable, understandable interface to the process, even though there may be continual change in the underlying plant configuration, feed and product compositions, and known and unknown disturbances.

We must provide the operator with easy and understandable ways to handle the job. Some of the nonstandard data types that flow back and forth to an operator are

- Job instructions
- Targets
- Safety and/or operating limits
- Repair instructions
- Operating instructions
- Diagnostic agents
- Operator comments (logbooks)
- Exceptions noted

These all contain great amounts of plant and process data, but not always in the form of numbers. In the next section, we will describe one manufacturing process—production planning—to illustrate how this architecture influences the client/server design. Operators also review and implement instructions from others while applying their experience wherever it is needed.

Shift supervisors

The immediate supervisors of the operators are the most senior and knowledgeable of the personnel concerned with the minute-to-minute operation of the processes. They must act as mentors for the operator plus implement the long-term plan for the processes, including operation within safe limits, profitability, and optimization. These are called *shift supervisors, foremen,* or some other title. Although not watching the process in a continuous fashion, as the operator does, these supervisors monitor the process in near real time along with their other duties.

Shift supervisors need information from all areas under their responsibility and other related areas. Information needs often cross unit boundaries and require links to different instrument systems. Even though the industry has spent years trying to get to a "single window," this has only been for the operator, not the supervisor or the engineers. As the main point of contact for other units, the shift supervisor handles much of the communication outside the unit. Supervisors in certain positions can spend as much as 50 percent of their time in communication with peers around the complex, answering and asking questions, exchanging information. For this reason, shift supervisors are the focal point of work group systems such as electronic logbooks, e-mail and best-practice forums. Shift supervisors also use, but do not maintain, many of the plant data such as the specifications, operating limits, mechanical limits, operator instructions, consumption (energy, environmental) guidelines, and incident reports.

In a work group orientation, the shift supervisor is more of a coach than a boss. She or he must anticipate problems and help keep the process running on an even keel. The shift supervisor will require sophisticated tools to assist such outage agents which compute the parameters that indicate the best time to take an outage; models and expert systems to allow easy what-if analysis of the process for rapid answers to new operating regimes (e.g., the process must go on oil at a certain temperature to save the gas supplies for the local community); and many more.

Staff

The staff at the plant site must handle the interface between the business and the process. Often, and incorrectly, the support tasks are maintained as staff functions rather than assigned to the appropriate business process. The "reengineering" of business makes these functions an important design factor for the information architecture. Organizations can seldom be changed, but the environment that people work in *can* be changed. Putting the right environment in place can lead to the evolution of the desired organization. A good example is the posting of control charts. No control has changed, but operators and other workers can see how they compare to the other personnel on performance, judged by metrics that are important to the customer. The information architecture is the most important element of this environment—how the organization, individual, or function is valued and reported.

Staff's needs are much broader than the shift supervisors—this statement is often interpreted as saying that staff need or can handle only summarized information, but they need plant information in real time just as much as others involved in the manufacturing process. Because of the potential data rates, staff need the information on an exception or ad hoc basis. Averaging, interpreting, and summarizing take information out of the data. Since staff are removed from the process, performance monitoring and data validation must be much more consistent and automated. Receiving data by exception allows a user to leverage his or her ability to accept unsolicited inputs, learning from both the presence and the absence of events. If a system is unreliable or loses data, it renders report by exception meaningless.

Long-range planning is a staff function. A workstation is desired which incorporates the real-time planning and scheduling tools. The workstation gets inventories, production rates, and qualities from the plants; committed schedules, prices, and demand from the corporate system; facilities capability (e.g., maximum blend rate) from engineering; and current problems from the operator. This is a prime example of how handling all levels as a work group provides the ability to more fully automate this function while giving good feedback to the planner.

Senior management

Some senior managers responsible for manufacturing have broader scope than the plant staff do. Timely, consistent performance data and other information presented by exception are a requirement for busy executives. Current systems provide very little pertinent information to managers in time for any response to be given, reducing the use of plant data to accounting and legal reports, analysis, or punishment. Real-time decisions made at the management level included sales, raw-material purchase, and scheduling around unusual incidents in the plants. For example, a decision may be made to standardize on particular vendor, but the only information available was ad hoc or anecdotal stories about incidents in the plants. If failure rates had been documented (from those incident investigations) and other metrics had brought insight to the equipment selection process, this would make the process data a valuable corporate asset. The alternatives are committee investigations and redundant efforts to dig out the same information from obsolete forms (paper) or make the wrong decision because the real metrics are not documented.

When reengineering, management systems must be overhauled to provide controls for senior management (measurements to provide senior management with the information concerning whether their decisions are on track). The work group can provide this information. If data were only in the individual personal computers (as would happen if the planning function were stand-alone rather than part of the work group), then the required information would be lost, unmaintainable, and (even if available) largely inaccurate.

System Applications

Once the database and network architecture are fixed, it is important to consider what information from the plant is required for the applications. From a maintainability perspective, the process database should be considered a series of resources rather than a single database.

Although many applications must run in the plant, let us consider a sampling of the more important ones, to see some of the effect on structure:

- Planning and scheduling
- Performance monitoring
- Operator task management
- OSHA/ISO 9000 requirements
- Process/technical support
- Data reconciliation
- Reports

There are many more specialized applications, but consideration of these will allow the database structure to emerge. In addition to the databases, there is the need to manage any change. For example, if a database is used to compute the sulfur emissions of a boiler and the computational method changes, it must be possible to reconstruct the computation for an audit.

Planning and scheduling

Planning and scheduling entail a coordination of the order procurement and order fulfillment processes. The actual planner is usually in the plant, but the results of her or his work are then available to the other business processes. Figure 2.5 shows schematically the planning application for a refinery. This is interesting because a refiner

must use a model to compute the proper blend ratios for products before the scheduling can be completed. *Scheduling*
This application to product blending makes extensive use of both *Data* configuration and historical information. The first step taken by the planner is to get a valid data set. The linear programming (LP) targets are loaded as a starting point; then the planner gets the amount of material in the component tanks (last values), qualities (average over several days), lineups (current values), and process flows. From the configuration information system, the planner needs the demand to be met, operating orders that show what is planned for unit rates *mode* over the next week, and tank limits. Next the planner obtains from the process information system the shipments that have already been made since the last session, current inventory in product tanks, and current flows for the process units. Finally, from the rest of the system, he or she gets the optimal blend ratios to use and the updated blending model. From these data, the planner can lay out the schedule for the time period of interest and predict the amount of components and products available at any time during the period. These figures are run through a rule base, usually an expert system, to ensure a complete data set that has internal consistency. The net result of this session is an updated model (if new field values are input) and blend ratios to use for the week.

Performance monitoring

Performance monitoring is not often considered part of the real-time information architecture, but it is, in fact, a critical part. Many people who will look at these data will not have the proximity to the process to be able to judge the quality or validity of the numbers presented. It is important for the performance monitor to be able to review and compare the computational method. Nomenclature is a problem since each plant, process, or unit may have its own naming convention brought in with the instrumentation. A way around this difficulty is to maintain, in the plant database:

- Plant data (current and historical)
- Definition of *standard* units and actual configuration *Std. UOM* *Config*
- Plant configuration changes
- Reference list of common names to tags *Ref/ Master*
- Standard ways of computing performance *Descript.*

There is much more to defining performance than simply mapping plant data to metrics via a set of equations. Part of the package is a definition of the units and ways of reviewing the calculations, including a comparison to a standard.

Operator task management

Operator task management includes documenting the actions of the operators via logbooks, instructions, and comments. In more sophisticated applications, the results of operator actions are compared to those expected and reported to the supervisors by exception. This implies that there is a database and communication means to relay this information to those who need it. A model of the organization including positions, relations, and people's names is central to this function (how else does one escalate an unacknowledged alert to the operator's supervisor since most e-mail will be to a person rather than a position?).

OSHA/ISO 9000 requirements

The OSHA Process Safety Management (PSM) and ISO 9000 (as well as other compliance software) will required additional information to support incident investigations, capital improvements siting, evacuations, safety/quality procedures, and many more. In addition to the above-mentioned models, these will require the following:

- Plot plans
- Recommendation tracking
- Investigation notes
- Procedure verification

Process/technical support

Process/technical support that is distributed and available to operators, supervisors, and peers is one benefit in this new architecture. The information needed by this application could be process models, process operating guidelines, material balances, and drawings.

Data reconciliation

To get more consistent data, data reconciliation software is needed. This software balances the raw material purchased, products shipped, inventory changes, and losses. Normally overall plant reconciliation is not done until a month after the fact. This result is clearly not useful for operations. However, a daily reconciliation requires up-to-date shipments, inventory measurement, and product shipments.

Reports

Reports are an important part of the information system, and their quality and timelines have a measurable effect on the ability of the plant to continuously improve. To maintain the integrity of the reports, the information system must contain procedures for managing change, supporting queries as to the origin of information presented, and ensuring that consistent calculations are used.

Backbone for Continuous Improvement

A major function of the system is to provide feedback for continuous improvement and compliance. Continuous improvement and the rigid methodology imposed by OSHA PSM, ISO 9000, and emission reporting have conflicting goals. Where safety is concerned, it is fair to say that innovation may not have a place; standards and practices are put in place to protect all. Quality and productivity improvement are different issues. An operator who may find a way to make a better or cheaper product is discouraged if there are paperwork and layers of procedures to go through when she or he tries anything different.

Systems to support continuous improvement become more important as staff are "flattened" and routine monitoring, the main feedback from the plant, becomes secondary to problem solving. After the "crisis handling," the little time that remains is consumed by compliance reporting and other paperwork. When plant data are integral to a person's job, they must be easy to use and understand. The spreadsheet has shown itself to be the best standard vehicle for interacting with a computer database.

Critical system functions

A critical function of the system is to provide feedback to those in the facility to promote continuous improvement. The spreadsheet is the prime reporting tool for staff, and there are many potential uses of spreadsheets, but we will cover these topics:

- *Plant reporting.* This includes the morning report, operations report, and technical service report. These give plant staff a clear picture of the current operation of the facility.

- *Model environment.* On-line models are much more valuable, and hard to install, than the off-line versions that have been used for years. The spreadsheet here is a mechanism of grabbing data, converting to an interesting format, and presenting to the user. A what-if analysis is a common part of the model environment.

- *Advanced scripting.*   Script languages can be used to provide advanced applications such as laboratory entry screens and statistical analysis where manipulation of the data is required.

Plant reporting   *Exception Formats*

The three kinds of plant reports discussed here are the morning report, the operations report, and the technical service report. These reports all share a common definition of the data from the process database.

Morning Report

It has been said that all decisions in a plant are made by 9:30, after the morning meeting. An automated morning report can help in two ways: The quality of the information is much better, and since it can easily be called repeatedly, this extends the decision making to later in the day. With an automated morning report, the question at the morning meeting can change from "What happened?" to "What are we going to do about it?" The effect of decisions is also clearer since many of the data on the report can be trended. The net result is that the decisions become more accurate and timely. The morning report also relieves operations and operations management of the collection, filtering, validation, and analysis of data.

The style of the morning report varies, but it contains major elements presented in some sort of exception format (e.g., highlight the out-of-specification condition, show the critical alarms for the last 24 hours). The hierarchical approach is better for top management—the initial report should contain, on a single page, every important fact and should enable navigation to greater detail only if desired. This is also important for extending the decision period, since the summary will be checked by management several times in a day to ensure proper plant performance.

At the next level are the operations report and technical service report. The critical elements of the morning report are

- Unit performance
- Inventories
- Shipments and receipts
- Compliance issues
- Plant targets, orders
- Comments and problems

- Scheduled maintenance
- Exception report

   Unit performance has only the metrics of the unit, not the detail or material balance. The key variables are the variables that show proper unit performance (crude units use energy to fractionate crude oil, reformers convert naphtha to reformate, etc.) A unit detail can be obtained from the operations report. The inventory report shows how much raw material and product are in the facility. The shipments and receipts will show what is planned into and out of the facility over the next few days. Compliance issues will show whatever compliance problems exist, outstanding recommendations and the deadline, and important parameters (e.g., compliance level and notes if higher enforcement procedures are possible). Plant targets and orders will document the targets currently set for the operators and any orders to change those over the next time period. The comments and problems are a listing of the comments made by the operating supervisor. These comments will include noted problems, exceptions, and explanations. Scheduled maintenance is important in that it may interfere with plans made at the morning meeting and should be documented in this report. The exception report is a list of exceptions thought noteworthy by the management agent; they could be alarms, ambiguities in the data, orders not followed, warnings when compliance dates pass, and many other possibilities.

Operations report

The operations report should coincide with the area of responsibility for a supervisor. It primarily shows detailed current operations compared to the previous period (e.g., yesterday) and can show some cumulative data if they are important. This operations report is a place for a supervisor or an operator to add comments. Some of the data on the operations report are also on the morning report, but in a different format.

   An *operations report* is intended for a definite time frame. The essential elements are

- Values from last shift
- Values this shift
- Plant targets, orders
- Comments and problems
- Scheduled maintenance
- Exception report

This report is often used as the basis of a manual input system if there is no DCS. In the case of comments, it is still the logical place to add comments.

Technical service report

A technical service engineer is looking at the longer-term view, and often the technical service report contains some data from embedded model. For example, if it is required to find the proper operation for the summer months of an olefin plant limited by the columns, it may be desirable to keep a few pieces of data (section loadings, heat duty) from the models in the process data historian, making them available to this report. At the minimum, the technical service report has a material-balanced view of the unit over some time. This report shows how the material balance as computed allows the technical service engineer some interactive capability.

The technical service report, at a minimum, has a material balance, but often will include data from model runs where more meaningful information is computed. The principal uses of a model are to compute variables that cannot be measured (e.g., tray loadings of columns or heat exchange duties) and to reference the behavior of a plant back to a standard.

Model environment

Models have been used routinely to assist in the monitoring and analysis of process units, but on-line models are much more valuable, and harder to install, than the off-line versions. Once run, the model can often deposit more interesting information back into the process data historian and for the technical service reports.

As a model environment, the spreadsheet has a number of uses including the collection of the base case, manual input of the missing parameters to control the cases and other information, a repository for the output of the model, a useful tool to generate a what-if scenario for the model (particularly a real-time what-if function), and a reporting tool for the results. If an engineer has automated the operation of the models, then a routine look at the unit could be taken quite rapidly and the result stored. This would provide valuable insight into the long-term behavior of the unit.

The models can also be used to reference a case back to the base case. This latter use will be of particular interest when the model environment is intended to support a process help line for several units of the same type. The additional function needed for this will have a separate cross-reference area where individual instrument tags could be referenced to meaningful names (e.g., *crude unit charge rate* makes more sense than *TK401 hot charge*). If there are several of these units, then the process help line could return to the system the comparison to an industry average, which could be of help in the long-term optimization of the unit and in troubleshooting problems.

There are two kinds of what-if techniques that are used. Models can provide *slopes* that can then be used in a spreadsheet to allow a user to predict what would happen for limited moves. The equations are also used to predict simple things like future tank levels. The two techniques are combined to do a what-if analysis for a gasoline blender. For example, a spreadsheet can be used to predict the levels of component tanks in a blender over the next week. The tanks are fed with run downflows, and the components are used to blend gasoline. The spreadsheet contains

- Rundown flows
- Blends scheduled
- Ratios of components to be used in each blend
- Blender lineups

From these data, the predicted level is computed. The spreadsheet is presented to the operator for any what-if analysis he or she may do.

Advanced scripting

Microsoft has announced that the scripting language of choice will be Visual Basic (VB), and Excel 5 uses VB as its scripting language. These applications are more difficult because building them requires more programming skills than the simpler spreadsheets. I have collected two examples of these, but with VB a user can do literally anything desired. In these two examples, the requirement was to be able to programmatically manipulate the data before putting them into a spreadsheet, which created a need for the VB, but Excel still handles the infrastructure part of the applications. Spreadsheets like Excel also provide statistical tools such as the Pareto chart, to show causes of downtime if the correct variables are measured.

Spreadsheets are also useful for data input. Many people combine the operations report with the operations logging—an input function. In other applications, such as quality control, the laboratory data for each product have to be entered manually.

Manual inputs are more complex than outputs since they must have programmed interaction with people. For example, it is often necessary to enter several values from a single sample and not accept these unless they pass some sort of test (e.g., add to 1.00).

Data Treatment and Storage

The techniques of data collection have matured over the last decade. The earliest systems were embedded in the control instrumentation which was designed for the operator, who cares about a relatively short-term window (1 to 3 days) of operation and is quite familiar with her or his process. These early systems would collect data (usually evenly spaced samples) for a short time. For the longer term, only averages were kept due to the limited storage capacity and the needs of the operations personnel. These data were stored as they were received, with little or no validation other than a range check, and they were indexed by the instrument tag.

In 1980, John Hale presented the Du Pont methods for data compression at nearly the same time as Bailey Controls introduced exception reporting in its instrumentation. These are two different, but important, contributions for plant data collection.

Exception reporting is shown in Figure 2.8. A small deviation d is defined for each point in the system. Instead of continuously sampling the value of a point, it is only broadcast when, beyond a minimum time, the point exceeds either the deviation or the maximum time. The minimum time eliminates the massive number of exception reports caused by a rapidly oscillating point. The maximum time is used by the network to assure itself that the transmitting nodes are still active and have not dropped off the line. Exception reporting was implemented in computer-based monitoring for power plants in the 1970s and in the Bailey Network 90 instrumentation shortly thereafter. It was ideal for digital networks that could become saturated if the system continuously broadcast redundant information.

Exception reporting is used for providing real-time data; compression is used for data storage. The early type of compression used a boxcar algorithm and is shown in Fig. 2.9. This type of compression requires a starting point; assume that one point is stored, and then

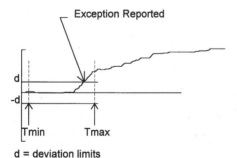

d = deviation limits

Figure 2.8 Exception reporting.

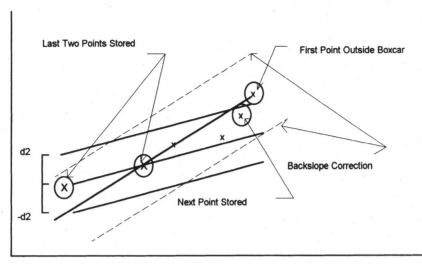

Figure 2.9 Boxcar compression.

draw a line to each new point that is received. Bands are then drawn (figuratively) at the same slope as the line joining the data points, and each new point is checked to see if it falls outside of the space defined by the dead band. Once a point is found that should be stored, it is sent to the archive and a new line is drawn from this newly stored value to the previously stored value and all the points between are checked to ensure they are within deviation bounds. This is called the *backslope correction,* shown by the dashed line. For many years, the majority of compressed-data archives were the boxcar with backslope correction. Minor variations (e.g., using a polynomial instead of a line) were tried, but were not in wide use.

To see the difference between exception reporting and compression, consider a point moving in a straight line of nonzero slope. Exception reporting provides reports of events with each passing of a deviation d, but no compression reports are generated until the slope changes. Thus applications that use current data, e.g., a process graphic, can refresh their values and stay updated in real time by using exception reports. Applications that require history, e.g., trends, use compressed data. An important characteristic of both methods is that they better support event-driven applications which are mandatory for the distributed computing environment for effective use of the networks.

Figure 2.10 illustrates the difference between compression and averaging (or sampling) in regard to preserving the shape of the curve. The X's are the time averages of the data at even intervals. The O's are the data stored by a compression algorithm. Note that the

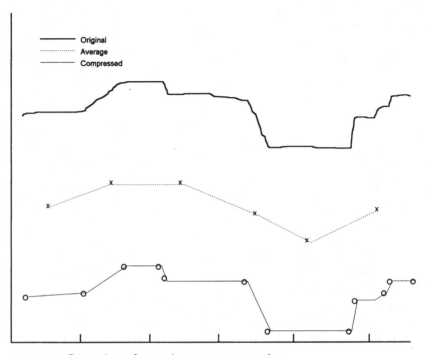

Figure 2.10 Comparison of averaging versus compression.

basic shape of the curve is altered by averaging and that most of the cause-and-effect information is missing or dramatically altered. It is impossible to tell, a priori, how many data points are needed to preserve the basic shape of the curve. It is clear that averaging or sampling markedly affects the frequency content of the time series data—this is the reason why advanced control vendors insist on very high-frequency sampling of the data to do the model determination.

Another method of compression, called the *swinging door,* has the advantages that a single point is needed for start-up, guaranteeing that all points are within the deviation band, and better least-mean-square reconstruction of the curve. Maximum and minimum times are handled as before and are not shown.

With the swinging-door algorithm, a value is stored if a straight line drawn between the last stored value and the next value does not come within the deviation specification of all the intermediate points. Figure 2.11 shows the slopes as dashed lines as they are initialized after a value is stored. One is drawn from the last point plus the deviation and rotated clockwise until all deviations are met. The other is drawn from the last recorded value minus the deviation and rotated counterclockwise until all deviations are met. A value is recorded

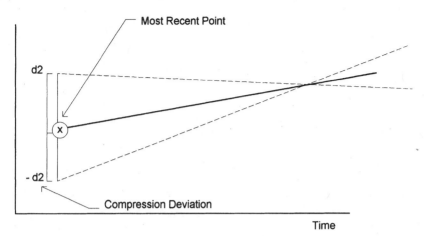

Figure 2.11 Swinging-door method after recording value.

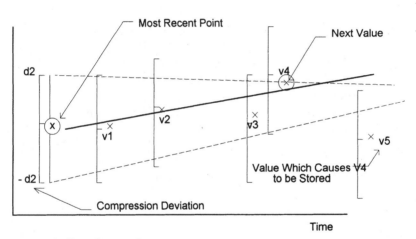

Figure 2.12 Recording a value.

when it is no longer possible to contain all the points within their deviation bands within the lines. This ensures that each value falls within the compression specification which becomes the maximum possible error. Figure 2.12 shows the system after four more values (v_1, v_2, v_3, v_4) have been received from the exception reporting. These values still do not cause a value to be stored because lines can be drawn which do not violate any of the deviation checks. The next value, v_5, creates the case where straight lines cannot be drawn that do not violate one of the deviation bands of the points and thus causes the v_4 to be recorded.

The net result of exception plus compression is a data flow shown in Fig. 2.13. Data enter the system and are immediately exception-

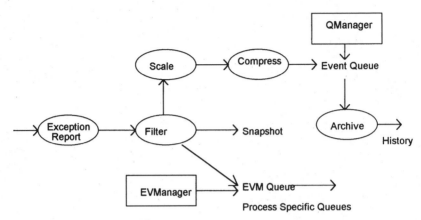

Figure 2.13 Data collection flow.

reported, which turns them into time-stamped events. After the filtering, these data are sent to the snapshot, compression, and user event queues, which are managed by an event manager. After compression, the data are sent to a different event queue and into the history. Since the data are time-stamped upon first recording, the processing is not time-critical.

This queue is managed by a queue manager so that the history can be backed up without data loss. Proper management of these event queues is a requirement for distributed processing. It is important to allow other applications to take advantage of the computations that have already been done by providing them with information by exception.

Metrics

In quality management systems, information derived from measurements is called a *metric,* and the design of a proper metric is very important. A rule of thumb is that whatever is reported as a metric will improve. Metrics may be the only numbers presented to management because people can only deal with relatively low-frequency data rates; these few numbers consequently take on great significance. Without well-designed metrics, managers will develop their own (each has favorite numbers that she or he uses as an "indicator"). Properly designed metrics allow people to see quickly the current state of the facilities.

For data collection systems, a rate of 200 to 300 points per second for each of 10 to 15 interfaces is not uncommon. People can only cope with a few points per second and, under stress, this decreases.

Establishing metrics is the way to reduce real-time data flows to people in addition to the commonly used summaries (reports, material balance, graphics); four are discussed in this section:

- Alarms and events
- Slow learn
- Measured metrics
- Agents

The ideal is to be able to communicate with the person (whether a process operator or manager) by exception presenting only needed information. The definition of *needed* is not static. It includes both deterministic (configured by the user) and unsolicited (sent by the system) information.

Alarms and events

Alarms and events can come in a large quantity and sometimes are more hindrance than help, often causing confusion (alarms are a specialized subset of events). Most instrument systems provide alarms and events in the form of digital states, numeric data, and text or journals. But these will be of no use until (1) they are converted to a common format and (2) tools are provided to allow the users to "sign up" for only the events that are meaningful to the job.

A good example of how a user extracted useful information from a mass of events concerns a large refinery complex. The system used an older Taylor Mod 3. This system was severely limited in the number of loops handled per module (512); thus there were 12 separate control networks in this very large complex, and each had its own alarm printer port. The designers knew that operators would never keep 12 printers on-line in a control room, and the system was installed with no printers—a poor solution to the problem.

The initial step to rectify this problem was to connect the ports intended for the printers to a PC and provide buffering and a reporting tool for the operations supervisor. All 12 instrument systems were connected into a single PC to document the alarms and events (loop on/off, setpoint change, mode change, etc.). The operating supervisor viewed a report every day to see what was happening and noticed that as operators became stressed, they tended to make more changes, which increased the traffic of events. In one incident an operator used the group-acknowledge function incorrectly and burned down a heater. The events archived on the PC were the only indication of what had happened—the continuous data did not show the (incorrect) group acknowledge, which was why the operator missed the hazardous situation.

To provide himself with a metric, the supervisor had the plant monitoring system compute the events per minute for the six operating areas and put these in as a normal variables. This provided a "stress monitor" for each of the six process operators. If the level went above a threshold, the operations supervisor would be paged. He would go to the control room unobtrusively to see if help was needed. In many cases, it was an operator having some trouble, and the experienced help was appreciated. In all cases, the experienced help appeared without request by the operator.

This is a good example of developing a few pieces of vital information from a massive amount of data; these 12 ports produced 60,000 events in a normal weekend.

Alarms are always a potential overload for people, but due to safety considerations, they are seldom filtered or "cut out." In addition to the alarms in the instrumentation, most plant monitoring systems can generate alarms for variables not in the DCS (violation specifications, operating limits, equipment limits). In addition to the process alarms, there are real-time *statistical process control* (SPC) plots which indicate when the plant is out of statistical control.

Other events are an essential part of detecting when to inform people by exception:

- Loop control on/off
- Device operation
- Backcheck and pattern monitors
- Operator comments and logbooks
- Sequence steps from batch processes

At present, event handling is an area that needs to be improved beyond the few ideas presented above.

Slow learn

The plant monitoring systems produce so many data that people are overwhelmed. Application engineers are always looking for ways to reliably indicate that there is a problem. There are a proliferation of simple methods to try to extract meaningful information from these data; consider a technique called the *slow learn* (see Fig. 2.14).

The slow learn is a technique whereby an action limit and a critical limit are imposed on important variables. When the system passes the action level, it is told to learn via algorithm (usually regression or

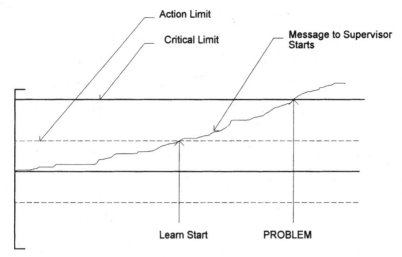

Figure 2.14 Slow learn.

neural net) the cause-and-effect relationship. If the variable has not returned to a value less than the action limit by the time the system has learned, then the system will predict when a critical limit will be reached and will report this by exception. In these calculations, both event information and continuous variables can be used. The system will continue to report on the problem until the critical variable returns to a state under the action limit. This is intended for problems that are building in a longer time frame (weeks) over which the supervisory personnel can keep a vigil, e.g., exchanger scaling, catalyst fouling, or degradation of the heat rate. These are the tools needed when one is faced with the tremendous amount of possible data. There is a need for background applications that simply indicate that it would be a good idea to look a little closer.

Many of the data required by supervision have very long cycle times, and a small reminder is needed as the scope of supervisory personnel expands in the ongoing downsizing.

Measured metrics

Measured metrics are variables derived from the measurements and their attributes (e.g., the rate). Typical metrics are energy per pound of feed, efficiency, maximum or average deviation from target, and percentage of uptime. These computations need to be designed to support the goals of the management system. Most executive-level personnel do not know which instrument tags to look at—this is another example of data useful for personnel close to the plant floor but not for management. Once defined, however, the metrics are a good way to provide a lot of information from the data. As an example, management spends quite a lot of money for a new instrument system. In one of our installations, managers decided to provide metrics to ensure that they were getting their value from the investment. The metrics were time in control (valve is between 10 and 90 percent), time in automatic, and time with no oscillation.

Management began accurate tracking of these metrics and directing the personnel (maintenance, operations) required to keep the loops on-line to look at these, rather than cycling throughout all the instrumentation; this resulted in a control uptime increase from 45 to 95 percent, clearly a better use of the multimillion-dollar investment.

Agents

Presentation of data is the area where we expect to see the greatest change in the next few years. Currently, the display system is used by personnel in the plant and consists of almost entirely deterministic reports and displays—fixed information built by the user or a systems person.

Examples are trending, graphics, reports, event logs, SPC charts, profiles, and others. Display systems have attributes in common: They present, in some form, history and other data irrespective of the viewer; and they have means for the user to change graphics of the plant, trend data, or SPC chart regardless of the plant or organizational model. This style of presentation is representative of the older hierarchy—a single monolithic system with central data presentation only. The new organization (peer-to-peer, distributed, highly motivated, and enabled) will have very different desktops between job functions. Two new types of new functions must be supported, and sometimes both are on the workstation. These are the collaborative work group and the strategic user.

Consider that what we have today does not work for management. Most of the PCs on the desks of executives are used only for personal productivity software, with the possible exception of e-mail. As pointed out by Vaskevitch (1992), 75 percent of software on a PC is spreadsheet, word processor, and database. A manager cannot use most of these in the job. Take the example of e-mail: Most e-mail is peer-to-peer—an unusual communication mode for a manager. When a problem has escalated to the long-term perspective, the manager must review and make decisions. Review of correspondence is only one example of software used within the collaboration work group called a *forum*. As a consequence of this lack of software directed at their needs, executives will use files, faxes, secretaries, and phones.

The missing ingredient is what is now known as the *agent*. Suppose that a manager gets the following message in her mail one morning:

IF YOU CONTINUE TO RUN THE SOUTH MOUNTAIN STATION OVER THE NEXT MONTH AS IT HAS RUN THE LAST TWO MONTHS, YOU WILL TRIGGER THE NEXT LEVEL OF EPA ENFORCEMENT DUE TO EXCESSIVE CEM VIOLATIONS.

These are not the words a manager wants to see, but it is much better to get the message while there is still time to take action. The value of this information is immense—it could make or break the company. The source of this information was her agent.

The agent must cull though the data and collect information from other applications to find the information required by management. The agent provides analysis, prediction of bad (and good) things to come, and feedback on the operation of the management system. The software would also support tools to show how it arrived at the conclusion, if asked by the manager. The presentation of the agent must be natural, informative, and aware of the managers' needs.

The agent is a program that acts as a user in the collaborative work environment, which also supports discussion topics, complex document management, replication across loosely connected links, and the other elements that make up this environment. In this situation, the communication becomes much more automatic, efficient, and direct. In the very flat organizational structures of the future, an operator may respond to queries from the top executives, and technical support may respond to operators in the normal conduct of their business.

This environment must also support the superuser. Probably there are several orders of magnitude of difference in ability and efficiency between the top 1 percent of the process troubleshooters and the average. The superuser is a person in that top 1 percent who should be surrounded with tools to increase productivity. A good example is the maintenance diagnostic engineer who specializes in vibration analysis—this user should have a workstation capable of performing and maintaining Fourier transforms in real time of any signal desired.

The agent is a program that acts as a superuser for someone else—its advantage is that it is faster, cheaper, and more predictable than a person. Its disadvantage is that people can still reason better and are more creative than programs.

System Support Considerations

Software that is not supported will die. This requires that the system designer provide sufficient tools from the beginning for supporting the system. Many aspects of maintenance have already been mentioned, but there are a few parts that were designed specifically for the maintainability of the system:

- Automated maintenance
- Stand-alone operation
- Buffering and redundancy

We have already discussed, in other sections, items that have to do with support such as the verify programs and I/O rates programs in the "Interface" section.

Automated maintenance

As the database becomes more distributed, the maintainability of the software becomes an important issue for reliability. Most incidents of network and control downtime during the early stages of a system are due to confusion or errors during start-up, shutdown, or routine maintenance; these have the same bad or dangerous effect as hardware errors. The client/server approach provides a completely automated maintenance and support system from the information network level.

Installation of the original system and upgrades of both the historian and the interface client should use VMSINSTAL procedures from Digital or equivalent automated maintenance procedures. This will be challenging with UNIX, since maintenance and management of the system are an area not currently specified by the open-system standards. After loading, the user should be able to log on and answer a few questions, and then the install procedure will install the historian, which will then install the interface clients automatically.

Once installed, the mother node is started up with a single command. This node then sends the required data to the daughter nodes and automatically starts the interface client. Once it is up and working, a copy is made on the local disks so that the daughter node can start up by itself in a stand-alone mode.

Management of change is automated; all changes to the database are made in one place and propagated to the daughter nodes automatically with the replication server. The mother node must also take care of time synchronization so that all the interface clients are synchronized.

Backup is also automated. A command file should be built that will temporarily stop all traffic from the interface client to the historian, but buffer the data in the queue manager. All users are suspended and files are closed, the system is backed up to local media, and then everything is restarted with no data loss and only loss of response for a brief time when the active archive is copied to a scratch file.

Stand-alone operation

Stand-alone operation is required so that the system on the control network can be restarted, after a failure, without the mother node. If advanced controls are contemplated, any data scanned by the daughter node continue to be updated by the instrumentation interfaces independent of the mother node. If data from the mother node are required by a control program, the data will be returned marked with an error code if the mother node is down. This allows advanced controls to continue to run even with no information coming from the network.

The interface client requires a menu system, similar to the mother node but with somewhat reduced functionality, so that control applications can be run locally. This makes it simple to define control applications to run with the information network gone.

Buffering and redundancy

One use of the daughter node is for advanced controls which should not be affected by the queries of users to the information system.

The data are very important to the information network. For this reason, the interface client should support redundancy of both interfaces and interface client nodes in nearly any combination. If redundancy for control programs is required, a dual processor is required; but failover can be done with no data loss without the hot standby.

The computers on the control network tend to be simple machines with few users resulting in high uptimes, so data buffering is supported for systems that do not require redundancy. In this case, if the information network were lost, the interface client would store the data in a time-stamped format for several days in a queue manager and, when the system was repaired, would supply the missing data. With certain DCSs, e.g., the TDC3000, failures in the interface client can be backed up by the history module within the DCS.

Another advantage of this style of buffering and redundancy is that it allows an upgrade of parts of the system with no downtime and no data loss. If no data loss is a sufficient criterion, then fault tolerance is not required at the host level.

Trademarks

- IBM, RS6000, IBM 1800, and OS/2 are trademarks of International Business Machines, Inc.
- SETCON is a trademark of Setpoint, Inc.
- HW4500 and TDC 3000 are trademarks of Honeywell, Inc.

- VB (Visual Basic), Excel, Windows, Windows-NT, and MS-DOS are trademarks of Microsoft, Inc.
- Sparcstation is a trademark of Sun Microsystems.
- HP-UX is a trademark of Hewlett-Packard Corporation.
- DECNET, VAX, and Decstation are trademarks of Digital Equipment Corporation.
- AAI is an abbreviation for Applied Automation, Inc.
- PI is a trademark of Oil Systems, Inc.
- Macintosh is a trademark of Apple Computer, Inc.
- ORACLE is a trademark of Oracle Corporation.
- SYBASE is a trademark of Sybase, Inc.

References

Kennedy, J. P. (1992): "Integrate Real Time Data with Decision Support," *Hydroc. Proc.,* vol. 71, no. 5, May, pp. 69–74.

Hale, J. C., and H. L. Sellers (1981): "Historical Data Recording for Process Computers," *Chem. Eng. Prog.,* November, pp. 38–43.

Vaskevitch, D. (1992): "Why Business Managers Are Empty Handed," *Computerworld,* April 5, pp. 93–97.

3

Databases and Information Management

Kirk Williams
Chesapeake Decision Sciences, Inc.

As a project manager and design consultant on five large oil refinery systems integration projects in the United States, Europe, and the Far East, I have had the opportunity to deal firsthand with the issues of designing and successfully implementing such systems. This experience has time and again reinforced the message that the information system is the window through which the users see and interact with the integrated system and that as a result, it is key to receiving the benefits generated by the overall system. The design and successful implementation of the information system, and its attendant database, must be driven by the following global objectives:

1. The long-term support and maintenance costs of the system resulting from design decisions must be minimized. Spending money on rigorous design, focusing on flexibility, and exploiting end-user tools are all key to the minimization of the total life-cycle cost of the system. A gentle reminder: System requirements specifications are always wrong, and this fact must be a design consideration; if it is not, the implementation and long-term support costs will explode.

2. There must be a change in the business culture; i.e., the information system must be used right from the outset as a vehicle for changing the business and operational practices at the manufacturing site. Move from focusing on quantities and utilizations to a money-based decision process at all levels.

It is perhaps cynical to suggest that a site manager's view of the operation and what actually occurs are not necessarily the same thing. However, with access to a database generated from a well-integrated system via a productive, user-friendly information system, the site manager will have an intimate knowledge of the real status of the production schedule, and so will all the operational, technical, and production or commercial staff. All site operations become visible at all levels and in any degree of detail. In short, there is nothing that can be hidden; meeting the plan means exactly that and nothing else.

3. The expectations of users, local management, and senior corporate management must be managed so as to ensure that the key steps in the project implementation are not cut short in an attempt to minimize short-term costs. In a sense, this is about education on the importance of design and the relative scale of design and construction costs compared to long-term support costs. Also there must be a serious attempt to sell the system to the users with the discipline of exposing users only to robust systems. Many systems implementations have failed simply because the users were exposed to immature and fragile systems too early, and as a result, their buy-in was forever lost.

4. The relational database is the only entity that subsystems communicate with; they must never attempt to interact directly with each other. This minimizes the complexity of the integration and can decouple processing to reduce interdependency and increase overall robustness and operability.

Concept of the Central Database

Traditionally there has been only limited integration of planning and scheduling systems with real-time process control systems and other data feed systems. This is due to the complexity of managing the numerous file-transfer interfaces and their temporal dependencies. In particular, failure recovery, file locking, data duplication and consistency, and operational dependency all combine to limit the extent to which integration can be achieved. This complexity stems from the numerous proprietary elements required to make up the total system. Vendors supplying supervisory control systems with purpose-built operating systems, planning and scheduling tools based on cumbersome card image or more recently spreadsheet input formats, and head office stocks accounting and sales systems implemented on proprietary mainframe systems all contribute to the problem of complexity. This is illustrated in Fig. 3.1.

Implementing a system where the integration is based on this type of discrete interface results in a highly complex operational environ-

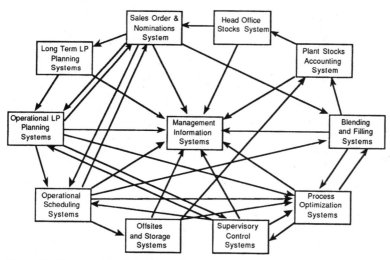

Figure 3.1 Discrete interface integration.

ment with high levels of data duplication and the attendant problems of data consistency, system interdependency, and operational fragility. Another major issue that arises is the currency and completeness of the management information generated. A system such as this is dependent on the operation of chains of discrete processes and interfaces. The management information database at the end of that complex chain is unlikely to be of any real tactical use in planning, monitoring, or controlling the manufacturing process. Attempts at this type of integration have been made by many manufacturing companies, but it is unusual for such systems to deliver their promised benefits, and the systems resulting from such developments are often significantly reduced in scope or fall into disuse because of their complexity of operation and long-term maintenance costs.

The explosive growth in open-systems computing and hardware performance and the very large improvements in the throughput and robustness of proprietary relational database management systems since the mid-1980s have combined to offer a solution to this integration problem. As a result of these fundamental changes in the computing environment, it has become practical to use relational database software technology as a vehicle for integration within the manufacturing process industry. A relational database and the available fourth-generation language tools offer a mechanism to significantly reduce the complexity of the interface problem. A central relational database becomes the interface medium for the subsystems making up an integrated planning, scheduling, management information, operational control, and monitoring system (see Fig. 3.2).

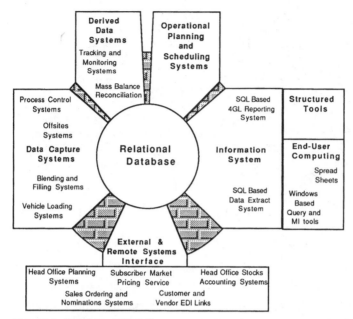

Figure 3.2 Database integration.

The central relational database within the integrated system must define the interface standard and fulfill the role of a message bus, linking all the subsystems and external interfaces. As a result, communications are necessary only between the subsystems and the database, rather than directly between the various subsystems. In this way, a layered system architecture may be developed, reducing interface complexity. This will greatly reduce data duplication and consistency problems and will allow increased operational independence of the subsystems. Within such an architecture the user need only deal with the information system or specialist tools fed from the database rather than many disparate systems.

Constituent Parts of an Integrated System

The subsystems linked into the central database and information system that make up an integrated manufacturing system may be broken down into four broad categories:

1. Data capture systems

2. Monitoring systems

3. Decision support systems

4. Real-time optimization systems

All feed data into the database, manipulate data held in the database to create derived data, or extract data for use by users or external systems. With a few exceptions, the systems linked to the database are background batch systems preparing data for presentation to the user by the information system tools. The obvious exceptions are the workstation-based decision support tools, the linear programming (LP) planning and scheduling systems, which require direct user involvement and have their own purpose-built user interfaces.

These are examples of the subsystems linked to the database:

- *Data capture systems:* real-time process control systems, tank gauging systems, blending and filling systems, laboratory automation/information systems, external nominations and sales ordering systems, public EDI links to customers and industry data services (e.g., market price quotation services), head office stocks accounting systems, head office long-term planning systems, and commodity trading systems

- *Monitoring systems:* mass-balance reconciliation systems, operational tracking systems (e.g., movement tracking to generate the data to enable the comparison of actual versus planned activities and verifying operational requests against current available resources and forward plans), derived data systems (e.g., cash flow calculations, process-level mass balancing, energy balancing, equipment performance parameters), reporting systems, trending and alarm systems.

- *Decision support systems:* These are characterized by three types of systems. First, linear programming (LP) systems are used for operation planning, blend optimization, buy/sell feedstock and product valuations, and evaluation of crisis management options (tactical decision support). Second, scheduling systems are used for planning short-term operations in detail, often consisting of several modeling systems covering different sections of the operation (e.g., process operations and filling and blending may be treated separately). Third, database reporting systems and end-user computing tools are used, such as stock accounting and valuation systems, statutory reporting, comparison of planned versus actual in physical and cash terms, and detailing contributions to cash flow.

- *Real-time process optimization systems:* Real-time optimization and constraint-pushing systems are usually a combination of LP and nonlinear programming (NLP) models and process models designed to give real-time advice to operation staff as to the economic optimum operation of the process in real time. These systems are sometimes linked directly to the process control systems to operate in a supervisory mode, although this is often ill advised because of the purely feedforward nature of most of these models and the long deadtime in the total system (i.e., process control systems and modeling systems). The data required to support on-line or real-time process optimization are collected from the process control systems, laboratory systems, LP planning systems, and mass-balance reconciliation systems. This optimization process is run external to the process control system and places the results into the database for communication to the process control system, again applying the principle of the subsystems communicating with only the database.

Critical Success Factors

There are many ways to construct the database and information systems to support the integration of the systems described previously; it is safe to say there is no one correct design and implementation strategy. Set out below are the key success factors for making it work and minimizing the total life-cycle cost of the system. A common theme runs through all these factors—good design, flexibility, and a sharp focus on long-term maintenance and support costs—because there is one inescapable fact: $1 spent in good design can save $1000 in maintenance and support costs over the life of the system.

Database design

Design objectives. It is a tired and well-worn statement that database design is everything in building systems using relational databases and fourth-generation languages. It is absolutely true, with no exceptions, particularly in attempting the integration of so many complex subsystems. I have been personally involved in the implementation of five major integrated planning, scheduling, and process control systems in oil refineries in the Far East, Europe, and the United States for a major oil company, and in every single case, the truth of this statement has been painfully reinforced.

There is very real management pressure on systems developers to cut short the database design in order to deliver early results. It is not usually acceptable for the project team to disappear behind closed doors for a year and emerge with only a good database design to show for the effort and expense. Some middle ground must be found that allows the demonstration of visible progress while a rigorous and detailed database design is completed. This may be achieved by first establishing the appropriate management expectations, bringing the senior management into the early project planning and quality assurance strategy process, and stressing the vital importance of good design. Also, deliver throwaway prototypes and demonstration systems to manage user expectations and establish or harden user requirements, but the database design work must be done. It cannot be allowed to just evolve.

A word on prototyping is called for. This is a powerful tool for developing reporting systems, but it is not necessarily as useful in designing relational databases. If a prototyping route is taken, then a final reengineering step must be included in the overall project cost. The final prototype evolution is not the finished product—just the completed specification. Then the real system must be constructed from this specification. Again, this is an expectation-management issue; unless this strategy is clear at the outset, there will be strong pressure to implement the final prototype as the production system. This is *always* fatal to the long-term maintenance budgets and system performance, because the build quality and database design resulting from this process are always filled with patches, work-arounds, so-called temporary fixes, and successive generations of changes and redundant code, all of which is a mine field for ongoing maintenance.

The use of a rigorous methodology implemented in the form of a CASE tool is also essential. The specific methodology is not that important, rather, the rigor and automation that the CASE tool brings to the process are paramount. The selection of a CASE tool with automated links to the chosen *relational database management system* (RDBMS) and fourth-generation languages is a significant advantage, as these tools often bring code generators to automate the construction of the information systems.

The database must contain a representation of the physical manufacturing process, its commercial environment, and all their attributes, values, and statuses through time. Changes to the manufacturing process are inevitable and must not impact the database design or that of the reporting systems. Similarly, the commercial environment within which the business operates is volatile, and this volatility is often structural, with new markets and demands continually replacing established ones. Again, these changes must be anticipated by the database design and transparently accommodated.

Therefore, in terms of design philosophy, there is one clear target: *flexibility*. The database that results from the design process must be proof against future changes. Careful attention to normalization and use of highly flexible metastructures for reference and master file data (refer to Fig. 3.3) will greatly reduce the cost impact of future requirements and changes to the system, the business it supports, and the physical and commercial environment it is attempting to model.

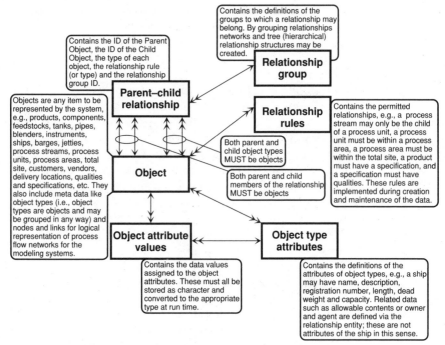

Figure 3.3 Flexible database metastructures.

Process and off-site data capture. This area of database design is the source of significant design problems. This is due to the synchronous nature of the database transactions and the enormous volumes of data involved; e.g., storing minute averages for 2000 data points for 5 days requires around 1000 Mbytes of storage in a well-indexed relational database.

Typically these data are also held at several levels of compression and length of history, for example, 1- or 5-minute averages for 7 days, hourly averages for 33 days, daily averages for 1 year, and monthly averages forever. The capture, processing, and storage of these data are a major database design problem and if handled inappropriately, will cripple even the largest database servers. Remember that the data compression (averaging) is also a heavy synchronous load, although without rigorous timing constraints, and must be accommodated in the overall system loading and scheduling analysis. A typical processing architecture is depicted in Fig. 3.4.

Relational database management systems are optimized for two types of transactions: the indexed select (query) and update, and the unindexed record insertion (creation) and deletion. This is due to the heavy overhead of index management associated with the creation

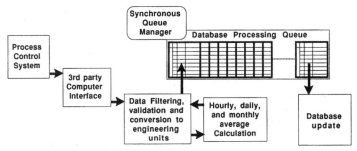

Figure 3.4   Process data capture processing.

and deletion of new data. The indices most commonly used by the RDBMS are modified B-TREE indices which must be resorted and balanced by the database management system once the extent of change to the data table pointed to by the index rises above a threshold value (the actual value varies depending on the proprietary RDBMS; for some, any change will trigger an index resort).

The RDBMSs are also optimized for short record lengths. The RDBMS usually only reads and caches physical storage blocks (or database pages), typically 2048 bytes. Record lengths that are either larger than the database page or sized so that there is a noninteger number of records per page will cause a significant increase in the number of database pages read from disk and hence will slow performance. Ideally, short records (and their free-space specification) should be sized to allow an integer number of records per database page.

These characteristics of the RDBMS combine to force a particular solution to the problem of capturing and storing large volumes of data in a synchronous manner. This design must also be able to deliver high query performance. After all, there is little point in capturing the data in a timely manner if they cannot be reported on with acceptable response time to the user. A structure supporting both high-volume data capture and high-performance queries is shown in Fig. 3.5. This structure has been implemented at a number of sites and has consistently demonstrated acceptable performance.

The key to the performance of this structure is its index stability. The process data table must be prewritten and populated with dummy data to the maximum length allowed in the database table definition and with the date/time pointer ID and the tag IDs written to their columns in blocks for each time-stamp ID value (i.e., the tag ID varies fastest). Then the indices may be applied to these two columns. In operation, these columns are never updated so the indices are completely stable. The process data table becomes a circu-

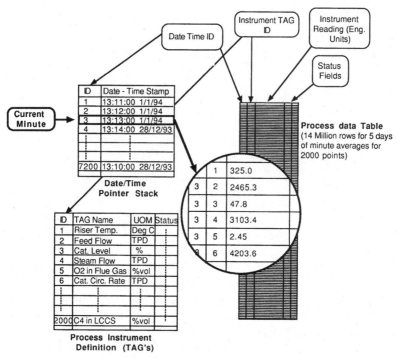

Figure 3.5 Database structure for process data capture.

lar buffer, with new data overwriting old, and the location of the data in the table is resolved by the date/time pointer table.

It is essential to fill the data fields in this table during this initialization process to the maximum extent allowed by the table definition; i.e., if the data field allows numbers of 15 characters and 4 decimals, then a 9999999999.9999 should be used to initialize the field. This is necessary because many database management systems only allocate space to store the data written; if later this is updated to a larger string, then a pointer is written and the data are written to free space elsewhere in the database. This RDBMS strategy is often referred to as *database chaining* and is implemented to minimize database space requirements. However, the side effect of this strategy is to prolong the write process and complicate (i.e., slow) data retrievals.

User acceptance and cultural change

The big money to be made from integrated manufacturing systems is not from advanced control, optimization, and scheduling in isolation but rather from a combining of the data generated from these systems—by making all the operations visible in real time to all levels of management and allowing the measurement of those activities in cash terms. However, to recover the benefits of the information system requires the enthusiastic buy-in of the user community. There are two prerequisites for achieving this buy-in; failing on either of these will certainly prolong the implementation of the system and reduce the benefits recovered. First, the software and hardware that the users are initially exposed to *must* be completely robust. What the users see first will color their perceptions of everything that follows. Second, users must see right from the start the usefulness of the system in the context of their day-to-day work.

In a very real sense, the information system is the window through which the majority of users will see the system and must be the carrot that leads the users to accepting the system. Key to this is the capturing of the imagination of the user community with simple-to-use reporting systems that replace and enhance their normal daily process monitoring tasks. As an example, a simple process data download to a spreadsheet of user-selected data (duration, frequency, and type) will quickly have great appeal to the process engineers, particularly if these data contain derived parameters such as heat-transfer coefficients, catalyst activities, and cost data. It is important to ensure that this type of functionality is entirely user-driven; i.e., the user chooses all the parameters and interactively initiates the download. In short, give the user control of the environment. Once the user's imagination is captured, the process of introducing the commercial thinking is simply a matter of incorporating cost/profit and cash flow data within the routine operational reports and setting operational targets in money terms.

At most sites, effective exploitation of the information systems and their attendant database requires a cultural change to bring commercial thinking to all levels of the operation. It must become second nature for all staff to think in terms of the dollar impact of their decisions and actions. It is the primary function of the information system to reinforce this culture by monitoring and reporting all activities in dollars. This is where the money is actually made.

Domain definition and data consistency

The consistent definition of data domains is a major factor in simplicity and ease of integration. This is rather like motherhood and apple pie, i.e., obviously good, but it is the most common problem in integrating the subsystems via a common database/information system.

To illustrate the data consistency issue, consider an LP planning system and a scheduling system. Both must contain representations of the physical process configuration, its yield and throughput constraints, product, feedstock and component qualities and attributes. Traditionally the two modeling systems would have had their own large databases containing these representational data (typically at least 10,000 records) expressed in terms specific to the modeling system. However, on integration of these two systems, one always experiences mismatches in definition due to the difficulties associated with the independent maintenance of two such large volumes of detailed representational data. Since most of these systems are constraint-driven, these representational mismatches not only were inconvenient to the mechanics of the integration but also undermined the relevance and quality of the solutions generated.

The simple solution to this consistency problem is to share a common database of representational data. Clearly the scope of the problem extends well beyond the example above, and all subsystems must share a common representational database. The major stumbling block to achieving this in practice is the often confused definition of the data domains within the subsystems. For example, it is often expedient to merge the domains of blending pools (physically tanks or in-line blenders), products, and process streams within an LP model formulation, and from the point of view of the mathematical formulation, they are treated identically. But from the point of view of the information system, these are very different. It is usually a simple matter to reformulate the LP model to accept these as separate domains, thereby eliminating the problem of merging input to match the model formulation and then dissecting the output to match the information systems domain.

In summary, an entity definition must have the same domain in all subsystems; e.g., the entity defining the list of salable products must be that and only that to all systems referencing it. The other key to ease of integration is the elimination of data duplication. Each subsystem must reference one and only one instance of any data item, never its own copy.

Object orientation, tools orientation, end-user configurability, end-user computing, and flexibility

Object orientation, tools orientation, end-user configurability, end-user computing, and *flexibility* are all massively overused buzzwords. What this is really all about is building user tools, not specific solutions against rigid specifications. In short, it is a design philosophy.

Too often, systems are built to meet specified requirements only to find that the requirements were incorrectly specified, were not understood by the users and/or the developers, or were just plain changed over the time required to build the system. In any case, the effort is wasted and the total systems cost goes up.

There is one immutable truth in building database systems: *the requirements specifications are always wrong.* This is the result of the knowledge gap between the users specifying the requirements and the systems developers implementing those requirements. The users usually have only a slim grasp of the possibilities and constraints of the system technology, and the developers' grasp of the business environment is equally fuzzy. So inevitably as the systems are delivered, the users become more and more aware of the potential of the technology, and this always renders the original requirements specified for the system obsolete. This is the major cause of project overruns and late delivery.

The solution to this problem is embodied in that list of buzzwords in the section title. Build tools that the users can configure to solve their own problems and fulfill their own requirements. This involves a process of interpretation of the original requirements into a set of tools capable of being configured to meet these requirements and with the flexibility to be extended and evolved by the users without the intervention of systems developers. The best example of this is the success of the PC spreadsheet and the way it has revolutionized end-user computing. A word of warning: The PC spreadsheet also brought some serious control and audit issues with its explosion of end-user-developed tools. A little constraint is a good thing.

A successful information system with supporting database is a tool kit from which the users can construct their own systems. The important issues are data and transaction consistency; robust, auditable, and secure operation; flexibility; and ease of use. An example of how this philosophy may be turned into a real system can be seen by considering the problem of reporting on process data. It would be simple enough to survey all the users on a site and write a set of reports that contained the range of views of the process data that the users required, e.g., material balances by parts of process units, whole process units, and process area over the entire site, by hour, 10-minute averages, daily, weekly, and monthly, perhaps rolling averages as well as fixed calendar averages. If you work through this, you will probably arrive at some 1000-odd discrete reports and burn up about 5 person-years of effort writing, testing, and implementing them. I have seen this very approach implemented in an oil refinery in Europe in which only 10 percent of these reports were ever run by the users.

Alternatively, give the user a tool kit consisting of a generalized report generator, a configurable system for synchronously calculating derived data (such as mass-balance closures) so they appear as real-time process data to the rest of the system, and an object-oriented master file system that can represent hierarchical relationships between reports and data sources. Then the user can generate his or her own reports over any period and any scope or content. The development and construction of such a system will use up about the same number of person-years of effort; but it will never be obsolete, and it will meet all the original requirements and any that users will dream up after implementation. In short, it is future-proof.

By taking this approach, ensuring that the supporting infrastructure is adequately generalized, auditable, and controlled, the use of end-user computing tools—custom-made or proprietary—will yield very large benefits in terms of reduced maintenance, cheaper development costs, and, more importantly, greater benefits recovery as users exploit the system much more widely than ever could be envisioned at the beginning of the system analysis and design.

Chapter

4

Data Reconciliation

C. Edward Bodington
Consultant

Gerard W. Cleaves
Manager, Chesapeake Decision Sciences, Inc.

Introduction

Data reconciliation is the adjustment of a set of data so that quantities derived from the data obey natural laws, such as material and energy balances. Measurements made on processes, such as flow, tank level, or temperature, are adjusted in some proportion to the standard error of the measurement. After adjustment, the material and, if considered, the energy balances are satisfied exactly. If a process model is used to assist in the data reconciliation, the model predictions now match process performance exactly for the current situation.

The fundamental purpose of data reconciliation is to reduce or eliminate as much as possible the effect of random measurement error on our analysis of process performance and on our predictions for future operation (Cleaves and Baker, 1987). Additional objectives are to improve our confidence in the calculation of unmeasured items, such as fractionating column internal reflux rates, and to identify process losses and faulty measurements (Lawrence, 1989; Brown and Lawrence, 1993).

Benefits of Data Reconciliation

The benefits of *data reconciliation* (DR) have been documented in the following areas (Ham et al., 1979):

1. Better monitoring of performance and higher accuracy of process yield measurements

2. Aid in detecting faulty instrumentation and in prioritization of instrument maintenance

3. More accurate operating data for technical analysis and process improvement

4. More accurate accounting and loss control

Some specific instances were also reported:

A catalyst evaluation using raw data led to an opposite conclusion, when compared to the use of reconciled data. Thus, the decision to change the catalyst would not have been made correctly if raw data had been used.

A process evaluation was performed in much less time with the help of a reconciliation program. The time requirement was reduced from about 2 weeks to a few hours.

A refinery observed that reconciled data led to improved credibility of planning predictions, reduced instrument maintenance cost, and earlier detection of losses and/or degrading performance.

Applicability of Data Reconciliation

Data reconciliation requires that a set of natural laws, such as material and energy balances, be applicable to the data set involved. Processes such as fractionation columns represent applications, since the laws apply easily to both overall rates and individual components of streams. However, many processes do not follow known natural laws that can be used for reconciliation purposes. For example, many physical properties measured for product blending, such as octane numbers or American Society for Testing Materials (ASTM) distillations, follow natural laws that are either unknown or only approximated by blending correlations. Only exact natural laws and near-exact relationships are useful in DR. Since many blending correlations are typically less exact than the measurements upon which they are based, such correlations are not usable for DR purposes. This means there is no substitute for accuracy in analytical data, from either a laboratory or a process analyzer. In the blending example, it means that components must be measured with the same care and diligence as the finished products are. The concepts presented below for gross (nonrandom) error detection and model tuning are applicable, and examples are given for such cases. Keep in mind that in cases where a true DR cannot be performed, gross error detection becomes more difficult.

Sources of Error

There are myriad reasons why a measurement will be found to be wrong. All measurements are subject to the random error of the measurement technology itself. The ASTM publications on their standard tests give ranges for the accuracy and reproducibility of the tests. For a process measurement such as an orifice meter for flow, the final result for a volume flow at some fixed temperature is dependent upon the flow instrument itself and additional measurements of the stream, such as specific gravity, temperature, and composition.

Unfortunately, measurements are also subject to many possible forms of nonrandom or systematic errors. For example, errors can arise from

- *Drift*—a slow change in the calibration of an instrument.

- *Bias*—a permanent one-sided error perhaps caused by an improper installation

- Deterioration of components, seals, etc.

- Wear of parts

- Corrosion of sensor equipment

- Fouling of sensors or measurement lines

- Improper calibration of an instrument

- Interference in an analytical procedure

- Improper analytical procedure

All techniques of data reconciliation assume that the error to be corrected is random, normally distributed in a statistical sense, and that the standard deviation of the measurement is known. Consequently, the procedures can help to identify the nonrandom errors noted above, but cannot really correct for them. In principle, first the nonrandom errors have to be removed by maintenance or adjustment of the instrument or sensor. Data reconciliation cannot be expected to function well in the presence of gross errors caused by any of the above problems. The real challenge appears when errors caused by the above are relatively small. The common presence of such errors might be thought to severely weaken the benefits of data reconciliation. However, experience has shown that such is not the case (Lawrence, 1989; Ham et al., 1979). Consistent use of a procedure for gross error detection and DR can pay for itself in leak detection, improvements in the efficiency of instrument maintenance, and higher accuracy and acceptance of predictions based on the data.

Redundancy

In the context of DR, *redundancy* means that a given measurement can be checked by a calculation based on other measurements. For example, a flow may also be calculated on the basis of several other flow measurements. The concept of being able to calculate a value to be compared with the direct measurement or another independent calculation is fundamental to DR. Without the extra information about error given by redundancy, DR cannot be performed. If there is no extra information, the system is just determined, and all measurements have to be accepted as is. Further, if there is even less information available, the system is underdetermined, and values have to be estimated (or guessed). It is very important to determine whether redundancy exists and, if it does not, which measurements should be added to gain redundancy at lowest cost.

The redundancy of measurements in a process can be determined by attempting to calculate the error in each of the natural-law balances to be considered. If all the data necessary are available, then the amount of process data is greater than the minimum necessary. Balance error is what the DR procedure works with and reduces to zero by data value adjustments.

In many processes, an overall material balance and its error can be routinely obtained, but internal balances that are important to a real understanding of the process performance are impossible to obtain due to a lack of instrumentation. Redundancy exists for the overall balance but not for some internal balances. Also redundancy may exist for some parts of the process or plant, but not others. For example, parallel heat exchangers may not have flow or temperature sensors to permit analysis of each one as an independent exchanger. A chemical reactor that uses hydrogen for temperature control may have total hydrogen flow measured, but not the distribution of hydrogen flow along the reactor, which is unmeasured and based solely on temperature control.

Many processes are instrumented in such a way that insufficient data are available on-line to calculate the balance errors. To perform DR, it will be necessary to add measurements. The determination of which measurements to add cannot be made in a simple, general way. The determination is important since adding sensors to a process is expensive and, in some cases, cannot be done without a process shutdown.

Several authors (Kretsovalis and Mah, 1987; Crowe, 1986; Mah, 1990) have described algorithms to classify data values as redundant, coaptive, and indeterminate. (*Coaptive* means that an unmeasured value can be estimated, but is not redundant.) Such a classification system is useful in organizing the approach to adding new measurements. However, no general implementations are known to be available for these algorithms. Actually setting up a trial DR application in one of the many nonlinear optimization systems that are available commercially would be a good first step.

Complexity of Data Reconciliation

The decision concerning how detailed data collection and DR should be is totally dependent on the use of the data. There is a hierarchy of uses for process data that requires more and more detail as we move down the list. (The order of items in the list is really a function of the process and its complexity. The list below gives one possible order. Your order may be different.)

Minimum detail:	Overall process rates
	Overall process performance
	Sensor maintenance advice

	Equipment performance
	   Heat-exchanger fouling factors
	   Catalyst activity
	   Compressor efficiency
	   Reactor conversion

	Component and atomic balances
	Control model tuning
	Optimization model tuning
Maximum detail:	Planning or design model tuning

The DR application to overall rates may only require a few measurements, while tuning an optimization or planning model may require hundreds. In general, the lower levels of detail can be handled with material balance DR alone. The intermediate levels may need energy balancing added. The most complex cases require a simultaneous DR and process model tuning.

Gross Error Detection

Before any DR can be performed, gross errors must be eliminated. As noted above, DR procedures assume that errors are random and not systematic. Removing systematic or gross errors is accomplished by one or more screenings of the data before the data are submitted to the DR procedure. Reasonableness checks via an expert system or simple range checks are very commonly used as the first level of gross error detection.

The next level of screening can be achieved by the use of *statistical quality control* (SQC) procedures. A measurement is tracked, and a gross error is suspected whenever the measurement goes out of its control limits. Tavary and Harris (1989) describe such an application to error detection for process analyzers. While these applications are really not DR (they consider only one variable at a time), they are an important relation that can be easily implemented with most process information systems that include SQC techniques. In addition to detecting gross errors, these procedures are very good for noise reduction for dynamic data measurements (Tham and Parr, 1994). Another approach uses the DR technique itself in a recursive way (Crowe, 1988). In this approach, the data are reconciled, and the changes made in the data values are examined. If any of the changes are larger than some criterion, e.g., more than 2 standard deviations for the measurement, then the suspect measurement is eliminated and the DR is rerun. If the improvement in fit justifies the elimination of the data value, the value is kept out and the results are examined for another suspect measurement. When this procedure concludes, the DR and gross error elimination have been accomplished simultaneously.

There are numerous variations on this basic theme (Rosenberg et al., 1987; Serth and Heenan, 1986). For the most part, the variations use a different criterion for selecting and eliminating the bad measurement. The simplest, known as the *measurement test,* is to calculate the ratio of the adjustment to the standard error of the measurement and then compare this to a cutoff value. The cutoff value is based on the probability of erroneously assigning a gross error when none, in fact, exists. This is commonly taken to be the 5 percent level, or a criterion of 2 standard deviations. Note that considerable redundancy is required in order to use this recursive technique. When measurements are eliminated, there still must be redundancy in the remaining measurements to perform DR and to estimate the missing values (Tham and Parr, 1994).

Fundamental Data Reconciliation Technique

The fundamental procedure for data reconciliation is to develop a set of natural-law balances within or around a process or a plant that must balance exactly. These balances are used as constraints in a mathematical minimization. An objective function is developed that is the sum of squares of the ratios of the measurement adjustments to the measurement standard deviations. This objective is minimized subject to the balance constraints. If the balances are volume or mass balances, the constraints are linear equations. The problem is a least-squares minimization subject to linear constraints (Ham et al., 1979). These problems can be solved by several techniques, but at present, using a nonlinear optimization system is likely to be most efficient (Cleaves and Baker, 1987). Even several spreadsheet programs available on personal computers have optimization systems built in that can handle this formulation. (The example to follow was solved with one of these programs.) The next level of data reconciliation requires component balances within streams and energy balances around heat exchangers, process heaters, furnaces, reactors, and the like (Charpentier et al., 1991). These balances all involve products of variables such as flow times composition or temperature functions (enthalpy). The objective function is the same as before, but the constraints are now nonlinear. Spreadsheet optimizers are capable of solving these problems, but may not be the best vehicle when the entire problem is very complex.

Redundancy may also be a problem when energy balances are added. The system may be very redundant when just flows are considered, but not at all when temperatures and enthalpy relationships are not well known. Because of this, adding the energy balances may not actually add very much to knowledge about the current state of the process. Forcing a balance when parts of the calculation are not exact or very well known may actually increase variable error. Even with adequate data on temperatures and compositions, items such as heat losses and heats of reaction may be known only approximately. Consequently, many applications move directly to tuning a process model rather than bothering with energy balancing.

Model Tuning and Data Reconciliation

A process mathematical model is a computer program that responds to submitted feed qualities and operating conditions in the same way as the real process, and it predicts product yields and qualities. Process models are fundamental to all procedures for internal model control, inferential control, model-based process optimization, and information feedback to planning and scheduling. The models need to be tuned to the process so that a model prediction for current operation will agree with what is actually happening. Tuning involves the adjustment of parameters within the model to make a model prediction agree exactly with the submitted data from the process.

Tuning a process model to data containing gross errors can only be misleading. The first step always must be not only detection of gross errors, but their elimination from the database or compensation for their effect. After some procedure has been used to detect a gross error, it is necessary to either fix the problem immediately or estimate a usable value for the measurement in error. The immediate fixing of the problem is often an unrealistic alternative. Perhaps the problem cannot be fixed as rapidly as desired, or the cause of the problem may not be understood yet. If the model is in a control loop, waiting for repair or adjustment means that control actions or a process optimization will be delayed.

There may be no alternative but to estimate the value for the suspect measurement. To do this, the DR procedure must be repeated with the measurement eliminated. This is exactly what is usually done anyway to confirm that the measurement is subject to gross error. Note that this procedure will not work unless there is sufficient redundancy in the measurements to permit an estimation of the missing measurement and still perform a valid DR with the remaining measurements. Tham and Parr (1994) describe an approach, which they call *data reconstruction,* for estimating a true value when a gross error exists.

The first model-tuning approach discussed is the simplest, which is to tune the process model to the raw data after some kind of gross error elimination as described above. This makes model predictions agree exactly with the data as measured and simplifies direct use of the predictions. However, this method takes no advantage of any knowledge of the measurement error characteristics, but combines those errors into the tuning constants in a way having nothing to do with standard deviations of measurements. It is likely that gross errors getting by the first screening would be hard to detect with this method. Nonetheless, this method is popular because of its simplicity. It is especially used and often is appropriate for neural network process models that were developed from raw, unreconciled data.

The next tuning procedure is called the *sequential approach:* DR is followed by model tuning. This requires three steps after gross error elimination: DR, model tuning, and model biasing. This approach is an improvement over the use of unreconciled raw data.

In this approach, DR is performed and then the model is tuned to the reconciled data. As mentioned above, this is almost universally done by adjusting constants in the model so that the model agrees exactly with the data point. The major weakness of this approach is that the values of some tuning constants really should be established by a DR procedure. For example, if the model contains a heat balance and the DR does not, the heat-balance error found by tuning will be carried along into predictions.

The third step in the sequential approach is to bias any model results that will be compared with current data from the plant. For example, if one of the model outputs is a set point or process target, the model prediction must be changed by the reverse of the DR adjustment so that the final value is directly comparable to the current process data. In effect, the error found by the DR procedure is added back to make the model result agree with the raw measurement. If this biasing were not done, then each model prediction would differ from the current measurement by both the desired target change and the estimated measurement error, added together.

Finally, the most sophisticated approach is to simultaneously perform DR and model tuning. This is accomplished by adding the DR balance equations to the process model. The advantage of this procedure is that some aspects of the process model are balanced with the DR procedure instead of being forced to fit with tuning parameters. For example, heat balances or atom balances across a reactor could be reconciled along with flow and component balances. Predictions need to be biased as above, to make them comparable to current operating data.

Regardless of the tuning approach used, the values of the tuning constants should be tracked in time and examined just as the DR error adjustments should also be followed. A large change in a tuning constant may be an additional indicator of a gross error that was missed by the first screening.

Complications

Up to this point, the assumption has been implicit that the data collected for use in DR or model tuning have been from steady-state operations. Indeed, most articles or examples of process optimization use steady-state models and do not make an optimization calculation unless steady-state operation is obtained. This means that the system in use must be able to detect steady-state operation.

Most applications use a simple approach of tracking the important variables and waiting until their values have not moved significantly for a period of time. The exact criterion on how much movement is allowed over what period of time is dependent on the process and the model, but some arbitrary percentage change over some period is typical.

The steady-state detection problem is really one of looking at the process and deciding if the state has changed. Several statistical techniques can be used to make the decision much less arbitrary than the typical criterion noted above. For example, see Narisimhan et al. (1986, 1987).

Some processes are difficult to run at a steady state, either because the process itself is not very stable or because the environment cannot be stabilized. For example, it may not be possible to stabilize the process feed quality. In such cases, it would be very desirable to be able to use the dynamic data directly and avoid having to achieve steady-state operation. Recently, much work has been done on data reconciliation in a dynamic environment (Darouach and Zasadzinski, 1991; Liebman et al., 1992). These articles are about the use of DR to improve the filtering of noise, consequently to improve the estimates of the dynamic trajectories of variables. Many process optimizations and applications of model predictive control use steady-state models. We would like to be able to tune these steady-state models on the basis of the dynamic data analysis. If the trajectories were continued to steady-state operation, the model could be tuned to that point. A serious question is whether the predicted steady state will be accurate enough for tuning a model to be used in planning, vis-à-vis tuning the same or a related model to be used for control.

A control model and the control strategy will be updated frequently, so an error in the predicted steady state will be continually corrected. Only the first time step of the many that may be required to get to steady state will actually be used. However, for planning use, the model would be tuned to the predicted steady state and then presumably used over a time period that is long compared to the recalculation frequency of the control application. If the process is far from steady-state, the quality of the prediction becomes very important. Industrial experience is needed to determine the validity of a predicted steady-state approach for tuning models for planning.

Computational Example

The example to be described is similar to that published by Ham et al. (1979). Although it is a very simple case, the example is complete from formulation through solution, so that an extension to more complex cases is straightforward. The flow sheet of the process, consisting of two distillation columns in series, is shown in Fig. 4.1. The input stream, all three output streams, and the intermediate stream from column 1 to column 2 are all measured. The measurements for both flow and composition are shown in Fig. 4.2. The balance equations are shown in Fig. 4.3. Note that only one of the component balances is shown, since there are 12 in total that all follow the same pattern. Applying the measured data to the equations shows that there is a problem with the data. As shown in Fig. 4.4, neither the flow balances nor the component balances are equal to zero, as required. The material balance closures overall and around each column are in error by 1 to 2 units, about 1 to 2 percent. The component balances are also in error by up to 1 unit.

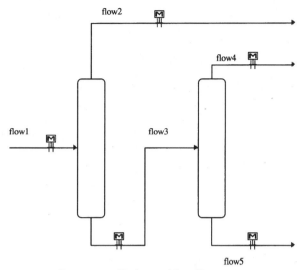

flow2

flow4

flow1

flow3

flow5

Figure 4.1 Data reconciliation problem diagram.

STREAM	FLOW	RELIABILITY (%)		
flow1	124	1.4		
flow2	64	1.2		
flow3	59	1.5		
flow4	32	1		
flow5	26	1.8		
STREAM COMPOSITIONS (%)				
	C1	C2	C3	C4
flow1	21	32	37	10
flow2	40	56	3	1
flow3		5	74	21
flow4		10	85	5
flow5			60	40
ALL COMPOSITION MEASUREMENT SDs = 0.4%				

Figure 4.2 Reconciliation problem input data.

On the question of redundancy, note that each flow can be calculated in two ways to compare with the measurement. For example, flow 2 can be calculated from flows 1 and 3 or from flows 1, 4, and 5. If we did not measure flow 3, we would still have redundancy for the overall balance, but each column would be nonredundant. Flow 3 would not have a measurement to compare to the calculated value. The estimate calculated from the reconciled overall balance would have to be accepted. This points out that even simple cases such as this one can have redundancy in one part and no redundancy in others. If, in addi-

BALANCE EQUATIONS

OVERALL
flow1 = flow2 + flow4 + flow5
COLUMN 1
flow1 = flow2 + flow3
COLUMN 2
flow3 = flow4 + flow5

COMPOSITION BALANCES
  COMPONENT 1, FOR EXAMPLE:

OVERALL
flow1*%c1 = flow2*%c1 + flow4*%c1 + flow5*%c1
Where: %c1 = percent in stream

Etc.

Figure 4.3 Reconciliation equations.

IMBALANCES, INPUT–OUTPUT		
BALANCE EQUATION		VALUE
OVERALL		2
COLUMN 1		1
COLUMN 2		1
COMPONENT IMBALANCES		
OVERALL	C1	0.44
	C2	0.64
	C3	1.16
	C4	−0.24
COLUMN	C1	0.44
No. 1	C2	0.89
	C3	0.3
	C4	−0.63
COLUMN	C1	0
No. 2	C2	−0.25
	C3	0.86
	C4	0.39

Figure 4.4 Initial imbalances.

tion, we do not measure, say, flow 4, the system becomes deterministic. All remaining measurements have to be accepted as is, and DR is not possible.

The reliabilities shown in Fig. 4.2 are in percentage of the measured value. As described above, the reliabilities are equivalent to the *standard deviation* (SD) of the measurement, taken at the measurement value. Since the SD may vary over the range of measurement, the SD should be that in effect near the current measurement. The usual assumptions made in using SDs are that the errors are normally distributed random variables. As stated previously, the presence of gross errors makes this assumption invalid. Because SD values will be used to indicate gross errors, the values should be as close to correct as possible. Estimates of SD values for various kinds of measurements are usually available from the manufacturer of the instrumentation.

The objective function that will be used is the least-squares form shown in Fig. 4.5. Some workers also use a weighting factor on each of the terms. For example, see Borsje et al. (1990), who call the weights *reliability factors*. Use of weighting factors is equivalent to a subjective biasing of the SD values, in effect increasing the SD for unreliable measurements relative to those considered more reliable. For the first example problem where we consider only stream flows, the constraints, also shown in Fig. 4.5, are seen to be the material balances from Fig. 4.3, in rewritten form. Although the constraints are all valid, they are not independent. That is, any one equation can be duplicated by combining the other two equations. Consequently only two of the equations need to be put into the matrix for the least-squares minimization.

The formulation is a quadratic objective function subject to linear constraints. The matrix structure for this optimization problem is shown in Fig. 4.6. The matrix shows the use of the measured values for the starting point (the RECON. values are set equal to the measured values). At this point, the objective is equal to zero (its smallest possible value), but the constraint equations are not satisfied, as shown under the column "RHS value." Figure 4.7 shows the optimum solution with the reconciled values. The largest adjustment was approximately one-half of a standard deviation, so no gross errors are indicated. The balance equations are satisfied within a very small tol-

---

$$\text{Objective} = \sum_i \frac{(M_i - R_i)^2}{(SD_i)^2}$$

M = measurements
R = reconciled values
SD = standard deviation of measurements

Constraints:

Overall	flow1 − flow2 − flow4 − flow5	= 0
Col 1	flow1 − flow2 − flow3	= 0
Col 2	flow3 − flow4 − flow5	= 0

Figure 4.5 Formulation of data reconciliation problem.

DATA RECONCILIATION MATRIX							
MEASUREMENTS	124	64	59	32	26		
STREAMS	R1	R2	R3	R4	R5		
RECON. VALUES	124	64	59	32	26		
						SENSE	RHS VALUE
OBJECTIVE	0	0	0	0	0	EQUAL	0
BAL. OVERALL	124	−64		−32	−26	EQUAL	2
BAL. COL. 1	124	−64	−59			EQUAL	1

Figure 4.6 Initial matrix—flow reconciliation.

erance. Note also that the column 2 balance is also satisfied, even though the constraint equation was not included.

Real industrial DR applications will be much more complex than this simple example which considers only stream flows. Hence our second example adds the component balances to the problem. Figure 4.8 shows the setup. We again use component balances overall and around column 1. The component imbalances in this case are multiplied by 100 compared to those shown in Fig. 4.4. As in the previous example, the reconciled values are set equal to the measurements for use as a starting point, as shown in Fig. 4.8. Note that the component constraints are nonlinear, since every term is the product of two unknown variables. This form is sometimes called *bilinear*. Again using the nonlinear optimization program with the same kind of objective function augmented with component adjustment terms, we get the results shown in Fig. 4.9. In this case also, none of the adjustments are larger than 1 standard deviation, so we conclude that there are no gross errors in the data. This problem took about 2 hours to set up in the spreadsheet program. The solution time was less than 1 min on a 33 MHz 386 CPU computer. Repeated use for new sets of data would take only a few minutes for each case, especially if the data were transferred from a database rather than typed in by hand.

A more complex application may include reactions and energy relationships. Balances would be, as in this example, for individual components around separation units, plus atom balances around conversion units, and enthalpy balances if sufficient data are available. In addition, other thermodynamic relationships, such as chemical equilibrium, can be included if the relationship available is rigorous.

By the time the DR problem has been augmented with component and energy relationships, the set of equations really constitutes a model of the process. This is why many applications go directly to a sequential or simultaneous DR and model tuning after gross error elimination.

DATA RECONCILIATION MATRIX—FINAL SOLUTION

MEASUREMENTS STREAMS	124 R1	64 R2	59 R3	32 R4	26 R5	SENSE	RHS VALUE
RECON. VALUES	123.458	64.3982	59.0598	32.24995	26.80985		
OBJECTIVE	0.149879	0.110115	0.001589	0.062476	0.202423	EQUAL	0.526482
BAL. OVERALL	123.458	−64.3982	−59.0598	−32.25	−26.8098	EQUAL	1.07E-14
BAL. COL. 1	123.458	−64.3982	−59.0598			EQUAL	0
ADJUSTMENT	−0.542	0.398203	0.059799	0.249952	0.809846		
RATIO TO SD	−0.38714	0.331836	0.039866	0.249952	0.449915		

Figure 4.7 Final solution—flow reconciliation.

DATA RECONCILIATION MATRIX

	R1	R2	R3	R4	R5	SENSE	RHS VALUE
MEASUREMENTS	124	64	59	32	26		
STREAMS	R1	R2	R3	R4	R5		
RECON. VALUES	124	64	59	32	26		
OBJECTIVE	0	0	0	0	0	EQUAL	0
BAL. OVERALL	124	-64		-32	-26	EQUAL	2
BAL. COL. 1	124	-64	-59			EQUAL	1

COMPOSITIONS

MEASURED	R1	R2	R3	R4	R5
C1	21	40	0	0	0
C2	32	56	5	10	0
C3	37	3	74	85	60
C4	10	1	21	5	40

RECONCILED	R1	R2	R3	R4	R5
C1	21	40	0	0	0
C2	32	56	5	10	0
C3	37	3	74	85	60
C4	10	1	21	5	40

IMBALANCE VALUES

	OVERALL	COL 1
C1	44	44
C2	64	89
C3	116	30
C4	-24	-63

Figure 4.8 Initial matrix—composition reconciliation.

DATA RECONCILIATION MATRIX—FINAL SOLUTION

MEASUREMENTS STREAMS	124 R1	64 R2	59 R3	32 R4	26 R5	SENSE	RHS VALUE
RECON. VALUES	122.4232	63.64353	58.77965	32.07451	26.70513		
OBJECTIVE	1.268557	0.088243	0.02158	0.005552	0.153461	EQUAL	3.339746
BAL. OVERALL	122.4232	−63.6435	−58.7796	−32.0745	−26.7051	EQUAL	7.11E-15
BAL. COL. 1	122.4232	−63.6435				EQUAL	7.11E-15

COMPOSITIONS

MEASURED	124 R1	64 R2	59 R3	32 R4	26 R5
C1	21	40	0	0	0
C2	32	56	5	10	0
C3	37	3	74	85	60
C4	10	1	21	5	40

RECONCILED	124 R1	64 R2	59 R3	32 R4	26 R5
C1	20.83128	40.06778	0.003012	0.000999	0.005429
C2	31.66197	55.96302	5.350055	9.8038	0.000832
C3	36.98454	2.99146	73.79048	85.20486	60.0811
C4	10.52221	0.977738	20.85646	4.990341	39.91264
SUM	100	100	100	100	100

OBJECTIVE CONTRIBUTION	124 R1	64 R2	59 R3	32 R4	26 R5
C1	0.177906	0.028713	5.67E-05	6.24E-06	0.000184
C2	0.714161	0.008546	0.765865	0.24059	4.32E-06
C3	0.001493	0.000456	0.274378	0.262296	0.041105
C4	1.704369	0.003098	0.128777	0.000583	0.047696

IMBALANCE VALUES

OVERALL	COL1
−1.1E-07	−2.1E-08
6.56E-07	6.26E-07
4.67E-08	−5.6E-09
−5.9E-07	−6E-07

Figure 4.9 Final solution—composition reconciliation.

Solution Techniques

Because the problem described in this chapter is so small, it is easy to solve with one of the spreadsheet optimizers that will handle nonlinear functions. In the past, many applications of DR required users to do their own development of a solution algorithm and the computer program to do the minimization of the least-squares objective. Numerous commercial nonlinear optimization systems are available now that make this development unnecessary. For example, GAMS from The Scientific Press, MIMI/LP from Chesapeake Decision Sciences, and MINOS from Stanford University, Systems Optimization Laboratory, are all in use for data reconciliation applications.

In addition, many commercial process models, especially those designed for use in on-line process optimization, include their own proprietary DR procedures. Commercial process information systems likewise may include their own procedures for gross error detection and DR. Consequently, it is unrealistic to think in terms of one DR technique being best for all cases. It is more likely that each process will use a different technique that is tailored to the needs of that process.

References

Borsje, H. J., G. A. Finn, and J. T. Christian (1990): "Real-Time Expert Systems and Data Reconciliation for Process Applications," *Adv. Instrum. Control,* vol. 45, part 4, pp. 1967–1971.

Brown, C., and P. J. Lawrence (1993): "Data Reconciliation. Making the Most of Process Plant Data," *Hydro. Tech. Intl.,* pp. 177–181.

Charpentier, V., L. J. Chang, M. C. Bardin, and G. M. Schwenzer (1991): "An On-Line Data Reconciliation System for Crude and Vacuum Units," Paper No. N.CC-91-139, National Petroleum Refiners Association Computer Conference, Houston, November 11–13.

Cleaves, G. W., and T. E. Baker (1987): "Data Reconciliation Improves Data Quality for Higher Level Control," *TAPPI J.,* March, pp. 75–78.

Crowe, C. M. (1986): "Reconciliation of Process Flows by Matrix Projection, Part II: The Nonlinear Case," *AIChE J.,* vol. 32, pp. 616–623.

Crowe, C. M. (1988): "Recursive Identification of Gross Errors in Linear Data Reconciliation," *AICHE J.,* vol. 34, no. 4, pp. 541–550, April.

Darouach, M., and M. Zasadzinski, (1991): "Data Reconciliation in Generalized Linear Dynamic Systems," *AIChE J.,* vol. 37, no. 2, pp. 193–201, February.

Ham, P. G., G. W. Cleaves, and J. K. Lawlor (1979): "Operation Data Reconciliation: An Aid to Improved Plant Performance," presented at the 10th World Petroleum Congress, Bucharest, Romania.

Kretsovalis, A., and R. S. H. Mah (1987): "The effect of Redundancy on Estimation Accuracy in Process Data Reconciliation," Paper no. 67A, American Institute for Chemical Engineers spring national meeting, Houston.

Lawrence, P. J. (1989): "Data Reconciliation: Getting Better Information," *Hydroc. Proc.* vol. 68, no. 6, pp. 55–60 June.

Liebman, M. J., T. F. Edgar, and L. S. Lasdon (1992): "Efficient Data Reconciliation and Estimation for Dynamic Processes Using Nonlinear Programming Techniques," *Comp. & Chem. Eng.,* vol. 16, no. 10, 11, pp. 963–986, October-November.

MacDonald, R. J., and C. S. Howat (1988): "Data Reconciliation and Parameter

Estimation in Plant Performance Analysis," *AICHE J.,* vol. 34, no. 1, pp. 1–8, January.

Mah, R. S. H. (1990): *Chemical Process Structures and Information Flows,* Butterworth, Stoneham, MA.

Narisimhan, S., J. W. Woodward, R. S. H. Mah, A. C. Tamhane, and J. C. Hale, (1986): "A Composite Statistical Test for Detecting Changes (in the) Steady States," *AICHE J.,* vol. 32, no. 9, pp. 1409–1418, September.

Narisimhan, S., C. S. Kao, and R. S. H. Mah (1987): "Detecting Changes in Steady States," *AIChE J.,* vol. 33, no. 11, pp. 1930–1932, November.

Pollard, J. F., and N. F. Zhang (1991): "Integration of Statistics and Engineering in a Petro-Chemical Environment," American Institute for Chemical Engineers 1991 annual meeting, Los Angeles, November 17–22, preprint 147e.

Rosenberg, J., R. S. H. Mah, and C. Iordache (1987): "Evaluation of Schemes and Detecting and Identifying Gross Errors in Process Data," *Ind. and Eng. Chem.,* vol. 26, p. 555.

Saha, L. E., A. J. Chontos, and D. R. Hatch (1990): "Optimization at Wyoming Gas Plant Improves Profitability," *Oil & Gas J.,* vol. 88, no. 22, pp. 49–50, 52, 55, 56, 59, 60, May 28.

Sanchez, M., A. Bandoni, and Romagnoli (1992): "PLADAT: A (Software) Package for Process Variable Classification and Plant Data Reconciliation," *Comp. & Chem. Eng.,* vol. 16, pp. S499–S506.

Serth, R. W., and W. A. Heenan (1986): "Gross Error Detection and Data Reconciliation in Steam-Metering Systems," *AICHE J.,* vol. 32, no. 5, pp. 733–742, May.

Swartz, C. L. E., K. H. Pang, V. S. Verneuil, and D. A. Eastham (1989): "Refinery Implementation of a Data Reconciliation Scheme," *Adv. Instrum. Control,* vol. 44, pt. 2, pp. 749–763.

Tavary, T. A., and J. W. Harris (1989): "Applying SQC/SPC Techniques to Process Analyzers," Paper no. CC-89-132, National Petroleum Refiners Association Computer Conference, Denver, November.

Tham, M. T., and A. Parr (1994): "Succeed at On-Line Validation and Reconstruction of Data," *Chem. Eng. Progress,* vol. 90, no. 5, pp. 46–56, May.

5

Advanced Process Control

Carol R. Aronson and John Gudaz

Introduction

Advanced control is the combined application of advanced methodologies and specific process knowledge to achieve improvement in process operations. Macroobjectives are largely economic: quality improvement, cost reduction, yield increases, etc. Methods are many and varied, but most commonly they involve determining, setting, and maintaining specific variable operating points and relationships, in the presence of physical plant and market constraints. A reasonable view is that advanced control is an attempt to have the best operator and best process engineer on duty 365 days a year, 24 hours a day.

For our purposes, any control other than basic regulatory can be considered advanced control. Advanced control is defined more by objectives and by the analysis applied to achieving objectives than by the choice of mathematical method. This is a functional view which is important to maintain. In today's and tomorrow's technology, physical and functional architectures often overlap, so the first-level control system physical components may very well be the execution platforms for advanced control modules. This blurring of classical lines—these probably should have never been viewed as lines anyway—and separate levels can create confusion. Analysis and reasoning must remain directed toward objectives and functional requirements that meet those objectives.

Recently, some advanced control functions have been implemented on *distributed control system* (DCS) modules, which in the past have been considered as first-level components. There are potential advantages in the increasing power of the DCS class of control system; but if control systems are not viewed from a functional perspective, it is very easy to get into the trap of considering the DCS as an advanced control system when, in reality, a DCS is an execution platform with components that may be suitable for some subset of advanced control requirements. Our view is that any preconceived physical control hierarchy can lead to loss of direction, and that a natural functional hierarchy will evolve from analysis, leading to an appropriate physical implementation.

Determining the execution platform prior to determining objectives and functional requirements is but one case of putting the cart before the horse. Many first-time implementers fall in love with existing packages, methods, and tools, disregarding practical considerations, such as how the tools might be implemented or applied, robustness, and most importantly its real relevance to the job at hand. For example, selecting an algorithm which exists in the form of FORTRAN code may immediately eliminate a number of otherwise completely acceptable execution platforms. Tools must be selected as part of the overall implementation strategy. A more robust tool is better than a tool which is more sophisticated but lacks the proper failsafe and what-if logic and is difficult to integrate into the overall system strategy.

In subsequent sections we will deal with the practical matters of project execution for advanced control. Key subjects discussed include

- Motivation and identification
- Context of advanced control within plant systems
- An approach directed toward a successful project

Elements of Advanced Control

The following provides a definition of functional levels of control used throughout this chapter:

- Regulatory control
- Advanced control

    Advanced regulatory control

    Constraint control

    Multivariable predictive control

    Optimization

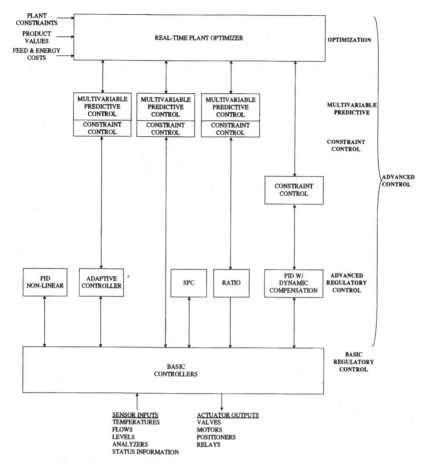

Figure 5.1 Functional control levels.

Although the physical placement of these elements will vary from implementation to implementation, the functions will still be present. A diagram depicting the functional levels is shown in Fig. 5.1.

Regulatory control

Regulatory controllers directly manipulate field devices—valves, pump drives, etc. Normally, proportional, integral, derivative (PID) or nonlinear PID algorithms are utilized. Regulatory controllers can be implemented in a DCS or can be single-loop board-mounted pneumatic or electronic instruments. In a DCS, the typical control loop execution frequency is from 0.25 to 4 Hz. A flow controller is an example of a regulatory controller. Regulatory control strategies are often designed by the process licensor.

Advanced control

Advanced controllers manipulate setpoints of downstream controllers. The downstream controller is placed into a CASCADE or COMPUTER mode in order to accept the setpoint from the advanced controller. Advanced controls are implemented in DCSs and/or computers. The strategy may consist of a hierarchy of advanced controllers. The execution frequency is determined by the desired closed-loop response time. Typical control periods range from 30 s to 5 min.

Advanced regulatory control. Advanced regulatory controllers utilize many different types of control algorithms, such as PIDs; PIDs with zone, nonlinear, deadtime compensation features; feedforward compensation; ratio controllers; adaptive controllers; or *statistical process control* (SPC). In addition there may be numerous configuration options for initialization, windup protection, proportional action based on measurement changes versus error, etc. These should be viewed as a set of tools for the control engineer. The controlled variable of an advanced regulatory controller may be a direct measurement from an instrument or a calculated variable. Advanced regulatory controllers using instruments as the controlled variable are often provided by the process licensor. Examples of advanced regulatory controllers include the following:

- The coil outlet temperature controller on a heater is configured to adjust the setpoint of the fuel gas flow controller. This strategy may also use feedforward compensation to reduce outlet temperature variations when the fuel gas composition or the heater inlet temperature or feed rate changes.

- A product yield controller is configured to adjust the setpoint of a flow controller.

- The 90 percent ASTM (American Society for Testing and Materials) point of a naphtha stream is calculated. This variable is controlled by adjusting the setpoint of the top temperature controller of a crude unit. This strategy may include feedforward compensation to the kerosene product flow to decouple the change to the top temperature.

Constraint control. Constraints on process variables and manipulated variables are almost always present and must be observed when one is operating a process unit. Constraints can be physical equipment limitations, quality constraints (such as product specification limits), or even market constraints set by product price and demand.

Consider a distillation tower that uses steam as the reboiler heating medium and cooling water to condense the overhead vapors (Huffmaster and Richard, 1988). A decrease in the column operating pressure will increase the relative volatility of the components to be separated. The same separation can be achieved while less steam is used, thereby reducing the energy cost. What are the limits to lowering the column pressure? Typical limits include the pressure controller output and the approach temperature of the cooling water exchanger.

The purpose of the constraint controller is to adjust the pressure setpoint to "ride" the most limiting constraint. The active constraint will vary. On a summer afternoon the limit could be the approach temperature. The advantage of the constraint controller is that it will slowly continue to decrease the pressure as the temperature cools off in the evening. This example is illustrated in Fig. 5.2. Note that when the feed composition changes to include more gas, the controller increases the pressure to enforce the maximum pressure controller output limit. Constraint controllers are typically tuned to slowly push a limit, but to react quickly if a limit has been violated.

In this example, the column pressure constraint controller is actually a simple optimizer. The economics determine that for this column minimum pressure maximizes profit and is therefore always desired.

The process objectives and economics determine whether a constraint controller is also a simple optimizer. Consider the heater outlet temperature controller of a crude unit. If the operating objective is to maximize the yield of the heaviest side cut (atmospheric gas oil), then a constraint controller is appropriate to maximize the heater outlet temperature. Typical constraints would be heater tube-skin temperatures, flooding in the bottom section of the tower, fuel gas controller output, and maximum product rundown temperature.

If, however, the operating objective is to produce an atmospheric gas oil with a pour point quality specification, then tube-skin temperatures and fuel gas controller output are actually constraints which may keep the pour point controller from meeting its target. In this situation, the optimum pour point setpoint is a function of the atmospheric gas oil value, disposition, fuel gas cost, and pump-around cooling limitations and costs.

Multivariable predictive control (MPC). Classical advanced regulatory control relies on the principle that changes to the manipulated vari-

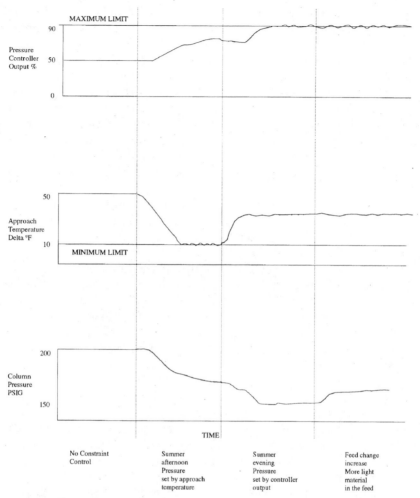

Figure 5.2 Constraint control action.

able will change the controlled variable. However, what happens if changes to a manipulated variable can strongly affect more than one controlled variable? A multivariable predictive controller uses dynamic process models to predict how a controlled variable will respond. This has been successfully applied to highly interactive processes and those with long dead times. The controller acts on *manipulated variables* (MVs) to keep *controlled variables* (CVs) at setpoint or within constraints. *Disturbance variables* (DVs) are measurements that are known to affect the process but that cannot be manipulated by the controller. These act as feedforward inputs. A good multivariable controller will always consider process constraints.

Consider a continuous catalytic reforming unit (Besl et al., 1993). The operating objectives are to control the reformate octane and the coke on spent catalyst while maximizing feed to the unit. Changing the reactor inlet temperature will affect both controlled variables. The multivariable predictive controller meets these objectives by simultaneously manipulating the reactor inlet temperatures, separator pressure, recycled hydrogen compressor speed, and feed rate. If one of the manipulated variables becomes constrained against an operating limit, the controller will observe the constraint limit and may change another manipulated variable to try to relieve the limit while attempting to maintain the octane and the coke on spent catalyst.

There are several proprietary multivariable controllers on the market. Distinguishing features are how they handle MV saturation and how they utilize available degrees of freedom.

Optimization.   In some process situations, economic tradeoffs exist between advanced control targets. An optimizer can help decide where the targets should be set. On-line, closed-loop optimization is the automatic adjustment of advanced control targets to satisfy an objective function. A typical objective function might be to maximize profit or maximize throughput. Optimization strategies usually require information from other systems, such as feedstock costs, utility costs, and product values.

Basic requirements to implement an optimizer are as follows (Cugini et al., 1984):

- A robust model based on incremental moves not absolute optimums, which can be automatically updated on-line

- A model that considers constraints

- Data reconciliation

- Valid economic data

- What-if logic, such as what if all the instrumentation is not available?

- A hierarchical set of controllers, including constraint control beneath the optimizer to implement the optimum targets

There are two types of models, simplified and rigorous. Good results can be and have been achieved with both types; however, there is a recent preference in the marketplace for rigorous open equation models. As computing power has increased, it has become easier to solve and implement rigorous models. Rigorous models still require reliable automatic updating techniques, so that the added rigor does not severely increase the maintenance requirements.

Typical periods for optimizers range from 1 to 4 h. Steady-state optimizers require periods between calculations that are several multiples of the steady-state plant time constant (White, 1990).

A good example of where profitability can be increased through the use of optimization is in an ethylene plant. Primary products of an ethylene plant are high-purity ethylene and propylene. An ethylene plant consists of a hot section and a cold section. The hot section can contain 6 to 10 cracking furnaces, and the cold side contains numerous distillation columns and utility systems, which provide condensing and reboiling for the columns. A variety of feedstocks of ethane, propane, naphtha, or gas oil can be used. The yields from the various feedstocks vary widely, as shown in Table 5.1 (Burdick and Leffler, 1983).

Each feedstock requires different operating parameters for the furnaces and the columns. Certain furnaces can handle a range of feedstock, while others are more specific. Normal operation includes bringing furnaces on- and off-line and changing feedstocks. Without an economic optimizer, how does one know where to set the advanced control targets?

The optimizer can have two objective functions—maximize ethylene production against plant constraints or maximize profit by considering feedstock costs, product values, and energy costs.

Please keep in mind that the use of the phrase *maximizing profit* is relative. Some would argue that advanced control cannot maximize profit, since it does not interact with the business functions. This becomes a semantics issue based on whether one has a control or a planning/scheduling perspective. Another way to view the situation may be to use the phrase *minimize cost.*

TABLE 5.1   Olefin Yields from Various Feedstocks

Feedstock	Ethane	Propane	Naphtha	Gas oil
Yield, lb/lb of feed				
Ethylene	0.80	0.40	0.23	0.18
Propylene	0.03	0.18	0.13	0.14

Motivation and Identification

A decision to apply advanced control should be motivated by the desire to improve operation and be based on identification of benefits, needs, and suitability. It is a business decision deserving of thoughtful and thorough analysis. Analysis includes previous experience, benefit potential, and cost estimation. A logical business decision is made when the analysis is sufficient to allow comparison with other investments and alternatives. Fortunately, experience has shown that analysis has a high probability of pointing to beneficial action that should be taken, with or without advanced control. Deciding to investigate advanced control as a potential investment is a pretty safe and sane decision and a logical extension of continuous analysis for improvement, which is a necessary part of plant operation.

There are several process and operation characteristics, listed with examples in the following paragraphs, which are good general indicators that advanced control is of potential benefit:

- *Highly integrated design.*   Over the last 10 years, heat integration has played a major role in the design and revamp of units. Consider a crude unit with an extensive preheat train. On many units the first exchanger in the preheat train is the overhead condenser. Assume the next exchanger in the preheat train is in the heavy gas oil pump-around, which provides reboiler heat for the downstream naphtha splitter. This means that the top section of the crude tower and the downstream naphtha splitter will see effects from a crude switch before the new crude has even reached the unit.

- *Frequent changes in feed rate, composition, and/or product demands.*   Depending on demand, a unit may be run at maximum capacity or to meet sales demand.

- *External disturbances.*   Loops must handle significant external disturbances. Rain can have a fast and significant impact on a fin fan condensing overhead vapors in a column.

- *Substantial time delays and lags in dynamic response.*   Consider a C3 splitter which separates propylene from propane. The boiling points of these materials are extremely close, 188.18 and 183.05°F, respectively. The separation typically requires 250 to 300 trays. It is not uncommon to observe a total response time of 8 to 12 h.

- *Unmeasured variables.*   Not all variables which should be controlled can be measured. Consider a coke drum. It is desirable to ensure that the drum is full at the end of the cycle. However, a 30-ft drum may only have indicators at the top of the drum. Once the coke reaches the level indicator, it may not be possible to increase the feed enough to fill the drum in the remaining time. It is therefore necessary to continuously calculate the level based on feed rate and vapor fraction and then to update the model when the level indicators are reached or at the end of the cycle when the height in the drum is measured.

A process can be examined for these characteristics as the initial step in analysis. In fact, some of this cursory analysis is part of normal operation monitoring. Process variability and economic performance will be used to determine benefits available from application of advanced control. Generally the direct payout will be in the following areas:

- Increase in maximum capacity
- Reduction of energy use
- Maximization of valuable product yields
- Increase in equipment life

This type of study cannot be considered conclusive, but it is a useful beginning for the identification of possibilities. Some caution should be exercised when one is working with general indicators, because a lot of the terms are relative and there is a tendency to look at only the major product variables, e.g., in a number of processes where compressor trains are service providers and the measurements for a compressor train would not be considered quality variables. However, we know that compressor operation is critical and that some control sophistication is required to balance efficiency and equipment life-cycle costs: Good compressor control strategy is advanced control with real benefits.

To reduce costs, it is tempting for some steps in an orderly procedure to be bypassed or foreshortened and/or physical equipment decisions to be made without analysis. Resist these temptations: The real cost benefit derived from incomplete analysis is small—no analysis is dangerous, and a good analysis does not cost a lot more than a bad one.

A decision to invest in advanced control should not be made for extraneous reasons. If advanced control is to yield positive, identifiable results, then it must have management support for real objectives. Some fallacious reasons for advanced control include these:

- *Desire for reinstrumentation.*   If the existing instruments and controls are not performing well, then fix those instruments and controls. Advanced control will not compensate for poor instrumentation. For example, some older systems only allow temperature to be controlled to $\pm 5°F$. Implementation of an advanced control strategy to manipulate the temperature controller will not improve the basic controller performance. Buying into an advanced control project as a means to get new instruments is an expensive way to do maintenance. New instrumentation must be justified on the basis of reliability, safety, maintenance, configuration flexibility, etc. Too often this type of justification is the output of an analysis with pre-ordained results, predicting fabulous returns to justify advanced control and the new instruments.

■ *Image.* Everybody else has advanced control; customers will be impressed by an investment in quality. This type of reasoning says that having it is enough. Any benefits are short-term, at best. Customers for products will eventually require that actual quality be produced and will not be especially impressed by the existence of a control system that does not deliver the desired quality and quantities.

■ *Elimination of personnel.* This probably will not happen. Good operators and engineers, and cooperation between them, are a requirement. There will most likely be a cost incurred for education of personnel, rather than an elimination of them.

True motivation is different from a desire to be proactive. You are motivated if you understand the realities of an advanced control project and have the tenacity and dedication to support it throughout its life. A successful control project must have the buy-in and support of operations. This includes the operators and the day-to-day unit engineers. There will be disturbances to production, some predictable, others as the result of invalid assumptions or human error. Management cannot force a system on operations and expect to obtain positive results. The authors have seen numerous instances where management's attitude has made the difference between success and failure. Cooperation between a variety of groups, companies, and individuals will have to be advocated and enforced—it seldom occurs naturally. Management support is a *sine qua non* for successful advanced control implementation.

Analysis

Analysis produces input to several decision-making paths, and it can properly occur in many different ways, for many different sets of circumstances. For that reason we will start with setting the general context of an advanced control system (Fig. 5.3) and defining the objectives of analysis.

Analysis can be considered the first phase of the project. Depending upon the results of analysis, it could also be the last phase. While

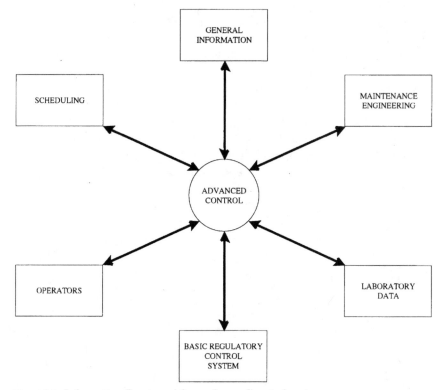

Figure 5.3   Information flow to and from advanced control systems.

process analysis should be an ongoing function of normal plant operation, our analysis phase is narrowed to focus on improvements available through advanced control. Information and knowledge gained from ongoing process analysis can contribute greatly to this phase of the project, and they may be the original source of interest in the investigation of advanced control.

Context of the advanced control subsystem

Advanced control is best visualized as an embedded subsystem. Interfaces exist between advanced control and

- Operators, process engineers, and maintenance engineers—people
- Scheduling—either people or people and system function
- Basic control system—primary interface to process
- Laboratory data systems—people and system function

- General information systems—plant database systems
- Maintenance engineering systems—either people or people and system function

Behavior and content of information flows across the interfaces are preferably determined by analysis. However, since subsystems are often purchased at different times, preexisting systems can be expected to affect advanced control system implementation. This cannot be avoided. All systems have inherent limitations. However, if we are resolute in our analytical approach, we incorporate these limitations in our description of alternative approaches and associated costs and benefits.

Analysis objectives

We define our objectives in terms of business decision making and an executable project:

- Provide cost/benefit analysis sufficiently comprehensive for determination of what, if any, advanced control will be provided.
- Give sufficient description of the control to be provided so that a project can be scheduled and executed with predictable results.

Analysis outputs

To achieve the objectives stated above, we need comprehensive descriptions that describe the advanced control, its costs, and its requirements. We can think in terms of the following models:

- Description of current operation
- Behavioral and functional model
- System analysis
- Financial decision-making model
- Build-or-buy decisions

Thinking in terms of models is not strictly necessary, but it is a helpful way to describe the outputs of analysis and to organize the analysis effort.

Description of current operation. To analyze costs and benefits, it is necessary to establish a baseline, which is a description of the key characteristics of the current operation. Primarily we are concerned with the state of instrumentation and control, process variability

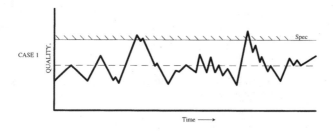

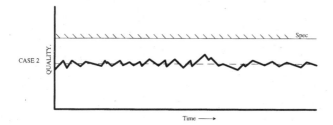

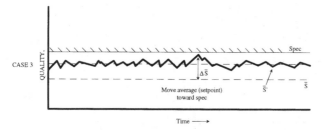

Figure 5.4 Control quality variations with time.

against specifications, and economic performance of target units. Current instrumentation should be analyzed for state of repair, tuning, and maintenance procedures. Control systems are implemented from the bottom up. Basic control and instrumentation must work effectively if advanced control is to achieve maximum benefit.

As an example of how to estimate the benefit of advanced control, we examine the product quality variability. For discussion purposes, consider the process variability shown in Fig. 5.4, case 1, and assume that it is normal butane which can be sold externally as a product or can be used internally for blending gasoline. An impurity specification exists for the normal butane. Depending on the situation, butane violating the specification may have no value (i.e., no customers) or will be sold for a reduced price. Therefore, operations will try to operate (on average) some distance away from the specification, so that there is room for upsets. Implementation of advanced control will reduce the variability, as shown in case 2. This allows operation to move the average setpoint closer to the true specification, as shown in case 3. The delta between the average setpoint represents an increase in yield at the same operating cost.

In reality, case 2 represents benefits, but they are more difficult to quantify (Latour 1992). Consider the normal butane used in gasoline blending. Gasoline has a *Reid vapor pressure* (RVP) specification. The major contributor of RVP is normal butane. Propane, an impurity in the normal-butane product, has a high RVP. Reduced fluctuations in the butane purity require less work at the blend center to "blend off" excess RVP.

Behavioral and functional model. The behavioral and functional model describes the required functions and behavior of the system:

- Define operating objectives.

- Proposed control strategies and alternatives.

- Operator interface.

- General use calculations.

- Failure-mode logic descriptions.

Define operating objectives. What are the operating objectives of the facility? Do they change? If so, how often? What drives the changes? These may seem like oversimplified questions, but they must be defined if the analysis is to remain focused. Energy conservation is a buzzword in today's process industries, but if your facility always flares excess fuel gas, it may not be a key objective.

Proposed control strategies and alternatives

- A block diagram describes the calculations and information flows associated with a strategy.

- Any instrumentation upgrades or replacements need to be identified and associated with the relevant strategy. Many existing facilities were built with the minimum number of instruments possible. Review current and proposed product specifications.

- Where logic for safety or sequencing systems is included, state transition diagrams or *sequential function charts* (SFCs) are generally useful tools.

- Identify which functions require the following: setpoint tracking, ramping, output tracking, setpoint limiting, output limiting, signal quality (good/bad) propagation, conditional controller execution, windup limiting and prevention.

As a general rule, state the requirements, even when they seem to be obvious. Not everyone makes the same assumptions; not every implementation of base control systems has features we consider to be obvious requirements. As an example, some DCSs make windup prevention extremely cumbersome to implement, and others provide good solutions, almost automatically.

A control objective is often achievable in a number of different ways. If analysis reveals an absolutely best way, describe it. Otherwise, the alternatives being considered should be described. If there is a significant difference in benefits achievable, then this should be described in the financial model. If an external subsystem limitation is the reason for stating an alternative, then this should be identified. For example, if implementing a function in a DCS platform precludes a preferred strategy, this should be identified. Eventually choices need to be made as to where control is executed: It should be made with clear knowledge of the ramifications.

Operator interface. The important characteristics of the operator interface are the following:

- Look and feel
- What is to be displayed to the operator
- Screen organization
- Generic display types required
- Operator inputs and the displays at which the entries should be made

Because look and feel and, to some degree, screen organization are so largely determined by the execution platform, effort should be concentrated on the data, specific displays, and display types. The look and feel of a platform will be part of the selection process.

A significant consideration is whether the operator interface will be a single window for all control functions or a separate window for the advanced control, called the *dual-window approach*. A single-window system presents all information to and takes all input from operators through a common interface—note that there may be multiple stations, but all are generically identical. We define an operator interface as single-window when

- The operator interface has a common look and feel for all functions and stations, regardless of whether it is a regulatory or advanced control function.
- Each operator station has access to the advanced control information as well as the basic system information.

■ Generic functions such as faceplates, trend displays, and operator entry procedures are common to all data. Trends, e.g., would be plotted identically whether the data were from advanced control functions or from the basic control system.

It is important to note that for a variety of reasons, such as capacity and security, certain stations will be configured to handle only certain functions or plant sections, even though from a system view every station could provide any of the functions using any of the data; this would still be classified as single-window operator interface.

The advantages of a single-window system are very simply that

■ Observations and manipulations of all functions can be made from any station—except as intentionally prevented.

■ Operators have to learn only one system.

There are no serious conceptual weaknesses to the single-window system. The real weaknesses lie in the difficulty of implementing a single-window system, or alternately the operational compromises made to force the system into a single window. The reality about single-window systems is that DCS suppliers and advanced control suppliers provide different functions and function types. Consequently, some functions will be force-fit, or special services must be provided to get to a single window. Some may argue with this view, pointing out that there are many single-window systems in operation; however, most were very simple, very expensive, or very much a compromise (Aronson and White, 1990).

A typical example of how single windows are achieved is *mirror controllers*. A mirror controller is a dummy block in a DCS module, to which the advanced control system sends information, via the control network, which is in turn displayed like a standard block at the DCS operator station. Operator entries such as setpoints, modes, or outputs follow the reverse path. This same general mirror approach is often used so that a status generated by advanced control can be incorporated in a process graphic or for simulated light or pushbutton displays. Additional difficulties arise in presenting information and functions which were not considered in the original DCS operator interface design, but are standard features of the advanced control system; for these situations, a compromise of the function is required, or features are added to the selected single window—at some cost.

None of this is meant to discourage the single-window approach, but to point out that between the concept and the reality there can be a big gap that needs to be filled. The degree of difficulty encountered in achieving a single window obviously will vary with the system components and suppliers involved.

The dual-window approach provides a separate window as the operator interface, and this has the disadvantage that operators need to learn two different interfaces. The advantage is that the advanced control window has been designed for the advanced control functions, and so the advanced control and the operator interface tend to be better integrated than in force-fit single-window approaches—this assumes that the advanced control is, in fact, designed and/or purchased as a complete subsystem. Most currently installed applications are dual-window in nature, and the approach has been generally successful.

Single- versus dual-window discussions can quickly become philosophical. It is much better to take a practical view: If the single-window approach is impractical, then use the dual-window; otherwise, use the single-window. *Practical* means that the requirements of the application functions can be met within the bounds of good system performance, reasonable maintenance procedures, and reasonable implementation ease. This decision requires systems analysis and judgment.

General use calculations. There are numerous benefits which are difficult to quantify and consist of having additional information available, such as on-line calculations of heat duties, fouling factors, efficiencies, reflux ratios, and inferred quality variables, such as a product flash point. This information allows operations to learn more about how the unit is really operating.

The analysis phase should also consider long-term data requirements within the facility. Who at the plant needs access to what type of data (second, minute, averages; 5-minute, hourly, daily, monthly, etc.)? Once more data are available, who else will be interested?

Failure-mode logic descriptions. As an embedded subsystem, an advanced control system will be affected by and can affect the performance of plant safety or emergency systems. Advanced control almost by definition uses multiple measurements and control devices and therefore, to be complete, must know how to respond to failures of the measurements and control devices. For example, a key aspect of implementing an optimizer is the failure mode or what-if logic: What if all the instrumentation is not available, or what if the unit is limited by process constraints? etc.

A description of what happens under all failure or emergency action conditions is imperative. If it does not exist, then it is quite possible to have control which is almost never operational, fails such that the process is left in an untenable state, or interferes with emergency action procedures or the recovery from such procedures.

Behavioral and functional model summary. A comprehensive behavioral model is a functional specification of the advanced control system to be built. It will provide implementers with sufficient detail to construct the system and provide information required for building the financial model. As such, it needs to be clear, complete, and concise.

System analysis. *System analysis* is the technical analysis of how the system will go together. It includes the selection of components and suppliers. System analysis is the transition from what (the behavioral model) to how (the implementation). It is necessary to get accurate costs and ensure that the components selected are correct for the functions described in the behavioral model.

Because there are always a variety of methods and configurations that can be used to perform advanced control, system analysis is highly iterative. In one configuration we may very well solve one problem, but the components are deficient when we look at another problem. In the beginning, it is necessary to accept the reality that a perfect solution is probably not practical, yet one must approach the job as if it were. Judgment is applied to know how to determine functional priorities and when to stop iterating. These are very simple guidelines: Give priority to those functions which yield the greatest benefit, and stop iterating when the solutions get more complex than the problem. System analysis consists of the following topics:

- Control execution platforms
- Operator interface
- Operating systems and communications
- Support requirements

Control execution platforms. In today's technology it is possible to execute advanced control functions in some DCS control modules. That in itself does not mean it is practical or even desirable. While initial cost is certainly an issue, the quality, complexity, and maintainability of the implemented control functions are more important. Implementing advanced control in a DCS controller is generally not practical if the controller does not provide the required features for advanced control—limiting, windup protection, quality propagation, etc. If the decision is made to include the advanced control in the DCS without these features, then either a very complicated implementation or a reduced benefit control strategy will result. It is our position that only control that is reasonably supported by the DCS should be implemented in the DCS. *Reasonably supported* means that implementation mechanics are straightforward and within the design considerations of the DCS base functionality. Just because it is possible does not mean it is practical. Distribution to execution platforms should not be determined until the control problem and requirements are known and the platform alternatives can be analyzed against the requirements. If the DCS controller does reasonably support advanced control requirements, it may very well be a logical choice for implementation.

These functional capabilities are generally required for advanced control:

- *Windup protection that handles output limiting, autoselection, and feedforward configurations.* Windup protection is key for feedforward applications because the feedforward action may very well force the total output into saturation. If not properly implemented, the feedback controller will wind up and not return to control properly when the saturation condition has cleared. Further, in normal operation without the proper windup protection, the feedback controller will stabilize with an offset. Constraint control often involves the autoselection of multiple controller outputs, which means that the windup protection in the unselected controllers needs to properly track the selected controller. Proper tracking prevents windup of the selected controllers and provides the capability to create a deadband to prevent chatter in the selection process.

- *Setpoint rate limiting or ramping.* Setpoints for advanced regulatory controllers often need to be changed slowly, as the process is being pushed toward a constraint. It is undesirable to detune the controller since the disturbance response and constraint violation normally need quick response. When one is bringing a process to a new state in a coordinated manner, setpoint ramping of multiple variables simultaneously is a useful feature.

- *Variable quality propagation and configurability.* Advanced control applications are multivariable in nature, often involving calculation of variables which are not directly measurable. It is necessary to know the quality of each individual measurement and from that to determine the quality of the resultant calculation, which in turn is used to determine whether the control function can generate an output or an alternate degraded control form should be activated. When calculations are chained, the quality of calculation results must be passed from one calculation to all succeeding users of the result.

If the DCS platform is capable of performing the control, then it is necessary to investigate the maintainability and general ease of use. For example, almost every DCS provides capability for windup protection for its controllers. However, some DCSs make it exceedingly difficult, requiring the linking of several calculation blocks and the construction of specific logic functions, while other systems provide a simple connection or option switch.

Keep in mind that one does not need a DCS to implement advanced controls, although it often makes it easier. DCS allows you to change the manipulated variables without rewiring. It may be expensive to convert the board-mounted instruments to accept an external setpoint.

Control systems, whether advanced or basic, should be considered dynamic systems that will need to be altered because of process modifications, because someone has an idea that will improve plant operation, or simply because mistakes were made and need to be corrected—this last is particularly true during plant or system start-up. The real question becomes not whether the control can be implemented, but whether it can be maintained and easily modified in the future. For example, one leading DCS provides capabilities to connect numerous types of function blocks to implement an advanced control strategy. A major problem with the architecture is that modification of the strategy, once it is on-line, requires a total reload of the module. More than one plant has been shut down due to a careless error.

One consideration that used to be important but is much less so today is the robustness of minicomputers versus DCS modules. Today minicomputers demonstrate about the same level of reliability as DCS modules, so this should no longer be a major consideration— assuming a good minicomputer is used.

Operator interface. As discussed above, a single-window operator interface has the implementation advantage that only one set of tools will be required for creating the advanced and basic controls. However, that set of tools may or may not be entirely adequate; so as in the control platform analysis, we have to look at its ease of use in implementation as well as the ability to modify and maintain functions. To paraphrase our earlier comment, use the approach that is the best for the job, and do not give too much precedence to the single-window versus dual-window philosophical arguments; either will work.

Operating systems and communications. In recent years there has been a lot of discussion about open-system architectures. Unfortunately too much of the discussion has centered on operating systems and communications, leading users to the conclusion that the use of common operating systems and communication protocols creates an open system. This is, of course, false. In a control system, the primary concern is not operating system compatibility and connectivity but interaction between the control system functions. As an example, two subsystems utilizing transmission control protocol/Internet protocol (TCP/IP) but without the application layer to interpret and convert data from one to the other are in fact not compatible; practically speaking, without that application layer, these subsystems are not open to each other.

Presently there are several operating systems that could be considered practical as application platforms for advanced control—UNIX, VMS, Windows/NT. All conform in one way or another to certain open-system criteria. But again, without the application interface between control system functions operative on each, there is no practical openness in the control system sense.

In reality, what the user should be primarily concerned with is the interfaces between functions. Are the hooks available to transfer and share data between various systems? The operating system and/or communication protocols are secondary. When this approach is taken, we concern ourselves with what can be communicated, at what frequency, and at what cost—how much work is involved. It is particularly important to maintain this practical view when the embedded nature of the advanced control system is considered. It does absolutely no good to connect two UNIX-based subsystems, say, a plant database system and an advanced control system, unless an application-level interface exists between the two.

Although the above-described view deemphasizes operating and communication systems, do not completely ignore them. Be sure that those being employed are well supported and have a reasonable life expectancy. Some indicators will help here:

- Who supports and who is doing development of packages for the operating system?

- Is the operating system in general use within the process industries?

- Are the communication protocol and hardware widely used within the control industries?

Support requirements. *Support requirements* are those activities required to support the system and the implementation of the system. The term should describe training and maintenance requirements as well as identifying the personnel that will need to contribute significant time to project implementation.

For many users, particularly first-time users, a key decision is whether a consultant should be hired for the analysis and implementation phases. The first question to ask is, Do you have the correct skill sets in-house for the project? If the answer is no, then you will need to hire a consultant. An advanced control project is not the place to learn on the job.

While a consultant with the proper background will be useful throughout the project, during the analysis phase of the project the experience brought to the project will be most valuable. During the analysis phase, the consultant's experience can prevent a lot of wheel spinning—analysis presents many opportunities for that. Additionally an experienced consultant can quickly outline the efforts required.

There are really two extremes in the use of consultants: Let the consultant do everything and make all the decisions, or ignore everything the consultant says. In the former, the user group develops no real capability for dealing with the system throughout its life. In the latter, the user spends money, makes mistakes that the consultant's experience could avoid, and then usually wonders why he or she hired the consultant. The proper utilization of a consultant is to use the experience brought to the table to avoid unnecessary problems, help organize efforts, and provide technical leadership in analysis. If the advanced control system is purchased, then the consultant provides a counterpoint to the supplier (not necessarily contention with the supplier) and will be able to better track project progress. If the system is built in-house, the consultant provides technical project leadership and some portion of the implementation, but should not be the only implementer. As with anything else, advanced control is learned by observing, listening, and doing. A general summary of the pros and cons associated with hiring a consultant is provided in Table 5.2.

A successful advanced control implementation requires a combination of the proper set of tools and techniques and process knowledge. These skill sets are required:

TABLE 5.2   Pros and Cons of Hiring a Control Consultant

Pros	Cons
Gets the job done faster.	After the project is over, you may have less specific knowledge of how to maintain it.
Can contract out long-term support and training.	May not be able to release proprietary information outside.
Requires less of your own workforce.	May be difficult to budget.
Access to knowledge that might not be available in your own organization. For example, your plant may be the tenth plant the consultant has put advanced controls on, built by the same licensor.	

- *Process knowledge.* Preferably, specific knowledge of the process being targeted is needed.

- *Advanced process control know-how and experience.* It is inadequate to just be conversant because there is a real project requiring real skill. This includes experience with the types of control relevant to the project at hand.

- *System engineering.* As described above, there will be a lot of options available. The ability to create and evaluate an implementation plan is extremely important.

- *Software.* Unless you are very lucky, software may need to be written to create interfaces between a DCS and the advanced control system, the advanced control system and plant information systems, etc. Additionally, it may be necessary to write or modify control algorithms and procedures.

Financial decision-making model. To complete the financial model, we need price/cost estimates for implementation of a project that will yield the estimated benefits. Prices will be provided by those selected to bid for the project.

A cost/benefit analysis can be made to determine the viability of a project and whether the project should be done by in-house client staff or provided by an advanced controls supplier. The information required to do the analysis is the price information, the information from baseline operations, the behavioral model, and support requirements.

Benefits to be achieved cannot be precisely determined and, in fact, are estimates, largely based on predicted reduction of variability and target shifting. Where possible, use previous experience to aid in establishing a potential range on specific benefit calculations. Historically, this has been a reasonably good approach when one is comparing similar process units.

Build-or-buy decisions. The question of whether to build or buy the advanced control system is very similar to the question of whether to use the consultant. If you do not have the skill sets in-house, then you cannot build it independently. At the minimum, you will need to contract the skill sets. Further, you will probably need to hire permanent employees with those skills to maintain the system, some of which at least are the same as those required to build it in the first place.

For one project it will generally be more expensive to build than to buy. For multiple projects, building may, over the long haul, be more cost-effective. But if you choose to build, it is necessary to provide all those features that would be expected in a purchased system, including maintenance features, configuration tools, debugging tools, control algorithms, upgrades as other subsystems change, etc. Keep in mind that in the 1960s and 1970s many large corporations built their own proprietary advanced control systems. In the 1980s and 1990s, many of these systems have been replaced because they were too expensive to maintain. Too many people underestimate the difficulty in building a proper control system, and then they reduce the requirements to match budget or personnel: In the end, somebody will pay. If you cannot put together the capability and budget to create a marketable system, then you should not build one for yourself.

Implementation

To get to the implementation phase of an advanced control project, the following items must be decided:

- What will be done
- Which application platforms will be used
- Who will be doing it

The implementation phase consists of the following steps:

- Detailed design
- Programming and configuration
- Off-line *factory acceptance test* (FAT)
- On-site integration
- Operator training
- Commissioning
- Documentation

Detailed design

The first step of the implementation phase is the detailed design. This document defines the specifics of "how." All engineering equations, assumptions, control algorithms, sequencing, and timing should be documented. The design phase may be a good time to do process testing, to determine response times to see whether the process actually responds as expected. However, if the analysis phase indicates that the existing instruments will be replaced with a DCS, then the amount of information from plant tests is reduced. All new instrumentation should be finalized. The decision to place advanced controls in the DCS or computer is made at this time. If the advanced control project will be implemented in a new DCS, additional planning is required. It is imperative that the I/O requirements for the advanced control be reviewed before the I/O is randomly configured in the DCS.

The design step should also include design of all interfaces to the advanced control system, such as the DCS, programmable logic controllers (PLCs), or board-mounted instruments to computer interface, the laboratory system interface, and the plant information and/or scheduling system interface. It is acceptable for the design step to be a phased activity, but the interface to the DCS, PLCs or board-mounted instruments must be in the first phase. Interface features or limitations can have a key impact on decisions of where to place advanced controls.

Robustness is more important than the latest technology from the university. Theoretical and actual are different. Compromises may need to be made during the design phase. Consider the following example: Operation of a crude tower is upset during certain crude switches. Operations suspects that the partial-product draw tray is going dry. It would be nice to calculate the liquid flow to the draw tray and then identify the minimum limit where operating problems occur. The calculated liquid flow could then be a constraint in the bottom pump-around controller, which is below the draw tray. As the liquid decreased toward the minimum limit, the heat removed in the pump-around circuit would be reduced, thereby forcing more material up the column. To calculate the liquid flow to the tray requires simultaneously solving material and energy-balance calculations around the tower. At this plant, the decision has been made to put all advanced controls into the DCS. What happens if the balance calculations cannot be easily implemented in the chosen DCS? The advanced control strategy will need to be redesigned to use another indication of drawing the tray dry. Perhaps the strategy will need to be redesigned to use a product flow controller, output override controller, or a reduced flow controller setpoint limit.

Prototypes of the *human-machine interface* (HMI) displays should be provided on paper. Please keep in mind that displays always change. It is important to get agreement on paper, before extensive time is spend configuring and fine-tuning the displays. A significant amount of time can be spent on displays because everyone who views them has an opinion. Make sure that the operations personnel have key input to accepting the displays, since the displays will be their tools for utilizing the new system.

A formal review of the detailed design should be done. All parties involved with the operation of the plant should attend the review.

Programming and configuration

Programming and configuration of an advanced control system often require specialized skill sets. It is the authors' experience that the most successful teams are small teams that have overlapping skill sets. Standards should be defined up front and followed throughout the phase. The authors do not support the idea of a handoff between phases. The lead engineer should be involved throughout the programming and configuration phase.

It is important that the team always have in mind the reason for the effort. The sooner the advanced controls are implemented, the sooner the facility can make money.

Think ahead in terms of long-term maintenance. If everyone at the facility knows FORTRAN but the decision has been made to implement the advanced controls in a proprietary vendor language, then make sure a significant amount of staff training occurs in the vendor language. Training only one person is a good way to have problems in the future.

If possible, stage all the equipment during the programming phase. It may seem expensive to lease DCS equipment, but the expense pays for itself by providing a safe testing environment. It is always easier to test and fix problems in an off-line environment. Having the correct equipment on-site helps eliminates surprises. System loading is the only item that is difficult to verify in an off-line system.

Off-line factory acceptance test

An off-line system test should be done at the conclusion of the programming and configuration phase. Calculations and control functionality should be tested.

At this point the following documentation should exist:

- Detailed design

- Program, configuration, and system environment manual

- User's manual

- FAT document

The FAT document should describe how to test the functionality of the system in a systematic fashion.

Process simulation may be used to verify *multivariable predictive control* (MPC) strategies; however, it is not necessary to build detailed process simulators to test advanced control strategies. The testing can be done with a static database. Punch list items should be noted, and decisions made on how the items will be resolved.

As much as possible, connectivity to other systems, such as the

DCS interface, laboratory, and scheduling systems, should also be verified during the off-line system test. Of course, there are practical limitations as to what can be tested in an off-line mode. Common sense should prevail. If the system fails the test, leave it in place until it passes. Moving the system on-site to try to maintain a schedule is a mistake.

A typical advanced control system consists of numerous layers of hardware and software, such as

- DCS firmware and operating system
- Supervisory computer operating system
- Network software, communication protocol
- Fill-in-the blank control system software
- *Graphical user interface* (GUI) communication protocol
- DCS interface software
- MPC software, etc.

Depending upon the scope of the entire project, the next step—on-site integration—could be days away or perhaps months or years. It is not uncommon for the advanced controls to be put on the shelf until the DCS reinstrumentation or grass-roots facility has been built. At the end of the off-line system test, a working system exists. Make sure that the upgrade to new versions of software is not taken lightly. Most software vendors provide upward-compatible software products. This means that if you build a graphic for version 2.5 of a GUI package, it will migrate to version 3.0. However, suppose the version of MPC software requires a specific feature in the GUI package which is obsolete in version 3.0. The migration path may require modification to the MPC package. The bottom line is that software compatibility issues are not under your control. Upgrades will be required in the future; just be careful, since there are no guarantees. Version upgrades should be tested in an off-line manner whenever possible.

On-site integration

The primary focus of this activity is to integrate the software demonstrated during the FAT onto the target machine. This may be as simple as unplugging the machine and transporting it to the control room. Or it may require integrating the software onto an existing machine, which is already performing advanced control on another unit. On-site integration should be viewed as a software task. Engineering problems will be identified, but integration is not the time to solve them.

A point-to-point checkout (DCS to computer) should be done on all instrumentation. Measurement behavior should be reviewed. Is the signal valid? Is there too much noise? A punch list of instrument problems should be assembled.

One by one, each regulatory controller that will receive a setpoint from the advanced control system should be turned on and checked. Is it initializing properly? Can the setpoint be changed? If not, there could be a problem with the interface software or in the configuration of the regulatory controller. Connectivity to all other systems (such as the laboratory or scheduling) should be verified.

All calculations should be reviewed from a software standpoint. Are the calculations running, are they changing over time, and do they make sense? For example, if a unit material balance is calculated, it should be approximately 100 percent. Too low or too high a value can indicate an instrumentation problem. The theory behind the calculations should have been checked during the previous phases.

At the end of the integration, all programs should be active, but manipulation of regulatory setpoints should be inhibited. This is the time to verify system loading. Monitor the CPU and memory utilization, check the response time on the GUIs, and verify the available disk space. If performance problems exist, fix them now, before you advance to the next phase. Trying to commission an inadequate system adds confusion and frustration to the task. Your goal is to provide the operators with tools to help them do their jobs. Providing them with inadequate tools will reduce their confidence in the system. This will only increase the amount of time it takes for them to feel comfortable with the tools.

Operator training

The responsibility for operator training should be determined in the analysis phase. Training should occur in two phases: formal classroom and on the job during the commissioning phase. Formal classroom training is best done at the completion of integration before the commissioning. This allows the trainers to demonstrate the actual system. Operators can learn how to enable and disable advanced controls, how to navigate around the system, etc. User manuals and reference material should be provided.

During the commissioning phase, the control objective and strategy should be reviewed with the operator prior to putting on the loop. Stay with the operator, and observe and discuss the performance. Actively encourage the operators to participate in the commissioning activity. Establish a logbook where any questions or problems with the advanced controls can be noted. The burden of communication falls on the control engineers. It is their job to facilitate information transfer between the shifts and to supply answers to questions in the logbook.

Operator training is a step which is sometimes overlooked or delayed in an attempt to accelerate a schedule. Do not do it! Make sure to emphasize that the system is a tool that will make the operator's job easier to do. It should always be the operator's choice to use the tool. If it will make her or his job easier, the operator will want to use it. Do not create a threatening "big brother is watching" environment. Make sure the operators feel that they are part of the team. Remember that a control system can be a success only if it is used by operations.

Commissioning

Stages of loop commissioning are as follows:

- Examine tuning of regulatory controllers.
- Enter setpoint high and low limits, output clamps, and ramp rates.
- Verify controlled variable.
- Turn loop on, and observe performance during the day.
- Obtain permission to leave on overnight—it requires technical supervision.
- Observe performance and fine-tuning.
- Conclude commissioning.

Commissioning is an iterative procedure. Tuning that works well one day may cause a disturbance the next day when the operating conditions change. Commissioning takes time.

The setpoint of each regulatory controller that will be manipulated by advanced control should be changed, and the performance observed. This is the time to resolve filtering and tuning problems of the regulatory loops, which were identified during the on-site integration. It is not unusual to find that regulatory control loops that ran well in the past require retuning. Consider a diesel product flow controller off of a crude tower. Under steady operation it is not unusual for the flow to be adjusted after receipt of a laboratory sample. Laboratory samples may be taken only once or twice a day. This loop may have a long reset time, so that it may take several minutes to reach the new setpoint. When advanced control is implemented, the response time may need to be sped up, since the advanced control may change the flow setpoint every 30 s.

Implementation of advanced controls can require extensive process testing. There are numerous testing methods, but the key to success is coordination with other groups within the plant. This includes planners, schedulers, operators, shift supervisors, and the laboratory (additional laboratory samples are often required to commission quality controllers). Communication goes in both directions. They need to know in advance what process changes the commissioning team will need to do. Likewise, it is extremely useful for the commissioning team to know when crude switches are scheduled, when specification changes are planned, and whether any special operating instructions are in effect due to maintenance or equipment failures.

All technical assumptions made during the design phase should be verified. Solve any problems. Consider the following example of a new main fractionator tower. Temperature measurements consisted of the following: liquid draw tray, pump-around exit and return, and internal vapor at various locations within the tower. Calculation of internal liquid and vapor rates inside the column requires interpolation of temperatures. During the design phase it was decided to use the vapor temperatures for interpolation. However, after start-up it was noticed that the vapor temperature several trays below the light-cycle gas oil draw tray was cooler than the draw tray. Thermodynamic principles state that vapor temperatures below a draw tray (in the absence of pump-around returns) will be hotter than the draw tray. Both instruments were checked, but the discrepancy remained. It is suspected that the vapor temperature is not actually being measured. The calculations were redesigned not to use the vapor temperature.

Verify that the tool is operating properly. An arbitrary limit on constraints can cause control never to reach or push against beneficial limits. The commissioning phase is the time to work with operations to identify realistic operating limits.

If the scope of the project includes regulatory instrument system replacement and advanced control, it is recommended that the commissioning be done sequentially. Attempting to mix regulatory and advanced control commissioning sounds good, but often does not work. Processes are interactive. Since advanced control is a hierarchical layer above regulatory control, it is important to have the entire regulatory system in place and properly tuned first.

A goal of the advanced control system is that it should be functional at all times except during start-up and shutdown of continuous units. In reality, there will be some upset situations or instrument maintenance during which the controls will not be operational. However, keep the goal in mind when you judge success. If the operators remove the controls whenever there is an upset, then the performance is unsatisfactory. Remember, advanced control provides the results of having your best operator and best unit engineer on the board 24 hours a day, 365 days a year. You do not need your best operator and best unit engineer when the unit is running smoothly—you need them to help transition out of problems.

Documentation

Documentation should never be left until the end, although it is often the last item to be completed. The detailed design, the program and system environment manual, and the user's manual should be updated to reflect as-built conditions. It is often helpful to mark the modifications during the commissioning phase when the changes are being made. Manual entries should be documented in a manner that facilitates easy access when operating modes change.

Documentation does not mean paper for the sake of paper. Many systems in the marketplace provide *self-documenting* features that automatically translate the configuration to documentation.

In reality, documentation is never completed. As the system changes over time, the changes must continue to be documented.

Was It a Successful Project?—and How to Keep It That Way

Long-term maintenance planning begins in the analysis phase. Maintenance never really ends. Advanced control is a tool. To get any benefit, it must be used and maintained. Do not expect to implement the system and then fire the implementers.

On-line loop time should be monitored after completion of the commissioning phase. If a loop is consistently not being used, the answer is not to keep turning it back on, but to discuss the problems with operations. There could be a number of problems, such as

- The process or operating objectives may have changed. There is a new constraint which has not been included in the design of the control system. There may be an instrumentation problem which has not yet been identified.

- There could be a tuning problem with the advanced control loop. Perhaps the unit is running at a vastly different throughput, and the tuning may need additional adjustment. Has the tuning of the regulatory control been modified? This impacts the performance of any higher-level controllers. At some facilities the instrument department will have responsibility for tuning DCS controllers, while the control department will be responsible for tuning advanced controllers. In this situation, additional communication between the various departments is required to keep a project successful.

- There may be a training problem. Perhaps a new operator has joined and has not received proper training on the advanced control objectives and how to use the controls.

As previously discussed, advanced control will reduce the variability of the process—that is the easy part. The hard part is getting operations to use the control to increase profitability. For example, assume the maximum specification for the heavy straight-run naphtha ASTM endpoint is 325°F. The average endpoint is 312.5°F, with a standard deviation of 12.5°F. Implementation of advanced control reduced the standard deviation to 4°F. However, to obtain more naphtha within the specification, the operator must increase the setpoint.

Another example where the tool must be used for the benefits to be realized is a maximum heater outlet temperature controller. If the operator enters a low maximum limit, the control will use the limit and never push against the true constraints.

Three to six months after completion of commissioning, a postaudit should be done on the unit. Postaudits are always difficult to do. The job is made easier if a set of "before" data is saved at the beginning of the implementation phase. It is not unusual to find that economic objectives or product specifications have changed since the time when the analysis was done. Still, it is useful to determine whether the anticipated results have been achieved. Do not be concerned with defining the exact source of the benefit. Odds are, it will be a combination of the new instrumentation, better tuning, more in-depth process understanding, and advanced control.

Implementation of advanced control should be viewed as a macro-control loop. Proper documentation of the most recent project provides feedback information on how to implement the next project.

Integration

In general, the possibility for good integration exists between the DCSs and computers. Most DCSs have application programming interfaces to supervisory computers. An exception is a lack of UNIX interfaces on the market today. However, in the advanced control field, interfaces are viewed as a necessary evil. It can be difficult to keep interfaces current—the firmware changes, the computer operating systems and compilers change, even the requirements change. Initially interfaces were only required to read measurements and write targets to and from the DCS. Today, interfaces may need read and write access to all point parameters such as limits, ramp rates, and initialization settings. No one should ever assume that an interface will work without problems. It should always be verified.

As of today, the best integration appears to be with laboratory data systems. The key to these systems is accurate time-stamp information and having the mechanism for operations to validate the information. Timely, accurate laboratory data provide information for advance control model updates and long-term performance analysis.

The typical method of communication between planning and operations is via daily written operating orders. If midday changes are required, new orders are issued. The authors have repeatedly seen facilities where planning orders specify operating targets that are physically impossible to obtain. What is even more surprising is that there never appears to be any dialogue on what the problems are. Also, there is no real discussion between planning and operations on the time criticality of mode changes. Sometimes operations wait 6 h, until the next shift is on, before implementing the changes. How significant is this?

Another area where integration occurs is with the plant information systems. Systems are now in place that transfer all process data to the information system. This is a situation where more data are not necessarily better information. One refinery provided real-time monitors throughout the facility, showing profitability. However, one must question the value of this information when the plot shows increasing profitability, with no indication that the crude unit has been flooded for the last 8 h, sending all products to the slop tanks.

An area where better integration is required is between advanced control and planning and scheduling. There is a gap between these functions (Baker and Shobrys, 1985). Quite often the economic data provided for on-line optimization are of poor quality. In the past, attempts have been made to use marginal values produced by the planning linear program, to determine the value of intermediate product streams. This provided a garbage-in, garbage-out situation. In one instance an ethylene plant optimizer, which was given prices directly from the planning LP, indicated that the plant should be shut down. This was an unrealistic answer. What was missing was a function to relate the marginal values in the LP to the short-term operating conditions and contracted deliveries.

Trademarks

UNIX is a trademark of AT&T, Inc. Windows/NT is a trademark of Microsoft, Inc. VMS is a trademark of Digital Equipment Corporation.

References

Aronson, and White (1990): "Implementation of Advanced Controls with 'New Generation' Distributed Control Systems," *Hydroc. Proc.*, June.

Baker, and Shobrys (1985): "The Integration of Planning, Scheduling and Control," Presented at the National Petroleum Refiners Association Computer Conference, October.

Besl, Cusworth, and Livingston (1993): "Advanced Controls Improve Profitability of UOP CCR Platforming," *Fuel Reformulation.*

Burdick, and Leffler (1983): *Petrochemicals for the Nontechnical Person,* PennWell Books.

Cugini, Kolari, Poje, Sourander, and White (1984): "Control and Optimization of Olefin-Cracking Heaters," *Hydroc. Proc.*, June.

Huffmaster, and Richard (1988): "Advanced Computer Controls Improve Tebone NGL Fractionation-Plant Operations," *Oil & Gas J.*, November 14.

Latour, (1992): "Quantify Quality Control's Intangible Benefits," *Hydroc. Proc.*, May.

White, (1990): "Applications of Advanced Controls and On-Line Optimization in the Chemicals Industry," Presented at the 2d Seoul International Chemical Plant Exhibition, April.

6

Scheduling

Dr. Donald E. Shobrys

Introduction

The purpose of this chapter is to describe the development and implementation of tools for scheduling. The existing literature is rich with articles on solution techniques that address specific aspects of the scheduling process or provide one-pass solutions for carefully defined problems. This includes contributions that date back to the 1950s (Wagner and Whitin, 1958) and more recent developments (Miller and Pekney, 1991). Unfortunately, these articles consider only one aspect of the implementation process, and the suitability of these techniques will vary from one application to the next. This chapter focuses on broader aspects of the implementation process, including

- Defining the size of the problem
- Identifying the issues to be addressed
- Selection of the appropriate solution techniques
- Data integration
- Describing the major steps of the implementation process
- Integration with other functions in the PSC hierarchy

A major impediment to more widespread use of modern, computer-based scheduling tools is a reluctance to acknowledge the potential benefits to the business or that these benefits can be achieved without major capital expenditures. There is a natural tendency to first spend money on the production process, or on manufacturing or financial control systems. The closing section of this chapter examines the benefits that can be achieved.

This chapter uses the words *continuous* and *batch* in describing production processes. *Continuous* refers to units that would normally have a continuous flow of materials going in and coming out. Examples are refinery crude units, continuous polymerization units, and paper machines. These units may come down for maintenance or clean-outs, but there are significant incentives for not shutting down these units. *Batch* refers to units that normally have intermittent flows of materials going in and coming out. This includes both units designed to operate in batch mode, such as batch reactors and blending kettles, and units that incur no real penalties for intermittent operations, such as packaging lines or compounding units.

Scheduling definition

A major problem with the discussion of planning and scheduling is that there is no standard vocabulary for describing the issues that drive the process. Different vocabularies exist, but they tend to be industry-specific. American Production and Inventory Control Society (APICS) terminology focuses on the mechanics of different types of analyses (master production scheduling, materials requirements planning, etc.) rather than the business problems that provide the motivation for this analysis.

To the business, scheduling is the daily link between the manufacturing process and the customer. The issues addressed by scheduling will vary with the characteristics of the production process and the nature of the market served. A more formal definition of scheduling is the specification of what each stage of production is supposed to do over some short scheduling period ranging from several shifts to several weeks. This includes defining or projecting the inputs to and outputs from each production operation. Although the horizon is a few days to several weeks, today's operation is the most important.

Operations are not averaged over the scheduling period. Time and operations move continuously from the beginning of the period to the end. The schedule is revised as needed so that it always starts from what is actually happening. Revisions typically occur each day or each shift. Scheduling is a reality check on the planning process. The objective of scheduling is implementation of the plan, subject to the variability that occurs in the real world. This variability can be in feedstock supplies and quality, the production process, customer requirements, or transport. Schedulers assess how production upsets and other changes will force deviations from the plan, and they determine how to make corrections that meet plan objectives.

If a valid planning process exists, scheduling consists of determining how close the plant can come to meeting planned objectives, given the actual timing of feedstock receipts, production operations, and product movements. Planning and scheduling typically take different views of feedstock arrivals and product shipments. Planning functions tend to consider totals within a time period as if all movements occurred instantaneously. Scheduling deals with the actual timing of movements.

There is often a great deal of emphasis on the optimization that takes place at the planning level. If the production process has any degree of complexity, it is difficult to realize the benefits of this optimization without effective scheduling tools.

Characteristics of the scheduling process

Process industry scheduling applications typically share the following characteristics.

1. Scheduling is the most active juncture of business and manufacturing systems. Schedulers are continually assessing how the capabilities of the production process compare to the needs of the business. On a daily basis, a scheduler has to react to process variability as well as business variability that can impact feedstock arrivals and product movements. Scheduling involves dynamic interactions with the business (marketing and customer service) as well as the manufacturing process and distribution. Human factors add unpredictability to these interactions.

Planning considers both business and manufacturing but is updated less frequently and considers less detail. Control applications focus on the manufacturing process, and *distributed control systems* (DCSs) provide control capabilities for specific portions of the overall process. At the control level, the visibility of the customer and the impact of human factors are greatly reduced.

2. Deficiencies in planning or control often create problems that appear in the scheduling process. Control deficiencies or bad data on the status of the production process can create customer service problems. Customer service problems may also occur because of either a planning process with an overly optimistic estimate of available capacity or a poor understanding of the capabilities of manufacturing. Operations staff may not be effective in executing activities as scheduled. Since these problems become visible in the scheduling function, the business often assumes that they indicate deficiencies in scheduling.

3. Projects that develop scheduling tools are prone to *mission creep*. As scheduling tools are designed and implemented, there is a tenden-

cy to address problems that occur in other functions since the problems often become visible in the scheduling process. This may involve considering the manufacturing process in the same level of detail as process control, or considering time horizons approaching those used in planning. Many projects have tried to go in both directions simultaneously.

There are several problems associated with this. If this mission creep is not contained, it is difficult to stay within project budgets and meet project schedules. In addition, mission creep can lead to tools that are no longer useful because they are too cumbersome to work with, too expensive to maintain, or too complex for the user to understand.

4. The emphasis in scheduling is *feasibility*. The scheduler must produce a workable schedule and must be able to accurately project the consequences of disruptions and schedule changes. Management often is fixated on cost minimization, but you first need an executable schedule before you can try to reduce scheduling costs.

5. Schedulers have to integrate information from a variety of sources. They need to know current inventories and expected product liftings to determine production requirements. The information on product liftings may be taken from customer orders, transport schedules, contracts, and sales forecasts. Schedulers have to know what is currently occurring in the production process, and they have to understand the production process so that they can predict the consequences of the current schedule. They have to know how the different process units or stages of production interact, and they have to be familiar with charge rates, yields, process times, batch sizes, run lengths, formulations, changeover costs and times, and any other parameters that describe the production process that they are working with.

This data integration is often so time-consuming that little time is available for analysis. The scheduler may have to manually integrate data from a variety of different sources. Some plants maintain the data in a single system, but their schedulers spend the majority of their time manually integrating data taken from multiple hard-copy reports.

Scheduling applications often differ in the following respects. These differences may occur between plants in the same industry or even the same company.

1. The organizational structure around the scheduling process may vary. A plant location may have a single scheduler, or the scheduling process may be subdivided. For example, some refineries will have

feedstock schedulers, hydraulic schedulers concerned with operations on the major units, and product schedulers who are concerned with blending and orchestrating movements from the refinery. The division between scheduling and transportation, scheduling and operations, scheduling and customer service, or scheduling and marketing may vary.

The range of a scheduler's activities is limited by the tools that he or she works with. If the scheduling process involves extensive manual manipulation of data, whether it is with pencil and paper or personal-computer spreadsheets, the scheduling process will often be subdivided across several individuals or consider a very limited time horizon. Effective implementation of computer-based scheduling tools can extend the range of activity of a single scheduler. This will focus the scheduling decisions into a smaller group of decision makers. More importantly, this will also make the scheduling process more responsive. The use of computer technology to expand the range of activity of a single individual is a key part of the business improvement process referred to as *reengineering* (Hammer and Champy, 1993).

2. The specific issues to be addressed by scheduling are dictated by the characteristics of the manufacturing process and the business. Units may operate continuously or intermittently. Production operations may be driven by the need to keep units running continuously or may be solely driven by customer requirements. The costs and time associated with changing operations may be a major consideration. They may be considered explicitly, they may be addressed with production wheels or cycles, or they may not be a factor in scheduling. Production operations are more predictable in plants with standard product slates or captive distribution systems. They can be less predictable if the plant produces make-to-order products, gets feedstock from spot markets, or sells into spot markets.

The interaction of scheduling with planning and control will also be heavily influenced by the characteristics of the manufacturing process and the business.

3. Data quality and availability can vary greatly and will control solution design and implementation priorities. Problems with data quality will limit the level of detail in any scheduling tools and will also limit the sophistication and complexity of the solution techniques that can be implemented.

4. A scheduler's familiarity with computer-based tools can vary greatly, and this will control the sophistication of the solution techniques that can be used. It is not a question of the techniques that can be used to solve each problem, but rather of the techniques

that the user will understand and have confidence in. The end user's starting point is often pencil and paper or the PC equivalent, which is a spreadsheet.

5. The availability of support resources will also vary, especially with the current emphasis on lean staffing. The more sophisticated the solution technique, the more intensive the support requirements.

Components of scheduling solutions

The development of scheduling solutions involves the following components.

1. *Definition of dimensions.* How big is the problem? There are a number of practical reasons for addressing this question. Size is a major factor in estimating project duration and cost. Size impacts the response time of solution techniques, and this plays a role in their selection. Documented estimates of model size also provide controls for project management.

2. *Scheduling issues.* Scheduling is part of the larger process of running the business. There are specific issues associated with each scheduling application that are a function of the business's needs and priorities.

3. *Supporting information flows.* What information is used currently for scheduling? What information could be used by improved tools? Where would it come from, and how would it get to the scheduler? Is this information currently in use, or would it have to be validated? Again, there are very practical reasons for these questions because the answers help define project cost and duration.

4. *Solution technology.* How do we find the optimal schedule? Is there an optimal schedule? What is the role of the scheduler, and what is the role of computer-based intelligence?

5. *Implementation and integration.* How do you put everything together? What are the risk factors? Can risk be minimized? What benefits can be realized from the finished system?

Dimensions of Scheduling Problems

There seems to be a *first law of scheduling dynamics* that can be expressed as follows: The human element determines the ultimate complexity of a scheduling function. The dimensions of the function will be adjusted to stay within the limits of the human element. The people who end up in scheduling positions tend to share a common characteristic: Somehow, they get the job done, no matter what tools are available to them. If the tools available to schedulers are limited, often schedulers have to simplify the job to make it manageable. They may focus on a key group of high-profile products or on a few key units or on a key stage of production. They may concentrate on the next crisis. They may take an aggregate view of inventories or production activities and may let operations staff sort out the details. Schedulers may have to take a simplistic view of the capacity available to them.

There are often opportunity costs associated with this simplification. These opportunity costs, which are discussed in greater detail at the close of this chapter, are often a good part of the motivation for implementing computer-based scheduling tools.

The process of defining a scheduling problem should begin with the dimensions of the problem. If the dimensions are very large, the production process tends to be simple and predictable, or the scheduler treats the process as if it were simple and predictable. If the production process is very complex or unpredictable, the dimensions of the scheduling problems will be smaller. The following paragraphs indicate the dimensions that should be measured as part of the definition of a scheduling problem.

Number of inventory items

The primary focus of the scheduling process is feasibility, particularly feasibility of inventory movements. The first step in addressing inventory feasibility is to define the inventory items that the scheduling function has to track. The scheduling function usually should follow inventory levels of feedstocks, intermediate inventories, and finished products. If products are packaged before they are shipped, each package product combination is another inventory item, and the function should follow the inventories of packaging materials as well. In many plants the scheduling function primarily follows finished products. Scheduling needs to follow these other inventory items since they will determine what production activities can take place.

In industries such as refining, it becomes important to follow the qualities of streams as well as their volumes. Stream qualities can influence throughput rates on units, along with unit yields and product formulations. Each stream-quality combination is another inventory.

Finished products deserve special attention in defining problem dimensions, since there may be multiple definitions of finished products. Marketing people may have a number of different identifiers for the same product because they are differentiating between different pricing schemes. Aggregated product definitions may be used in forecasting, planning, or management summaries. Examples are product families in the chemical industry or generic products such as unleaded gasoline in refining.

Common problems in the chemical industry are that product on hand may be subdivided into multiple grades (based on quality), or that a customer may ask for a selection of a product based on specifications that are narrower than the normal product specifications. It may be possible to drive the process to produce the desired grades or selections, or the allowable end use may have to be determined as part of the quality control process.

The scheduler has to define production activities required to meet customer requirements. Thus she or he has to know how inventory can be applied. For scheduling purposes, a unique product identifier should be assigned to each unique set of specifications or manufacturing instructions.

Defining units or stages of production

The next step is to define the major units and stages of production to be considered in the scheduling process. This step requires an understanding of the production process and the issues considered by scheduling. A "no brainer" default is to consider every piece of equipment, pump, and section of pipe separately. While this might be a reasonable approach in building a detailed simulation model of the plant, it will generally result in a tool that is too cumbersome for use by the scheduler. This is another area where we see *scope creep,* as people try to extend scheduling tools to address real-time control of the process or movements.

For scheduling purposes, a stage of production or piece of equipment should be considered only if the scheduler will be making decisions about the timing, sequence, throughput rate, or volume of production operations on that piece of equipment.

Time horizon

The emphasis in scheduling is on the near term. The definition of *near term* is a function of the normal run lengths of production activities. If the run lengths for operations are typically a few hours, the scheduling time horizon may be a few days. If run lengths typically span weeks, such as on polymerization units, the scheduling time horizon may be 2 or 3 months.

Another key consideration is how far in advance the plant sees the customer orders or contracts that it will have to fill. Ideally, scheduling is driven by firm orders or contracts, while planning is more heavily dependent on a demand forecast. The scheduling time horizon should coincide with the time horizon for which the plant has a majority of the firm orders that will have to be filled. This could range from 3 days to 10 weeks. If this is shorter than production lead times, then scheduling will have to be driven by a combination of firm orders and forecast demands.

This is another prime area for scope creep, as the time horizon considered by the scheduling tool is extended to address planning functions.

Number of production activities

As a very rough rule of thumb, a scheduling tool becomes cumbersome to work with if it considers more than 1000 production activities at a "scheduling" level of detail. This threshold may drop to several hundred activities if tight synchronization across the different stages of production is critical, or if the production process is unpredictable.

Number of customer orders or contracts

If the scheduling process does not see or deal with individual customer orders or contracts, this number may not be very significant. A large number of orders may be met out of finished inventory, but only a few production activities may be required to replenish that inventory.

The number of orders is more significant if production activities are primarily driven by customer orders, especially if products are specific to a customer. In those situations the number of orders is an indication of the number of production activities required to meet existing demand.

The number of new and modified demands on a daily basis indicates the amount of demand-driven change that can occur in the schedule each day. This will be in addition to the change coming from variations in the production process and raw-material availability.

Number of schedulers

It is dangerous to simply consider the number of schedulers currently in the process. The function of each scheduler must also be examined. Schedulers may actually be the staff members who make scheduling decisions. However, you will often find "schedulers" who are primarily information gatherers. If each scheduler is actually a decision maker, you may find that a relatively small portion of the scheduler's time is spent on analysis and decision making. Most of the time may be spent on collecting and manipulating information.

Well-designed computer-based scheduling tools should integrate and manage the information needed for scheduling. This will either extend the range of activity of the scheduling function or change the staffing requirements, requiring a smaller number of schedulers who will spend the majority of their time on analysis and decision making.

It is important to estimate the change in function and/or in staffing requirements for the revamped scheduling group prior to the start of the project. The number of people in the "to be" scheduling function will indicate the training burden and the amount of coordination required in any new scheduling tools. The change in function and change in workforce indicate the size of the organizational problem to be dealt with when implementation occurs.

Scheduling Issues: Examples for Different Industries

These issues vary with production process and business characteristics, as described below. A common thread across all industries is the dynamic aspect of the scheduling process. There is a common need to be able to quickly react to changes in the process, raw-material availability, customer requirements, and the timing of movements.

Refining (continuous processes)

A refinery is a good example of a *push* production process. Most refineries have the same major units, and these major units operate continuously. Crude oil is usually the primary feed. As it goes through the crude unit, it is separated into component streams. Some of these streams are desirable. Either the undesirable streams are converted to desirable streams on conversion units such as crackers, reformers, and alkylation units, or else they are blended with the desirable streams into finished products. Undesirable streams may also be sold off or used as low-cost fuel. Given their high volumes (40,000 to 400,000 bbl/day), refineries have a relatively small number (50 to 200) of finished products. The primary products of most North American refineries are motor gasolines.

Refinery units have different modes of operation. Changing the mode of operation on a unit will change the qualities and volumes of the streams coming off the unit. Although the mode of operation of a refinery unit can theoretically vary continuously over a wide range, actual practice is to operate units in distinct modes or in a relatively narrow range. On most units there is no cost or time associated with changing the mode of operation. Examples of exceptions are solvent extraction and dewaxing units.

The qualities of the streams feeding a unit will affect the yields and qualities of the streams coming off the units, and may also limit charge rates to the unit.

The refinery planning process typically provides scheduling with volume-based information. Planning determines the volumes of different feedstocks that will be consumed. Planning also selects the modes of operation on the units and determines the volumes to be processed in each mode. Planning sets budgets for the purchase of secondary feedstocks and for sales of blend stocks and products. Planning does not provide very much guidance on timing, since the tools used by the planning process consider time in discrete-time buckets that are still typically a month in size.

The function of the scheduling group within a refinery is to define charge rates and the timing of mode changes in response to product requirements and containment problems. This group is also responsible for scheduling the movements of material in and out of the refinery.

A number of refineries decompose scheduling into crude (or feedstock) scheduling, hydraulic scheduling, and products scheduling. Crude schedulers react to the timing of crude arrivals, determine which tanks the crude should be placed in, blend crudes as needed to meet targets for yields and qualities off the crude unit, and determine the charge rate to the crude unit. Hydraulic scheduling is concerned with operations on the major units and inventories between the units. It includes defining charge rates and the timing of mode changes so that the components needed for finished products are produced while intermediate inventories stay between minimum and maximum tank limits.

Product scheduling is concerned with defining the timing of blends and the activities required to move finished products out of the refinery, while ensuring that component and finished-product tanks stay between minimum and maximum levels. The scheduling of blends and of movements of finished products such as motor gasolines is closely linked to the generation of blend recipes. Recipe generation is influenced by component availability and containment problems. The recipes determine component drawdowns, which in turn impact availability and containment.

Interactions between scheduling and process control occur with regard to unit operations and movements. Charge rates and the timing of mode changes are communicated from scheduling to process control, usually via refinery operations staff. Setpoints, or volume and quality targets that determine setpoints, usually come from planning, although scheduling may make short-term adjustments. Feedback from process control to scheduling concerns the status of the production process. The schedulers need to know rates, inventory levels, and key stream qualities. Some industry experts take the position that if a pump fails or trays are damaged in a column, the scheduler must be informed. Schedulers would probably prefer to know the consequences of those events in terms of their impact on rates, inventories, and qualities.

The area of oil movements is fertile for scope creep around scheduling applications. There is a tendency to expect the scheduling function to take a control-level view of movements. Scheduling determines the need for movements, which are based on projections of production and consumption. The control system is responsible for the execution of each movement, and this requires a detailed description of the topology of the movement system. One objective of scheduling is to look far enough ahead to identify potential containment problems before they can become crises. This may cover a period of one or more weeks. The control system is focused on the movements that have to occur now, so it can handle a level of detail that would make a scheduling system unusable.

Batch process plants (specialty chemicals, lubricants)

Similar types of plants also produce food products, pharmaceuticals, paints and coatings, and health care products. Within these plants, production activities can occur intermittently at each stage of production. These are examples of *pull* types of production processes, since production activities are often primarily driven by specific demands. These plants are small in volume compared to refineries, but they may have hundreds or even thousands of products across all product-package combinations. If the plant supplies products for retail sales, the same material may be sold in dozens of different types of packages.

Products may be customer-specific. It may be very important to address the needs of specific customers, and customer service problems may result in lost sales. Schedulers may interact with order acceptance functions to ensure realistic ship dates for customer orders, and they may be involved in addressing customer service problems.

A schematic of a lubrication plant is shown in Fig. 6.1. Base oils arrive at the lubrication plant and are stored and sometimes blended in field tanks. Base oils are combined with additives in batch kettles, in-line blenders, or high-speed batch blenders. Small-volume blends occur in batch kettles. They will move from the kettles to bulk loading racks or packaging lines. The in-line blenders and high-speed batch blenders typically blend into dedicated tankage or swing tanks. Swing tanks provide temporary storage and are emptied when the product is put into packages or shipped in bulk. Management of swing tankage becomes increasingly critical as the throughput through the automated blenders increases.

Other batch plants might include batch reactors, separation units, and drying lines. In specialty chemical plants, these facilities may be

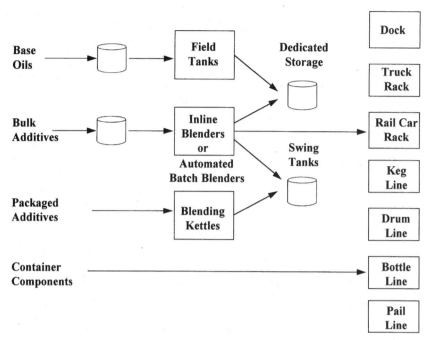

Figure 6.1 Batch plant example.

combined in a variety of configurations depending on the products being produced. Instead of blending lubricants, kettles might be used for foods, beverages, paints, coatings, specialty chemicals, or health care products that are then packaged.

For each stage of production, there often are several facilities where a product can be made or packaged. Reactors, kettles, drying lines, and packaging lines may exist in parallel. There may be significant costs or delays associated with changing operations. Kettles, reactors, and drying lines may require cleaning when you are changing from one product to another or when you are deviating from the desired sequence of operations. This may create off-specification products that have to be disposed of or blended off in small amounts. The time and amount of off-specification product may be a function of product compatibility. Packaging lines may incur downtime when changes occur in the product being filled, package size, or package footprint. The fastest lines often require the most time for changeovers.

Sometimes these transitions are considered on a case-by-case basis. Another approach to controlling the impact of these transitions is to impose product cycles, or wheels, which define the order in which products can be made. To move between two products, it may be necessary to produce a third intermediate product, whether there are orders for it or not. There may be minimum and maximum limits on production volumes. These may be imposed by the equipment. A blending kettle or batch reactor has a maximum volume based on its size, and usually it has a minimum volume that it can effectively process. Minimum production volumes may also be imposed in an effort to limit the impact of transition costs and times.

There are usually quality assurance tests at each step of the production process. The time required to perform these tests may vary from minutes to a day or more, and the product may not be usable until the results have been obtained.

The general trend has been to reduce the time required for testing, either by providing the ability to get results back more quickly or by reducing the need for testing by making improvements to the manufacturing process. This has direct implications for scheduling. In the past, the results of quality control tests were often not available until the next shift, or the next day, or even later. This tended to simplify coordination between the different stages of the production process by allowing schedulers to consider the different stages of production independently. Production activities that occurred today on the first stage of production would feed activities in the second stage of production tomorrow, which in turn would feed the next stage of production on the following day. This made it easy to distribute scheduling responsibilities by stage of production. Coordination between schedulers could occur on a daily basis.

The reduction in test times has made synchronization across different stages of production more critical. In addition, process reengineering efforts frequently remove the storage capacity used to hold these buffer inventories in an effort to force lean production. Feeding and consuming production activities may occur within a single shift. If scheduling is distributed across several schedulers, they may have to iterate continuously over the course of the day.

A second trend in the chemical industry that impacts scheduling is that the requirements of individual customers are becoming increasingly selective. A product that meets the manufacturer's quality control criteria may not be acceptable to all customers. The acceptability of a batch of product to a specific customer may be determined by grade level or other end-use criteria. It may be necessary to net existing inventory against customer orders and selection criteria on a batch-by-batch, or lot-by-lot, basis to get an accurate indication of production requirements.

If a planning function exists, it may often interact with scheduling indirectly. The planning process must often depend heavily on forecast demand because actual orders may be available only over a limited time horizon. The commitment that a business will make based on forecasts will also vary. A planning process driven by forecasts may be used to determine material requirements, staffing levels, or overtime. In these situations, the communication between planning and scheduling occurs in the material and workforce availability that the scheduler sees. Some plants may go one step further and actually produce certain high-volume products, or products with long manufacturing lead times, based on forecast demands.

The planning process may determine two other parameters that affect scheduling. Safety stock levels may be revised periodically by planning based on changes in forecast demand. Planning may also provide target or minimum production quantities that consider trade-offs between changeover and inventory holding costs. These safety stock levels and production quantities can only be used as guidelines at the scheduling level for two reasons:

1. These calculations are based on some type of forecast, and actual orders may deviate from the forecast.

2. The safety stock and production quality calculations often do not consider limits on production or storage capacity.

It may be difficult to find a formal planning process at some of these plants. They often operate in a highly reactive, highly intuitive mode, and plant staff are very proud of their "fire-fighting" skills. The lack of a formal planning process may create a variety of difficulties that are often attributed to scheduling. Typical examples are that the accepted orders exceed capacity for a portion of the product slate, creating customer service problems. Raw-materials warehouses may be full, but production delays still occur because of particular raw-materials shortages, because raw materials are managed based on intuition or historical data.

Since custom service is important to these plants, there should be constant interactions between scheduling and the order acceptance process. Scheduling is a key part of the order fulfillment process. The interactions between scheduling and order acceptance fall under the heading of *available to promise* (ATP), and they are intended to ensure that customer orders are given order ship dates.

Rather than allow a dynamic ATP process, some companies will use fixed order lead times to govern the acceptance of customer orders. Unfortunately, these fixed order lead times are often defined without consideration of manufacturing lead times or without providing a mechanism for checking capacity availability. This can result in customer service problems that are again attributed to poor scheduling.

Interactions between scheduling and control will primarily consist of a download from scheduling to control of the activities to be performed, and feedback from control on the work completed and the status of the production process. There are two types of control systems that scheduling may interface with in batch plants. There may be a *distributed control system* (DCS) or *programmable logic controllers* (PLCs) in place on the manufacturing process. These systems are not always found in batch plants, particularly in older plants. They may be in place only around certain parts of the production process. It can be very expensive to install the instrumentation required to automatically monitor the process, and it may be difficult to justify the cost in older plants.

The second type of control system is *shop floor control*. These systems control the distribution and execution of work orders. These are often form-driven systems. A work order is created for each production operation to be executed. The work orders are distributed to the production areas. Operators on the plant floor either receive printed copies or view them on computer terminals. The work orders are often used to log partial or full completion of production activities, either on the printed copies or via terminals. A key issue in the interactions between scheduling and shop floor control lies in defining the mnemonics used to identify work orders. Work orders are typically created by the scheduling system. Depending on how far in advance the work orders have been created, the scheduling system may have to inform shop floor control of changes to or deletions of work orders. It is also convenient if scheduling can be quickly informed of the activities that have been partially or completely executed.

Continuous and batch hybrids (polymer plants and paper mills)

These plants are a combination of the prior examples. A key stage of production runs continuously, while subsequent stages run intermittently. One example is a polymerization plant, such as the one in the schematic shown in Fig. 6.2.

Monomer is fed into polymerization units. These are continuous (or semicontinuous) units that run blocked operations, moving from one product to the next. The polymer coming off the units may go to compounding, where it is mixed with other polymers or agents, or it may go to packaging lines that operate intermittently. The compounding units may have intermittent operations, and they also feed packaging lines. Product transitions on the polymerization units may require clean-outs, or they may generate lower-value transition (twilight) material while going from one product to another. The transitions are often defined by the production wheels, or cycles, discussed in the previous section. Some plants may have dryers between the polymeriza-

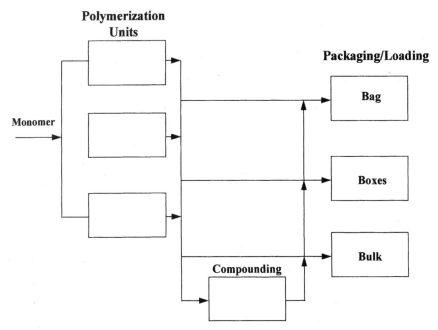

Figure 6.2   Hybrid example.

tion units and packaging. Another example of this type of plant is a paper mill, where the paper machine operates continuously, going across different grades of paper and different colors and basis weights within grades, while downstream of the paper machine the rewinders, embossers, and converting lines operate intermittently.

The interactions between planning and scheduling will vary by stage of production. Planning will largely determine production operations on the continuous stage, while scheduling creates and sequences the activities on the other stages of production in response to containment requirements and customer orders. The plant will maximize production efficiency if the product runs on the continuous stage are as long as possible. Unfortunately, this can create customer service problems. The issues of how frequently a product is made, and volumes that are produced when it is made, are also referred to as *campaign frequency* and *lot sizing*. Decisions on campaign frequency and lot sizing must often be based on demand forecasts because of the length of time required to cycle through the products made on a unit. The process used to determine production operations on the continuous stage will vary with different business strategies. Some businesses will lay out a plan that has good transitions and tries to meet monthly forecasts. This plan is given to customer service staff, who use it as a guideline for committing to customer ship dates. The business tries to maximize production efficiency by trying to get customers to place orders that conform with the plan.

Other businesses will have the planners go through one or more rounds of negotiations with marketing, sales, and customer service. These negotiations may even include the customer, as the business tries to balance the tradeoffs between customer service and production efficiency. There are also companies that commit to meeting customer demands, irrespective of the impact on planned production. The factors that determine the strategy used by a business include the variability of customer demands, the stability of the production process, the amount of competitive pressure in the marketplace, and business objectives such as maximizing margin versus maximizing or protecting market share. The planning process may also address material requirements for raw materials with long lead times, the feasibility of meeting expected demand with available capacity, operating calendar and staffing levels, and the timing of major maintenance activities. The role of scheduling on the continuous stage of production is heavily influenced by business strategy. If the business emphasizes production efficiency, the continuous stage of production may run to plan with only local adjustments by scheduling. If the business emphasizes customer service, the scheduler may constantly be trying to minimize the impact of disruptions and recover to plan.

The scheduling issues addressed in these plants are often a combination of the issues described in the two previous sections.

The output from scheduling is the definition of the timing, sequence, and volume of production activities. Just as in the batch plants, this information is often passed to distributed control systems or shop floor control systems for execution.

Summary of potential scheduling issues

The following scheduling issues or functions appear across batch, continuous, and hybrid scheduling environments.

Creation of production operations. The scheduling function must create the production activities required to meet customer requirements, particularly for batch operations. The planning function generally defines the required production operations for continuous processes.

Dynamic rescheduling. This is the process of modifying the schedule in response to changes in demand for finished products, raw-material availability, and production upsets. The ease of doing this controls the frequency of updates and often defines the credibility of the scheduling function in the plant. The harder it is to do dynamic rescheduling, the larger the number of inventory and capacity buffers in the scheduling process.

Inventory feasibility. This is a key aspect for customer service and order fulfillment, and it is often a focal point for interactions between scheduling and the customer service staff accepting customer orders. The scheduling function often must adjust production volumes, throughputs, and the timing of production operations to ensure inventory feasibility. The effort may also involve balancing production volumes across multiple stages of production.

Detailed sequencing. The sequence of production activities can have significant time and cost implications. Delays may occur in moving from one production operation to another, reducing the effective capacity available for production. Product volume may be lost as well. The time and volume lost are often a function of the differences between the two products (color, composition, physical properties). It is often possible to reduce the time and material lost by carefully sequencing production activities to minimize the differences between adjacent production operations. Some plants control the impact of these transitions by using a product wheel that defines a fixed sequence which includes all the products made on a unit.

Synchronization of activities. Inventory buffers decouple stages of production. With adequate inventory between the stages of production, the different stages can almost be scheduled independently. The current emphasis on lean production and faster quality control procedures is reducing those buffers and increasing the need for careful synchronization between the different stages of production.

Scheduling Data Requirements

Data requirements fall into two categories. You need the data that let you define the finished-product volumes that must be produced, and you need the data that let you define the production operations which will result in the production of the required finished products. These data requirements may seem obvious, but there are often difficulties in getting accurate data.

Data defining production requirements

This includes the following data categories:

Customer orders or contracts. The scheduling function needs a snapshot of the orders or contracts that are currently open. Even if scheduling is not driven by customer orders or contracts, they define the timing of product movements. This information tends to be very dynamic, not only because new demands are added over time, but also because existing orders may be modified or canceled. The order information required will include the product or product/package combination required, quantity, ship date, and order number. If schedulers are actively involved in customer service interactions, they may also need to know the customer and customer location. If customers have special selection or end-use criteria, schedulers need to know this as well.

Net forecast. The extent to which the forecast impacts scheduling will vary from one application to another. The plant may use a forecast only to order raw materials; or it may use a forecast to reserve capacity but only produce to actual customer orders; or it may actually produce to the forecast. Within a plant, each of these options may be applied to different portions of the product slate. The forecast may be generated with statistical techniques, it may be based on business intelligence, or it may simply consist of historical data.

The forecasts that schedulers receive are often too coarse to be useful. The most common problem is that the forecast is for a monthly time span. Forecasts are also often aggregated. A scheduler working at a product/package level may receive forecasts at a product or product family level. To be useful for scheduling, the forecast must be disaggregated to the product/package level and distributed over time in a manner that is consistent with the movements seen by the plant. A month may be front-end-loaded or back-end-loaded. Movements may occur in periodic lumps (24,000 gal every 6 weeks) based on a customer's inventory policies rather than in uniform increments over time (4000 gal/week).

The scheduler should work with the most complete set of demand information available, which means combining the forecast with orders. *Net forecast* refers to a forecast that has been reduced to reflect existing orders. The process of netting forecast against orders should also consider the treatment of *unconsumed* forecast, which is any forecast for which orders never materialize. Some businesses may ignore unconsumed forecast, while others may roll it forward for some period of time.

Inventories. The scheduling function needs to know current inventory levels for raw materials, intermediate products, and finished products. The inventory data must be detailed enough that the scheduling function can see how much available inventory can be applied against every order. Thus if customers have special selection criteria or end-use classifications, the scheduling function must be able to see inventory by these selection criteria or end-use classifications. Inventory data must also be synchronized with order data. This issue is discussed further below.

Process status. To know what additional production is required, the scheduling function must know where the plant is with regard to the current schedule. This includes receipt of raw materials and production of intermediate inventories as well as production of finished products. This information must also be synchronized with the order and inventory data. There are several ways of obtaining this information. Schedulers may have to "walk the floor" when they arrive to determine the status of the production, or they may receive that information verbally from area supervisors. A shop floor control system could send the schedulers a list of work orders that have been partially or completely filled since the last production update, showing the items and volumes produced. A distributed control system may send the schedulers the volumes produced since the last production update.

These data should be updated at least daily, and a key issue is synchronization of data sources. The inventory update should contain the inventory levels at the time that the snapshot of open orders was taken. The process status should reflect the status of the production process at the time that the inventory levels were recorded and the snapshot of open orders was taken. It is usually possible to get a synchronized update on a daily basis because most businesses will close out their systems at a specific time each day. More frequent synchronized updates of open orders, inventories, and process status would be of value, but they are often unavailable. Updates over the course of the day on any new orders, order modifications, or order cancellations that have accumulated since the last synchronized update are also of value. Periodic updates on only inventory levels or only the process status are not nearly as useful. Schedulers may use the inventory or process updates to infer whether a key production operation has been completed, but they cannot use only this information to update the plant schedule. Inventory may be on hand because it was produced or because a shipment has been delayed.

Two common problems exist in obtaining these synchronized updates. First, batch update procedures may be in place around "real-time" systems. As an example, a real-time inventory system at a chemical plant logged production continuously, but product shipments were only entered once a day. Second, problems may exist with data from accounting systems. The timing often relates to billing procedures rather than actual movements. An order may be closed when it is invoiced, or when the invoice quantity is confirmed, rather than when it is shipped. Accounting data may be accurate only at the end of an accounting cycle, which may occur once a month. The product identifiers used in accounting systems may often be much coarser than those needed for production scheduling.

Data defining required production activities

This consists of the data describing production operations at the plant. These data are used to determine what operations are required and their characteristics.

Facility use. This defines which streams or inventory items are produced on each facility. For example, a polymerization unit will produce specific types of polymers. If the timing and sequence of loading and unloading activities must be addressed by the scheduling function, then docks, barge slips, truck racks, and loading bays are included as facilities. Facility use data define the inventory items that could be loaded or unloaded in these locations.

Sometimes the word *routing* is used to refer to this type of information, particularly in batch applications. The notion is more applicable to some discrete manufacturing applications, where a specific item may go through a series of operations on different facilities. In process industry settings, the product from one stage of production may often go into a number of intermediates or finished products, so the notion of a single routing for a finished product is not really applicable.

Material use and production at each stage of production. This consists of defining the inventory items consumed and produced in each production operation. This information is needed to determine which production operations will be needed to meet a finished-product shipment. This information is also needed to determine the feasibility of production activities. Shortages of intermediates or of raw materials may prevent the plant from shipping finished product on the required date. For continuous units, this information is referred to as *yield data*. In a batch environment, this information is referred to as *formulations* or *recipes*.

If the plant has packaging operations, then material use data are also required for packaging operations. They define the volumes of bulk products and the packaging materials needed to produce one inventory unit of each packaged product.

In batch applications, the reader may encounter the notion that scheduling should only consider capacity feasibility and not deal with material use. This is a carryover from the days when the capabilities of existing computers limited the issues that could be considered by scheduling tools. These limitations are no longer relevant. Material use data are a key factor in determining whether a schedule can actually be executed and in identifying possible solutions to production upsets or problems with material availability.

Data on production quantities. There may be minimum, maximum, and target volumes for production activities. The minimum and maximum values may be defined by physical limitations of production equipment (such as the size of a batch reactor or a finished-product tank that a blend is going into) or maintenance policies (frequency of clean-outs on a polymerization unit). Target volumes will often come from the planning process.

Data on timing. These data define how long a production operation will tie up a unit and how long it takes for inventory to become available after the start of a production operation. The duration of continuous operations will be determined by minimum and maximum production rates. Operations on batch reactors may have fixed durations. Packaging lines may run at a fixed rate for each product/package combination.

The delay between the start of an operation and the time when the resulting inventory becomes available is a function of the time required for testing and time required to move the inventory to the next stage of production. These testing and movement times are usually a characteristic of batch operations.

Transition times and costs. Product transitions on a unit may involve downtime, production of low-quality material, and the loss of the feedstocks used to flush out the unit. These transitions are a major concern to the scheduling function in some plants, and they can significantly reduce the capacity available for production. Two key characteristics of these transitions are the time that the unit is out of production and the cost of the transition. The time that the unit is out of production can be the time required to clean the unit, the time that it will take to produce off-specification product, or the total of these two. If this time is significant, it has to be considered in determining the timing of production activities.

The cost reflects the degradation of any feedstocks used in cleaning the unit and the loss in revenue from the unit being out of production or the reduced value of the product made during transition. Sometimes there may actually be disposal costs for the transition product. These costs indicate the severity of different transitions, and the costs can be used in trying to resequence production operations to minimize the impact of product transitions.

If a dollar cost is not available, the time lost, flush volumes, or the volume of off-specification production may be used as surrogate measures of the relative impact of transitions.

Other costs.   The costs used in scheduling should be variable manufacturing costs, with no fixed-cost allocation. Allocation of fixed costs will distort decisions made over the near term. For example, a foundry modernized a casting line, purchasing automated equipment that dramatically increased throughput rates and quality while decreasing labor requirements. Shortly after the modernization was completed, there was a major business downturn that dictated that a portion of the foundry be closed. The accountants recommended that the new line be closed because it had the highest per-unit production costs. The production supervisor for that area pointed out that the accountant's per-unit costs were so high because the accountants included a per-unit allocation of the cost of the improvements to that line. On the basis of variable production costs, the new line had the lowest per-unit production costs in the foundry.

In addition to the transition costs mentioned previously, variable manufacturing costs include operations costs (including materials, energy, labor), inventory holding costs, and customer service costs (i.e., low sales or meeting customer due dates by using more expensive truck shipments instead of rail).

The availability of a full range of cost data is not always essential for improving the scheduling function. A scheduler must first produce a schedule that is feasible with regard to capacity and inventory, given the existing demands on the plant. A completely feasible schedule is one with no late or incomplete shipments. Fictitious penalty costs can be used to measure the extent of capacity or inventory problems. If extensive economic optimization occurs in the planning function, these penalties indicate how far the schedule and the actual pattern of product movements are from the optimal plan. The consideration of the other costs mentioned above can often be a refinement.

In addition, within the time horizon used for scheduling, one or two cost categories will often dominate. If transition costs are significant, they will often far exceed any other cost component except for customer service costs.

Any costs taken from accounting systems should be treated cautiously. In addition to potential problems with the allocation of fixed costs, accounting systems tend not to handle transition costs very well. The collection of the data needed to describe the production process is often challenging. Many of these data may reside only between people's ears. Traditional MRP II systems often serve as repositories for these data, but it may be difficult to extract them in the form needed for scheduling. The description of material and facility use (bill of materials) is often aggregated across multiple stages of production, multiple facilities, or both. In addition, traditional MRP II systems do not provide any place to put data on transition costs and times.

Solution Methods

The refining industry was a leader in planning and scheduling technology through the 1960s and 1970s. During the 1980s and 1990s, the disruptions associated with downsizing and an extreme emphasis on cost containment resulted in stagnation of the refining industry's planning and scheduling technology. Some companies actually went backward, as their centers of planning and scheduling expertise were reorganized out of existence.

At the same time, the chemical industry viewed improved planning and scheduling as a way of reducing the cost of doing business while improving the responsiveness of the order fulfillment process. As a result, the chemical industry currently has more widespread use of leading-edge scheduling technology than any other process industry segment (e.g., see Singh and Miller, 1993). A number of companies deliberately do not publicize the details of their efforts in this area because they view them as a strategic advantage.

A wide range of techniques can be applied to scheduling applications. Unfortunately, zealots abound who promote one technique or approach to the exclusion of all others, usually using jargon specific to their approach. Their arguments are analogous to the notion that a carpenter should need only a hammer in building a house, rather than considering all the tools in the toolbox. New technology provides incremental improvements in our ability to address scheduling problems. It expands the set of tools available, but it does not provide a universal panacea.

The responsiveness of the scheduling function is controlled by the time required to make decisions and the ability to communicate with the other decision-making functions. The use of *intelligent technology,* such as simulation, mathematical algorithms, linear programming and its variations, and expert systems, can reduce the time required to make decisions. These techniques can quickly generate or identify cost-effective solutions. This intelligent technology must be coupled with flexible model management systems so that the decision support tools can quickly adapt to changing business conditions.

Improving the quality of decisions requires realistic treatment of process behavior and explicit consideration of economics. Scheduling tools should be interactive for all but the simplest scheduling applications. Management often would like to remove the human element completely from the scheduling process, but it is usually far more cost-effective to interactively assist the scheduler. The solution criteria to scheduling problems vary over time, and humans are good at dealing with dynamic tradeoffs. For example, a scheduler's options in responding to a product shortage are often influenced by which customer was shorted last. Humans are also good at mitigating the impact of bad data, while one-pass solution procedures are usually very legalistic and can be severely disturbed by relatively minor data errors. The most cost-effective solution often is to let the scheduler manually resolve some portions of the scheduling problems because there are diminishing marginal returns for each increment of automation added. The budget required to automate 95 percent of the scheduling process may be twice that required to automate 90 percent of the process. Support and maintenance requirements may increase dramatically as well. The amount of automation that can be accomplished is a function of data quality and the variability of both the production process and customer requirements.

A major limitation in past efforts to provide tools for production scheduling was the computer resources available at the plant level, both for addressing the scheduling process and for managing the information needed for scheduling. These limitations often dictated that only a portion of the overall scheduling process could be addressed, and often decision support was restricted to a single technique. These computer-based limitations no longer exist.

Interactive scheduling tools using combined solution strategies have been successfully employed for a wide range of process industry settings. A number of examples are cited below:

- Process and transportation scheduling (Baker, 1982)

- Lubrication plant planning and scheduling (Thomas and Shobrys, 1988)

- Scheduling blocked operations in chemical plants (Faccenda and Baker, 1990)

- Chemical plant scheduling (Singh and Miller, 1993)

- Planning and scheduling for refinery blending (Salas et al., 1993)

The key aspect in the selection of solution techniques is that users have to understand what they are doing. They have to understand the behavior of the solution process, rather than the technical details of execution. The implementer may have to take the end user along a growth path from a simple approach to more sophisticated methods.

Implementation of solution techniques also involves another trade-off. In general, the more application-specific a solution approach is, the faster it will work. At the same time, the more specific the solution approach, the more difficult it becomes to adapt it to changes in the business and in the plant configuration.

The most commonly used types of computer intelligence currently applied to scheduling problems in industrial settings are briefly described below.

Simulation and graphics

Simulation is an essential tool for scheduling problems because of the emphasis on feasibility. Simulation provides feedback on the consequences of a schedule as evaluated in continuous time. The consequences of the schedule include capacity utilization over time, material utilization over time, and total schedule cost.

The widespread computer graphics capabilities currently available provide an efficient way of presenting this feedback interactively. A Gantt chart is a classic way of presenting capacity utilization, and the display of inventory profiles over time presents information on inventory use and inventory feasibility. An example of this type of display is shown in Fig. 6.3.

The top portion of Fig. 6.3 is the Gantt chart. It shows purchasing (PUR), high-density polyethylene units (HD-1, HD-2, HD-3), extruders (E-1, E-2, E-3), and low-density polyethylene units (LD-1, LD-2). The rectangular bars represent operations on these units, and their names can be displayed by scrolling through the legend in the upper right-hand corner. The lower portion of the display shows inventory profiles over time. One limitation of using simulation without any additional computer intelligence is that the solution of scheduling problems becomes a trial-and-error process.

Optimization

There is often confusion over the use of the word *optimization* in reference to scheduling. In common use, *optimize* can mean "to seek improvement." In a mathematical sense, *optimize* means to find the best possible solution to a given mathematical problem.

The ability to optimize a problem depends on how "nice" the problem is mathematically. Mathematicians use terms such as *continuous, discrete, convex, linear, nonlinear,* and *NA complete* to describe whether a problem is nice. Scheduling problems are usually not very

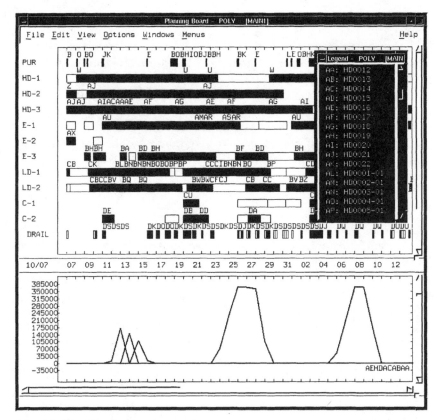

Figure 6.3 The planning board.

nice mathematically, so it is difficult to guarantee an optimal solution unless you are willing to be liberal with the definition of the problem.

Any mathematical model is an approximation of the real world. Hopefully, the model is realistic enough that the optimal solution to the mathematical problem is a cost-effective solution for the real world. The practical value of an optimization algorithm is that it knows when to stop, and you can often estimate an upper bound on solution times as a function of model size. You can always get an optimal solution if you redefine the problem so that it is mathematically nice. People will do this at times so that they can solve a problem with their pet technique.

Linear programming (LP) is the most commonly used optimization technique. Most scheduling problems require an extension of linear programming known as *mixed-integer programming* (MIP). MIP can consider the integer decision variables required to deal with sequencing issues, minimum production quantities, and other yes/no types of decisions.

There are three potential limitations in applying MIP to scheduling problems:

1. Solution times

2. Controlling the solution process

3. Interpretation of results

MIP problems tend to get very big very rapidly, and solution times can become very long, even with modern solution codes and modern computers. People will often stop the MIP solution process before it converges on the optimal solution because they do not want to wait that long. They may use an expert system to clean up the answer they obtain.

Most schedulers prefer to update schedules in a *net-change* fashion, protecting some portions of the schedule from changes while allowing changes to occur in other areas. Passing this information back to the MIP solver is not easy. If you are not careful, you may describe an infeasible problem.

The ability to interpret MIP solutions must be developed over time. Optimization techniques can utilize a large amount of information, and they can change many things all at once. Users have to understand the relationship between data and solutions. There is also the problem of translating from discrete time periods to continuous time. Optimization models tend to view time in discrete buckets, and everything in a time bucket happens instantaneously to the solver. The scheduling process has to consider time in a continuous fashion. One approach is to have many time buckets, which results in huge models. It is usually more effective to take a first cut with an optimization model and then to refine the solution with a simulation-based tool (see Faccenda and Baker, 1990).

The application of optimization to scheduling problems is a fertile area for future development. High-performance workstations are simultaneously becoming less expensive and more powerful. *Graphical user interfaces* (GUIs) coupled with expert systems allow more intuitive user interfaces. Expert systems also have the potential for giving MIP solvers more application-specific knowledge, reducing solution times.

Heuristics

Heuristics are intelligent searches for improvement. They often have intuitive appeal for schedulers because heuristics mimic the thought processes of schedulers and can be structured to make a limited number of changes at one time.

Heuristics can take the form of mathematical algorithms or sets of expert-system rules. The mathematical techniques may perform an intelligent search. An example is to try to find alternative sequences of production operations that would reduce transition costs. Alternatively, an optimization technique may be applied to a particular aspect of scheduling, such as inventory balancing, capacity balancing, or synchronizing production activities across stages of production.

Virtually any mathematical heuristic can also be implemented by using an expert system, although it may execute more quickly if it is written in a procedural fashion. One of the dangers of expert systems is that they can be used to reinvent the wheel. Their strength is that they can be used to embed application-specific knowledge into the solution process. Examples are dealing with product wheels, shutdowns, start-ups, and weekend transitions.

The diagnostic capabilities of expert systems can be used to identify schedule problems and invoke problem-specific solution methods. This may be coupled with manual intervention facilitated by graphics, context-sensitive views of scheduling data, and feedback on the economic impact of schedule changes.

Implementation and Integration

Implementation

Implementation of computer-based scheduling tools poses some unique problems. These tools often contain technology that is new to the scheduling function. The clients (both the business and the end users) often cannot articulate their requirements until they have had some experience with the technology. The implementation process has to give them this exposure and incorporate their feedback. *Rapid iterative prototyping* (RIP) is one method of doing this. RIP follows the definition of project dimensions and project issues and consists of repetitive iterations through the following cycle:

- Design
- Development
- Use
- Incorporation of user feedback

An experienced applications person can usually predict the number of times this cycle will have to be repeated for a given application. This approach is efficient because it lets the users move up the learning curve before they finalize their requirements. It may create some concern in information systems (IS) organizations because it conflicts with traditional system methodologies that emphasize detailed predefinition of user interfaces and procedures.

Any implementation effort is an imposition on end users, since the business has to continue to function while new tools are implemented. There may be changes in the roles of scheduling staff. There may be "schedulers" who primarily perform a clerical role in collecting and organizing data. These individuals may be become stressed out if they have to perform an active decision-making role.

The most cost-effective way to implement scheduling tools is with heavy involvement from the end user. This keeps the development effort focused on high-priority issues and minimizes the amount of rework required when the user starts to use the tool. Surrogates can be used for the end user, but this usually increases the time and budget consumed by the implementation effort.

Scheduling tools should be developed with live data, and validation should occur in parallel to actual operations. The use of static or fabricated data creates opportunities for development activity to be distracted by red herrings that may not really be issues of concern. The resulting development activity often does not add any useful functionality, but still consumes the project budget. It is far more cost-effective to stop development until data become available.

There is a need for continuous improvement around every scheduling function. Change occurs in the systems environment, the business, and end-user skill levels and requirements. As the applications around scheduling evolve, a flexible scheduling system should be able to take advantage of these improvements and become more effective. As end users work with new technology, their skills evolve. There should be continuous improvement in scheduling to utilize these improved skills. The business itself will go through changes.

Integration

There are three types of integration that must be considered.

- Data integration (automating the collection of data needed for scheduling)

- Integration with other functions in the *planning, scheduling,* and *control* (PSC) hierarchy

- Integration with other business functions (such as ATP)

It is unlikely that users will accept scheduling tools without data integration, unless the scheduling application is very simple.

Schedulers often spend the majority of their time manually collecting and manipulating data, reducing the time available for analysis. The first step in improving scheduling productivity is to automate this data collection as much as possible. This should also involve consistency checks on the data as well. Expert systems are well suited for performing this data checking.

Integration with other PSC functions is required to fully realize the potential benefits of work done in those other functions. The benefits of optimization at the planning level can be largely lost without effective scheduling tools. Up to 50 percent of the potential benefits from advanced control applications are based on the assumption that valid targets will be received from higher-level functions (Van Horn, 1985).

The information that moves between scheduling and planning or control has been discussed earlier in this chapter. Efforts to expedite the movement of this information may run into problems with naming conventions and data definition. Planning often takes an aggregate view with both naming conventions and data. For example, it may be necessary to disaggregate planning information from product families to products, or from bulk products to product/package combinations, to make it useful for scheduling. Control functions take a more detailed view of the process than scheduling does. Naming conventions may relate to points of measurement (tag names) rather than inventory items. Information from control may have to be aggregated, averaged, or filtered.

Technology exists to allow dynamic on-line interactions between scheduling and other business functions. For example, consider how the confirmation of customer orders [also referred to as *available to promise* (ATP)] occurs at a company with plants in North and Central America. Orders are received at a central location. As the orders come in, the order takers can release queries across a network to the scheduling tools at the individual plants. The order takers get a response within seconds on whether the order will be available on the requested data or the date on which the product will be available. Similar interactions can take place between scheduling and transport, sales, and customer service.

Benefits

There are two primary objectives for improving planning, scheduling, and control functions:

- Improve the responsiveness of the entire manufacturing logistics management process.

- Improve the quality of the decisions made in that process, with resulting improvements in profitability.

Computer-based scheduling tools can reduce response time by focusing decision making on a smaller number of participants. For example, a major lubrication plant went from seven schedulers when scheduling was done manually to one scheduler and backup with computer-based scheduling tools.

Improved scheduling tools increase profitability by reducing or exposing the hidden costs in the current process. Inventory and capacity buffers occur at person-to-person interfaces and at organizational boundaries. The scheduler's primary responsibility is to produce product when needed. If I am dependent on another scheduler's decisions, I will try to protect my ability to meet the demands I am responsible for by keeping buffers of inventory or capacity in reserve. The lower the visibility of the other scheduler's decision process, the larger my reserves will be. If I am dependent on information from another organization in the company, or if I have to make commitments to other organizations, then I will try to keep buffers to protect myself from mistakes, misunderstandings, and variability in production and demand.

The number of buffers will increase with the number of participants and organizational boundaries that are spanned by the process. The size of the buffers will increase with the amount of variability in the production process and in customer demands. The size of the buffers also increases with the difficulty of projecting the impact of upsets or schedule changes. Over time, these buffers may become embedded in rules of thumb and other routine practices in the scheduling function. Using buffers to hedge against uncertainty is a reasonable course of action as long as the buffers are visible, so that they can be managed. If the current scheduling process is largely manual, people may not even realize how many buffers are in the process. As improved scheduling tools focus decision making, they reduce the number of places where these buffers can exist. This reduces the amount of inventory that the plant carries and results in more effective use of production capacity. The scheduling tools can also provide a common view of the total scheduling process across different scheduling functions and with other organizations such as transportation and order management.

Improved scheduling tools also generally allow consideration of a longer time horizon, moving the scheduler from a reactive mode to a proactive mode. This benefits the stability of the schedule. There are fewer schedule changes, which improves communication and coordination on the plant floor.

The longer time horizon also benefits production efficiency, providing a larger window for resequencing operations to reduce the impact of transitions. This resequencing can be enhanced with the use of mathematical algorithms and expert-system rules. The use of mathematical algorithms and expert systems adds structure to the scheduling process and forces clearer definitions of process parameters, such as capacity availability and capacity consumption. These better definitions, coupled with a reduction in downtime from product transitions, result in increased throughput. The increases range from 1 to 4 percent for plants running blocked operations on continuous units, to 20 percent for batch plants.

Improved scheduling tools can dramatically improve customer service. The computational abilities of computer workstations, coupled with mathematical and expert-system-based intelligence, give high visibility to individual customer orders, movements, or contracts. Schedulers can quickly assess how a change to an individual order will impact the existing schedule and how a production upset or modification to a production operation will impact individual orders or movements.

A closing note: Any lessons of value were learned from my coworkers and clients. My education still continues. Any mistakes are my own.

References

Baker, T. E. (1982): "Algorithms for Interactive Scheduling," presented at the SHARE meeting, Los Angeles.

Faccenda, J. F., and T. E. Baker (1990): "An Integrated AI/OR Approach to Blocked Operations Scheduling," paper no. CC-90-134, presented at the National Petroleum Refiners Association Computer Conference, October 29–31.

Hammer, M., and J. Champy (1993): *Reengineering the Corporation: A Manifesto for Business Revolution,* HarperCollins, New York.

Miller, D. E., and J. F. Pekney (1991): "Exact Solution of Large Asymmetric Traveling Salesman Problems," *Science,* vol. 251, p. 754, February 15.

Salas, O., J. Critchley, P. Smit, and J. Howard (1993): "Blend Planning and Scheduling at Engen's Durban Refinery," paper no. CC-93-133, presented at the National Petroleum Refiners Association Computer Conference, New Orleans, November 15–17.

Singh, H., and D. L. Miller (1993): "A Modular System for Scheduling Chemical Plant Production," Foundations of Computer Aided Process Operations (FOCAPO), Crested Butte, July.

Thomas, L. R., and D. E. Shobrys (1988): "Planning and Scheduling Lube Blending and Packaging," *Hydroc. Proc.,* November, p. 111.

Van Horn, L. D. (1985): "Integrating Process Control and Operating Target Decisions," presented at the Instrument Society of America (ISA) Convention, Philadelphia, October.

Wagner, H. M., and T. Whitin (1958): "Dynamic Version of the Economic Lot Size Model," *Management Sci.,* vol. 5, no. 3.

7

Planning

James N. Fisher and James W. Zellhart

Introduction

Why plan? Historically, the reasons to plan process industry operations were to determine a feasible operating plan while attempting to maximize profits or minimize costs. Planning helped to develop guidelines to meet these objectives. Today, these objectives have not changed. The only difference is that the planning requirements of the process industries have become more difficult. These difficulties arise from the necessity to make more varied, higher-quality products and to meet tighter environmental requirements.

What do we need to plan? Planning methods vary with the problems studied. Planning can be for the entire company or for making an individual product at a specific site. Well-run companies have goals and do planning to meet their objectives. Company plans are done at varying levels of detail and often use different techniques. Also, a company's general plan will not involve the fine detail in modeling needed to plan for the manufacture of a specific product at a given site.

When is a plan made? Planning can be for a horizon as long as 5 to 20 years for things such as new facility planning or as short as the next few hours to make a specific batch of product. An operating plan for a company's site may be for the next 6 months (long-range planning), 1 month (short-range planning), 1 week (a short-range plan to pass to a scheduling or blending system), or 1 day. Product manufacturing plans (blending in petroleum refineries) often are used for a single product to be made over the next few hours.

Where should planning be done? Planning is done from corporate headquarters on down to specific process sites. If planning were done only at process sites, the plan would not encompass the corporate vision. Therefore, many companies do corporate planning to set guidelines which are then passed on to each processing site for more detailed process planning. These guidelines include distribution of feedstocks and sites where primary products will be manufactured. Historically, many companies that planned in the corporate offices did not do much planning with models at individual processing sites. With the increasing complexity to meet more and more stringent customer and legislated requirements, the necessity of sophisticated planning at individual processing sites cannot be ignored.

Most planners and plan users have perceptions of what can and cannot be accomplished in planning. There are probably as many different perceptions as there are those who think about it. The objective for planners is to do as good a job as possible and to continue to be diligent in improving the accuracy of planning model predictions. Results should be neither oversold nor denigrated. There will always be some parts of the results that are not as sound as others. But a planning model is not a daily scheduler or a process controller. When the model determines unit severities or predicts process yields, one should not then expect these processes to use these predictions to the letter in operations. Plans are almost always averages over time, not what should happen at any given instant.

The fundamental objective of planning is to develop a good set of operating goals for a future period. Plans can never be perfect because the future is never precisely known. Realistically, operations management looks for a plan that will coordinate activities and unify individual objectives; management does not look for the best possible plan that can be followed blindly or imposed on process operations.

Traditional Practices

The two main technologies used for planning in the process industries are *process simulation* and *linear programming* with its extensions to nonlinear optimization. These are described in turn here.

Process Simulation

Planning in the process industry is frequently done with process simulators of one form or another. Simulators range from single-process mathematical models to process flowsheet simulation systems that consider the unit operations, such as heat exchangers and reactors in detail (e.g., the systems provided by Aspen Technology, Inc.,

Chemshare, Inc., and Simulation Sciences, Inc.). These and other modular systems connect individual models together to represent an entire plant. When applied to a single process, the term *simulator* is synonymous with the term *model*. Single-process simulators predict process yields and product physical properties. Their predictions are based on a single input set of operating conditions and feed qualities. They are often run multiple times while using various scenarios of feed and operating parameters to determine a range of solutions, which are then used to help develop operating plans. Unless coupled with an optimization system, simulators do not directly find the best way to operate a process. Their use is therefore different from that of planning models using linear or nonlinear optimization that also simulate process operation, but find a single best solution given a possible range of conditions.

The process simulators are usually, but not necessarily, more accurate in predicting yields and properties for a specific case than the optimizers that find a "best" case within the range of parameters allowed. This is because the models used in the optimization programs are usually a simplification of the simulation model. Simulators, whether for a single process or for many processes, are often run for numerous cases to find a satisfactory case for the operating plan. However, planning for single-process operation is often restricted to a narrow set of conditions, and a single simulation case is all that is necessary to aid the planner in developing the processing plan.

There are some applications of process flow sheet simulation systems to integrated planning optimization and control. For example, Chaps. 16 and 17 describe applications to an ethylene complex and to a crude unit, respectively. In these cases, the simulation models are very detailed at the unit operation level and are coupled to a nonlinear optimization.

Single-process simulators

Kinetic simulations. The most desirable simulators for conversion processes, from the standpoint of accuracy and breadth of applicability, are those based on the chemical reaction kinetics. These simulations divide the reactors into segments in each of which the chemical reactions that are taking place are modeled directly. Each molecular type in the feed is considered independently. Because of this level of detail, development of kinetic simulations is more difficult and expensive than that of empirical simulations. This is especially true for most petroleum refining processes. Petroleum is a mixture of many types of organic molecules. The higher the boiling point of the petroleum fraction, the more difficult it is to identify and assign reaction rates to all the types of molecules present. Historically, pilot plant work on the various processes has not obtained enough of the required kinetic information. Kinetic information was acquired on the effect of unit operating conditions but not on a sufficient variation in the feed quality. Often the operating information was obtained on only the presumed feed that the unit was being designed for. In addition, analytical instruments capable of measuring or classifying heavier petroleum feedstocks were either not available or thought to be too expensive. It is easy to see that developing the database for a kinetic simulation is both expensive and time-consuming.

Once developed, kinetic simulators have continuing extensive data requirements to keep up with changing unit capabilities, goals, feeds, catalysts, etc. The simulators are usually not very capable of extrapolation to make yield forecasts outside the development environment. Modeled process ranges normally never should exceed the ranges of the development database. Because commercial kinetic simulations are expensive, often they are not available to many small companies. Also, refineries that do not vary operations significantly usually cannot justify the cost of a kinetic model.

Empirical simulators

Most process simulators are developed by using empirical methods. The reason is that most of the historical data, whether pilot plant data or actual processing data, are empirical. As noted above, kinetic information is available concerning processing conditions, but the feed quality classification is usually empirical. Therefore, many simulators are kinetic concerning processing (reactor) conditions and empirical with regard to feedstock variations. Empirical equations are most often used as the process model in linear and nonlinear programming applications.

Planning and/or refinery analysis using simulation

Simulators have been, and still are, used extensively for planning in the process industry. It is not uncommon for companies with more than one refinery to have one refinery plan with a simulation system and another plan with a linear programming system. Simulation for planning can be done on a process-by-process basis, by running one model at a time, or by use of a system that links the simulators together. Simulators are very useful in monitoring individual process operations and are more valuable if the same simulator can be linked to a system to simulate the whole refinery.

Process flow simulators are used extensively to aid in process design. Process design usually requires knowledge of reactor kinetics, which is why the favored process simulators include reactor kinetic correlations. Simulators that are built for process design consider process equipment, such as pumps, heat exchangers, and flash drums, in detail. Consequently, these simulations are usually difficult to use in day-to-day operations planning. Day-to-day planning keys on variations in feedstock quality and types of products manufactured, and not on details of the unit design. The feed characterization required for a process design simulation is usually more extensive than the information available to the planner. Therefore, flow sheet simulators used in day-to-day planning often run with many parameters fixed.

In 1982, Han described a system specifically designed for planning applications, which combined a modular simulator and nonlinear optimization: "System/B is a refinery planning tool designed to make it easy for the refinery planners to generate detailed nonlinear applications. The system is a combination of two existing systems." One is a program that "hooks together process models to simulate a refinery section or a complete refinery." The other "is an in-house developed non-linear optimizer. System/B incorporates an interface subroutine to pass information between the simulator and the optimizer" (Han, 1982).

Data preparation using simulations

Simulators are probably the largest and most efficient source of data for other planning systems such as *linear programming* (LP) and *nonlinear programming* (NLP) models. The simulators contain the detailed correlations required to simulate operations for various types of processing. These simulators either are built and maintained by the companies that use them or are purchased from the various vendors that study and model the different types of petroleum and petrochemical processes. Often the simulators are then further calibrated to fit specific plant operations. Even simulators designed for process design can often be used if they are restricted to existing process equipment measurements. The simulators then can be used to generate data reflecting base operating conditions, limited changes in operating conditions, and more broad changes in feedstock characteristics.

Simulators are very efficient data generators. Their use is much more efficient than the use of data obtained from commercial operations, especially when data are needed outside the normal-range operating conditions. These data are frequently needed to evaluate alternate feedstocks and changes in unit operations. Also, with changes in the operating environment, only simulation data are usually obtainable.   Feedstock

Linear Programming

Linear programming is the most heavily used mathematical programming technique for planning. While simulations may be more accurate, use of LP is usually much faster in obtaining a feasible plan. A short explanation of linear programming is in order before we describe the various types of LP models.

Simulation models, be they kinetic or empirical, are a series of equations that estimate process yields and product properties. These estimates are based on feedstock properties, given operating conditions and other needed data that help define the processing environment. There is an equation for every unknown. The unknowns can therefore be determined uniquely by solving each equation. If all the equations are linear, there is only one possible value for each unknown.

In planning, much of the purpose of the function is to choose between alternatives. If there are alternatives, it means that there are not a sufficient number of equations to determine all the unknown values uniquely. There are more unknowns than equations, so there is not a definite single answer. In this situation, we want to choose the best alternative based on the value of what is called the *objective function* or *equation*. We want to determine the final values of the unknowns that give a maximum profit or minimum cost when used to calculate the value of the objective equation. These same values must satisfy the equations that are available. In 1947, G. B. Dantzig invented the simplex algorithm that finds the best value for the objective function, subject to satisfying a set of linear equations, known as *constraints*. The procedure was named *linear programming*. Occurring at about the same time as this invention was the beginning of commercial availability of digital computers. This made linear programming a viable alternative in planning (Bodington and Baker, 1990). Linear programming is limited to solving only linear equations. However, many times a nonlinear relationship can be represented by procedures to be described below.

Linear Programming Formulations

Full-scale models

A *full-scale LP model* is one that considers each process in detail and uses the most accurate model available for each process. These models represent the major feeds, intermediate streams, and products for the processing being modeled. For a planning model of a petroleum refinery, the model will normally contain one or more crudes fractionated in one or more ways. Full-scale models normally optimize on one or more cut point temperatures within the crude unit. Crude unit products then are represented as feeds to downstream processing and/or for making finished products. Downstream processing models may contain variable operating conditions that allow the model to find the best condition to maximize the refinery's profits or minimize its costs. Modeling of product blending includes the limitations in manufacturing these products to meet the specifications. Other products may be blended to given recipes or are single refinery streams.

The earliest full-scale LP models often contained many variables that represented different severity operations for each feed in a process. The representation of a single process within the LP is called a *submodel*. These submodels would make a different type of product consistent with the mode of operation. As an example, a reformer model might make four or five different reformates for each severity operation for each feed. Figure 7.1 illustrates this type of modeling for three feeds and three conditions. Models contained as many as 100 variables for the range of severities and for the range of potential feedstocks. This type of modeling caused many problems and was probably the primary reason for the use of linear programming for planning to lose favor in the late 1960s. The problem with this type of

Old Style LP Modeling — Example LP Structure of a vector for each condition for each feed.

Reformer

	Feed A			Feed B			Feed C			ETC. ->>>
	low sev	med sev	Hi Sev	low sev	med sev	Hi Sev	low sev	med sev	Hi Sev	
Feed-A	1	1	1							
Feed-B				1	1	1				
Feed-C							1	1	1	
*										
*										
GAS	-0.020	-0.030	-0.044	-0.024	-0.036	-0.053	-0.018	-0.027	-0.040	
Propane	-0.040	-0.060	-0.088	-0.048	-0.072	-0.106	-0.036	-0.054	-0.079	
Butane	-0.052	-0.078	-0.114	-0.062	-0.094	-0.137	-0.047	-0.070	-0.103	
REF-AL	-0.880									
REF-AM		-0.840								
REF-AH			-0.780							
REF-BL				-0.870						
REF-BM					-0.830					
REF-BH						-0.770				
REF-CL							-0.890			
REF-CM								-0.850		
REF-CH									-0.790	
*										
*										

Figure 7.1   Old-style LP modeling.

modeling is that a solution may show a high-octane reformate derived from feed A going into premium gasoline and a lower-octane reformate from feed B going into regular gasoline. This usually was impossible at the refinery since its single reformer did not batch-process nor was there separate tankage available for different grades of reformate.

Another problem arises when streams from various sources are combined and then distributed to more than one destination. The quality to be distributed downstream has to be assumed, since the composition, and therefore the actual quality, of the pool is unknown until a solution has been obtained. This problem is called the *pooling problem*. There are many pooling problem possibilities in an LP model, and the original linear programs had no mechanism for avoiding them. The solution to this problem is discussed under "Recursion in Linear Programming" below.

The first attempt to minimize the problem of picking and choosing operations that really could not be simultaneous was to develop what are now called *delta-base models*. Figure 7.2 shows an example of a base-delta model for the reformer. Delta-base models assume an average feedstock to a process and one or more variables that are the yields on this feedstock. The reformer is a process that has multiple yields at varying severities (octane levels). The model's yield assumption is based on an average feed to the reformer, and the products are

Delta Base Modeling

Example LP Structure – Feeds Accumulated Base Vector each condition

Reformer

	Feed A	Feed B	Feed C	BASE low sev	Base med sev	Base Hi Sev	Free Variable N2A
Feed−A	1.0						
Feed−B		1.0					
Feed−C			1.0				
*							
*							
Feed Pool	−1.0	−1.0	−1.0	1.0	1.0	1.0	0.008
Feed N2A	−40.0	−30.0	−50.0	40.0	40.0	40.0	−10.0
GAS				−0.020	−0.030	−0.044	−0.005
Propane				−0.040	−0.060	−0.088	−0.009
Butane				−0.052	−0.078	−0.114	−0.012
REF−L				−0.880			
REF−M					−0.840		
REF−H						−0.780	

This example is similar to early (1970) versions of a reformer model where the model has only one N2A corrector which increments the amount of feed. Newer versions often pool for each severity and the correctors can be more responsive with different delta yields at each severity. The N2A corrector in this example is the average yield change over the severity levels.

Figure 7.2 Delta-base modeling.

those that would be expected with this base feed under the base operating conditions. The process product properties are those that would be expected under these conditions. Most planning submodels have only one base variable, which is for the normal severity level at the unit, and the yields are on the assumed average feed under the base conditions.

A *delta* is the change in yields and product properties that would be expected if the process were operated at a different condition from the base. For example, if the assumed base feed to a catalytic cracker has a K factor of 11.5 and the linear program's best condition had a K factor of 12, then a delta variable for a change in K factor is employed. This variable changes the yields from the base by a delta consistent with the new K factor of the feed. The delta variables represent the first derivative of yields and qualities with respect to a change in the value of the delta variable.

The primary assumption made in this type of modeling is that a linear representation of a change is sufficient to determine new yields and properties with changes in the process away from an assumed base condition. There is a delta variable for each feed quality and operating condition being considered. The second assumption is that the sums of the linear deltas are cumulative. A catalytic cracker may have a delta variable showing changes in yields based on the feed's K factor, its basic nitrogen content, and its sulfur content. It is possible that the LP case may show that all three of these delta variables are activated.

Delta-base modeling helped to reduce the number of pooling problems in a linear program, but the problems were still there and other techniques were needed. Improved techniques were also needed to get around the major limitation of linear programming, which is that important nonlinearities could not be handled even by clever linear modeling.

Figures 7.1 and 7.2 show a typical LP matrix setup for modeling the nonlinear reformer yields with increasing severity. Modeling yields at multiple severity levels works well for a process where the change is convex in relation to the increase in profit; it does not work for changes that are concave with profit. Linear programs drive on value, and the value in a reformer is the quantity of reformate and its octane. Figure 7.3 shows the nonlinear relationship taken from the example in Fig. 7.2. The arrow reflects the direction of an increase in refinery profit as a function of reformate yield and octane with increased severity.

A full-scale model usually includes blending the major products made at a plant site, which for a refinery would include motor gasoline, jet fuel, diesel, and fuel oils. These products are blended to specifica-

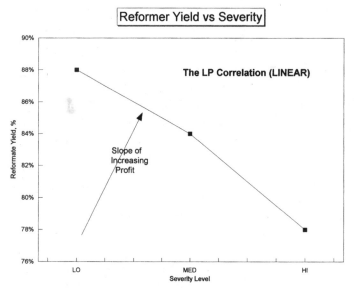

Figure 7.3   Reformer yield versus severity.

tions. Many specifications can be blended linearly, on either a volume or a weight basis. Other qualities do not blend well linearly. Over the years, many techniques have been employed to make blending in linear programs more accurate. The most widely used technique is the linear blending index. These indices are generally determined by running multiple linear regression analyses of many blends and studying the qualities of the components in the blends and the blends' final quality. Most linear indices employ a logarithmic or exponential factor to find the linear correlation that fits the nonlinear blending relationships.

As an example, the *Reid vapor pressure* (RVP) is a quality that does not blend well linearly. If butane (RVP = 52) is blended with reformate (RVP = 4) in a 50:50 mix, the blend's final RVP will not be the average of the two (RVP = 28). A commonly used index for RVP is $RVPI = (RVP)^{1.25}$. Therefore, the RVPI of butane is 139.6 and of reformate is 5.7. The 50:50 blend's RVPI is 72.7, and therefore its calculated RVP is 30.8. Some properties often converted to indices for linear blending include the viscosity, pour point, flash point, and beginning and final boiling points.

Some properties do not work well, even with indices. One reason is that the property measured often has the same value for samples containing different types of molecules. For example, blending octane numbers has always been a problem. Straight linear blending of octane is the most common way of modeling this property in large-scale models, even when it is widely known that it suffers in accuracy. Techniques used to improve the accuracy of octane blend modeling have included these:

- Add bonuses or biases (positive and negative) to each component for each type of motor gasoline blend.
- Develop interaction coefficients for each component with respect to the others.
- Develop quadratic equations for types of blends within a refinery and update the refinery's coefficients periodically.
- Use a technique first proposed in 1981 (Rusin et al., 1981) called *transformation blending.*

All the methods except the bonus method require that the linear program be recursed (recursed means that the problem is modified as a result of examining a solution and then is repeatedly resolved until the procedure converges; see also Fisher and Baxter, 1970). We are not aware of any full-scale refinery models successfully using the transformation octane blending method with recursion. We do know of many applications of the transform octane method with recursion for stand-alone gasoline blending models.

Modeling blending volatility, usually measured according to the ASTM D-86 Distillation, is a problem in linear programs. Many have developed volatility biases for all blend components. This technique can be a problem when it is decided to change process cut points. Specifications are normally in terms that state a blend's distillation points, such as that the 10 or 90 percent point temperatures must not exceed a certain value. (For example, for premium motor gasoline, the maximum temperature at 90 percent off is 320°F.) The first obvious modeling technique tried was to volume-average each component's 90 percent temperature and set the specification to a maximum of 320. This method works very poorly. If the modeler insists on using this technique, the modeler must use biases that are normally derived through regression analysis. If the specification changes (from, say, T90 maximum of 320 to 310), then a new regression analysis will be required to determine the biases needed at the new specification. Also, any new component or change in boiling range of components requires that they undergo a new regression analysis. If the modeling technique is turned around and, instead of using the temperatures, the modeler uses the percentage off at a given temperature then the resulting "percentages off" do blend almost linearly. Therefore, specifications can be simulated by encompassing temperatures surrounding the specification levels.

The 1990 Clean Air Act requires that motor gasoline manufactured after 1994 meet product qualities that cannot be measured either on-line or in the laboratory. These new qualities are determined by non-linear statistical models (Tennessen and Di Nello, 1993). Further in the future, on May 1, 1997, the EPA nonlinear complex models for toxicity, volatile organic compounds (VOCs) and NO_x (nitrogen oxides) will be in effect. Today's linear tools will no longer be able to handle the planning problem.

Others (Bain et al., 1993) forecast that "reformulated fuels legislation will present extremely difficult technical challenges for gasoline blenders—almost to the point that blending without good models will be impossible or impractical. Balancing the component usage against the plan will require that both the gasoline blenders and the planners use the same models with a practical update strategy."

Some say that the EPA's reformulated gasolines cannot be modeled in today's linear tools, and others say that the blenders need to use the same models as the planners. Most companies that market LP systems developed for refinery planning have announced that they have the EPA's complex formula working in their systems. Will these systems be successful in handling the EPA's complex formulas? We have had a little experience in using one commercial system's beta version of modeling the EPA's complex formula in a stand-alone motor gasoline model. It worked well. We wonder whether it can be done in full-scale refinery models. On our one attempt with a full-scale refinery model, where we used a preliminary commercial beta version, it cycled badly and did not converge to a solution. This may be because it was a beta version that was not quite ready. Or, it may not be a problem for a more normal full-scale model that is more tightly constrained. Since we were never successful in getting the transform octane blending procedure to work well in full-scale models, we will wait and see about modeling the complex formula in full-scale models.*

Ensys Energy & Systems, Inc., has developed "best-fit linear blending values for gasoline components for each emission equation" (Dunbar et al., 1993). They state, "Good accuracy has been achieved using linear emission equation 'blending values'...over a wide range of gasoline properties, compositions and emission reduction targets." Ensys notes the procedure does not need recursion once the factors have been developed for a given refinery.

Minimodels

When linear programming was first used to do planning (in the late 1950s and early 1960s), computers' capacity was so limited that the

---

*As of January 1995, these procedures are working well in full-scale models.

models had to be minimodels. They were not called that at the time, but it was recognized that the models could contain only the most critical processing limitations. Today, the most important criterion of minimodeling versus large-scale modeling is that the minimodeler has to have a more thorough understanding of the environment being modeled. Large-scale models usually contain highly accurate, very detailed submodels for the processes. For a refinery, process submodel correlations often come from the experts in each processing area. Full-scale models determine the optimum severity levels for many processes and optimize processing cut points. For minimodels, a single severity level is the normal way for units to be modeled, and unit products will have no optimization on cut points, for example. Often processes are compacted. The modeler fixes many conditions that are optimized in a full-scale model.

Because many conditions are fixed in a minimodel, some types of problems and studies are eliminated and cannot be correctly solved. For example, sulfur tracking through a refinery will probably not be done. If the model represents the manufacture of ultralow-sulfur diesel, it will probably consider only components that all meet this specification individually. The model probably tabulates only the quantity of diesel manufactured with little or no actual specification blending. Many specification blends in a full-scale model become recipe blends in a minimodel. Processing required to meet these specifications is likely to be fixed at typical conditions.

For specification blends such as motor gasoline, only the specifications that are usually limiting are likely to be modeled. Reformers will probably have only a single severity, and the hydrotreater could be combined into the reformer to minimize the number of rows and columns.

Minimodels usually do not use recursion. Minimodels are similar to extreme-point models discussed below in that they are useful in larger systems such as supply and distribution models, time-staged models, or multirefinery models or any combination of these three types of models.

Of course, what is and is not included in a minimodel is up to the modeler, but the objective is to reduce the size of the model and yet obtain answers similar to those obtained in a large-scale model.

Extreme-Point Models

As the scope of a problem studied increases, the level of model detail usually decreases, so that the problem can be solved at reasonable cost and/or in a reasonable time and so that the model solution can be understood. The tradeoffs between model scope and level of detail are

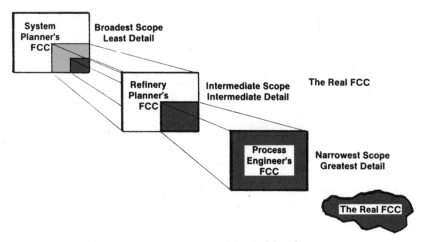

Figure 7.4 Tradeoffs between model scope and level of detail.

represented in Fig. 7.4. At the corporate level, the level of detail is minimal. But at the fluid catalytic cracker (FCC) process unit level, it's maximum.

An *extreme-point LP* (EPLP) model formulation for refinery planning is an extremely condensed version of a full-scale refinery model which, when given the same problem premises (crude price and availability, product volumes and values, and unit capacities), will give the same answer as the detailed refinery LP model. EPLP models take about one-tenth of the LP rows required by a detailed planning model, which represents each crude slate, each process, and each product blending operation in the refinery. EPLP does not attempt to represent all the piping in the refinery. Instead, it represents only those major "handles" or "modes" that the planner has available to alter refinery operation. As Fig. 7.5 illustrates, the EPLP model for-

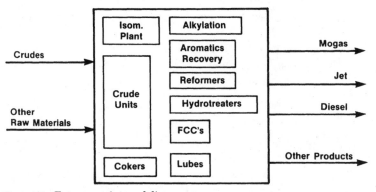

Figure 7.5 Extreme-point modeling.

mulation represents the refinery in the same manner as a detailed model represents an individual refinery process (e.g., an FCC).

EPLP models are often developed by running the detailed or "complete" LP model many times at varying conditions (often extreme points), to develop variables such that each variable in the EPLP model represents a complete stock balance around the whole refinery for one mode of operation or "handle." It represents the ultimate effect on the refinery for planning questions of a selected raw material or product made under a given set of premises. As a result, the EPLP model will usually contain only constraints on raw materials, products, unit capacities, and product specifications. If a case premise were submitted that exactly matched one of those developed when the detailed model was run, then the EPLP model's answer would be exactly the same as that of the detailed model. If a problem premise is submitted that does not match a prior detailed-model case, then the assumption is made that the linear combination of selected variables would closely match what normally comes from the detailed model.

This method provides an adequate representation of an individual refinery for planning questions that do not involve significant changes in the refinery operation, i.e., stream reroutings. And it allows us to represent a complex refinery in only 100 to 140 LP rows.

The submatrix in Fig. 7.6 illustrates the difference between a *complete* or detailed LP model formulation that represents all the piping and the *ultimate* yield model formulation that represents the differ-

		Complete				Ultimate
	Crude	Naphtha to Reformer	Gas Oil to FCC	PP to Alkylation	Purchase Iso-Butane	Crude
Propylene/Butylene			15.0	-100.0		
Iso-Butane		3.0	5.0	-140.0	100.0	
Gasoline	10.0	90.0	70.0	180.0		58.0
Naphtha	20.0	-100.0				
Kero/Jet	10.0					10.0
No. 2 Fuel Oil	20.0		10.0			23.0
FCC Chg. Stock	30.0		-100.0			
No. 6 Fuel Oil	5.0		5.0			6.5
Crude Unit Op.	100.0					100.0
FCCU Operation			100.0			20.0
CRU Operation		100.0				30.0
Alky. Operation				180.0		9.0
Naphtha → CRU		100.0				20.0
FCC Chg. → FCCU			100.0			30.0
PP → Alkylation				100.0		4.5
Purchased iC$_4$					100.0	4.2
Refining Fuel Pr.	5.0	5.0	15.0		10.5	
Loss/(Gain)		2.0	-20.0	60.0		-3.8

Figure 7.6 Ultimate versus complete refining yields.

ence or the delta effect on raw materials, products, process unit limits, and key process feedstocks. The net savings, for this example, by the ultimate model formulation, is four LP columns and five rows. In addition to representing the ultimate effect on a refinery, EPLP variables represent an *incremental* change, or *delta,* from a *base* or *plan* operation for the refinery. As a result, these variables are both incremental and ultimate:

- *Incremental* means that they represent a relatively small change from the base operation, say, 5000 barrels per day (bbl/day) crude charge to a 100,000 bbl/day refinery.

- *Ultimate* means that they represent only whole refinery changes, not changes in intermediates (Fig. 7.6).

EPLP models are sometimes called *base-delta* models, which comes from the description of its two major parts:

- *Base* or *plan case:* The plan case is an optimized *refinery plan* operation for some period such as a week or a month. It contains raw material purchases, product sales, intermediate stream volumes, capacity utilizations, and key product qualities based on output from a detailed refinery model.

- *Delta raw material and process shift logic:* This part of the model defines the *ultimate* yield effects (on a refinerywide basis) and delta capacity utilizations for changing raw materials or varying process alternatives (Fig. 7.7). The data come from a detailed model.

Process shift logic defines the process changes available to the refinery planner in day-to-day operations (Fig. 7.8). It defines processing modes (topping, cracking, coking) for crudes; processing limits, i.e., key process unit capacities; and stock balance capabilities (e.g., range of motor gasoline, jet, or diesel manufacture).

Delta or shift vectors in the EPLP model formulation adjust the refinery operation for changes in a "swing" crude charge, for a product shift (jet to diesel), for an intermediate process stream shift (naphtha to jet), and for a process stream quality shift (cetane index on diesel for a jet-to-diesel shift). The optimum solution to an EPLP model formulation of a refinery consists of starting with the solution to a base case, then turning on various shift vectors or deltas to satisfy a specific what-if planning question (Fig. 7.9).

Advantages of EPLP model formulation

Since the data for the EPLP model formulation are calculated from the detailed model formulation, a properly formulated EPLP model

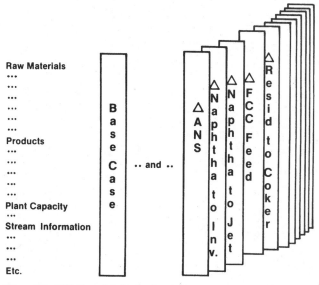

Figure 7.7   EPLP model: base plus deltas.

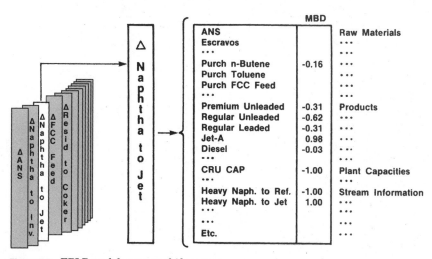

Figure 7.8   EPLP model: process shift vectors.

solution will closely match the detailed model solution for most day-to-day planning questions. And since the EPLP model formulation is only about 10 percent the size of the detailed model,

- It solves much more quickly.
- It is easier to use and understand.

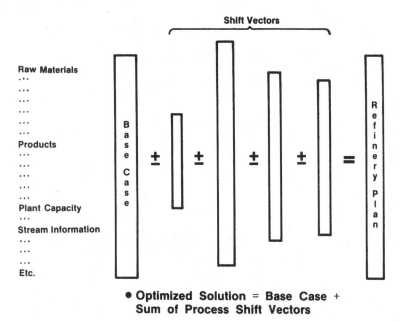

- **Optimized Solution = Base Case +**
  Sum of Process Shift Vectors

Figure 7.9 The optimized solution.

- Time staging is more feasible.

- Multiplant models are more feasible.

Refinery EPLP model formulation is a very powerful tool for quick stock balance optimizations and raw material evaluations. Because of the relatively small size, a planner can represent a 6-month plan with six 1-month periods. Time staging improves the current-month plan by allowing the planner to anchor it on her or his forecast of operations 6 months out. Inventory levels at the end of each month must satisfy the processing and product specifications for 5 additional months.

Limitations of EPLP model formulation

EPLP model formulation requires careful construction and use. The model builder must provide sufficient flexibility to handle the range of possible what-if questions. Of course, if every possible handle is allowed, there is no advantage in moving from a detailed model formulation to an extreme-point formulation. And the cost of developing, solving, and updating the EPLP model becomes too great.

While the EPLP model formulation based on a base-delta operations approach is well suited to developing routine plans and many economic studies, it is not adequate for

- Economics of rerouting internal process streams. It does not represent internal piping in enough detail.

- Economics of asphalt or lube oil manufacturing from different crude oils. It does not retain identity of crude oil through downstream process units into product blends.

- Product blend optimization when more than one quality specification applies simultaneously. It does not represent the flexibility available through blend optimization in a detailed model.

- New facility evaluation. It does not represent internal piping in detail necessary to measure impact.

The hazard of using an EPLP model is that a problem's premise may go beyond the bounds of the extreme points modeled. This is not an exclusive problem of EPLPs models. Full-scale models also cannot solve problems that exceed the refinery capability modeled.

EPLP model formulation

The most important step in EPLP model formulation is the definition of the process logic required to represent a refinery:

- What variables are used to optimize processing?
- What limits are required?
- Which product specifications need to be carried?

After the model definition is complete, use the full-scale refinery LP model run to calculate the base case and each delta effect on the entire refinery material/quality balance for each delta crude or for each process shift. Updates are needed when there is a major change in the refinery (e.g., new plant, stream rerouting). Of course, simulation models and spreadsheet models may be used to develop EPLP variables.

Variances on an EPLP structure

An EPLP model can have variances upon its structure relative to the above description. For example, the refinery EPLP model may make blend components instead of finished products.

Often, a single variable represents a typical operation in a refinery. This variable would be called the refinery's BASE variable, similar to a full-scale refinery's process unit base yields. The other EPLP variables, instead of being stand-alone complete scenarios of varying refinery operations, are then delta variables off the refinery's base conditions. The advantage of this type of modeling is that when conditions change significantly from a refinery's base, only the base variable need be changed. The assumption is that all the delta variables are still realistic. This technique is employed when much is known about a specific refinery and the refinery's planning staff uses the EPLP model.

Short history of EPLP

To our knowledge, the first commercial use of extreme-point modeling was with a system developed by Bonner and Moore Associates for the Federal Energy Administration's World Resource Model developed in 1974. Later, Gulf Oil entered into a joint effort with SRI (then Stanford Research Institute), to develop a supply and distribution (S&D) system using EPLP technology. Gulf's final version of their S&D system was called *RSDM*. It was in heavy use when Gulf was acquired by Chevron in 1984. Chevron continued using this system, until it was rewritten for the personal computer (PC) platform (Fisher, 1993).

EPLP applications

EPLP models are used in at least two modes:

- Single-refinery basis by refinery planners to generate optimal stock balances or raw material valuations.

- System basis, where the refinery or plant EPLP model is a part of a larger model representation, such as a manufacturing division or a company by a planning group organizationally above the refinery or plant level to answer division or company-level questions, e.g., products distribution, exchange valuation, intermediates valuation, price sensitivity.

System planning EPLP applications

Chevron's RSDM (Zellhart, 1987) model coupled several individual refinery EPLP models with a products distribution model. It was used as a tool to manage inventories around process unit shutdowns over a 6-month or longer time frame for a manufacturing region that consisted of several large refineries which distributed products to many marketing terminals. The alternatives to inventory management were to alter the crude slate, to shift processing, to purchase/sell product on the spot market, or to purchase/sell intermediate feedstock.

When asked for the best shutdown strategy for all process units in one refinery, the manufacturing region planners considered several options:

- Shut down the entire refinery, purchasing product needs on the cargo market.

- Stagger process unit shutdowns, managing inventories to minimize purchases.

- Manage other refineries to cover the product shortfall.

The RSDM model allowed them to quickly determine the best action plan.

When asked for the best strategy to accommodate high inventory levels for several products, planners used the RSDM model to determine the best plan for reducing the manufacture of several products without backing down on the manufacture of other profitable products.

Individual refinery planning EPLP applications

Refinery planners use the individual refinery EPLP models for most planning questions, except product blending and new facility planning. Since the EPLP model is easier, faster, and cheaper to use than the full-scale model, the refinery planner can make more runs in the same amount of time. Instead of one good answer, the planner can probe his or her assumptions to establish the sensitivity of the results. As a result, the planner is able to spend more time on analysis (what-if's) and less on number crunching.

Multiperiod Models—Time Staging

Linear programming can be used to do scheduling with multiperiod models. Multiperiod models are typically a normal planning model dropped into an LP system multiple times. The models are tied together with variables that represent the transfer of streams from one period to the next. These transfers are normally limited by known inventory tank limits. Each period model will represent a period of time, often from 2 weeks to 1 month. Not every period modeled has to have the same period length. The transfer variables are limited by a point in time, but the amount of a stream coming in to the variable is the days' sum for the incoming period, and the quantity going out is the days' sum going out. Therefore, if period A has a different time frame than period B, the transfer variable for, say, stream X will have different in and out coefficients. As an example, assume period A is for 30 days leading into a 15-day shutdown for period B. Period C is then a 60-day period after the shutdown. The tank farm has a limited capacity to hold 75 Mbbl of component X. The variables shown in

TABLE 7.1

	A_TO_B	B_TO_C	FCC_FDA	FCC_FDB	FCC_FDC
BOUNDS_UP	75	75			
STRM_X_INA	$\frac{1}{15}$		1.0		
STRM_X_INB	$-\frac{1}{30}$	$\frac{1}{60}$		1.0	
STRM_X_INC		$-\frac{1}{15}$			1.0

Table 7.1 could represent the buildup of inventory and transfers from period to period for component X.

This example shows, in Table 7.1, stream X in period A having the option of going to inventory via the variable A_TO_B or being fed to the FCC unit in period A through the variable FCC_FDA. In linear programs, the normal way to model the making of something is with a negative coefficient and the use of something is with a positive coefficient. Variable FCC_FDA is a variable in a period submodel that is normally on a daily basis. If the multiperiod models are modeled for a daily period, the interpretation of each period's result is easier. Then the transfer variables control the time length of each period.

The variable A_TO_B represents the sum of the daily buildup of component X over period A that is passed on to period B in a daily amount. Therefore, since period A is twice as long as period B, the magnitude of the coefficient coming into the variable must be twice that going out. The easy way to model this is to invert the in and out coefficients to the length of each period; i.e., the in coefficient for the variable is $+1$ divided by the length of period B, and the out coefficient is -1 divided by the length of period A. A system could then be set up to build or modify the multiperiod models so that the time periods could vary from study to study. The bound on the variable is the total inventory limit given in the example, 75 Mbbl.

Multiperiod linear programs are not as efficient for scheduling as scheduling systems, but for inventory control over major shutdowns, a multiperiod model has the advantage of more accurately determining optimum inventory control of unit feedstocks and crude utilization.

We have seen other structures for multiperiod models. There is no apparent limit to how multiperiod LP modeling can be done. Some modelers have developed models such that each period is not on a daily basis but for a total period. Many people model each period for the same length of time. The most common use of multiperiod modeling in the petroleum field is for scheduling motor gasoline blending. Here, it is not uncommon to find the first seven periods of the model representing the next 7 days and the latter one or more periods representing weeks and/or months. This type of model normally contains only blending. Manufacturing is represented with assumed production rates of blending components. The advantage of using LP for this type of scheduling is the capability of optimization considering specification blending, which is difficult to successfully represent in other types of scheduling algorithms. However, Chaps. 14 and 15 describe applications of integrated planning and scheduling systems, where the planning application optimizes the recipe generation for immediate use by the scheduling system.

A less common use of multiperiod modeling that we have seen is in facility planning, where each period is normally 1 year and there is no assumed inventory carryover from period to period. The purpose of this type of modeling is to determine when facilities are best constructed to be used for subsequent periods. Therefore the transfer variables in this type of modeling are unit capacities.

Multirefinery Modeling

Multirefinery modeling is used to study synergisms associated with interrefinery transfer of intermediates and in supply and distribution modeling. The discussion of extreme-point modeling above illustrates that as more refineries are tied together, the greater the need to condense the size of each refinery model. And if an extensive distribution system is also tied into the model, the need for refinery model condensation increases.

Goal Programming

Goal programming is a term used for a technique that encourages solutions of planning systems toward certain goals. The encouragement could be similar to trying to make the next batch of regular gasoline as similar as possible to the last regular blend. These techniques build stability in blending and minimize blender personnel dissatisfaction problems that would occur with widely different blend compositions for the same grades of gasoline. Also, with similar blend compositions, there is less concern about incompatibility of the same grades with widely different formulas being mixed in the field.

Goal programming in linear programs can be done in either time-staged models or single-stage models. There are varying methods of goal programming, but almost all include the use of small economic penalties if goals are violated. The models should not be constrained to force goals, but should be encouraged toward goal consistency. Nix (1979) notes that refinery modeling often has alternate optimum solutions, and goal programming minimizes the number of alternate solutions, pushing instead toward a single satisfactory solution.

Goal programming has been very effectively applied by Chevron in its single-blend nonlinear optimizers called GINO and DINO over the last 15 to 20 years (Fisher, 1982). These two systems never called the way they held product blends close to an optimal formula goal programming, but their techniques are quite similar to the goal programming methods applied in normal linear programs.

Short-Term Planning

Most initial short-term planning is done on full-scale models. Short-term plans determine how best to operate existing facilities. Full-scale models contain known process limitations and capabilities. The short-term plan for an entire facility is normally a plan for the next month. That is the definition we will use for the short-range plan. Often short-term plans are the beginning of long-term plans, such as the plan for the next 6 months. Planning is needed to ensure product shipments, obtaining the right raw materials and meeting changing product specifications. Specifications are constantly changing due to seasonality and sometimes due to products being made for different marketing areas.

Planners and users of the plan must recognize that the plan is a forecast for an uncertain future. Planners should not spend an excessive amount of time trying to develop processing yields that are accurate to the nth degree. Processing yields should always be as accurate as possible, but not to the extent that "paralysis of analysis" sets in because of worry that the yields are not perfect. Sensitivity analysis often shows that if yields are within 1 percent of the correct value, that is good enough. Yields for each process should be checked for mass balance, hydrogen balance, and other balances, such as sulfur, when applicable. The planner should worry that the planning system being used does not find cracks in the way things are modeled and create mass.

The best short-term plan is the plan that can be, and is, carried out. Implementation usually is effected by passing down economic drivers (value of feedstocks and products) to single-process optimizers from the full-scale model. This allows the planning for specific processes such as catalytic reforming, fluid catalytic cracking, and product blending.

One step in the short-term planning process that is often overlooked but may be the most important step is the reconciliation or performance-monitoring step. If this is not done periodically, planning models are likely to get farther and farther away from reality. Also, "if profitability is a planned objective, and the plan is approved, then an information system feedback on the plan is necessary to keep management appraised on actual vs. planned..."(Bannayan and Treat, 1993). If the actual values vary significantly from what was planned, then a review is needed to determine why. Is it that the planning model's yields are not realistic, or were there other causes? If there were other causes, should there have been an update on the planning process? Planners need to keep looking back to ensure that they know what is happening in the plant *today,* to plan for tomorrow. They also need to ensure that their planning is being used as much as possible. If significant changes occur in the plant after a plan is made that were not planned for, then it is good practice to redo the plan. This improves the credibility of planning and gives guidance as to the best course of action to take, given the changes that have occurred.

Redoing the plan will become even more important in the future, when planning is tied to scheduling and ultimately to control. And as the world gets more complex, modeling becomes more important and ensuring the credibility of planning model results requires constant diligence.

Once the full-scale model's short-range plan has been accepted, then smaller specific process planning models will usually have even shorter terms. A gasoline blending model will often plan for the next week. Blending models, and the full-scale models, should incorporate some "safety factors" into their blending specifications. Most companies follow certain practices to ensure that their blends will always meet specifications, and these practices need to be incorporated into the planning models. Examples include octanes 0.2 above specification or an RVP specification 0.2 below specification.

Facility Planning

Facility planning is often done with linear programming. Facility planning with linear programs can be a full-scale grassroots refinery study or a study for the expansion or debottlenecking of existing facilities. The methods of study are the same; it is the magnitude of the investment that changes. With facility planning, there is a greater degree of the unknown in forecasting. Normally the economic consequences of this type of planning are great, and the forecast is a projection farther into the future. Therefore, the unknowns are the types of feedstocks and their costs, the demands for products and their prices, and the unknown of whether the process yields and costs of construction are realistic. *Decision and risk analysis* (DRA) is playing an ever-increasing role in improving companies' evaluations of capital ventures. Planning models, be they linear programs, simulators, or spreadsheet balancers, are being used as the source in developing product yields for varying premise scenarios used in DRA (Fisher, 1992).

The decision to build a process or not is a yes/no decision. In linear programming, this is called an *integer-type decision* that, when employed with the rest of a planning model, becomes a *mixed-integer programming* problem (MIP). There have been many papers on this subject (McMahan and Roach, 1982). Planning models have been getting larger and larger with the improvements of optimization codes and faster computers. Solving mixed-integer models is not as time-consuming as it once was. The problem is that with a grassroots study, the number of integers becomes large. If the problem is to evaluate the expansion of existing facilities, then many scenarios will be needed and using integer variables normally is unrealistic because of the solution times required. One has to remember that a single case is never run. One case always brings up more questions that need more runs, and the time to run multiple cases on extensive time-consuming MIP models often becomes prohibitive. If the facility planning LP is used to prepare data for a DRA model, then many cases will be necessary to cover the ranges being studied.

For grassroots studies, recursion on variables that represent capital expenditure has been employed successfully since the early 1970s (Bonner and Moore's RPMS system). The problem for the modeler is to determine the proper criteria for representing each major capital expenditure. Figure 7.10 shows the economies of scale of a hypothetical unit X. The assumption is that unit X costs $45.5 trillion for a 20 Mbbl/stream day unit and has a 0.6 slope, reflecting the economies of scale. The figure shows total average investment plotted versus daily stream barrel capacity.

Figure 7.11 shows the investment versus capacity curve and then an assumed linear average investment per barrel versus daily capacity. The initial assumption for this average-cost slope is for a 10,000 band per stream day unit. [In a linear program, this investment per barrel is divided by the stream day barrels ($30 million ÷ 365 days/yr × 10 Mbbl/stream day) and then multiplied by a capital recovery factor (approximately 0.15 for a 15-year life and 10 percent recovery) needed to recover capital costs over time.] Recursive methods have been employed to change the capital costs based on the average cost at an assumed capacity level or the incremental cost at the assumed capacity level. Once a linear program reaches a converged solution, the capital cost recursion routines review the assumed capacity levels versus the results and correct the costs for those that exceed the allowable range of error. The normal procedure is to assume incremental costs to a given minimum capacity and then shift over to average costs.

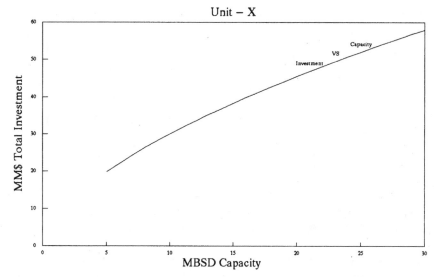

Figure 7.10   Example of economies of scale.

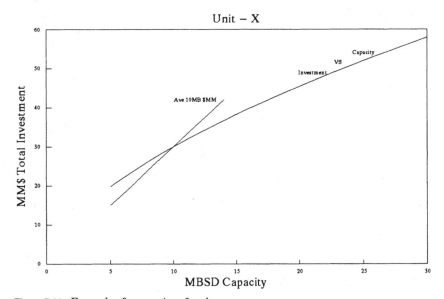

Figure 7.11   Example of economies of scale.

Process Optimization

Process design or plant operation problems usually have an unlimited number of feasible solutions. Process optimization involves choosing the best feasible solution based on performance criteria. Process engineers strive to improve upon the initial design and upon the operation of a process unit to increase the yield of valuable products, to decrease operating costs, or to do both. To find this process optimum, it is necessary to carefully identify the objective, the constraints, and the degrees of freedom in a process.

Optimization can be applied at many levels in a company ranging from a combination of plants and distribution facilities at one extreme to an individual process or unit operation at the other. For an individual process or unit operation, optimization may apply to process design or process operation. Process design simulators are available to optimize process design and equipment questions. While process design is carried out once, optimization of process operating conditions is carried out monthly, weekly, daily, hourly, and perhaps every minute. The optimization of plant operations is concerned with selecting operating controls for a given unit (temperatures, pressures, flow rates, etc.) that are best set by some measure. Generally the engineer tries to set operating conditions to meet demands while running at minimum cost.

One way to accomplish process optimization is to run off-line process models that simulate the process mathematically. Plant engineers run many cases, analyze results, and recommend operating targets and/or strategies. While this approach is useful for studies of performance or design questions, it is not practical for operations that require immediate operating-condition recommendations. To achieve the full benefit of advanced control technology, plant engineers must provide timely, accurate operating targets. This has to use on-line closed-loop process unit optimization technology. Estimated benefits from advanced controls and on-line optimization range from an incremental benefit of 15 to 60 cents per barrel (Hydrocarbon Processing's *Advanced Process Control Handbook VII,* September 1992).

On-line optimization usually consists of the following steps (Stramwasser and Davis, 1993):

1. Process data monitoring
2. Program scheduling
3. Data reconciliation
4. Model update and optimization
5. Results to advanced controls

After the process data are checked for consistency and validity, they are used to calculate a plant material balance. If key process variables and the material balance are within specific tolerances over a suitable time interval, the process is deemed to be at a steady state and the process model may be updated. Next, the program scheduling step determines whether execution of the optimization sequence is allowed.

If a model update or an optimization is scheduled, the data reconciliation step is executed. In this step, key model inputs are adjusted through data reconciliation techniques to guarantee a consistent mass balance. Next, the process model is updated: Key model parameters are tuned so that the model accurately fits the current process operation. Then the nonlinear process is perturbed to obtain numerical derivatives for the optimization system to use in obtaining the optimum solution. The most heavily used optimization procedure is successive linear programming, but other algorithms also are in use. Finally, the optimum process values are sent to the advanced controls as optimum targets.

Nonlinear Programming

Methodology

In their text *Optimization of Chemical Processes,* Edgar and Himmelblau (1988) suggest that there is no single best method or algorithm of optimization that can successfully solve all problems. The methods chosen for a specific case will depend on

1. The nature of the objective function
2. The nature of the constraints
3. The number of independent and dependent variables

Edgar and Himmelblau give six general steps for the analysis and solution of optimization problems:

1. Analyze the process to define variables.
2. Determine optimization criteria, using variables defined in step 1.
3. Develop mathematical expressions that specify process, using physical principles (mass balance, energy balance), empirical relations, implicit concepts, and external restrictions. Identify independent and dependent variables.
4. If model formulation is too large in scope:

   a. Break it up into manageable parts.   and/or
   b. Simplify the objective function and model.

5. Apply a suitable optimization technique.
6. Check the results and examine the sensitivity of results to changes in coefficients and in the assumptions.

Steps 1, 2, and 3 deal with the formulation of the mathematical model to represent a process, i.e., specifying the variables, objective function, and constraints. Step 4 suggests we simplify this model formulation as much as possible without losing the essence of the problem, e.g., elimination of variables that do not greatly affect the objective function. Step 5 is the selection of the appropriate solution methodology. And step 6 is the checking of the candidate solution to determine if it is optimal. In addition, step 6 determines how sensitive the optimum is to changes in problem parameters. See *Optimization of Chemical Processes* for more detail.

If the objective function and constraints in a model are "nicely behaved," optimization is fairly straightforward. If the objective function and all constraints are linear, so that linear programming can be used, then a unique or globally optimum solution will be found, if any feasible solution exists. Upon initial formulation, most mathematical models of real-world processes are not linear. We usually modify our original model description of the physical process so that it fits the available methods of solution. Unfortunately, model users usually do not appreciate the relationship between the original model and the simplified model.

Edgar and Himmelblau and Lasdon point out that the most direct approach to solving the general nonlinear programming problem is to linearize the problem and successively apply linear programming techniques:

1. Formulate a model with a nominal operating point, and linearize all the constraints and the objective function about that point. Then solve that linear problem.

2. Successively linearize the constraints and the objective function of a nonlinear problem as successive improved feasible solutions are reached. Once the solution to the optimal linear program proves nonfeasible, locate the nearest feasible point and again linearize the constraints and objective about the new point.

3. Linearize the functions in a piecewise fashion so that a series of straight-line segments is used to approximate the objective function and constraints.

Successive linear programming

One of the more obvious methods to approach a nonlinear problem is by repeated linearization of both the objective function and constraints at some estimate of the solution. This is the basis for the approach called *successive linear programming* (SLP), in which at each stage a linear problem is solved. The use of SLP has increased over the years because the underlying LP algorithms have enjoyed steady improvements. SLP is widely used in the petroleum and chemical process industries because it can solve large problems and because they are fairly easy to implement with an efficient LP code. It is very efficient on highly constrained or mostly linear problems (Edgar and Himmelblau, 1988). Starting with a nonlinear problem, we linearize the nonlinear terms with a Taylor series expansion. Then we solve the linearized problem, relinearize about the new solution values, resolve, and stop when the linearized problem converges to an optimum of the original nonlinear problem. Bodington and Randall (1979) reported on the SLP algorithms used in Chevron's product blending tools to handle nonlinearities. The paper by Lasdon and Jaffe (1990) compares two common approaches for handling nonlinear behavior in refinery planning and product blending.

Successive quadratic programming

Quadratic programming is the name given to the procedure that minimizes a quadratic function of n variables subject to m linear constraints. A quadratic programming problem is the simplest form of nonlinear programming problem with inequality constraints. It usually takes fewer iterations than SLP, but more work per iteration. The smaller number of iterations makes *successive quadratic programming (SQP)* the most efficient method when the nonlinear model is complex and the computation is time-consuming. SLP is very efficient and fast for the case where the optimum is at a corner point, i.e., a constrained optimum. For interior optimum solutions, SLP can be very slow. SQP is usually much faster overall when the optimum is not at a corner point (Edgar and Himmelblau, 1988).

Generalized reduced gradient

The best current general algorithm using interactive linearization, according to Edgar and Himmelblau, is the *generalized reduced gradient* (GRG) algorithm. GRG (Abadie and Carpentier, 1969) is an extension of the Wolfe algorithm for linear constraints modified to accommodate both a nonlinear objective function and nonlinear constraints. In essence, the method employs linear or nonlinear constraints, defines new variables that are normal (i.e., perpendicular) to the constraints, and expresses the gradient in terms of this normal basis. (Wolfe has shown that the original reduced gradient method is related to the simplex method for linear programming.)

This approach introduces slack variables to convert inequality constraints to equalities. GRG algorithms use m equality constraints to solve for m of the variables, called *basic variables* (as in LP), in terms of the remaining $n - m$ nonbasic variables. The original problem is transformed to a simpler reduced problem, with a reduced objective and its reduced gradient. Thus, GRG algorithms solve the original problem by solving a sequence of reduced problems, which are usually solved by a gradient method. Following Murtaugh and Saunders (1978), the nonbasic variables are further divided into s superbasic variables, which are strictly between their bounds, and $n - m - s$ remaining nonbasic variables, which are at one of their bounds. In GRG2 (Lasdon and Waren, 1980), the reduced gradient with respect to the current superbasic variables is used to determine a search direction. Then a one-dimensional search is initiated to solve the problem. Computational experience (Schittowski, 1980) shows that, if properly implemented, GRG can be both reliable and efficient.

The code MINOS (Murtaugh and Saunders, 1978) is a very efficient GRG code for linearly constrained problems, having solved problems with more than 1000 rows. Its success supports the view that GRG methods are the most efficient and robust for linearly constrained problems. The GRG methods should also be considered strong contenders for handling nonlinear constraints.

Reduced-gradient algorithms seek to maintain feasibility on a set of nonlinear constraints while reducing the value of the objective function. As a result, the dimensionality of the search is reduced to the total number of variables less the number of independent constraints. The difficulty with this approach lies in returning to a feasible point if the solution of this subproblem with the linearized active constraints is not feasible relative to the original constraints. Thus, differences among GRG algorithms are the result of different approaches on how to conduct the search, how to reduce the objective function, and how to return to a feasible point.

Recursion in Linear Programming

What is recursion? *Recursion* is a technique used when certain parameters of an LP model are only estimated and when their values depend upon the LP solution. These estimates are used to find an initial solution. Once the solution is reached, the estimate values are compared to what the solved model determines the values should have been. If the estimates are in disagreement with the solution, the values are updated and the model is resolved. This continues until either the estimated values agree within a stated tolerance with the solution values or a maximum number of recursive steps have been

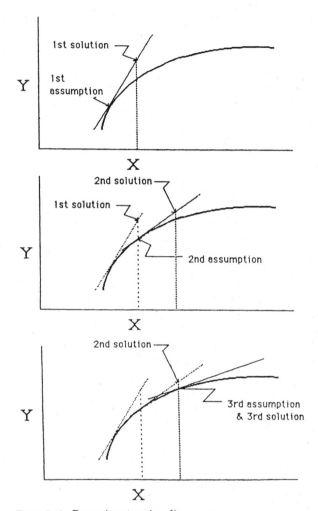

Figure 7.12   Recursive steps in a linear program.

reached. This is illustrated in Fig. 7.12 with a set of three recursive steps shown on a simple curve, where the tangent to the curve is the estimated value which is then updated from recursive step to recursive step (Fisher, 1986).

This simple recursion involves replacing coefficients in the LP problem with new values at each step. Without any control over the use of the new values and with no information about previous solutions left in the problem, there is no guarantee that simple recursion will ever converge to a solution. In fact, if more than a small number of values, say 10 or 20, are changed from step to step, the LP solutions will often not converge, but will wander or cycle from one solution to the next. An enhanced procedure was developed in the 1970s to solve not only the above nonconvergence problems but also the LP pooling problems. The technique, known as *distributive recursion,* not only incorporates updating of the estimated values, but also accounts for the imbalance between the current pool actual versus assumed quality.

A definition that shows the close relationship between recursion and SLP was given by C. A. Haverly (1982): "Recursion handles non-linearities by approximating them by their local derivatives. The derivatives are calculated at the values of the variables which correspond to the expected optimal solution variables. If the actual optimal solution turns out to have different values for the variables, then the system calculates the derivatives again and, at new assumptions for the variables, alters the LP matrix accordingly and reoptimizes." While linear programs using this distributive recursion may occasionally not converge, the method is generally robust and reliable for problems with hundreds of recursed variables.

Recursion involves the modeling of nonlinear problems in a linear model. An early attempt at changing linear programs from solution to solution is called *parametric programming.* "It starts with an optimal solution and then varies in an arbitrary but preassigned manner constants on the right hand side until one of the basic variables becomes zero" (Garvin et al., 1957). This early paper talked about making changes to a linear program on the rim (right-hand side or an objective function). This article discussed ways to represent the nonlinearity of octane blending with tetraethyl lead. It lead to the first commercial applications of recursion in which lead susceptibility was modeled.

In the late 1970s and early 1980s, associates at Haverly System did numerous studies on the pros and cons of distributive recursion to solve pooling problems in linear programs. Many of these papers were "white papers" presented at their yearly Magen Users Group meetings, and some were then republished in issues of *SIGMAP Bulletin.* Haverly (1979) stated that he had "used recursion models on real problems without serious difficulty. However...it has been fun to make a model and do rather extensive research on its behavior over a wide range of conditions. There have been a number of surprises. Hopefully, the results will help lead to recursion application models which have good behavior over the broadest possible range of data input." Some of his conclusions were that users should not assume that the linear program will always find a global optimum. Good starting estimates are important, and finding the global optimum is more likely with high economic driving forces.

A *global optimum* is the best possible answer a model can find. Models that are recursed or altered with various types of nonlinear techniques can find what is called a *local optimum*. That means the model has taken a certain path and has stopped at what it finds is the best possible answer; but in reality, if a different path, or a different series of model changes, had been used, a better answer would be possible.

In the 1970s, both computer and program limitations narrowed the scope of just how extensively recursion techniques could be used. In 1978, Chevron began testing the method called *distributive recursion.* At that time, computer hardware improvements and the robustness of optimization codes allowed the industry to expand its recursion horizons. Distributive recursion caused model sizes to double or triple. But it was the first successful method to really solve the LP pooling problem. [See Fisher (1986) for details on the method.] Paul Nix (1989) did a study using distributive recursion and concluded that "improper treatment of pooling relationships may cause significant errors in LP solutions and in the decisions based on those solutions. Distributive recursion provides an effective way to model pooling problems so as to reduce the likelihood of significant error."

Lasdon and Jaffe (1990) did an extensive study looking at distributive recursion (DR) versus successive linear programming (SLP). Their conclusions were that "as process models for production planning become more accurate and sophisticated, they will include more nonlinearities. Solution procedures for these models will require more sophistication as well. We believe that the DR/SLP framework is very promising in this regard, but that improved algorithmic logic will be necessary."

Distributive recursion has attained wide industry acceptance and is operational in most of the commercial planning systems (e.g., systems from Bechtel, Bonner and Moore Associates, Chesapeake Decision Sciences, and Haverly Systems).

There is no guarantee of convergence for any of the nonlinear methods. In practice, the most robust current algorithm using iterative linearization is the generalized reduced-gradient (GRG) algorithm. Studies have shown GRG methods are not the fastest, but are the most robust algorithms for solving nonlinear programming problems. Again, please see Edgar and Himmelblau (1988) for more details.

Integrated Planning

The past

The petroleum industry has invested considerable effort in developing sophisticated mathematical programming models to help planners provide overall strategy and direction for refinery operations, crude oil evaluation, etc. In addition, a considerable effort has been made in advanced process control for process plants to enable plants to run close to their optimal operating conditions. Unfortunately, a gap has existed between the two activities, with inadequate attention and effort invested to providing tools that aid the planner, the scheduler, and the operator in an integrated environment.

The refinery scheduler attempts to use the monthly LP model strategic plan to develop a detailed day-to-day schedule for refinery operations based on scheduled crude and feedstock arrivals, product liftings, and process plant availabilities and constraints. The schedule usually includes details of the operation of each process unit, the transfer of intermediates to and from the tank farm, and product blending schedules. But the scheduling is performed for each tank instead of for a pool.

In practice today, most refinery schedulers have few sophisticated computer tools to accomplish this task. Many use spreadsheets that contain individual operating modes for the primary processes and for the main feedstocks based on the same data used in the LP model. The scheduler uses the spreadsheet to generate manufacturing plans on a daily or weekly basis. Some use paper, pencil, and calculators as their only aids in daily scheduling.

For many years it has been a goal in the process industry to integrate planning with scheduling and control—a goal that has met with little success. Problems of getting integration to work have been many. Claims of success have been many, and usually the claims were premature. Often successes were not significant and would then be lost with changes in personnel. The NIH (Not Invented Here) syndrome killed many a budding development. Some problems stemmed from

- Turf wars

- Poor or no communication between company departments responsible for the three disciplines

- Easy-to-make products and usually inexpensive raw materials

- Lack of computer power

- No systems capable of carrying a plan all the way through to control

- Lack of good planning or faith that planning is well founded

- No commitment by upper management to tie it together

Industry has continued to work toward integration and is beginning to succeed in some areas to tie in planning with scheduling or control.

The present

It appears that integration is closer to reality than ever before. Many reasons for its failure to work in the past are no longer valid. Systems and computers are certainly better. Turf wars still exist, but management is beginning to realize that it cannot allow this to continue. The world is becoming so complex that integrated planning, scheduling, and control will be essential to manufacture product. The future is today. If a plant cannot survive today, it will not be around for the future. Many plants have shut down owing to the high cost of doing business and the lack of capabilities to make the new products required to meet higher customer and EPA standards.

Attention is beginning to be focused on integrating planning, scheduling, and control.

The future

Much of tomorrow or what is likely to be needed in the future is known, and industry is working with more purpose than ever to integrate planning because of the future and its complexity. The EPA has legislated that refineries must produce motor gasoline that meets specifications for a "simple" formula which begins in 1995. The formula then converts to a more complicated formula, called the *complex formula,* in 1997 or 1998 if it is not allowed to delay by Congress. The complex formula depends on several gasoline properties. It is a highly nonlinear formula containing qualities that cannot be measured by a single instrument. The purpose of the formula is to force air quality improvements by reducing emissions of pollutants relative to 1990 baseline gasolines. Gasoline properties will be tightly monitored, giving even more reason to integrate planning with production.

A common theme in the 1993 National Petroleum Refiners Association (NPRA) Computer Conference was the critical need for integrated planning, coupling blending operations with refinery planning and scheduling functions because of the difficult technical challenges presented by reformulated-fuels legislation. Balancing component uses against the plan requires that both the gasoline blender and the planner use the same models. Most believe the companies that succeed in the integration of planning, scheduling, and advanced process control will have a significant competitive advantage.

The federal 1990 Clean Air Act requires refiners to manufacture *reformulated gasoline* (RFG) in 1995, with new stringent product qualities. The cost of noncompliance is severe, with penalties of up to $25,000 per day of violation plus the amount of economic benefit to the refiner.

Planning and Scheduling Functions

Traditionally, planning and scheduling for a refinery encompass three areas:

- Crude management
- Process unit optimization
- Product scheduling and blending

Crude management entails crude segregation and crude unit operation. Process unit optimization deals with downstream (of the crude unit) process unit operations that handle crude unit intermediates. Product scheduling and blending deals with developing a product shipment schedule and an optimum blend recipe based upon information from process unit optimization and current operating data.

A major problem in refinery planning begins at this foundation: the crude unit and crude unit yields. Not only is the future price of crude not known, but also the actual composition of the crude is often only an educated guess. Crudes vary from shipment to shipment because of the mixture of sources actually shipped. It is expected that the quality does not significantly change over a short time, but this assumption can be hazardous to one's plan. If the actual crude composition does not closely agree with that modeled, then an error is made that often snowballs through the rest of the refinery model.

A second, very common source of error in the crude unit submodel is the assumption that the crude cuts are produced as modeled. Often, models are not even adjusted to show cut overlaps. This is caused by taking the easy way out in developing crude cut yields and qualities. One of the typical crude cutting procedures assigns distillation temperatures directly from the true boiling point crude analysis and makes no adjustment for the actual refinery degree of fractionation. This is especially a bad procedure as we go into RFG and CARB Phase 2 type of gasolines that have tight 90 percent point limits. The fractionation efficiency of gasoline and distillate components from all processes will have a significant effect in controlling aromatics and other hydrocarbon types.

Planners will have to be more diligent in the future, looking back on their plans and comparing to what actually happened to upgrade the prediction accuracy of their models.

Product scheduling and blending is usually handled by preparing both a short-range and a long-range plan, using the same model of the blending process. The long-range plan, typically covering 30 days, provides aggregate pools of products for a production schedule. The short-range plan, typically covering 7 days, fixes the blend schedule and creates recipes for the blender. Desired output from the long-range model includes

- Detailed blend schedule
- Optimal blend recipes
- Predicted blend properties
- Product and component inventories
- Component qualities, rundown rates, and costs
- Product prices
- Equipment limits

Desired output from the short-range model includes

- A detailed product blend schedule
- Optimal blend recipes
- Predicted properties of blend recipes
- Component and product inventories as a function of time

Blending Operations

Traditionally, blending operations are responsible for the actual production of fuels based on the optimal recipes provided by planning and scheduling. Operating objectives are usually prioritized:

1. Meet quality specifications.
2. Meet shipment schedule.
3. Minimize quality giveaway.
4. Minimize blend cost.
5. Maintain inventory targets.

On January 1, 1995, a host of new EPA regulations will take effect, requiring gasoline to be *reformulated* to improve the air quality. Blenders will have a difficult time trying to manually control many blend properties. Traditional trim control will not fare much better than manual control. A control approach capable of handling nonlinear behavior will be a plus, and it needs to link the blend operator with the refinery planning and scheduling group by using a cascade-like control strategy (Tennessen and Di Nello, 1993).

The planning and scheduling steps are the primary control loops that drive the blend control system. It is the output of the planning and scheduling step that provides the control set points for the blending operations loop. While mid-blend results provide feedback to blending operations, final-blend results are feedback to planning and scheduling.

To close the loop, data must be electronically available from a database.

A Successful Integration—P2/GINO

Chevron has enjoyed success over many years of practice in integrating planning, scheduling, and control by using two gasoline blending tools (Hurst et al., 1983). For planning and scheduling optimum gasoline blends, they use P2, a program that starts with component productions (from a refinery planning linear program, a simulator, estimates, etc.). P2 provides optimal recipes for each grade of gasoline based on a daily, weekly, or monthly period, using manufacturing costs for that period.

Blending the individual gasoline product in a tank is done with the gasoline *in*-line optimization (GINO) program. GINO is run on a batch basis, one blend at a time, by using the P2 recipe as input. Using a goal programming approach, GINO adjusts the optimum P2 recipe as little as possible while handling adjustments for the actual current blending situation (e.g., minor changes in component qualities, tank heel, stock excess, pump problems). In addition, GINO minimizes quality giveaway (Stadnicki and Lawler, 1983). The GINO objective is best stated as "Come as close as possible to the planner's P2 recipe while making on-test gasoline with minimum giveaway and while satisfying local constraints." GINO is normally run by the blender several times in making a blend to make midcourse corrections and update biases.

The control program uses the GINO database, operator setup information, and on-line analyzers to automatically adjust the blend recipe set points in the blender. The control strategy objective is to make on-test blends with minimum giveaway. The control system consists of two parts, called a *fast loop* and a *slow loop*. The objective of the fast loop is to regulate the tail line "critical" inspections at the tail line inspection targets predicted by GINO. This is accomplished by automatically adjusting the blend recipe by changing the ratio set points in the blender. "Critical" inspections are expected to be on test with zero giveaway for the finished blend. The objective of the slow loop is to reset the tail line inspection targets of the fast loop, to allow for nonperfect tail line inspection control and bias updates (using GINO).

Concluding Remarks

When you write about the state of mathematical programming, it is a lot like an article on the state of computing. The article is out of date before the ink dries. However, there are those who need the information even if it is dated. I'm reminded of a recent conversation with a client who had just attended a brush-up class on mathematical programming. The instructor was speaking about the state of the art of linear programming and had given an illustration using an 18-row model. When he was finishing the lecture, he noted that this was a very small problem. He noted that solution algorithms today could handle models with as many as 900 rows. My client wanted to correct the instructor, but didn't for fear of embarrassing him in front of the class. At the end of the class he pointed out to the instructor that linear programs with well over 10,000 rows were now routinely being solved. He also stated, "And the coefficients, they change." The instructor had trouble believing this.

References

Abadie, J., and J. Carpentier (1969): "Generalization of the Wolfe Reduced Gradient Method to the Case of Nonlinear Constraints," *On Optimization,* Academic Press, New York, pp. 37–47.

Bain, M. L., K. W. Mansfield, J. G. Maphet, W. H. Bosler, and J. P. Kennedy (1993): "Gasoline Blending with an Integrated On-Line Optimization, Scheduling and Control System," presented at the National Petroleum Refiners Association Computer Conference, New Orleans, LA, November.

Bannayan, M. A., and M. G. Treat (1993): "Decision Making Based upon Integrated Information Systems," presented at the National Petroleum Refiners Association Computer Conference, New Orleans, LA, November.

Bodington, C. E., and W. C. Randall (1979): "Nonlinear Programs for Product Blending," presented at The Institute of Management Science/Operations Research Society of America joint meeting, New Orleans, LA, April/May.

Bodington, C. E., and T. E. Baker (1990): "A History of Mathematical Programming in the Petroleum Industry," *Interfaces,* vol. 20, no. 4, July/August.

Dunbar, D. N., M. R. Tallett, and J. Leather (1993): "Linear Blending Values Produce Accurate Results for EPA Gasoline Emission Equations," internal report, Ensys Energy & Systems, Inc., Flemington, NJ.

Edgar, T. F., and D. M. Himmelblau (1988): *Optimization of Chemical Processes,* McGraw-Hill, New York.

Fisher, J. N. (1982): "Goal Programming in LP," internal report, Chevron Research Company, April 19.

Fisher, J. N. (1986): "Chevron's Experience with Distributive Recursion in LPs," presented at the National Petroleum Refiners Association Computer Conference, Salt Lake City, UT, October.

Fisher, J. N. (1992): "Decision and Risk Analysis in PIMS," presented at the Bechtel PIMS conference, Houston.

Fisher, J. N. (1993): "Evaluation of the Refining Segment of California Energy Commission's CAPE Model," Hearing, Sacramento, CA., December 10.

Fisher, J. N., and W. W. Baxter (1970): "Non-Linear Applications of Mathematical Programming in the Refinery Environment," presented at the National Petroleum Refiners Association Computer Conference, New Orleans.

Garvin, W. W., H. W. Crandall, J. B. John, and R. A. Spellmann (1957): "Applications of Linear Programming in the Oil Industry," *Management Sci.,* vol. 3, no. 4, pp. 407–430.

Han, D. D. (1982): "System/B—A User Friendly Optimizer," paper CC-82-118, presented at the National Petroleum Refiners Association Computer Conference, San Francisco, CA, November.

Haverly, C. A. (1979): "Behavior of Recursion Models," *SIGMAP Bull.* no. 26, April.

Haverly, C. A. (1982): "Recursion," presented at the Haverly Systems 16th MUG Users' Conference, Snowmass, CO.

Hurst, C. V., C. E. Bodington, D. L. Burgan, G. Garrett, J. T. Ranney, and D. E. Weber (1983): "Question and Answer Session on Blending Optimization, Scheduling, Control," National Petroleum Refiners Association Computer Conference, Tulsa, OK, October 30–November 2.

Lasdon, L. S. (1982): "Large Scale Nonlinear Programming," Working Paper 82/83-3-1, Department of General Business, University of Texas at Austin, December 6.

Lasdon, L. S., and B. Jaffe (1990): "The Relationship between Distributive Recursion and Successive Linear Programming in Refining Production Planning Models," paper CC-90-135, presented at the National Petroleum Refiners Association Computer Conference, Seattle, WA, October.

Lasdon, L. S., and A. D. Waren (1980): "A Survey of Nonlinear Programming Applications," *Oper. Res.,* vol. 28, no. 5, pp. 34–50.

McMahan, W. L., and P. A. Roach (1982): "Site Energy Optimization, A Math Programming Approach," *Interfaces,* vol. 12, no. 6, December, pp. 66–82.

Murtaugh, B. A., and M. A. Saunders (1978): "Large-Scale Linearly Constrained Optimization," *Math. Program.,* vol. 14, pp. 41–72.

Nix, P. S. (1979): "A Linear Programming Model for Daily Gasoline Blending," presented at the Haverly Systems MUG Users' Conference, San Francisco, CA.

Nix, P. S. (1989): "The Pooling Problem and Distributive Recursion," presented at the Haverly Systems MUG Users' Conference, August, Nashville, TN.

Rusin, M. H., H. S. Chang, and J. F. Marshall (1981): "A Transformation Method for Calculating the Research and Motor Octane Numbers of Gasoline Blends," *Ind. & Eng. Chem. Fund.,* vol. 20, no. 3.

Schittowski, K. (1980): "Nonlinear Programming Codes—Information, Tests, Performance," *Lecture Notes in Economics and Mathematical Systems,* vol. 183, Springer-Verlag, Berlin.

Stadnicki, S. D., and M. B. Lawler (1983): "An Integrated Planning and Control Package for Product Blending," presented at the 2d Annual Control Engineering Conference, Rosemont, IL.

Stramwasser, R., and J. Davis (1993): "On-Line Optimization at El Palito Refinery," presented at the National Petroleum Refiners Association Computer Conference, New Orleans, LA, November.

Tennessen, R. H., and R. P. Di Nello (1993): "Closing the Loop between Blending Operations and Planning and Scheduling," presented at the National Petroleum Refiners Association Computer Conference, New Orleans, LA, November.

Zellhart, J. W. (1987): "Refining, Supply, Distribution, and Marketing Model," presented at the National Petroleum Refiners Association Computer Conference, Kansas City, MO.

8

Expert Systems

Joseph F. Faccenda and Duncan A. Rowan

Introduction

Expert systems technology is playing an increasingly important role in process industry planning, scheduling, and control. The applicability of expert systems extends throughout the *planning, scheduling, and control* (PSC) hierarchy, although the functions performed and the degree to which expert systems contribute to a solution vary at different levels in the hierarchy. Furthermore, in most instances, the key to realizing the maximum benefits from the application of expert systems lies in the effective integration of expert systems technology with other technologies.

In this chapter, we explore the role of expert systems at different levels of the PSC hierarchy. In each case, we will discuss how expert systems technology is applied, both from a theoretical viewpoint and through experiences with the application of expert systems to industrial problems. Examples are provided to illustrate these concepts. We begin with a brief introduction to expert system fundamentals.

Expert systems defined

An *expert system* is a computer program that is able to perform within a limited domain (a field or application area) at the level of a human expert in that domain. This is accomplished via the two major components of the expert system: the *knowledge base* and the *inference engine*. The knowledge base is the place where the domain knowledge is stored. There are a number of different ways to represent the knowledge base, with the most common being the production rule. These rules take on the general form

IF <conditions>

THEN <actions>

where the actions are executed whenever the conditions are satisfied.

The inference engine controls the execution of the rules in the knowledge base. The ability of the inference engine to search the knowledge base and execute the appropriate rules in a nonprocedural manner is what distinguishes expert systems from other heuristic problem-solving approaches.

The inference engine may use one or more strategies to move through the knowledge base. An example of one common strategy is *backward chaining*. This strategy is driven by the inference engine's attempts to prove a hypothesis. The inference engine selects conditions which, if true, will prove the hypothesis. If the conditions encountered by the inference engine have not already been resolved to be true, then the inference engine continues searching for other rules to resolve these conditions. This process continues until the original rule is proved true or false. This and other strategies are discussed in more detail in Harmon and King (1985).

Special significance in process industry manufacturing

Process industry production processes are generally configured to manufacture many of the key intermediate products in a limited number of large, high-volume facilities. There may be several such production stages for a given product. In many cases, the intermediate product which is output from one of the production stages may be transported to another production site as input to a subsequent stage. In some production processes, the production facilities involved in this manufacturing chain may be located in different parts of the world. Optimally planning the use of these interdependent facilities is a key to the success of the business. Control of these process while they are running is another important factor. And a factor which cannot be overlooked is the importance of proper planning and execution of the transitions between different products on a facility.

Subsequent manufacturing steps usually involve further differentiation of the product through operations such as (1) introducing additives and colors, (2) blending or otherwise combining production from earlier stages, (3) slitting or chopping sheet products to order sizes, and (4) packaging the final product into one of several different containers. These production stages present more of the operational scheduling difficulties which are found in other industries. However, there are also some problems which are unique to the process industry. For example, since the intermediate products must often be stored in finite-capacity vessels such as tanks, staying within tank limits is as important as keeping enough in-process product inventory for the subsequent production stage.

Because of these unique problems faced in process industry manufacturing, naturally expert systems technology plays a key role in their solution. From planning the use of facilities, through their scheduling and control, human experts have traditionally played a key role in the decision-making processes. Although mathematical optimization models, simulation models, and sensor-based process control systems continue to provide the foundation for computer-aided benefits in these areas, expert systems–based extensions are providing significant additional value.

The role of expert systems through the PSC hierarchy

The role of expert systems varies throughout the PSC hierarchy. The roles range from complementing an optimization or simulation procedure to serving as the primary decision-making vehicle in a rule-driven procedure. The remainder of this chapter focuses on three major application areas, each of which benefits in different ways from the application of expert systems. These areas are

- Production and distribution planning
- Production scheduling
- Process control

Production and Distribution Planning

In this section, we focus on the higher-level planning functions that deal with where to produce products, usually encompassing multiple production stages, to achieve the best overall capacity utilization, manufacturing cost, and distribution cost while meeting a specified mix of marketplace demands for the final products. When the products can be made on production facilities located in different parts of the world, this decision process is also sometimes referred to as *global sourcing,* i.e., determining which global facilities should be used to source products. This level of planning is particularly important to businesses which do not have a large number of parallel production facilities located at a single site. In these cases, a good global sourcing plan can provide an important extra degree of flexibility and can significantly increase effective production capacity.

This production and distribution planning function can take on different forms, depending on the characteristics of the business. This function falls between multiyear strategic planning and short-range production scheduling, and thus it may span a time horizon in the range of 3 months to 3 years. Businesses which do this type of planning for a time horizon of 3 months have relatively short raw material and distribution lead times, and they can change their production sequences with minimal impact to the facilities. At the other end of the spectrum, approaching the 3-year time horizon, are businesses with longer lead times, highly geographically dispersed production facilities, and highly seasonal customer demand patterns. In some cases, a business will divide this level of the planning hierarchy into two pieces, a long-range piece and a midrange piece. For the purposes of this discussion, we will treat this as a single level in the planning hierarchy.

Depending upon the business situation, expert systems technology will play varying roles in developing these production and distribution plans. Although the primary tool used to deal with these problems is mathematical programming-based optimization, expert systems can be used effectively to complement the mathematical techniques. The complementary role of expert systems takes several forms, including

1. Incorporation of heuristic decision rules which are used by business planners, but which cannot be completely expressed in mathematical models

2. Direct integration into the mathematical solution process

3. Interpretation of results, including reporting, marginal cost analysis, and infeasibility analysis

4. Translation of planning information into a starting point and constraints for short-range production scheduling

Heuristic decision rules

Although it has been proposed that business planning can be accomplished by developing an expert system around the heuristics of the business planner, it is often an unsuccessful approach. This approach suffers from two types of problems. First, it is usually difficult and/or inefficient to encode the rules used at this level of planning. The rules vary significantly with changing external business conditions and internal corporate financial goals. Second, the rules which are developed usually perpetuate a problem found with the human decision processes. This problem is that the rules will reflect one limited style of decision making, which hides new opportunities that become available with changing conditions. Mathematical modeling does not suffer from these types of problems because the decision processes can be parameterized via costs and constraints. Under ideal conditions, the mathematical model will reflect the actual costs and value of decisions, restricted only by actual physical, regulatory, and policy constraints. Thus, new conditions can be reflected via these parameters, and the model remains robust in its ability to gain the maximum advantage from any set of conditions.

Unfortunately, this ideal state is also difficult to achieve. In reality, many of the relevant costs are not easily obtained, and the changes in constraints cannot always be reflected via parameterization. This is one place where expert systems can play an important complementary role.

Expert systems have been successfully used to develop the appropriate incidence structures used in generating the coefficient matrix for a mathematical model. These rules can interpret physical and policy information which often affects different parts of the coefficient matrix. While this task would be difficult or impossible for a business planner who is not trained in mathematical programming, the expert system can perform this function easily. This approach allows the model to reflect the planner's knowledge, without restricting the model solution to a limited set of planning rules and without requiring the intervention of a modeling expert.

As an extension to this idea, we have considered the use of expert systems to help develop the relative costs needed to properly reflect tradeoffs in the absence of real costs. This is an area which does appear to have potential, but we have seen very limited success for this application in practice.

Solution process integration

Linear programming (LP) formulations are able to reflect a large percentage of the framework required for long-range planning. They provide the ability to simultaneously optimize the potentially thousands of decision variables involved in the production and distribution plan over the planning time horizon. LP solutions can now be obtained very quickly for even the largest problems of this type.

The major problem with the ability of a linear program to accurately capture production planning situations is the discrete nature of some of the decisions that must be considered. A simple example of the weakness of the linear formulation when applied to semicontinuous batch-process plants is the tendency of the linear program to assign unrealistically small quantities of material to production facilities. An alternative mathematical formulation is a *mixed-integer* LP formulation, which considers the minimum acceptable production (and distribution) quantities of products. However, traditional branch-and-bound solution techniques used on problems of this type will not always produce a sufficiently improved solution to warrant the computation time required.

An even more difficult problem arises when the long-range plan needs to balance product transition (setup) and inventory costs plus facility capacity utilization. This must be accomplished by simultaneously determining batch sizes, allocating batches to facilities, and sequencing the batches on the facilities. This problem is further complicated when operation is in the context of a multistage production environment and/or when the product transitions depend on the sequence in which the products are run. Often some of these complexities can be ignored at the planning level and dealt with for a shorter time horizon at the detailed scheduling level. However, it may be necessary to deal with enough of these factors at the planning level to create significant computational complexity.

For many of the problems of this type, a combined approach which uses embedded expert-system rules to help deal with the discrete variables is very effective. Under this scenario, rules are run to examine the LP solution, and discrete constraints are added to the linear program based on this analysis. These rules are partly based on the decision logic that the planner uses to manually make production and distribution decisions. The rules also usually reflect information which is extracted from the linear program, such as objective function deltas and other marginal-cost information. Thus, the knowledge of the modeler also becomes part of the solution process. This combined knowledge base, integrated with the optimization capability of the linear program, produces better production plans in a much shorter time than is possible by other methods. It has been found that planners have a high acceptance level and confidence in solutions generated by this method.

Depending on the problem structure, another strategy which can be effective is the decomposition of the discrete parts of the problem. The idea here is to use expert-system rules to decompose the problem and then use traditional branch-and-bound rules to solve the subproblems. Rules also control the links between the subproblems and the master problem. This strategy is effective when the problem is decomposible and when the problem requires a tighter solution than can be achieved by the previously described method.

An approach which has the potential of producing even better solutions is to integrate expert-system rules directly into a branch-and-bound procedure. This method involves running rules to decide on the branch variable and the branch direction (up or down). As was the case in a method discussed earlier, the branching decisions can combine problem knowledge that the planner has with the knowledge of the model builder. The major difficulty in implementing the apparently powerful approach has been due to the lack of flexibility in the available software. The software needs to interact at a low level of the optimization algorithm, but still must provide a good environment for the development and maintenance of the expert system rules.

As more complexities are introduced to the problem, particularly any consideration of sequence-dependent setups, more specialized solution procedures are required. We have seen limited success with one approach which combines expert system rules with a linear program for production allocation, capacity balancing, and inventory analysis, along with a traveling salesman sequencing formulation. Including the traveling salesman sequencing formulation as part of the linear program allows production allocation decisions to simultaneously consider available capacity, production cost differentials by facility, and setup costs and times based on transitions to other products allocated to the same machine.

A well-known problem with using this type of formulation for traveling salesman problems is that it cannot prevent the occurrence of multiple unconnected product sequences (also known as *subtours*). Thus, the primary role of the expert system is to help quickly find reasonable integer solutions, so that subtour constraints can iteratively be added to the formulation until all subtours are eliminated. This is discussed in greater detail by Faccenda and Baker (1990).

Analysis of results

The interpretation of model results is particularly important to the production planning process. One reason is that the longer-range time horizons under consideration will naturally incorporate data elements which carry a greater degree of uncertainty. Another reason is that the policy decisions reflected in the model may not be completely rigid. Thus, the planner needs as much help as possible in understanding the solution to a model, and she or he must be able to easily relate the solution to other model solutions run with input data perturbations. Furthermore, these solutions must be communicated to managers across various functional areas, such as manufacturing, marketing, distribution, and facilities planning. Solution interpretation can be aided by expert systems in different ways. One way is through the creation of custom reports, which are built via interactive dialogue with the user. These reports can be customized to include the most relevant information required to address the questions at hand in a compact format. This is an especially powerful idea when the reports contain information which spans multiple model runs. The marginal-cost information which is generated as part of a standard mathematical programming solution can be important. However, we have found it impractical to expect someone to understand this type of information in its raw form. Expert systems can help by picking out and interpreting suspicious marginal-cost values.

Another area where expert systems can help is in the analysis of infeasible model formulations. We see this function being more appropriate for the model developer, since the model design and data screening should prevent most models from generating infeasible formulations after the model is in the hands of an end user. Although we have used expert systems for infeasibility analysis, researchers in this area are continually developing improved specialized tools for this purpose. It appears that the role of expert systems is moving to complement these specialized tools.

Translation to detailed scheduling

An important result of the production planning function within the hierarchical decision process is to provide a framework for short-term production scheduling. This involves translating information from the planning solution to goals and constraints in the scheduling model. Depending on the production processes involved, this may include disaggregation of bulk product types into subgrades. As another example, in a refinery situation, blend streams from the planning level may be aggregated into blend operations with the recipes determined from the plan. In most cases, the planning model results are also translated to bounds on starting and ending times for production activities, as well as target inventory goals.

Expert systems rules have been found to be an excellent way to facilitate the translation between the planning and scheduling levels. The rules are able to interpret the numerical results from the planning model to create a good set of goals and constraints for the scheduling level. These expert-system rules attempt to maintain the integrity of the planning solution while leaving as much room as possible for dealing with short-term problems that always arise at the scheduling level.

Production Scheduling

As the popularity of expert systems grew, their application to production scheduling has received a good deal of attention. Many have contended that operations research–based mathematical optimization approaches have been unsuccessful when applied to production scheduling problems and that an expert systems approach is superior. The rationale is that the best human production schedulers appear to be those with an ability to recognize and deal with problems based on many years of experience in the job. Therefore, why not simply automate the solution to parallel the human decision processes, rather than cast the problem into an optimization or simulation framework? In practice, we have found several answers to that question. To start with, the question becomes easier to address when we divide the production scheduling problems into two major classes. The first class encompasses the more traditional view of production scheduling, where a time-based series of customer requirements are to be assigned to a set of production facilities under various constraints. This class of scheduling problem in process industry manufacturing involves tradeoffs between product-to-facility allocations, production run lengths, product-to-product transitions, and inventory levels. Constraints may include customer delivery dates, facility availability, planned maintenance, shift patterns, customer priorities, and labor or other secondary resource constraints. Our experience, which is supported by much of the literature on the subject, is that the best solution is obtained by applying a combination of expert systems, optimization, and simulation technology. It is also critical to apply this technology within a solid database framework. We discuss this class of scheduling problem in the next section.

The second class of scheduling problem is real-time reactive scheduling, also referred to as *dispatching*. This class of problem deals with very short-term unplanned upsets to the calculated production schedule. These upsets may have a variety of causes, but they always require that decisions be quickly made to solve the immediate problem with minimum disruption to the planned schedule. It is with this class of problem that we find expert systems can be applied as the primary solution tool. The keys here are to build a solid rule base that is able to recognize short-term requirements and constraints, connected to real-time process data so that the expert system can quickly assess the problem and generate a solution. We discuss this in detail in a later section.

Developing a production schedule

As described previously, the development of a production schedule should ideally start with the framework provided by a higher-level plan. Schedule development proceeds from this initial starting point to take many additional details into account. For example, the production plan is usually developed by aggregating time into buckets. At the scheduling level, these buckets must be transformed to a continuous-time representation, which may reveal problems within the time buckets that were not recognized in the plan. The planning level often deals with aggregations of subgrades, which must be disaggregated and dealt with explicitly in the schedule. Furthermore, the schedule must account for the details and resulting complexity involved with precisely sequencing production batches on a facility.

As indicated earlier, these problems are best addressed by a combination of optimization, simulation, and expert systems technologies. This combination allows the structured, highly quantitative parts of the problem to be handled by mathematics-based methods of optimization and simulation. The qualitative, inexact aspects can use expert systems to take advantage of the scheduler's knowledge and experience. These technologies are then applied in a total system which includes strong database links and allows the scheduler to easily perform manual interactive manipulations of the generated schedule, preferably within a graphical environment.

There are numerous ways in which expert systems are used in combination with operations research techniques for production scheduling. One approach is to combine the two techniques into a hybrid solution algorithm, as described in the previous discussion of planning models. Another approach which has been very successful in practice is to generate an initial solution by using operations research techniques and then to analyze and modify the solution to incorporate the aspects of the problem which are difficult to code into a mathematical model. A useful extension to this technique is to embed expert-system rules into a simulation model. The simulation model then executes rules at various points in simulated time, which are triggered by different classes of events. Thus, localized scheduling rules which are typically applied by human schedulers can be utilized in the simulated execution of the mathematically generated schedule.

There are several examples of the need for combined expert systems and operations research solutions in the literature. Kusiak and Chen (1988) surveyed some 20 scheduling systems based on expert systems technology. Most of the systems from this survey also reference some type of simulation and/or optimization interaction. The most notable exceptions are examples of robot scheduling, which is more of a reactive than a planning environment.

A specific process industry example of combining these technologies is described by Casto and Slater (1990). Their "production scheduling adviser" features a modular approach which includes an interactive Gantt chart, expert system module, and optimization module. Faccenda and Baker (1990) describe the advantages of combining operations research, expert systems, database, and interactive Gantt charts to solve process industry planning and scheduling problems. Collins and Baker (1989) cite several additional examples of the application of expert systems and operations research to these problems.

Reactive/dispatching scheduling

Reactive scheduling is now receiving more attention, as processes are being operated nearer to capacity with very little downtime. Industry is trying to achieve up to 5 years between major shutdowns (H. Sinclair, Dow Chemical Co., Texas A&M Instrumentation Symposium, January 1994). Greater utilization of plant facilities is critical to reducing costs. Industrial engineers and business reengineering specialists strive to reduce the *cycle time,* which is defined as the time that material spends in a plant being transformed from raw material to the finished product. The cycle time can be reduced by increasing the throughput, by reducing intermediate and product inventory, or by doing both.

For example, in a new batch process being designed in Du Pont, the batch cycle time will be reduced (versus the existing process). The new process is much "tighter" and less forgiving of misoperation or slow turnaround of product release information. The intent is to have the product meet quality specifications immediately after the run, and not require holdup for postrun quality adjustments. The operating group has recognized the need for more careful operational planning. The approach being taken is to capture the knowledge for executing the production plan based on experience gained from operating a pilot facility. Each product run requires proper sequencing of process steps which are contingent upon equipment constraints. The products are specialized to the degree that chemists must work closely with production personnel in order to produce a successful run. There is the expectation that after the procedures and methodologies are documented and reviewed, the knowledge can be converted to an expert system. This will be done in phases. As is very common, automating this task will require integration with existing databases and control systems. This is an example of money being saved on the capital facilities, but more will be spent on intelligently operating the facility.

Several examples of the use of expert systems for reactive scheduling are appearing in the literature. These include Martin (1992), Whitworth (1993), and Dubois and Opdahl (1993). In these applications, expert systems play a more dominant role, compared to applications directed at developing an initial schedule. The focus of the database interfaces is also different, relying more on direct connections to real-time process information. Another common thread in these examples is some use of simulation modeling in combination with the *expert systems* (ES) rules.

Reactive scheduling opportunities using ES technology can be particularly dramatic on processes which transition frequently. Transitions, caused by product changes, grade or rate changes, and maintenance outages, often introduce product variability and increase off-specification production. In some processes, we have found that at least half of product variability occurs during process transitions. Typically, transitions in a continuous process produce material which is not within specifications for the before-transition product or the new product. Thus, with careful planning the losses due to transitions can be minimized. In a Du Pont process, a study during which knowledgeable engineers orchestrated the transitions showed that losses could be reduced 50 to 60 percent! The reasons for the reduction included

- Proper planning, including having all necessary equipment ready for use

- Development and communication of the schedule to operators and maintenance personnel

- Aggressive operation, i.e., making moves in parallel, starting moves early where acceptable, etc.

These issues are being addressed primarily with labor practices and training. However, ES technology is particularly appropriate for addressing the last issue. Making aggressive transitions involves the application of engineering knowledge (i.e., making calculations, process dynamics) and experiential knowledge (previous operating experience, empirical knowledge). ES technology is a natural fit for capturing and applying this knowledge.

The predictive system also includes process transition advisers, which are becoming more prevalent as products become increasingly specialized and rapid turnaround time is required to meet customer demand. Thoroughly understanding and carefully executing a response plan for a transition can provide significant economic benefits in terms of improved first-pass yield and waste reduction.

Process transition adviser applications

Currently, Du Pont is applying expert systems to coordinate production schedules across a synthetic fiber production facility. The economic value of performing optimum transitions was demonstrated in a 1990 plant test that showed significant yield improvements were achievable. In this process, the spinning operation schedule is propagated back to the upstream polymer operation. A spinning machine production schedule is produced by a semiautomatic system that is networked to an on-line expert system. The expert system monitors current process conditions and determines the required future production rates. Knowledge is embedded in the system in the form of models, procedural calculations, and rules. The information is displayed to the operator in a simple 5-day schedule that is updated for each 8-h shift.

In this process, the spinning operation is extremely sensitive to changes in upstream residence time; therefore, the residence time is maintained as constant as possible. Although this is not possible during rate transitions, the impact on the downstream spinning operation can be minimized by carefully managing the transitions. To achieve this, the expert system must solve a material balance that is complicated by constraints on the magnitude, rate of transition, and timing. The ES input includes the desired production rate information and estimates of the machine outage duration as well as on-line process data. The system generates the optimum polymer transition, given any reasonable set of initial conditions. Normal transitions occur approximately twice per month per line. The expert system does not attempt to accommodate infrequent unscheduled production interruptions. After a transition is completed, the system switches into a steady-state mode that maintains a constant residence time until the next transition begins.

Deploying the process transition adviser application required a thorough understanding of the transition process. The implementation team soon discovered that the engineering knowledge needed to coordinate the entire process was spread over several people in different organizations. By having the experts work together and arrive at a mutual understanding of the problem, the plant was able to institute more rigorous efforts to reduce the number and magnitude of transitions. This cultural change resulted in capturing some economic benefit. Even though the frequency of transitions is now somewhat lower, the expert system is still needed to capture the remaining financial stake.

Another common problem in the operation of processes in the face of transition disturbances is that operators may overcontrol the process. In one process it was observed that operators were making about twice the necessary rate adjustments in an upstream polymer process in response to fluctuations in the downstream processes (two different downstream processes). However, in many cases the downstream demand was fluctuating around some mean value; these fluctuations could be absorbed by intermediate storage tanks. This polymer process is sensitive to changes in rate, and therefore minimizing rate changes is beneficial.

Further investigation revealed that the demand by the downstream operations was planned and could be accurately forecasted for 24 h in advance. An expert system has been developed to predict the storage tank inventory for the upcoming 24 h based on the current upstream (tank inlet) rate and the projected downstream (tank outlet) rate. The system will plot the predicted inventory and notify the operators when rate changes are required. This system is under test at this time. The most challenging aspect of this application was the integration with the existing human interfaces—both the operator interface and the interface for manufacturing supervision to enter the operating forecasts. The necessary calculations are a simple mass balance around the storage tanks. As is typical, some engineering "workarounds" had to be developed to account for problems such as unmeasured recycle flows.

Process Control Expert Systems

Expert systems applied in the process control arena are typically on-line expert systems that receive data primarily from sensor-based process control systems and respond in real time to process problems. These ES applications should be viewed as extensions to rather than replacements of traditional process-control technology.

The general demand for higher-quality domestic products is induced by worldwide competition. Improving quality requires us to have better data and analyze them to make appropriate decisions. As discussed by Laffey et al., (1988), real-time, on-line expert systems can benefit problem-solving situations in which humans suffer from cognitive overload, fail to monitor all available information or resolve conflicting constraints, are expensive or scarce, make high-cost mistakes, miss high-revenue opportunities, or cannot simultaneously manipulate all the relevant information to obtain optimal solutions to provide a solution quickly enough.

High-revenue opportunities certainly exist in the process industries because incremental improvements in operation typically have high economic returns. Automation in general and expert systems in particular do this by helping to prevent costly, unscheduled shutdowns due to equipment failure. Expert systems can also improve the percentage of time the process produces top-grade products by interpreting errant process behavior and advising corrective action. Companies understand that much of their competitive advantage results from knowledge about how to operate the process and process equipment most effectively. Because human expertise is perishable, interest in capturing this knowledge in expert systems is growing.

Much of the motivation for building on-line systems in the process industry is consistent with the published benefits for knowledge-based systems in general; i.e., expertise is scarce, vague, and dispersed and should be preserved, made precise, focused, and applied continuously. Also, once captured, knowledge can be distributed among similar applications. Another motivating factor for applying on-line expert systems is the reduction in plant staffing. However, this is not a primary justification since operating labor typically represents a very small percentage of the total production cost. But reducing the routine technical assistance to manufacturing required of process engineers is of great interest. If expertise is leveraged in expert systems, engineers could move to more productive, creative, and valuable tasks.

To date, the entrance of ES technology into process-control applications has been gradual and continues to evolve slowly. On the whole, this industry is rather conservative when it comes to using novel technology. Any misapplication can have severe consequences in terms of capital equipment and product losses, human safety, or possible environmental contamination. Despite this operating philosophy, the motivation for applying ES technology is too compelling to disregard, and tools and techniques have evolved until beginning system implementation is cost-effective. Application areas that have benefited include sensor validation, data reconciliation, on-line equipment diagnosis, and model-based knowledge systems. We frequently find applications with 10:1 rates of return or higher.

In the past, computer-based applications have approached what we call *artificial intelligence* today. In many cases, these systems were designed for one-of-a-kind applications related to a critical process problem. Generally, they take multiple-process sensor inputs, analyze the data, make nonroutine decisions about process operation conditions, and adjust process target values. In most cases, these applications have been written in procedural computer languages.

In one example, a water-cooled process reactor for an exothermic chemical reaction is operated at maximum cooling to gain the greatest product-to-ingredient yield. Increased cooling promotes a fouling problem that reduces heat transfer from the process fluid to the cooling water and eventually causes a severe loss of cooling and subsequent shutdown (with the potential for a runaway reaction). A supervisory computer monitors the differential temperatures of the process fluid and the cooling water to calculate a heat-transfer coefficient. When the supervisory computer determines that heat transfer is inadequate, it ramps the process temperature upward until the fouling clears and then gradually ramps the temperature back down to approach optimum yield once again. This system definitely embodies process expertise, although it was not designed as an expert system.

In the case of this computer program, the sensor data exist and change fairly slowly with time; i.e., the heat-transfer coefficient will change over tens of minutes. Such long time constants are typical for many petrochemical processes. However, much smaller time constraints, on the order of tens of milliseconds, are involved in diagnosing electromechanical interlock systems. In one case, phantom shutdowns of a $3 million, 20,000-hp compressor result in downtime costing $15,000 per hour. Capturing and quickly analyzing data for one of 40 possible interlock conditions capable of shutting down the compressor are absolutely necessary. A high-speed event recorder has been developed to log data such as vibration, stator temperature, overvoltage or overcurrent conditions, and high process temperature or pressure every millisecond.

This data collection rate is required to obtain sufficient resolution since the dropout time for the interlock relays is about 20 ms. After an interlock event, experts determine the trip's cause. In this case, data analysis has not been reduced to an expert system, although such an operation is possible. The key to this application is having the available data with sufficient resolution to diagnose the problem. In this example, responding with any kind of corrective action during the tripping process is impossible; however, by aiding the postmortem analysis, the system reduces the mean time to repair, thereby increasing the compressor availability.

In terms of process dynamics, we find some extremely long time constants in chemical processes with large residence times; this means that the effects of a process disturbance will take a long time to propagate through the process. These time constants can be several hours, which means that the process response to adjustments made by one operator may not be fully developed until hours later or perhaps until the next operating shift has taken over. (The new operator may not be aware of the previous action.) In these cases, great expertise and patience are required to control the process. The long time constants and large inertial loads of these processes make operating them much like navigating a supertanker: Any need for corrective action must be anticipated, and patience is required to allow process response to develop. Because these are not natural human tendencies, automatic process control and expert systems can benefit the operation of these processes.

These examples emphasize a point regarding real-time process-control systems, including expert systems: Real time depends completely on the time constants of the process. A real-time system must collect and analyze data and issue a response within a time acceptable for solving a problem.

ES applications

The industry has explored many application areas: sensor validation, data reconciliation, process and equipment diagnosis, and model-based expert systems. Individual measurements generated by on-line process sensors are fundamental to on-line expert systems. These sensors range from basic physical measurement devices such as thermocouples to extremely complex devices such as on-stream process analyzers (complex chemical or electrical processes). The sensor's characteristic behavior reflects its design, specific installation, and process behavior. Many sensors are critical to process operation because they supply feedback and closed-loop control. In typical wet-chemical processes, about one-third of all process measurements serve as interlock sensors or are used in closed-loop control systems. These systems operate on the principle that the incoming measurement signal accurately reflects the process condition. Typically, these control systems recognize a sensor fault only for extreme conditions (open circuit, short circuit, and so on). The objective of using expert systems for sensor validation is to improve the measurement system's overall reliability. This may simply mean recognizing that the sensor is suspect and that an alternate measurement or control strategy should be instituted. A further objective is to improve the overall availability of the process measurement by providing troubleshooting assistance to the maintenance technician, thus reducing the mean time to repair. In general, systems that perform sensor validation can be used in multiple applications, accessions, generating more compelling economic incentives for their development.

Process engineers and plant operators develop experience in distinguishing normal from abnormal behavior of specific sensors. As an elementary example, consider the reactor temperature (Fig. 8.1). Due to the large thermal inertia of the process, this signal is not expected to make an abrupt shift in value but will exhibit smooth, highly damped behavior. Therefore, any sudden shifts indicate a faulty signal (probably an electronic failure).

Other common physical-process measurements are pressure and flow detection. These signals exhibit a certain level of high-frequency noise, as shown in Fig. 8.2. A change in the noise band such as an increase or a decrease in the noise level may indicate a faulty signal. A typical low noise level may indicate that the sensor has become detached from the process, e.g., by a closed block valve. While the average pressure

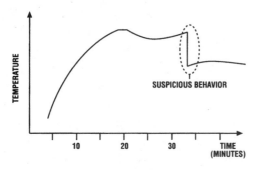

Figure 8.1 Reactor temperature trends.

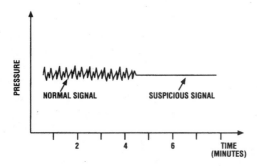

Figure 8.2 Pressure and flow detection.

remains unchanged, the noise level will drop to zero. An increase in noise may indicate instability in the measurement. Engineers and operators recognize the typical signal patterns on strip-chart recorders or equivalent cathode-ray tube displays. This process has been automated by developing algorithms to detect suspicious sensor behavior. With a short-term history of process data, these algorithms compute the rate of change, moving average and standard deviation, and other variables. These data validation techniques have been used by the author to provide a "watchdog" monitor of data interfaces to real-time expert systems so that any interruption of data flow is detected and appropriate personnel are notified automatically by e-mail.

Du Pont has an expert system that performs sensor validation on complex process analyzers. This system diagnoses mechanical and electronic failures in the analyzer, abnormal sample presentation to the analyzer, and adverse ambient conditions relative to the process or analyzer. The expert system is segmented into a monitoring component that continuously scans and processes on-line data and a rule-based component that analyzes a snapshot of information and manually entered data. The expert system monitors on-line data for suspicious behavior, including the signal stability of the measurement and reference signal and the characteristics of internal signals, such as the automatic gain control.

If the expert system determines that a fault has occurred, the ES alerts the operator. The maintenance technician can then activate the diagnostic expert system, which reads a snapshot of information from the on-line scanner, processes the data, and collects the additional information necessary to diagnose the problem from the technician. As in most other applications, human observation enhances on-line data. In most cases, a complete data set does not exist on line because some measurements or observations cannot be performed on-line cost-effectively.

In a well-instrumented chemical process, redundant process data exist because of the inherent physical interaction of the processes. Consider the process by which inflow, outflow, and tank level are measured (Fig. 8.3). These measurements are related by the mass-balance equation, which states that any difference between inflow and outflow results in a level change; the rate of level change is proportional to the difference in the two flows. Any of the three measured variables could be calculated from the other two by using the mass-balance equation; however, all three are usually measured. This creates redundant data, allowing cross-checks on all signals. Knowledge in the form of these governing equations is deep and provides additional information about the health of individual sensors and the process in general.

Drift in individual sensors may occur over a long period. Although it may not be detectable by sensor validation techniques, it can often be detected by data reconciliation techniques. Much work has been done in this area by using both traditional data reconciliation techniques (Tamhane and Mah, 1985) and ES methodology. In both approaches, noisy, imprecise measurements impede data reconciliation; however, sensor repeatability may be sufficient to allow data reconciliation even though sensor precision may be poor (Rowan, 1988). Relationships other than mass-balance relationships, such as energy-balance and reaction rate equations, can reconcile process data. In addition, data reconciliation techniques can be applied to process measurements and control-system outputs associated by feed-

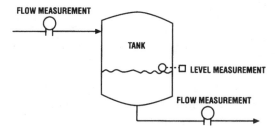

Figure 8.3 Tank-level measurement process.

back control. Since feedback controller outputs often control variables such as the pump speed or the automatic valve position, they provide a crude indication of process flow.

The reconciliation scheme can also include laboratory data. Since laboratory analysis is considered the ultimate proof that product properties meet specifications, laboratory data are of major importance. In addition, laboratory methods are sometimes required because techniques for on-line measurement of specific product composition may not be practical. In reconciling laboratory data with on-line process data, care must be taken to adjust the data in time. Because it may take several hours for a sample to be taken and processed in the laboratory and for the results to be returned, the laboratory data must be compared to the corresponding historical data taken on-line. Laboratory data can provide the final validation of on-line sensors and process operation.

Sensor validation and data reconciliation techniques allow process measurements to be validated wherever measurement methods may fail or drift from the necessary accuracy. If measurement data are considered highly reliable, these steps may not be necessary. In any case, once process data have been judged reliable, individual data values may be combined into patterns, providing higher information level. Sensors which have known failure or drift behavior can be monitored for these conditions. Monitoring of on-line viscometers is one example where these techniques have been applied.

Diagnostic systems have also been applied to malfunctions of the process itself. A number of applications in the petrochemical industry have been reported by Prasad and Davis (1992). Also Calandrais et al. (1990), have reported on the diagnosis of a large-scale boiler power plant. The author has been involved in applications such as diagnosing plugged vacuum jets, coating of in-line mixers, heat-exchanger fouling, control-valve failures, and other specialized applications such as diagnosing malfunctions in spinning machines, film casting and coating lines, and paper manufacturing problems.

In addition to diagnosing process malfunctions that affect the product quality, diagnosing supporting equipment, such as refrigeration machines, boilers, compressors, and instrumentation systems, is frequently desirable. The analyzer diagnostic system previously described is also an example of an equipment diagnostic application. Another example of this type of expert system is a diagnostic package for refrigeration equipment, which uses pressure and temperature data from both the process and refrigerant sides of the machine to detect degrading performance. Problems may occur in the compressor, condenser, evaporator, or purge unit and consist of abnormal conditions, such as compressor surging, loss of heat transfer, lubricating-oil problems, and bearing failure. The system is being prototyped in an off-line mode but will be developed into an on-line system. Both of these examples represent systems that can be applied in many similar (though not all identical) applications because the supporting equipment is common to many processes and plants.

Model-based expert systems involve deep knowledge about the process. Models are derived from first-principle relationships of physics and chemical engineering and from empirical models based on statistical regression of process data. Incorporating this type of deep knowledge into an expert system allows for a very compact, precise system design. This has been proved true in diagnosing electronic circuits and detecting chemical plant faults (Rowan, 1988). On-line models have been used for process control strategies relying on the model to make process measurements unattainable on-line with physical methods. Product properties or chemical components may be computed indirectly by using available sensors to supply data for the model.

A simple example uses a model to calculate the polymer viscosity from the pressure, temperature, and flow measurements on a transfer pipeline. The biotechnology industry applies models to determine cell growth in bioreactors from the measurements of bulk properties, such as oxygen feed, ammonia evolution in the off-gas, and biomass temperature. Du Pont has developed expert systems that interact with process models and use the model-generated results as input information to the inference engine. On-line dynamic models can reason about the projection of process variables into the future. Modern ES tools allow model parameters to be included as object attributes (in an object-oriented tool). Combining the power of object-oriented modeling with that of object-oriented expert systems can be very powerful, yet easy to understand and maintain.

Knowledge-base development

Much has been written about knowledge extraction and knowledge-base development. Du Pont's experience has not been unique in these areas. We have found the accuracy and validity of the resulting expert systems to correlate directly with the quality of the domain expert's knowledge and ability to communicate this knowledge. To apply ES technology demands the same understanding of the industrial process as required to apply conventional control strategy and modeling techniques. In many cases, knowledge extraction has contributed valuable information and produced new insights into the experts' reasoning. Therefore, performing initial problem analysis can be valuable even before the expert system is constructed. Du Pont has succeeded in staffing these projects by providing ES education to engineers experienced in process control. Using so-called knowledge engineers unfamiliar with this domain has proved impractical. In process-control applications, domain experience outweighs ES experience. Other companies have come to similar conclusions (Ricketts, 1988).

In many applications, the existing domain expertise is adequate. It may exist in many forms: heuristics and empirical understanding from operating experience, fundamental understanding of first principles, existing models, and so forth. In our applications, most knowledge comes from engineers who have practical experience with the process or technical specialists who have studied it from a fundamental point of view. Senior operators' experience has also been included in some applications.

For applications in which cause-and-effect relationships are vague, we have run statistically designed experiments or less formal step tests to obtain better knowledge of these relationships and to map cause and effect. Although these techniques are not novel ES technology, they clarify knowledge in another way.

Du Pont has applied various tools and knowledge representation techniques, including induction and rule-based, objective-oriented, and frame-based systems. We have found that object-oriented knowledge powerfully represents the physical entities (such as sensors, pumps, valves, and pipes) and conceptual entities (such as mass and energy balances). The object structure affords much more efficient development of large applications. Logic has generally been represented in the form of production rules and procedures.

Du Pont has employed straightforward inferencing techniques for on-line expert systems. These systems are usually data-driven; they use forward chaining but employ some backward chaining for gathering data with respect to specific goals. [See Harmon and King (1985) for descriptions of forward and backward chaining.] Using tools that allow the knowledge base to be partitioned into compact modules that can be activated at the appropriate time has been very advantageous. Our expert systems run in several modes. Some systems run in a continuously scanning mode, monitoring for certain events to occur. Other systems are executed by periodic scanning when fresh data are available, usually once per minute (but perhaps more often). Still other systems are activated by external events such as the input of laboratory data, while others are activated manually as needed. The inference engine must be able to continue processing real-time data while it seeks manually entered data; the system must not freeze under any conditions.

Several approaches to system validation have proved acceptable. For simple systems designed to detect process phenomena, some applications have been built simply and put on-line. The performance of these systems is monitored as the particular process condition recurs. In most cases, however, capturing data related to process phenomena is desirable so the system can be tested off-line. The sets provide case studies for alterations and refinements to the knowledge base. These data sets may be derived from archived plant data or captured during designed experiments. Validation of a system around very rare events, such as detection of catastrophic failure, requires process simulation as the only source of test data.

To validate the Falcon fault detection system, we used a benchmark data set of 11 sets of actual process data and 10 sets of simulated data (Rowan, 1988). Many interactions existed in this knowledge base, and subtle changes were thoroughly tested by using the benchmark data set. In general, we prefer testing the system in fast-forward mode (i.e., faster than real time) to speed up the validation process.

Human-machine interface

The ideal human-machine interface for plant operators would integrate directly with an existing control console. To date, this has been difficult because control systems and expert systems have not been offered by a single vendor. Many Du Pont process-control systems also include company-proprietary, host computer systems with additional consoles that display information generated by expert systems. Several plants use Digital Equipment Corp. (DEC) workstations (VAXstations) as ES-operator interfaces.*

Operators desire a very intuitive interface with basic functionality. Whereas system developers may function efficiently by using a graphic interface with multiple overlaying windows, operators prefer to interface with hard boundaries and simple pushbuttons to call up other information on the screen. Display areas on the screen include scrollable, time-tagged, text-alarm messages; areas that will call up trend recordings, enter comments, and indicate the value of critical process variables; and the facilities for activating these features. In addition, the engineers and production supervisors can call up an area of logged messages, including alarms and operator comments. In some instances, process graphics are also useful; however, these appear on other control consoles and may not be duplicated in the expert system.

In addition to sensor data, some process-diagnostic applications often require observation by a human operator. This applies less to

*DEC and VAXstation are trademarks of Digital Equipment Corporation.

highly automated wet-chemical processes and more to sparsely instrumented mechanical operations, such as paper manufacturing processes and film or sheet drying operations. In film or sheet processing applications, about 50 percent of the information required for a process-diagnostic system must be entered manually. Expert systems for these applications must have a well-designed operator interface. Applications in the utility (Osborne et al., 1985) and paper manufacturing industries (Myers et al., 1989) use manually entered data.

Since Du Pont regards the operator as the customer for these expert systems, we request assistance from operators when designing the human-machine interface for an application. Including operator suggestions in the design results in a more acceptable product and generates ownership by user contribution, which facilitates the technology transfer process.

Development tools

On-line, real-time system applications provide a genuine challenge for software designers building ES tools. Capabilities essential to these applications include data scanning over networks, temporal reasoning (collecting and analyzing time-varying data), calculation, logic solving in rule form, and other pattern-matching facilities. To handle time-varying data, the tool should have an internal historian for buffering data used to establish trends, rates of change, and other signal characteristics (such as the noise level). A library of common signal processing functions is also useful. Highly desirable characteristics include an object-oriented structure, allowing for multiple levels of classes, subclasses, and instances. Class (generic) rules are essential for efficiency in reasoning about common objects in the process; e.g., a single rule should be able to check all temperature sensors against a high limit.

Although text editors may be a plausible development environment for small applications, graphic editors are decidedly more efficient and desirable. The editor should make as many syntactic and semantic checks as possible and provide on-line assistance for developing the proper rule grammar. Validating capability using canned data files and run-time debugging facilities such as break points, watch points, and single-step mode should be included. Facilities for constructing an operator interface as previously described are necessary; this interface should allow operator data entry.

Because these applications are critical, the on-line system and its tool must include facilities for error handling when communication errors occur, data supply systems go down, or bad data are returned from the process. Because these events are inevitable, the tool and application must be designed to cope with them, adding yet another level of complexity to the on-line application.

Summary

Expert systems now play an important role in process industry planning, scheduling, and control (PSC). The most successful ES applications depend on proper integration of ES technology with other technologies. This integration is different at various levels of the PSC hierarchy, but almost always includes database integration, an appropriately designed human interface, and integration with traditional solution methodologies such as sensor-based process control, mathematical optimization, and simulation.

References

Calandrais, J., G. Stephanopoulos, and S. Nunokawa (1990): "DiAD-Kit/BOILER: On-Line Performance Monitoring and Diagnosis," *Chem. Eng. Prog.,* vol. 86, no. 1, pp. 60–68.

Casto, J. Craig, and John H. Slater (1990): "An Intelligent Graphics Solution for Production Scheduling," paper CC-90-131, National Petroleum Refiners Association Computer Conference, Seattle, WA, November.

Collins, Dwight E., and Thomas E. Baker (1989): "Using OR to Add Value in Manufacturing," *OR/MS Today,* December.

Davis, Randall, Howard Shrobe, Walter Hamscher, Karen Wieckert, Mark Shirley, and Steve Polit (1982): "Diagnosis Based on Description of Structure and Function," *Proceedings of the National Conference on Artificial Intelligence,* pp. 137–142.

Dubois, L., and P. O. Opdahl (1993): "Products and Systems for Scheduling," *Journal A,* vol. 33, no. 3, pp. 38–40.

Faccenda, Joseph F., and Thomas E. Baker (1990): "An Integrated AI/OR Approach to Blocked Operations Scheduling," paper CC-90-134, National Petroleum Refiners Association Computer Conference, Seattle, WA, November.

Harmon, P., and D. King (1985): *Expert Systems: Artificial Intelligence in Business,* Wiley, New York.

Kusiak, Andrew, and Mingyuan Chen (1988): "Expert Systems for Planning and Scheduling Manufacturing Systems," *Eur. J. Oper. Res.,* vol. 34, pp. 113–130.

Laffey, Thomas J., Preston A. Cox, James L. Schmidt, Simon M. Kao, and Jackson Y. Read (1988): "Real-Time Knowledge-Base Systems," *Expert Sys. Mag.,* Spring, pp. 27–45.

Martin, John (1992): "Expert Systems Solve a Scheduling Problem for Carpenter Technology," *APICS,* November.

Myers, Douglas R., James F. Davis, and Charles E. Hurley (1989): "Application of Artificial Intelligence to Malfunction Diagnosis of Sequential Operations which Involve Programmable Logic Controllers," abstract 37B, Extended Abstracts of American Institute of Chemical Engineers Annual Meeting, Houston, April.

Osborne, Robert L., Avelino J. Gonzalez, J. C. Bellows, and J. D. Chess (1985): "On-Line Diagnosis of Instrumentation through Artificial Intelligence," paper 85-0985, *Proceedings of the Instrument Society of America Meeting,* Houston, TX, October.

Prasad, P. R., and J. R. Davis (1992): "Framework for Implementing On-Line Advisory Systems in Continuous Process Operations," *Chem. Eng. Sci.,* vol. 47, pp. 3713–3720.

Ricketts, Grant V. (1988): "How to Do More in Less Time," *AI Expert,* January, pp. 46–52.

Rowan, Duncan A. (1988): "Applying On-Line Expert Systems: Technical Issues and Business Concerns," *Making Change Work* (Chemical Manufacturers Association Sixth Process Control Users Forum), New Orleans, LA, April.

Tamhane, Ajit C., and Richard S. H. Mah (1985): "Data Reconciliation and Gross Error Detection in Chemical Process Networks," *Technometrics*, vol. 27, no. 4, November, pp. 409–422.

Whitworth, Mark (1993): "An Approach to the Development of Reactive Scheduling Systems," paper 93-302, Instrument Society of America Conference.

9

Detailed Process Modeling

C. Edward Bodington
Consultant

Introduction

A process model today is a mathematical representation of a process available as a computer program or as a set of equations written into a spreadsheet on a personal computer (PC). In this chapter we discuss how to go about developing the computer program or the equations to put into the spreadsheet. We cover why models are so important, the tradeoffs in the buy/build decision, the gathering of data for developing a model, and some considerations about which techniques to use for model development. Finally, we describe some uses for models and give two examples of ways to approach simple and complex model development.

The Central Purpose of Models

A process model is a mathematical structure that responds to its inputs in the same way as the real process responds. The central purpose of a model is to predict the behavior of a process under new, proposed, or experimental conditions. Models are used in design when the process plant itself does not exist. Process engineering or modification studies are also an important use that has a long history. Usage for planning, process control, and optimization also goes back a long way, long before anything more sophisticated than a slide rule was available.

The various models used in engineering or planning or control developed along different lines because they were used by different groups for different purposes. Recently the desire to integrate planning, engineering, and control uses has brought about a joining together of the models, so that in many cases the same model and the same modeling system are used for all three functions. It is also common for the planning model to be a simplification of the more complex model used for control or design. The model used in scheduling may be simpler yet and may consist of just a yield structure predicted by the more complex model.

The term *mathematical model* was not used extensively until computers were being used in its development and use. The earliest models were a computerization of the charts, equations, and procedures that were formerly done by hand. Modeling skills grew extensively in the 1950s. By 1955 books and articles were available on solving problems with the technique of *linear programming* (LP) (Symonds, 1955; Garvin et al., 1957), all of which involved modeling. The earliest use of model-based on-line process optimization was reported in 1961 (Griffith and Stewart, 1961). Since that time, the literature on the use of models has become voluminous. The process model is now ubiquitous. It is hard to imagine a study, plan, or forecast made without some kind of model involved.

The range of complexity, while increasing continually as techniques become more sophisticated, continues to be rooted in the simple yield structure. The volume or weight percent of each product from a process remains the simplest model, but the high end is continuing to expand in the direction of process simulation systems coupled with reaction models as needed. The range of complexity is enormous.

The Continuum of Complexity

The complexity of models forms a continuum, starting with the basic yield structure. The yield of products for a given feed and mode of operation was used before computers were invented, and continues to the present. The extensive prior use of yield structures made for an easy transition to the use of these very basic models within linear programming systems. Some processes, like crude units, are still probably best modeled within linear programs in this way. Scheduling systems also tend to use just yield structure models, since the main concern of scheduling for the process industries is inventory management, not the details of process operation.

The next level in complexity is the *base-delta model,* which has become very popular in LP planning systems. The base part of the model is the basic yield structure model. The delta part of the model is formed by generating the first derivative of the yields with respect to some feed characteristic or operating condition. For example, Fig. 9.1

	BASE	SEVERITY DELTA	NAPHTHENES DELTA
SEVERITY	850	1	
NAPHTHENES	17		1
REFORMATE	87	− 0.1	0.4
GASES	12	0.1	− 0.4
HYDROGEN	1		
OCTANE	86	0.1	0.2

Figure 9.1   Example of reformer base-delta model.

depicts a reformer model using deltas for reformate octane number and a feed property. The predictions from such a model can be very good if the base is current with actual operation. In developing and updating these models, use is commonly made of a more complex model, such as that used in design studies. An important consideration in developing base-delta models is that the base must be weight-balanced and the deltas must not disturb the balance, when invoked.

It is also possible to develop the delta columns by experimentation on the process or by analyzing the results of special test runs. This procedure was common before more sophisticated models were available.

Combinations of yield structure and base-delta models are sometimes used when the linear approximation of the delta is not accurate enough. For example, a group of base points can be used to model the nonlinear yield-octane relationship for a reformer. These columns are then coupled with a delta for a feed property relationship.

The availability of computers led to an upsurge in statistical analysis and the development of empirical models based on experimental design. These models use the main effects of variables, the cross products between variables, and can be expanded to include quadratic effects. A *main effect* is the effect of a variable by itself, independent of all other variables. A typical model equation would be as shown in Fig. 9.2. By the early 1960s, this modeling technique had established

$$Y = A*X(1) + B*X(2) + \dots + C*X(1)*X(2) + \dots$$

Where:

Y is the dependent variable
$X(1), \dots$ are the independent variables
$A, B, C \dots$ are the unknown coefficients

Figure 9.2   Model equation basis for designed experiments.

the practice of designing experiments to fit a predefined model form. The purpose of the design is to determine the coefficients in the equations with highest precision and to avoid confounding some effects with others. Many users of these techniques found that the experiment design helped in obtaining a high-quality database even if some other equation form was fit to the data. *High quality* in reference to a database means that the data cover the experimental space well. That is, the experimental variables are moved in a pattern that avoids confusing the effect of one variable with that of another (which is known as *confounding*).

A patent (Bodington, 1966) obtained by the author was a direct result of running a designed set of experiments on a dewaxing process, developing a model, and then using the model in an off-line process optimization. The indications of the optimization were tried in the laboratory and were found to work. The process itself was subsequently changed, and an improvement in throughput of about 10 percent was achieved. The literature abounds with other examples of successful computer analysis of empirical models. Despite successes, the empirical model was found to be unreliable for extrapolation to regions not covered by the database. Sometimes an extrapolation would be correct, at other times it would not be. Extrapolation beyond the database is always risky, no matter how the model structure is obtained. However, model forms based on more theoretical grounds are much more reliable.

Theoretic-based models have consequently supplanted the pure empirical model, mainly because they are better under extrapolation. Before we describe theoretic-based models, two other techniques of lower complexity need to be covered: the *response surface* models and the use of *neural network* technology. Response surface models (Bodington, 1987) are an old concept rediscovered and now seeing some use for refinery planning models. In a response surface model, the database that would be used for development of a process model is used directly, without any actual attempt at modeling (see Fig. 9.3). The data points themselves represent a response surface for the process. In the implementation described by Bodington, a small linear program is used to pick out and then interpolate from the nearest neighbors to the desired set of operating conditions. Since no model is actually involved, the response surface model does not extrapolate reliably. In some cases, the use procedure will not allow any extrapolation.

One very interesting property of these models is that the inputs required for a given output are just as easy to determine as the usual outputs for a given set of inputs. Any subset of the variables can be taken as the inputs, and the remaining values are determined. Each

	1	2	3	4	5
SEVERITY	800	850	900	800	850
NAPHTHENES	15	15	15	20	20
REFORMATE	90	86	80	92	88
GASES	9	13	19	7	11
HYDROGEN	1	1	1	1	1
OCTANE	80	85	90	81	86

Figure 9.3   Example of a response surface model.

data point in the database represents a valid way of operating the process, so the only assumption being made is that a linear interpolation is correct. More complex nonlinear interpolations are also possible. Each data point must be accurate to avoid noise in the interpolations. Base-delta models can be calculated directly from the database, but for this use it is even more important to minimize error in the database. One can readily see that the values for the delta columns would be greatly affected by noise or errors creating bumpiness in the response surface.

The latest entrant in modeling technolgy is the use of neural networks. This technology comes from the field of *artificial intelligence* (AI) and attempts to mirror the learning and processing characteristics, albeit in a very limited way, of the human brain. These models, like the response surface type, do not depend on knowledge of the underlying process technology. They also tend to not extrapolate reliably, but some models extrapolate very well (Chitra, 1993). In addition to not needing any process technology input, these models appear to be able to make predictions that are relatively insensitive to noise in the input. The model will simply reproduce the error characteristics of the database. Reasonable predictions can sometimes be obtained even if an item of input is missing. It is possible to determine derivatives of result variables with respect to inputs directly, without having to resort to repeated executions of the model. This would save time in generating or updating base-delta models for LP use.

In neural network model development, the database is divided into a training portion, on which the model is actually developed, and a comparison set, typically about 15 percent of the database, used to test the accuracy of the model predictions. This is a good procedure to use in other techniques of model development as well.

However attractive the use of raw, noisy data may be, it is good to remember that neural network technology has not repealed the law "garbage in equals garbage out." The more accurate the database, the better the resulting model. Chitra (1993) describes some very successful uses of neural network models in solving process engineering problems and gives an excellent reading list for anyone wishing to use the technology.

The models based on theoretic and fundamental principles form their own continuum from single equations representing chemical reactions to the very complex process simulation systems now available that achieve remarkable precision for most processes. A typical equation-based process simulation may contain upward of 25,000 equations. These systems are detailed to the point of considering pumps, compressors, heat exchangers, flash drums, distillation columns, and reactors. For reactors, the modeling may require empirical or quasi-theoretical equations if the reaction is not well understood. Even very large models are being used in on-line, real-time process optimizations, involving as many as 60,000 equations. These models represent the high end of complexity. However, the complexity exists because they are so detailed, not because they are necessarily difficult to develop or use.

Many applications of process simulators, process optimizations, and model predictive control need detailed models of the process reactions. Since many of the complex petroleum and petrochemical reaction mechanisms are not well understood, reaction models are not readily available within commercial process simulation systems. Even with the most sophisticated simulation system available, it may be necessary for the user to provide a detailed process reaction model.

The Model Development Decision

Build or buy? That is the question. The three most important considerations in making the buy/build decision are the database, the database, and the database. The fourth consideration is whether it is possible to buy a model that will satisfy your requirements. If a suitable model exists on the market and you lack a database of good experimental data for the process, you should buy the model.

Unless historical operating data can be used, the development of a good database is very expensive and time-consuming. For empirical models, the number of data points must be large, usually in the hundreds, and the range of variable values must be extensive. The more theoretically based the model equations, the fewer data points will be required. You must also determine the quality of the database (by the procedure that is described later), to ascertain that measurements of variables are reasonably independent of one another.

It is rare that historical process operating data will be adequate for model development, because the values of some variables or feed characterizations are not measured routinely, the process operates over a very narrow range of conditions, and several variables are usually confounded with each other. Given these limitations, a possible exception is the training of a neural network for dynamic model control or for some limited process troubleshooting.

If you must experimentally acquire a database, it could cost several thousand dollars for each data point. Historical pilot plant data may not be adequate, particularly if the data were taken without model development in mind. Consequently, it is very important to realistically assess the requirements of model use and then the adequacy of the database relative to those requirements. Do not assume that the data on hand are adequate. Narrow-focus models designed to predict the effect of changes in only a few variables are usually much easier and faster to develop than broad-focus models designed to predict the effect of extensive process modifications. Historical data from the process or pilot plant might be adequate for a narrow-focus model. Models designed to solve a specific process problem can be developed, used, and then discarded. This can all be done at low cost by using empirical equation forms or neural network technology. In these cases, building the model in-house is a clear choice.

Process models have a maximum longevity of about 10 years. The need to update the model as the process itself changes must be anticipated. Every time some new process modification is invented and then implemented, the model must be revised. For example, the inventions of high-temperature regeneration and complete regenerator combustion required modification of fluid catalytic cracking models. If the model is developed internally, then you must maintain a staff of experts who can modify the model when needed. If a model is purchased, you must count on future purchases of updates.

Processes themselves seldom run for over 10 years without modification to improve their efficiency, yields, or quality. A new type of catalyst can completely change the characteristics of a process. Keeping ahead of these developments with an internal modeling group is possible, but expensive. As above, an expert staff must be maintained who can update the model in a timely fashion. Many suppliers, of catalyst, e.g., have a model available that was used in their own development of new products. It is sometimes possible to license use of this model along with use of the catalyst. This is usually a desirable alternative to internal development.

The buy/build decision comes down to one of lowest cost, given not only the direct costs affected by the considerations described above, but also the benefits to be achieved by using the model to improve performance. If a suitable model can be purchased, it will almost always be more profitable to purchase it than to embark on a development project.

A model development project will be unavoidable if no commercial model exists or if the ones available do not satisfy your requirements. However, in this decision it is important that your requirements be in terms of model functions, not features. If you decide to buy, buy the best technology regardless of the ease of use or other "packaging." Use features can always be added later at low cost. This is easy stuff that surrounds the technology. No amount of fancy features will make poor technology shine.

The Model Form Decision

The more fundamental theory that can be embodied in the model, the better the model will be. The fit to the data and accuracy of predictions under both interpolation and extrapolation will be improved. For example, if the process is a chemical reaction, the effect of temperature on rate is better represented by the Arrhenius form (Fig. 9.4) than by any other functional form. The theoretically correct shape of a function will always fit better under the wide ranges of actual use than any other form. Most really useful model equations are a combination of theory, as far as possible, and empiricism. An excellent example is the equation published by Wollaston et al. (1975) for predicting conversion in a fluid catalytic cracking process (Fig. 9.5). Conversion is the percentage of products boiling below some defined temperature. None of the feed boils below this chosen temperature, so conversion with no reaction is zero. The conversion function is cv/(100 − cv). This function is typical for completion percentage or percentage of reaction modeling. This conversion function is set equal to the product of several functions for catalyst activity, feed properties, temperature, space velocity, and catalyst/oil ratio.

$$\text{RATE} = K^* \text{EXP}(- E/RT)$$

Where:

K = rate constant
E = reaction activation energy
R = gas constant
T = temperature
EXP signifies e raised to the following power

Figure 9.4 Reaction rate dependence on temperature.

$X/(1 - X) = f(A,Z)*(C/O)^N*(WHSV)^{N-1}*\exp(E/RT)$

Where:

X = volume fraction conversion
$f(A,Z)$ = function of catalyst activity and feed properties
C/O = cat-oil ratio
$WHSV$ = weight hourly space velocity
E = cracking activation energy
R = gas constant
T = temperature

Figure 9.5   Catalytic cracking conversion model equation.

Activity is conversion under some standardized conditions of a specific feedstock. The equation is therefore attempting to adjust the standard activity to the actual feed and operating conditions. The activity to be used here in this function is not the measured standard activity, but the activity estimated to be effective in the catalyst coming from the regenerator. The activity is a function of the catalyst makeup rate, the carbon level on regenerated catalyst, and an activity loss rate on reused catalyst. This function is therefore a mixture of theory and empiricism.

As in this case, the feed property correction term is likely to be empirical. The temperature term is theoretically correct. The space velocity and catalyst/oil ratio functions are empirical but reasonable and are based on the observation that many yields of products plot as smooth curves when plotted against these parameters.

If the parameter N and the activation energy E are known (values are given in the paper), then a linear multiple regression program can be used to determine the activity and feed property coefficients. This is a desirable result, since it simplifies the mathematical analysis. However, nonlinear regression technology is robust and easy to use, so a limitation to equations linear in the coefficients is not at all necessary. Fundamentally nonlinear relationships should not be approximated just to fit a linear analysis technique.

A development reported by Powell (1989) is a very good example of the kinetic model. By *kinetic* is meant that the reactions themselves are modeled in some detail by dividing the feedstock into numerous pseudocomponents whose typical reaction properties are taken to be known from specific experiments. The reactors are then modeled by calculating the reaction progress over small slices from inlet to outlet. In this hydrocracking example, a reactor is divided into 30 slices; and reactions for cracking, desulfurization, denitrification, aromatic and olefin saturation, and naphthene ring opening are considered. In this particular development, a detailed analysis of the feed is not used to partition the feed into pseudocomponents. Rather, an analysis based on bulk properties (such as gravity, distillation, refractive index, bromine number, sulfur, and nitrogen) is used, and then correlations are used to perform the partitioning. This is a common approach that avoids a very complex feed characterization. Another important aspect is that using bulk properties makes it easier to relate the feed to properties typically available from other models that represent feed supply processes. The distillation is, of course, not a bulk property and contains information on the distribution of boiling points of compounds in the feed.

Fundamental basis aside, another major consideration to examine to help set the model form is how the model is to be used. The purpose of the model should be clearly in mind before you decide on the model form. If the use is specific to a particular process unit or known to be short-term, perhaps a response surface or neural network model would be the best choice. These techniques bypass the model form question entirely. If the purpose is predictive control or optimization of several units, then care with formulation and a broader-based technique are justified. The data that will be available during use also will limit model form and complexity. Feed quality characterization is probably the most severe limitation, especially with high-boiling-point and almost opaque stocks that do not lend themselves to continuous analyzers. This limitation will determine whether the model can ever be used on-line. Bear in mind that the number of truly independent bulk feed properties in petroleum or petrochemical-based stocks is actually small—six or seven at the most. Most on-line model applications can be handled with two or three feed properties measured and the rest inferred, if necessary.

Almost all model use involves either analytic or numerical derivatives. Most optimization techniques, predictive control applications, planning model development, and engineering uses depend on derivatives and predicted changes from one point to another (Bodington, 1989). Consequently, the model must either be differentiable or deliver stable, consistent numerical derivatives.

An Approximate Method for Checking Database Quality

Before an existing database is used, it is important to test its quality. The variables to be used in the model are supposed to be independent of each other. A high-quality database will show a high degree of independence in the variable values. A low-quality database will show values for several variables that tend to move together, so that their values are not independent of each other.

$Y = A*X(1) + B*X(2) + C*X(3) + \dots$

Where:

Y = any dependent variable
$X(1), X(2), \dots$ = independent variables
$A, B, C, \dots$ = coefficients

Figure 9.6   Linear regression equation.

The concept of database quality is admittedly rather subjective. However, an approximate quantitative measure can be obtained by using the data in a linear regression while just looking for main effects. The equation form is the simplest possible (Fig. 9.6). The purpose of the regression is to examine the covariance matrix. The off-diagonal elements of this matrix give the correlation coefficients between the row and column variables (the diagonal elements all equal 1.0, indicating that a variable is perfectly correlated with itself). Any off-diagonal elements greater than about 0.7 should be suspect. Any values of 0.9 or above indicate a strong correlation, which means that the variables in question are not independent at all. In such a case, both variables should not be used in the model development. If both variables are known to be important, then additional data points will have to be obtained, specifically designed to separate the effects of the two variables.

Bear in mind that the variables used in this quality determination are not necessarily just single variables. They can also be combinations of variables known to be important to the process. For example, one could use the catalyst/oil ratio for a catalytic cracking process.

Assembling a Database

Assembling a database for a model development is the most important part of the project. If new data points have to be obtained, assembling the database may also be the most expensive part of the modeling project. It makes economic sense to try to reuse existing data as much as possible. It is also desirable to try to generate a single database with complete data points, each one having values for all the variables to be considered. When data from several sources are combined in a database, it is important to identify the source of each data point in the database.

The typical problems with attempts to combine existing databases are that the values of variables now needed are missing and the analytical techniques were different from those now in use.

Different procedures for obtaining the data mean that every database collected at a given point in time is biased with respect to others. This bias must be accounted for by adding bias variables to the database and to the model equations. A similar bias exists between pilot plant and commercial data. Reproducibility of analytical measurements is more important to the model than absolute accuracy is. It is also important to use the same analysis technique as will be used when the model is in actual use. Use of one procedure for development and another in practice will introduce an unknown bias into the predictions. Sooner or later, each data point will have to be checked for validity. It is best to build in a data reconciliation procedure as part of the mechanism for adding data points to the database. For example, the weight-balance closure, component-balance closures, and the like should be included directly as database elements.

It is common for data from a real operating process to show high correlations between many of the operating variables. Stable operation tends to require synchronized movements of set points, and the response to a change in feed quality may always be the same. For example, assume a reformer that is at or very near maximum heat input. Suppose the feed quality drops so that it is harder to reform. Under these circumstances, the feed rate will have to be reduced whenever the feed quality drops, to maintain the same reformate quality. This confounds feed rate with feed quality, so that the separate effects are impossible to determine. In the quality test described earlier, the correlation between the two would be very high. To separate the effects, runs would be required with feed rate held constant for varying feed quality, and vice versa.

Historical data from an operating unit may also be subject to time bias since the data are available in time sequence and cannot be random. The range of variables is usually narrow, and the data may represent not steady-state but dynamic conditions. In addition, some important variable may not be measured, or its importance may not be understood. If this "hidden" variable changes after model development is concluded, the model will go astray no matter what technique of model development is used.

Historical data are, of course, entirely satisfactory for some models, such as for dynamic response. In this case, time-sequenced data are exactly what is wanted. Despite the narrow range and variable confounding, useful models can be developed for particular units. However, unaccounted changes in "hidden" variables can cause gross prediction errors, and it is unlikely that the model can be applied to another unit.

Required Number of Data Points

How many data points are really needed depends very much on the extent of knowledge represented by the equation form and the inherent accuracy of the data points themselves. For example, if the equation is theoretically based on known chemical or engineering fundamentals and the data are perfect, then the number of data points needed is equal to the number of unknown coefficients in the model equation. However, since all data will contain some measurement error, some experiments need to be repeated to measure the basic experimental error in the results. In addition, some runs need to be made to form a trial set, upon which to try out generated models. A practical minimum is therefore approximately double the number of coefficients in the model. Again, this assumes that you know what the equation form should be.

The practice of changing one variable at a time from a base operation leads to the absolute minimum number of data points, but assumes that only main effects of variables are important and that there are no interactions or level effects between variables. This kind of experimentation is suitable only for very simple systems, such as determining dynamic response in a noninteracting system. If variables interact, the one-at-a-time approach will prove to be misleading. More data points and a more complex model concept will be required.

Another estimate of the number of experiments required can be made from experimental design considerations. These estimates depend upon the number of independent variables rather than the number of coefficients in the model. For what is called a *complete two-level factorial design,* the number of data points required will be 2 raised to a power equal to the number of independent variables to be considered. Thus, for two variables, four experiments are the minimum required. For three variables, eight experiments are required.

Clearly, the number of experiments needed rises very rapidly as the number of independent variables increases. This rapid growth is due to the equation form assumed by the experimental design. The equation is assumed to contain all main effects, all two-variable cross products, all three-variable cross products, etc., up to a final term that multiplies all variables together. Our experience is that successful, useful equations can be obtained with only a small subset of the complete factorial, so that many fewer data points are actually required. Practical experiment designs usually use what is called a *fractional factorial,* typically one-half, one-quarter, or one-eighth of the full factorial. The equation is kept to that shown in Fig. 9.2. Only main effects and two-factor cross products are considered. For example, in the case of 8 variables, only 64 (instead of 256) experiments are required. If some of the two-factor interactions are known to be unnecessary, the number of data points may be further reduced. The classic text by Box et al. (1978) is the best source of information on the design of fractional factorial designs. By using their procedures, the number of data points can be held to a reasonable amount. However, note that the above text recommends that all experiments be duplicated to obtain an accurate measure of the error in the dependent variables. Using a designed set of experiments presupposes that algebraic or regression techniques will be employed to calculate the model coefficients. If response surface or neural network techniques are to be used, then several hundred data points are usually required. The more data points, the better. For this reason, these techniques are usually used with historical data collected from the actual operating unit. As Chitra (1993) points out, neural network models can be superior to regression models when historical data are used.

Model Validation Data

In addition to the minimum number of data points needed for model development, it is necessary to obtain several more data points just for model validation. Nothing stresses a model more than the attempted prediction of a data point which was not used in the model development. It is common to add about 15 percent more data points than the minimum.

Sequential Experimentation

The technique of *sequential experimentation* couples model determination with experimentation. As soon as a few more experiments have been made than a minimum equal to the number of coefficients, the coefficient or model determinations can begin. As more and more data points are added, the values of the coefficients or the character of the model will become more and more stable. The model can be used to predict the value of the next data point before it is added to the database. This technique is really appropriate only when the form of the model equation is well known.

Experiment Design: Which Experiments to Run?

Tightly coupled with the question of how many experiments are needed is the question of exactly which experiments should be run. The independent variables can be set to values over a continuum. Without some kind of plan, a large number of random experiments could be made without obtaining a quality database by the measure described above. The quality may be maximized and the cost of assembling a database minimized by using statistical principles to design the experiments in advance. The purpose of experiment design is to measure the effects of the variables with maximum efficiency. The benefits of the technology have been proved over and over. The database developer needs to become conversant with the technology. The cost of learning how to design the experiments or of obtaining the advice of a statistical consultant will be returned many times over. As described by Hunter (1966), it is easily possible to run major test runs on operating units without causing trouble in operation. However, each one has to count and cannot be a time waster.

A formal discussion of the technology of experiment design is beyond the scope of this chapter. However, numerous books and articles are available on the subject; e.g., see the classic Box et al. (1978), Box and Draper (1987), or Hunter (1966). Many statistical consulting firms also give classes in the subject.

The basic idea of experiment design is to go through the following steps:

1. Select the independent variables that will be used for the model. These include some variables that would in some cases be called *parameters,* in that they are not actually under direct arbitrary control. Items such as feed qualities, e.g., octane or aromatics content, are parameters rather than true independent variables. However, we still want to determine the effect of these parameters independent of other variables.

2. Select possible upper and lower values for each variable above that can be easily achieved in the experimental runs.

3. Define the model equation that will be fit to the data.

4. Design the experiments. Each run is defined by, e.g., a series of 1s and 0s, indicating the level of each variable in the test run. A 1 means that the variable is at its high level; a 0, at its low level. Thus in an experiment labeled 1111, all four variables are at their high levels. Where effects are known to be nonlinear, four levels may be chosen rather than two. In this case an experiment could be defined, e.g., as 20_1. The 2 signifies the top level and _ the lowest, with 1 and 0 signifying the intermediate upper and lower levels.

In learning how to actually do the experiment design, the reader will find that much of the literature and many of the techniques of statistics are aimed at discovering or proving relationships between variables where some kind of causality is suspected, but is not known to be true in advance from fundamental principles, e.g., the relationship between smoking and lung cancer. These kinds of problems are very different from that of this chapter where we want to determine the coefficients in a predefined model. Many books on statistical analysis do not even mention our model-fitting situation. However, the references given at the end of this chapter are pertinent and will form a good starting point.

On operating units it is common to use one-at-a-time changes in the variables from a base point of operation. This kind of experimentation is fine for most dynamic response models and for cases in which the experiments will be repeated periodically to update the measured responses. The problems with the one-at-a-time procedure are that it gives (1) no information on interactions between variables (in other words, no information on the effect of the levels of other variables) and (2) no averaging of the main effect of a variable as other variables are changed. The two-level designs outlined above do give all this kind of information, albeit at a cost of a greater number of experiments.

Developing the Model

Once a database has been assembled and checked for quality as described above, we are ready to determine the coefficients in the model equation, use the database directly as a response surface, or use the database to train a neural network.

Use of Regression

The first topic to be discussed is the use of a linear or nonlinear regression computer program. Not only are these programs inexpensive, but also they give numerous quality indicators about the resulting correlation equation.

The most useful indicators are the values of t, also named the t *ratio,* and the correlation coefficient R. Almost all regression programs use this terminology. The t values are the coefficients divided by an estimate of the standard error of each coefficient. Thus, values around 2 or 3 indicate that the coefficient is well determined and is important to the equation. Values around 1 or less indicate that the coefficient is not very important and could be zero. That is, the term multiplied by the coefficient is not important to the equation.

The correlation coefficent R is related to the overall fit of the equation to the data. Specifically, the square of the R value is equal to the fraction of the variance of the dependent variable that is explained by the equation. Realistically, R should be over 0.95 before an equation is considered acceptable. At this level only about 10 percent of the variance is unexplained by the equation. However, this residual variance cannot be lower than the variance of the measurement of the dependent variable, which would set a maximum to the value of R.

In a few remarkable cases, one run is made and the answers are obtained to complete the project. However, most of the time the standard error of prediction will not be low enough to really be satisfactory in our intended use. It is also possible that the equation we are trying to fit has alternate forms or terms in it. The job is really to find the best form or to select the best combination of possible terms in the equation. One of the usual options is to use a stepwise linear regression program so that we obtain the best single-term model, the best two-term model, and so forth up to a point where adding more terms does not improve the correlation. In doing this work, we need to pay attention to the following considerations:

Determine the standard deviation of the dependent variable you are trying to predict by using the duplicate experiments in the database. The standard error of the prediction cannot be lower than this value.

Use graphs of the prediction errors (actual value − predicted value, also known as a *residual*) versus several variables or equation terms to discover any regularity or obvious nonrandom behavior. Many regression systems produce these residual graphs automatically. The graphs will lead you to add terms that will improve the predictions.

Try predictions on the reserved trial set of data that was not used in the regressions. If the prediction error on the reserved set differs markedly from that for the correlation itself, then the model equation is probably faulty. Graph the residuals for this set of data against the model variables as above.

It is possible that a stepwise regression will produce a correlation that is quite good (has a high value for R) but is nonsensical. The program uses a set of variables or a combination of variables that cannot be correct or is very unlikely, based on knowledge of the process. This behavior is more likely when data are used from experiments that were not designed with this model development in mind. The real solution is to obtain more data points, designed this time to emphasize the effect of variables or terms that we know, from fundamentals, must be important in the model. If it is not possible to obtain more data, we have little choice but to fix the equation structure to what we know is correct and no longer use a stepwise approach. However, this situation strongly points out that the database is not very good, since it does not produce an acceptable regression equation using terms that are known to be necessary. Obtaining an acceptable model from such a database is unlikely.

Outliers are data points that are not predicted within some multiple of the standard error of prediction. Using 3 times the standard error is common, but some workers use 2 times. Outliers are sometimes simply eliminated from consideration and removed from the database, and the regressions are repeated. The justification is that such a large error is not really possible, so there must be something wrong with the data point. This is not necessarily the case. It is preferable to rerun the data point if nothing can be found wrong with the experiment. We must always ask, Is it the data point or the equation that is wrong?

Use of Neural Network Modeling

With this modeling approach, no explicit equation form needs to be formulated. The database itself is relied on to contain all the information needed, without assistance from an equation structure based on fundamental principles. However, the input data used for training are not necessarily just raw data values from the database. It is becoming more common to use functions of the data that are more appropriately related to the desired prediction result. For example, the Arrhenius temperature function (Fig. 9.4) can be used instead of temperature alone in the model of a chemical reaction. Here again, the more fundamental theory that can be exercised in developing terms for the model, the more robust the final model will be.

Some statistical techniques are being used to help generate appropriate combinations of variables to use in the training. *Principal-components analysis* or *factor analysis* and *canonical correlation analysis* (Chakravarty, 1993) are some of the techniques currently in use. Books by Hair et al. (1987) and Green and Caroll (1976) are good references on these topics. Topologically, these techniques try to shift the origin of the data and then change the angle of the coordinates to coincide with a ridge or other feature of the response surface. The purpose of these techniques is to reduce the number of variables that must be considered by developing a smaller set of independent data combinations, called the *factors,* that represent the database. The data combinations or factors are then used in the neural network training rather than the larger number of original data values.

If the training of a neural network model is viewed as a special way of doing nonlinear regression, then a proper attitude toward the effort will be engendered. Using a database and data combinations developed with equivalent care will result in a much higher-quality model compared to that resulting from a haphazardly assembled database.

One of the attractions of the neural network approach is its seeming ability to tolerate noise in the data and even missing data values when it is used for prediction.

A very lucid explanation of neural networks is given by Zupan and Gasteiger (1993). Since the technology arose from the field of artificial intelligence (AI) rather than via statistics, there is a completely different set of terms and jargon associated with the procedures. For example, the network structure is known as the *architecture*. The desired output values are known as *targets*. The data points are called *objects*. Performing a calculation through the network for one data point is known as *propagating an object*. Once the terms are understood, the technology is actually not all that difficult or esoteric and should find an increasing audience among model developers.

Use of Response Surface Modeling

In response surface modeling, the database itself is the model. No explicit equation structure is used. Since each data point represents a valid way to operate the process, only noise or error in the data points limits the prediction accuracy. For intermediate operating points, it is usually assumed that a linear interpolation can be used. Figure 9.7 shows the interpolation procedure graphically. From the figure, it is easy to see that errors in the data points will cause the same error to be in the predictions. Using this approach to obtain derivatives for

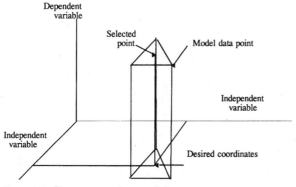

Figure 9.7 Response surface model.

the effects of variables would not be very accurate unless the database were essentially noiseless, with data errors smoothed out.

One way to use response surface models for predictions is to use a small linear program to pick out the nearest neighbors in the database closest to a desired point. This is equivalent to using the linear program to do the interpolation shown in Fig. 9.7. The procedure, suggested by T. E. Baker and L. S. Lasdon about 1985, is described in Bodington (1987). Also see Box and Draper (1987).

Tuning Process Models

Only the uninitiated think that the tuning of a process model by adjusting constants in the model to make it fit reality is somehow dishonest and an admission that the model is no good. In fact, even the best of models will need tuning to account for two sources of error:

- Prediction error of the model itself, however small

- Analytical and measurement error in tuning data

Disagreement between theory and practice, prediction and actual, forecast and reality is a fact of life. Many techniques have been developed at increasing levels of sophistication to improve accuracy. For example, chemical equilibrium, vapor-liquid equilibrium, and thermodynamic parameter calculations have achieved a remarkable level of prediction accuracy for many chemical and petroleum systems. Unfortunately, many other needed predictions are in areas where theory, correlations, and background are not so accurate. In all cases, some form of tuning constant is needed to make the necessary prediction agree with practice.

In the following discussion, the tuning constant will be termed a *bias factor* (BF). The bias factor is the difference between an actual determination and an estimator at some given time:

$$BF = actual - estimate$$

The principle involved is that a best estimate at a time T2 is equal to the estimator value at T2 plus the bias factor measured at T1:

$$Best\ estimate(T2) = estimator(T2) + BF(T1)$$

Note that as T2 approaches T1, the calculation becomes exact:

$$Best\ estimate(T2) = actual\ determination(T1)$$

$$T1 = T2$$

A variant of this approach makes use of a multiplicative BF as opposed to use of an additive term only. In this variant, BF is a ratio of actual to estimated value, and the best estimate is equal to the estimator times BF.

As an example of the use of the bias factor, the prediction of blend qualities that result from mixing several components is subject to estimation errors from several sources: Blending correlations are not accurate, and component analyses are subject to error and were not necessarily made on the exact stock being used for blending. For these problems, the bias factor is equal to an actual determination minus the blending correlation prediction. The best estimate for the next batch is then the correlation prediction plus BF for the last batch.

This procedure has been in use for gasoline blending systems since the 1960s at least. Experience shows that it is very effective in improving accuracy as long as three principles are adhered to:

1. The quality information and therefore the bias values are accurate.

2. The measured BFs form a time sequence, consistently measured on each batch.

3. The BFs are consistently used on each prediction.

Thus the calculation and use of the bias factors are actually in a feedback system similar to a process control loop. In this case the objective of the loop is to improve accuracy, rather than control to some set point.

When calculated and used in this consistent fashion, the predictions become very accurate because the values from one time period to the next show a high degree of what is called *autocorrelation*. The past is therefore a good predictor of the future. Numerous applications of process optimization, predictive model control, planning, and scheduling owe their success to the working of the bias factors. Note that in some cases, a moving average is used rather than the direct time series of bias factors.

More sophisticated time-series analysis of the sequence of BF values or techniques of statistical process control could be used if this simplest approach is not adequate. For example, see Tham and Parr (1994).

Using Process Models

Process engineering

The major use of process models in process engineering is to detect changes in the operation of the process that are indicative of problems that will reduce process profitability, or—to put it the other way around—to discover the cause of a problem that is reducing process profitability. For example, a reformer model can be used to calculate an effective catalyst activity. Doing this periodically enables a forecast of catalyst fouling rates and, therefore, of when catalyst regeneration will be necessary. Fractionator modeling can sometimes be used to determine the internal condition of a column so that the extent of maintenance required at a shutdown can be forecast.

Process models always have adjustable parameters in the model for the purpose of tuning the model to agree exactly with a set of data from the process. Once the model has been tuned, there are two options in common use for assessing the process condition: (1) One or more of the tuning parameters can be used directly as a measure; or (2) the model is tuned, then resolved for a particular set of feed and operating conditions, and the results are used as a measure.

Design engineering

Process models are heavily used for the design of new process plants and modifications to existing processes. Most applications now involve use of a commercial process simulation system with a model for the chemical reactions added. For example, in Part 3, Chap. 16 is about the use of a commercial process simulation system wherein the users added their own model of their ethylene cracking process. Many engineering and construction firms have models for the processes that they offer, or companies that license processes or special catalysts have models available that they use in their own development. Many times it is possible to obtain a copy of the model along with the process, or at least to have a usable version installed on your own computer equipment.

If you do intend to get a model along with a process, try to get the model delivered in a form that uses your central database system for input and output. In this way, it will be possible to easily integrate the model into the rest of your systems. A model that stands alone, especially from an output standpoint, will be difficult to integrate.

Data reconciliation

As described above, process models always have adjustable parameters that can be used to make a prediction agree exactly with a set of data from the process. Predictions can then be made for different conditions. Unfortunately, any errors in the data will be carried over to the prediction. The change in model results may appear to be correct, but may actually be misleading because tuning of the model does not necessarily correspond to a data reconciliation. For example, a discrepancy in an enthalpy balance calculated during tuning may be allocated to an imbalance parameter and carried through to subsequent predictions. A true data reconciliation would demand that the enthalpy, weight, and component balances all be satisfied exactly. The data themselves would be modified based on the probable error in each measurement to achieve closure on all balances simultaneously. Chapter 4 on data reconciliation describes these aspects in detail.

In practice, some gross error detection procedure is used before the data are used for model tuning. Then some criteria need to be established for the values of the tuning parameters. If a value, which is ideally zero, becomes larger than its criterion, then the data set should be investigated for excessive error in one or more of the measurements. This procedure warns about errors that are not gross errors but are indicated to be large enough to cause misleading predictions. While this procedure is not true data reconciliation, it is often sufficient to guarantee meaningful results.

When true data reconciliation is used, the data themselves are modified to make weight balances, etc., close exactly. A problem always arises then as to what new value is reported to the process operator or what exact new set point value is sent to the control system. It is almost universal that a bias factor will be calculated between the reconciled value and the measurement and then used to bias the prediction or the set point obtained from the model. Consequently, as long as there are no gross errors, the net result can be essentially the same as simply tuning the model to the measured data in the first place. However, it is not adequate to simply assume that the workings of the model will be unaffected by being tuned to raw data, rather than to reconciled data followed by use of a bias factor. The adequacy of the simpler approach must be validated by trial use.

Process optimization

Model-based process control and optimization are becoming ubiquitous. Numerous books, articles, and classes are available on the subject. Detailed process models are used in a segment of the applications where a steady-state model can be used. In a process optimization, the common cycle is to take data from steady-state operation, reconcile the data, recalculate the optimum targets for the process, and then modify the process set points as necessary. The cycle time frame can be from a few minutes to several hours.

The complex process models that are the subject of this chapter are usually large enough to require a large number of data items, which usually include several analytical measurements that are periodic. The analytical data cycle time will limit the frequency of set point updates.

When used for optimization, complex process models are almost always simplified to fit the data that will be available. For example, a few feed qualities will be used instead of a larger number actually required for the model input. This can be done for a particular process plant because the quality of various feeds will not change completely in character except over a long time.

Planning model development

Complex process models are also used to develop simplified models for inclusion in planning models. For example, runs on a complete process model can develop the base and delta columns used in a linear programming (LP) planning model. This use and that for process optimization are very dependent on the ability of the model to predict the correct derivatives of model results with respect to changes in the operating variables. In nonlinear optimization, the base-delta values will be updated repeatedly, making it even more important that derivatives obtained from the model be accurate and repeatable.

Simplifying models for various uses

For many applications, including planning and process optimization, use of the complete complex model is not practical. For example, a planning model may use only a subset of the feed qualities that are actually required as input to the full model. A few feed properties will act as an alias for others that are really needed by the model but that will not be measured. Derivatives of the complex model must be taken correctly to avoid getting misleading results. If a numerical or analytical partial derivative is taken, the derivative is based on holding all other variables constant. However, if the variable is an alias for others as well as representing itself, this constancy is not the desired effect. When the variable changes, all aliased variables must also be changed in correct harmony.

In real feeds to a process, when a property changes, several other properties also change at the same time. If we are to represent entire feeds with a single property, then the numerical derivatives must be obtained by varying all the properties in correct fashion from one run to the next and then dividing the difference by the change in just the one property (Bodington, 1987). Since the relationship between the properties depends upon the source of the feedstock, every process installation will get a different answer for the derivative, which is as it should be.

If analytical derivatives are available, the correct derivative can be obtained by using the chain rule with the partial derivatives for each

$$dY/dQ_1 = \partial Y/\partial Q_1 + dQ_2/dQ_1 * \partial Y/\partial Q_2 + \ldots$$
Where:

Y = dependent variables
Q = qualities 1, 2 …

Figure 9.8 Obtaining correct derivatives by using the chain rule.

of the aliased properties, coupled with derivatives for the effect of the main property on the others, as shown in Fig. 9.8.

Examples of Process Models

Fractionation columns

Today, the commercial process simulators have no equal in their ability to model fractionation. This is mainly due to the strides made over many years in the ability to predict the vapor-liquid equilibrium concentrations and tray efficiencies. However, on many occasions a simpler model is more appropriate. When only minor changes in operation need to be forecast, or when a specific column needs to be modeled within another more complex model, simpler approaches can be used. One really easy way to model a simple splitter or three-product column is to use the *Fenske equation* (see Fig. 9.9) with the number of trays obtained from back substitution of measured performance. This approach works very well for simple cases such as depropanizers, debutanizers, alkylation plant columns, and chemical plant rerun columns. While clearly limited in the kinds of uses for which it is useful, the model can predict the effect of changes in feed composition, or of changes in reflux if coupled with another correlation for the effect of reflux on the effective number of trays. This is an example of a theoretical model, since the Fenske equation is based on fundamental principles. Only one parameter is needed if the relative volatility is known, and two parameters are needed if this is not specified in advance. Thus only one data point is needed to develop the model; two data points are needed if the volatility is not predefined.

$$(X_a/X_b)_{top} * (X_b/X_a)_{bottom} = A^N$$
Where:

X = mole fractions
A = relative volatility
N = theoretical trays equivalent
a = light key, b = heavy key component

Figure 9.9 Fenske equation for distillation.

The second example refers to the equation for fluid catalytic cracker (FCC) conversion shown in Fig. 9.3. This equation is part theoretical, part empirical. Since there are empirical segments for the equation, determination of the numerous coefficients must be done as if the equation were completely empirical. Numerous data points will be required. The theoretically based terms really only ensure that the basic shape of the curve will be closer to true and that predictions involving those terms may extrapolate better than empirical forms. Derivatives involving the theoretically based terms also will be more accurate under extrapolation away from the original database. Note that this equation covers only the major operating variables for an FCC unit. In particular, the catalyst activity is a base value measured in a pilot plant. Thus, the equation is of no help in determining catalyst activity from other properties of the catalyst.

A full FCC model could be based on this equation, but it is only a starting point. The complete model would also contain equations for predicting the yields of light ends, gasoline, and cycle oils. Additional equations would predict properties of the products, such as gasoline octane numbers and olefin content. Then equations are needed for the coke burning reaction in the regenerator, heat of cracking and combustion, and a heat balance to make sure that heat produced by the regenerator is sufficient to satisfy heat requirements in the reactor. The catalyst stripper at the exit of the reactor then needs to be modeled so that the effects of steam rate and catalyst circulation on coke production can be properly represented. The final model is a very complex assemblage that can require years in development. In addition, every new catalyst that affects product distribution or product properties will require an update to the equations. To create the database for an FCC model development by using unplanned historical data from an operating process is almost impossible. Because the regenerator and reactor have to be in heat balance, some of the variables are always going to be moved simultaneously. For example, if the feed changes so that the coke yield will be higher, then conversion will usually be dropped to keep actual coke made at the regenerator maximum. No matter what happens, some compensating change will be made to keep the process stable. This hopelessly confounds several variables with each other. Pilot data or special test runs have to be obtained to separate the effects.

References

Bodington, C. E. (1966): "Dewaxing Process," U.S. Patent 3,249,526, May 3.
Bodington, C. E. (1987): "Adapting Process Models for Optimization," in *Computer Aided Process Operations,* eds. G. V. Reklaitis and H. D. Spriggs, Elsevier, New York, pp. 663–668.

Bodington, C. E. (1989): "Formulation of Process Models for Optimization," in *Proceedings of the Eighth Annual Control Engineering Conference,* Control Engineering, Des Plaines, IL, pp. XI-15–XI-22.

Box, G. E. P., and Draper, (1987): "Empirical Model Building and Response Surfaces," Wiley, New York.

Box, G. E. P., W. G. Hunter, and J. S. Hunter (1978): *Statistics for Experimenters,* Wiley, New York.

Braden, W. B., T. Graettinger, A. Federowicz, and N. V. Bhat (1992): "A Neural Network Based Control and Optimization Program," Operations Research Society of America/The Institute of Management Science national meeting, San Francisco, November.

Chakravarty, T. (1993): "Use Canonical Correlation Analysis instead of Regression," *Chem. Eng. Prog.,* vol. 89, no. 10, October, pp. 76–83.

Chitra, S. P. (1993): "Use Neural Networks for Problem Solving," *Chem. Eng. Prog.,* vol. 89, no. 4, April, pp. 44–52.

Fenske (1932): *Ind. & Eng. Chem.,* vol. 24, p. 482.

Garvin, W. W., H. W. Crandall, J. B. John, and R. A. Spellmann (1957): "Applications of Linear Programming in the Oil Industry," *Management Sci.,* vol. 3, no. 4, pp. 407–430.

Green, P. E., and J. D. Caroll (1976): *Mathematical Tools for Applied Multivariate Data Analysis,* Academic Press, New York.

Griffith, R. E., and R. A. Stewart (1961): "A Nonlinear Programming Technique for the Optimization of Continuous Processes," *Management Sci.,* vol. 7, no. 2, pp. 379–392.

Hair, J. F., R. E. Anderson, and R. L. Tatham (1987): *Multivariate Data Analysis,* 2d ed., Macmillan, New York.

Hunter, J. S. (1966): "Quality Control and Process Improvement—4. Statistical Experiment Design," *Chem. Eng.,* vol. 73, no. 7, March 28, pp. 111–118.

Powell, R. T. (1989): "Kinetic Hydrocracker Model Helps Engineers Predict Yields, Targets, Operations," *Oil & Gas J.,* January 9, pp. 61–65.

Symonds, G. H. (1955): "Linear Programming—The Solution of Refinery Problems," Esso Standard Oil Company, New York.

Tham, M. T., and A. Parr (1994): "Succeed at On-Line Validation and Reconstruction of Data," *Chem. Eng. Prog.,* vol. 90, no. 5, May, pp. 46–56.

Wasserman, P. D. (1989): *Neural Computing, Theory and Practice,* Van Nostrand Reinhold, New York.

Wollaston, E. G., W. J. Haflin, W. D. Ford, and G. J. D'Souza (1975): "FCC Model Valuable Operating Tool," *Oil & Gas J.,* September 22, pp. 87–94.

Zupan, J., and J. Gasteiger (1993): *Neural Networks for Chemists,* VCH Publishers, New York.

Management

C. Edward Bodington
Consultant

Introduction

The integration of planning, scheduling, and control functions presents several management challenges. This chapter describes four areas in which such an integration project will require changes in organization or attitude:

- Organization and management structure
- Safety and environmental issues
- Quality and quality improvement issues
- Training

Organization and Management Structure

In most nonintegrated situations, the planning is done by one organization close to the marketing and supply functions, but not part of them. Planning buffers sales opportunities, commitments, and feed purchases and tries to set achievable targets for the plant. Scheduling is done by another organization that is between planning and operations and tries to get a schedule that is feasible, if not optimal, to meet commitments. Process control is done by yet another organization, usually segmented by process, that operates the processes as well as possible, given the information available. The three organizations have different objectives and probably have entirely different reward structures and different ideas about what constitutes a job well done.

Chapter 1 pointed out that the planning function particularly, and the scheduling function to some extent, developed from the top down in the company hierarchy, whereas process control developed at the individual process level. These separate developments used different people, skills, and technology and led to a gap in knowledge, communication, and understanding among the functions (Baker and Shobrys, 1985; Van Horn, 1985). Where the gap exists, the people in each functional area use different terminology and entirely different kinds of models for the processes and are unused to involving the other functions in decisions. The separation of the functions may be reinforced by the company organization and reward structure, which tends to maintain the separation, even though that may not be the actual intent. For example, planning may be rewarded for not over-committing the plant production capacity. Planning will therefore not commit to demands that would risk pushing the processes beyond their capabilities. Scheduling may be rewarded for keeping the plant away from inventory problems. Thus the scheduler will keep too much inventory and try to limit the range of inventory variation, even if it means delaying a shipment. Operations may be rewarded primarily for safe, low-cost operation. Thus, the processes will be backed down, away from critical limits. All three functions have built in a cushion consistent with their reward structures, resulting in a plant that is operating way below its capabilities.

When planning, scheduling, and control are integrated, the view presented to each function is widened to include more of the other functions. The close coordination now possible has to be built into the objectives of the functions. The gaps among the functions will not go away simply by installing computer systems. The organization and its reward structure have to be changed to enhance cooperation and teamwork.

There is general recognition that the organization in existence prior to integration should not be kept intact. In many projects, e.g., several of those in Part 3 of this book, a major organizational change was part of or preceded the integration project. In some cases, a corporate cultural change was part of the justification for the integration. However, since there are very few plants with completely integrated systems operating at present, there has not been a consensus developed regarding the best form for a new organization and its reward structure. The best organizational structure may be different for each company. It is obvious that any barriers caused by departmentalization have to be eliminated. Extensive organizational changes cannot come from the bottom up in the company hierarchy. Consequently, the impetus for change and the initiation of the drive to implement an integrated system have to come from the company top management. The project described in Chap. 18 is an excellent example. Once the drive has been initiated, lower-level employees can form teams to implement the changes and the systems. Top management must continue to be involved and provide support, throughout the projects and into the future (*The Economist,* 1994a).

Recent Changes in Organizational Structures

Over the last decade or more, numerous corporations have reduced the number of levels of management and given more responsibility and authority to people in lower levels (Drucker, 1988). The term *empowerment* is now in vogue; it basically means moving decision making down in the company hierarchy to people who before were simply "controlled and commanded" to perform a certain function. This new look fits the concept of the integrated system very well. The integrated system and its incumbent information technology are one of the tools that lead to empowerment. To empower an employee, it is necessary to change the system of production to give that employee control over aspects that were not under the employee's control before. If the system of production is not changed, what is thought of as empowerment may merely mean that the employee's workload has been increased.

The elimination of layers of middle management has been accompanied by the more severe reduction in staff, euphemistically called *downsizing* or *right-sizing.* Where a company has gone through waves of layoffs, employees who have survived thus far are correctly fearful that they may be next. In such a circumstance, it is hard to believe that the remaining employees will give the company's future even equal consideration to their own. The essence of a successful enterprise is that employees submerge their own personal immediate goals and instead align them to those of the enterprise, recognizing that they themselves will be better off in the long term if the company prospers. Since a laid-off employee does not share in the company's prosperity, people who fear the next layoff are loath to wholeheartedly support changes that might eliminate their jobs. Consequently, companies that have recently downsized may have difficulty getting more than lip-service support for productivity improvement projects—especially since productivity is measured as performance divided by the number of people on the job. Only top management can remove the fear of layoff and get the employees again pulling together for the benefit of both the company and themselves. Fortunately for our subject, the areas of planning, scheduling, and control have not been hard hit by downsizing. These functions are generally already at low or minimum staffing levels. Consequently, the integration of these functions is more likely to enhance productivity by an improvement in performance (the numerator) rather than by a reduction in staff (the denominator).

Another organizational change that is ongoing is the modification of reward systems to make sure that the rewards for good work reinforce the overall optimization objective of the integrated system (Hammer and Champy, 1993). In their book *Reengineering the Corporation,* Hammer and Champy give many examples of reward systems, good and bad, that enhanced or subverted the objectives of the company.

The other side of the reward structure change is the elimination of policies that inadvertently reward malperformance or that demotivate employees. Edwards Deming (1982) gives numerous examples of such cases in his book *Out of the Crisis.*

Enhancing Cooperation and Reducing Resistance

Technical articles about projects for process optimization or control seldom describe the serious impact that such a project may have on the people involved. If the project is not introduced properly, operators who have been told for years how good their work is now are told that the new computer control system is going to improve process performance. Even if it is not directly stated, there is the strong implication that the new system will do a better job than the operators ever did in the past.

From the first introduction of a project, it is important that everyone understand that the integrated system is going to change the way the processes need to be operated. New demands and requirements to be imposed will make it very difficult to operate without the new computer tools. For example, the production of reformulated gasoline adds numerous specifications that must be considered and met. In the past, only octane, vapor pressure, and sometimes distillation points were critical, limiting specifications. The new gasoline will involve many more limiting specifications, such as oxygen, benzene, aromatics, olefins, and additional distillation points (Bodington, 1992).

The first hurdle, therefore, is to convince the ultimate users of the integrated system that there is a need for improvement. The key is to involve users in the formative stages of the project, whether it be for complete integration or just for improvement of a single process. For example, in an advanced control project, the operators need to understand that the reduction in variability will allow a closer approach to targets and physical limits in a safe manner. If they do not understand, they may not be willing to actually move the set points closer to limits.

The history of computer applications is replete with examples of technical successes but financial failures because the users would not use the system or actively subverted it. "I don't need some damn computer to tell me how to run my plant." Projects are still "going on the rocks" because the users were not involved early enough. The managers thought they were empowering the users; the users did not feel empowered—they felt rejected and diminished in job function, but with a larger workload.

If a project is developed in private, without direct user involvement, the developers will always miss something. It is impossible to get everything right the first time. Consequently, when a new system is implemented, the users will have to honestly and seriously use the system, discover and point out the problems with it, and work with the developers to get the system to really be correct. If the users have not really accepted the need for the system and have not been imbued with a desire to have it work well for them, they can kill it. All they have to do is practice what is termed *malicious obedience*. The users do exactly what the developers tell them, they do not point out where the system needs to be fixed, and most surely the system will perform poorly and eventually will be abandoned.

Resistance to change is natural, especially if the person's level of perceived control over job activities appears to be in jeopardy. Resistance must be confronted wherever and as soon as it appears. Trying to ignore it or waiting to handle it later, while hoping it will go away, is tantamount to development without the person's involvement—it is always a mistake.

The significant change in the organization that will accompany the integration project will eliminate some of the resistance and inertia. However, the ultimate users still need to "buy into" the project.

As an example of what can happen, a company installed a computer control and optimization system on a process. The project was carried out by a special team that did not directly involve any of the operators or their managers. Actually, the installation was opposed by the process operators and their management. While the developers were in residence, the new system worked very well and made a good return on the investment. As soon as the developers left, the system was simply neglected. In short order, it no longer worked correctly and was shut off. Soon the computer was actually removed from the process.

A second attempt was mounted by other developers at a different plant of the same company. The results were the same! As soon as the developers of the successful installation went away, the system was simply neglected and eventually turned off. What happened? In these instances the users did not buy into the project, and the organization and its reward structures were not changed. The resistance should have been met head-on and the organization changed as necessary to get user support.

Unless the ultimate users have a personal, career, and financial interest in the success of the project, it is likely that the project will fail. If the integration of planning, scheduling, and control is to be successful, users must feel that they themselves will have an expanded role in the company due to the new system, that their careers will be more interesting and secure, and that they will participate in financial gains made through their efforts. Management must make sure that these "feelings" are actually true. Users must have an expanded role, their jobs must be more interesting and secure, and users must gain financially as a result of project success (Pfeffer, 1994).

An integration of planning, scheduling, and control should also be accompanied by a new vision or *mission statement* for the integrated functions. All users should understand the new vision and their role in achieving it. For example, one of the major benefits of the project may be reduced response time to customer inquiries, or increased market share by becoming the preferred supplier by being able to supply highest quality at lower cost than one's competitors. Whatever the benefits, everyone must understand their roles in accomplishing the mission.

What Can Go Wrong?

Suppose the integrated computer systems are in place and the organization and reward structures have been changed to support the new procedures. Is success now guaranteed? Unfortunately, death and taxes are still the only sure things in this world. Hypothetical case 1: Top management thinks that by installing the computer system it has empowered the employees. In fact, managers have merely added to the employees' workloads. Employees now have less time to be concerned about quality and customer satisfaction than before. Quality and customer response stay the same, at best, and may actually worsen.

Hypothetical case 2: A new person is given a knowledge worker job, such as tactical planning, without much training or turnover from the previous job occupant. During the learning process, the people who depend upon the output of this job for information do not get what they need and become frustrated and exasperated. Quality and productivity suffer. Instead of showing continuous improvement, the company regresses.

What has gone wrong? Assume that the functions have been reengineered by using the principles published by Hammer and Champy (1993). In the first instance, case 1, the cause is that the reengineering of the functions has been only partially implemented. In a worst case, only the parts of the procedures that reduce cost have been implemented. For example, many companies are now changing (or trying to change) their salary administration to a fixed salary coupled with a monthly or yearly bonus that depends upon the profits of the company. No annual change in base salary is made on the basis of merit in the same job (ignoring the erosion of real income due to inflation). If this is done with a view to sharing with employees the success of the company, all is well and good. If, however, this is a disguised attempt to avoid compensation in order to reduce labor cost, then the insincerity of management will be found out and quality and productivity are bound to suffer. If the organization is to be changed to enhance cooperation and teamwork, the whole job has to be done; one cannot pick and choose parts of the reengineering process based on some other objective. Although we have used the reengineering of Hammer and Champy as an example, the same situation would exist if one were implementing only some parts of the 14 points of Edwards Deming (1982) or of future theories of management yet to be developed.

All management theories fit some companies at some time. After all, the theories are developed as an example of what works for some subset of companies. But companies and cultures change with time, leading to continual modification or replacement of one theory implementation with another (*The Economist,* 1994b). Regardless of the theory application being attempted, any insincerity on the part of top or middle management will be found out and will subvert any benefit that might have been achieved. In case 2, the cause is a leftover from obsolete management attitudes that considered one employee as completely interchangeable with others. Interchangeability and learn by doing are obsolete concepts when it comes to knowledge work. A knowledge worker is one who possesses special knowledge that is required to perform a particular job. On-the-job training is usually necessary to become proficient, with training done by an expert. Training by an expert distinguishes on-the-job training from learn by doing. As the control systems on processes have become more complex, more attention has been paid to operator training. It is recognized that the operator needs special knowledge in order to utilize the very complex functions of the new control systems with some intelligence. Many companies use training simulators, classroom instruction with examinations, etc., to impart the necessary knowledge in addition to on-the-job training.

Planners and schedulers are also knowledge workers, but formal training for them has been lacking in most companies. With an integrated system, planning and scheduling are part of the control loop for the processes. Without formal training and knowledge transfer, every time a new planner or scheduler comes on to the job, all the knowledge possessed by the previous person will have to be relearned by the new person. This is not continuous improvement—this is falling back and starting over again. The value of the knowledge possessed by the knowledge worker must be recognized, adequately compensated, and preserved to be built on when there are personnel changes. Without an adequate training and turnover period, how could you tell that a new prospective planner will not be able to come up to the expertise of the present one? Are you willing to let a drop in profitability signal that a mistake has been made?

Safety and Environmental Issues

The Clean Air Act Amendments (CAAA) and the Occupational Safety and Health Act will continue to impose layers of requirements for record keeping and analysis of daily operations (Lohry, 1994; Nimmo, 1993; Parkinson, 1992). For example, the Occupational Safety and Health Act "management of change" requirements call for an auditable trail of documentation and approvals for changes to operating processes that can affect process safety (Franke and McGuire, 1993; Hoskins and Worm, 1993). Other aspects of the regulations concern the drawings pertaining to the process and training of personnel in operations, maintenance, and engineering. The training aspect concerns not only how to find information about the status, configuration, or materials processed, but also operating procedures and objectives. The environmental considerations will require records on daily and long-term average performance and product qualities.

There is clearly a considerable overlap between the recording and training requirements that are or will be mandated by government regulations and the requirements of a system for integration of planning, scheduling, and control. Many of the resources needed can be shared, thereby reducing the cost of both implementations. Both systems need a central database, communications, and input/output devices such as video terminals. In addition, much of the information to be kept will be collected in the normal course of operations by the process information systems on the processes.

Quality and Quality Improvement

Much has been written about quality control, continuous quality improvement, and the concept of total quality management (TQM) (Deshpande et al., 1993; Shaw, 1989; Schmidt et al., 1986; Edwards Deming, 1982). The culmination of efforts to change a company to "live-and-breathe quality" seems to be registration to the ISO 9000 standards (International Standards Organization standards for quality assurance). The key point of this registration is that an outside, independent auditor certifies that a company has systems and procedures, in place and working, that allow measurement, control, and assurance of all aspects of product quality.

The ISO 9000 standards fundamentally provide a model for a comprehensive system for quality assurance. It is very important to note that the products themselves are of little concern. The standards speak to the procedures in place to deliver to a customer the quality of product desired. For this reason, many customers now require or will require their suppliers to have ISO 9000 registration. The standards apply to the entire supply chain through order entry, planning, scheduling, manufacture, and shipping. Thus, it is not product quality alone that is important, but the response to the customer from order placement to on-time delivery of the specified product. A moment's reflection will convince you that integration of planning, scheduling, and control is a prerequisite to ISO 9000 registration. These functions are in the middle of the supply chain.

The procedure for ISO 9000 registration is time-consuming, but it probably results in a different company that is better coordinated, more efficient, and more profitable and has better access to markets (Mancine, 1994). The registration process involves

- Training personnel who will be doing the registration work
- Comparing procedures with the standards
- Modifying procedures to conform to the standards
- Conducting a preliminary audit
- Correcting or adding procedures
- Conducting a final audit
- Having a follow-up audit, if necessary

Once registration is achieved, then periodic repeat audits are required to certify that all aspects are in compliance over time. No company that has achieved ISO 9000 registration has been left unchanged. Since almost everything that a company does affects the supply chain, and the standards try to leave nothing to chance, every aspect of company operation will be involved. Every employee will understand how her or his actions affect the supply chain and his or her part of the quality process. Integration of planning, scheduling, and control would be a good first step along the path.

What is *quality* in a process industry business? Edwards Deming would probably have defined it as the amount of variability in the performance of the company and in the properties of the company's products. The lower the variability, the higher the quality. It is easy to find examples in which a reduction in variability will increase productivity and lower costs:

- Reducing specification giveaway on products reduces product costs and increases production.

- Steady operation of a process allows a closer approach to targets and/or limits. Almost all the benefits for advanced control systems are due to a reduction in variability by better process control.

- Reduction of variability in the properties of products increases the efficiency and lowers the costs for all downstream uses. This is also true for intermediate products consumed or transformed internally within a plant. The economic benefit of a reduction in the variability of the quality of intermediate streams has long gone unrecognized.

The ISO 9000 standards can be thought of as providing a model for the measurement, control, and reduction of variability.

Employee Training

Training to gain, renew, and improve skills has been touched on in several contexts in this chapter. We pointed out that continuous quality improvement is impossible unless replacement personnel start out with the same expertise as those who are leaving a position. It would appear that government regulations will specify a certain level of training for safety and environmental considerations. However, the mandated training will be narrow in scope. The training that will have to be available for companies to achieve ISO 9000 registration includes the mandated training and goes beyond to form an excellent basis for continuous quality improvement.

For the purposes of the integration of planning, scheduling, and control, the training of people in these functional areas needs to be expanded so that, e.g., the planners will understand the needs of the scheduler, control engineer, and operator. In short, each function must be aware of the information needs of the other functions and how to provide what is needed. The purpose of this chapter has been to stimulate thought about the organizational structure that will best serve an integrated system for planning, scheduling, and control. No specific structure can be recommended since each company must follow its own culture. Integration team members should read widely about management theory and formulate their own ideas about what will work in their own company. The books or articles by Pfeffer (1994), Hammer and Champy (1993), Edwards Deming (1982),

Drucker (1988), Peters and Austin (1986), and Halberstam (1986) are enthusiastically recommended.

References

ANSI/ASQC Q90 ISO 9000 Guidelines for Use by the Chemical and Process Industries, ASQC Quality Press, Milwaukee, WI, 1992.

Baker, T. E., and D. E. Shobrys (1985): "The Integration of Planning, Scheduling and Control," paper CC-85-97, National Petroleum Refiners Association Computer Conference, New Orleans, LA, October 27–30.

Bodington, C. E. (1992): "Use of Nonlinear Optimization for Gasoline Blend Planning and Scheduling," Operations Research Society of America/The Institute of Measurement Science national meeting, San Francisco, November 1–4.

Deshpande, P. B., R. E. Hannula, M. A. Bhalodia, and C. W. Hansen (1993): "Achieve Total Quality Control of Continuous Processes," *Chem. Eng. Prog.,* vol. 89, no. 7, July, pp. 59–66.

Drucker, P. F. (1988): "The Coming of the New Organization," *Harv. Bus. Rev.,* January-February, pp. 45–53.

The Economist, (1994a): "Re-engineering Reviewed," July 2d, pp. 66.

The Economist, (1994b): "A Survey of Japan," July 9, Special Supplement.

Edwards Deming, W. (1982): *Out of the Crisis,* Center for Advanced Engineering Study, Massachusetts Institute of Technology, Cambridge.

Edwards Deming, W. (1985): "Transformation of Western Style of Management," *Interfaces,* vol. 15, May-June, pp. 6–11.

Franke, R. R., and M. L. McGuire (1993): "Integrating Plant Management Systems for OSHA Compliance," paper CC-93-129, National Petroleum Refiners Association Computer Conference, New Orleans, LA, November 15–17.

Halberstam, D. (1986): *The Reckoning,* Avon, New York.

Hammer, M., and J. Champy (1993): *Reengineering the Corporation,* HarperCollins, New York.

Hoskins, R. K., and G. H. Worm (1993): "Develop an Effective Management of Change System Manual," *Chem. Eng. Prog.,* vol. 89, no. 11, November, pp. 77–80.

Lohry, E. J. (1994): "Small Business: Make the Most of Process Safety Management," *Chem. Eng. Prog.,* vol. 90, no. 2, February, pp. 60–62.

Mancine, B. J. (1994): "Succeed at ISO 9000 Registration," *Chem. Eng. Prog.,* vol. 90, no. 2, February, pp. 55–61.

Nimmo, I. (1993): "Start Up Plants Safely," *Chem. Eng. Prog.,* vol. 89, no. 12, December, pp. 66–69.

Parkinson, G. (1992): "Refining's Clean New Jingle," *Chem. Eng.,* April, pp. 35–39.

Peters, T. J., and N. K. Austin (1986): *A Passion for Excellence,* Warner Books, New York.

Pfeffer, J. (1994): *Competitive Advantage through People,* Harvard Business School Press, Cambridge, MA.

Schmitt, N. E., J. Jarvie, and J. Chowdhury (1986): "Statistical Process Control," *Chem. Eng.,* vol. 93, no. 11, June 9.

Shaw J. A. (1989): "SPC for the Process Industries," *InTech,* vol. 36, no. 12, December, pp. 34–37.

Van Horn, L. D. (1985): "Integrating Process Control and Operating Target Decisions," Instrument Society of America conference, Philadelphia, PA.

Waterman, R. (1994): *What America Does Right,* W. W. Norton, New York.

Implementation and Justification

Implementation

C. Edward Bodington
Consultant

The Combination of Elements

In this chapter we describe the combination of the elements of the chapters of Part 1 into a functioning integrated system. A block diagram showing the relationships and information flows between the elements is given in Fig. 11.1. We use this diagram to explore the details of the information generated by one element that is needed by another. Throughout the discussion, the term *plant* refers to a complete refinery or chemical complex, and the term *process* refers to the individual units that make up a plant.

The diagram in Fig. 11.1 shows only the major relationships between the elements. For example, data reconciliation uses data from the process information system, and model tuning uses the reconciled data. The success of an integration project depends to a significant degree on the details of this information transfer between elements. Many transfers require an interpretation of the results in one element before the results can be useful to another element. For example, planning results must be related to runs on particular feedstocks, batches of products, and specific operations on processes in the scheduling element. The functional elements are arranged in a hierarchy. Business functions such as customer order handling and strategic planning are usually said to be at a high level, and the plant itself is at the lowest level in the hierarchy. This ranking has to do with the usual way in which the elements are placed on an organizational chart, but has nothing to do with relative importance or real information flow. All the elements are

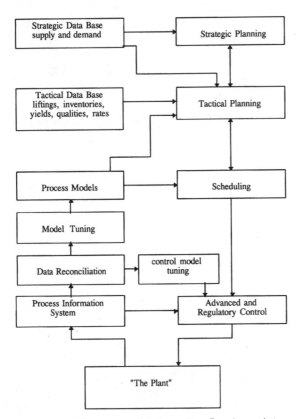

Figure 11.1 Elements and information flow in an integrated system.

essential in an integrated system, and all will be present in one form or another. As shown in Fig. 11.1, the arrangement of the elements from tactical planning down is more a loop structure than hierarchical.

We describe a reasonably complex case. The description is of an integration in a complex petrochemical or refining plant, one with numerous processes and many different products. For simpler plants containing fewer processes and making similar or a small number of products, all the elements are still required to be in place, but may be combined or so simple that it is difficult to recognize some elements as separate entities. For example, process models range in complexity from a simple material balance to a small set of correlation equations, to a process simulation containing thousands of equations. In the simplest case, the presence of a process model would hardly be noticeable.

A plant with nothing but continuous operations may not require a separate schedule. For such a plant, the average operation calculated by the planning system corresponds to actual daily or hourly operation of the plant itself without modification or interpretation. In this case, planning and scheduling are combined.

It is also possible for the situation to be much more complex than the one to be described. For example, the plant may not be independent of other plants from a feedstock or demand area standpoint. In this case, the tactical plan would have to consider several plants as a group. Strategic planning also becomes more complex and may require a scheduling application in addition to the planning function.

Thus, the complexity of each element in a given implementation depends upon the plant itself. We must leave it to the reader to adapt our analysis and recommendations to the specific plant or plants in question.

A Brief Walk-through

Strategic planning, also called *long-range planning,* is commonly used for monthly to yearly feed selection and demand allocation for a group of plant sites. *Tactical planning* is short-range planning for each site, each one done independently, typically over a day to a month. In large companies, the strategic plan may be a multiplant, multiperiod model run by a central group apart from the plant. In small companies having only one plant, both the strategic plan and the tactical plan probably are drawn up by the same person, using different versions of the same model.

The tactical plan, typically for a week or a month, is translated to a schedule of detailed operations, for 1 week or 10 days. The schedule is then translated to the information needed by each of the process advanced control systems. To make the transfer of information possible, the tactical plan must contain a representation of the current operation of each process. Data collected from plant sensors and combined with results from the analytical laboratory system are presented for use by the process information system. Data reconciliation is used to verify data quality, guide instrument maintenance, etc. Reconciled data are then used to tune process models for both planning and, if needed, control. In some cases, these models are the same.

Tuned and updated process models are then interpreted for use by planning, scheduling, and controlling elements. For example, the process models may be used directly by control, but a simplified model may be generated for use by planning.

What we have described is a multilevel feedback control system from the individual processes to tactical planning and back. The integrated system really is structured as in Fig. 11.2, but in this diagram, which better demonstrates the central role of the database, it is more difficult to appreciate the feedback loop from control to planning and back,

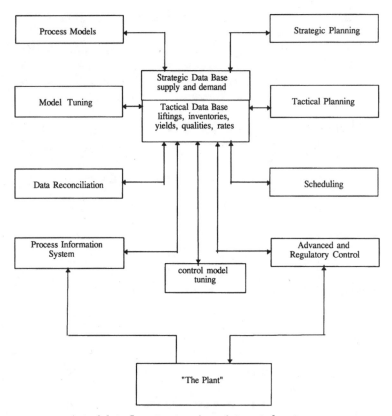

Figure 11.2   Actual data flow structure in an integrated system.

including the other elements. Each element may also have its own private database, and some elements may share a private database.

Critical Success Factors

What has to be done correctly if an integration of planning, scheduling, and control is to be successful? A consensus is emerging that a complete system will contain an adaptation of each of the elements described in Chaps. 2 through 10:.

- A process information system for real-time data collection and analysis of process operations

- Data communications networks for easy, standardized transfer of information between elements

- A central database for storage and dissemination of all inputs and results

- Model-based data reconciliation both for the overall plant and for the individual processes

- Advanced process control including process optimization

- A formal computerized scheduling system to manage process interactions and inventories and to translate planning results to a form useful to the advanced process control systems

- A responsive tactical planning system with real-time updates to the process representations; a plan redeveloped as often as necessary to maintain coordination between customer requirements and the processes

- Expert system (ES) applications embedded in all the other elements to interpret data and results and to improve the efficiency of data analysis

- Process models tuned in real time so planning predictions for current operation agree with actual performance

- An organizational structure that rewards cooperation and teamwork

We will now expand on these characteristics to justify their inclusion and to amplify their implications to the system design and operation. The chapters in Part 1 described each element in detail, so little is repeated here. The major purpose of this chapter is to adequately describe the interactions between the elements when they are working together.

A Process Information System for Real-Time Data Collection and Analysis of Process Operations

The popularity of process information systems demonstrates their usefulness. Because they are central to data collection and analysis, these systems can be justified on their own merits. These systems often consolidate data from other systems, such as tank gauging or laboratory systems. Their data analysis and presentation features help process operators understand better what the process is doing. They often perform *statistical quality control* (SQC) calculations and the control chart plotting. When used for SQC, these systems become part of the control system. Process engineers use them for problem analysis assistance and for tracking of equipment performance parameters such as the fouling factors for individual heat exchangers. Many systems include gross error detection procedures to pinpoint erroneous data values and guide instrument maintenance. Process information systems are a fundamental building block for the integrated system.

When you are preparing for a process information system, you must decide which items of available data to collect and store. The best advice is to collect everything that has a measurement. If something is important enough to have a measurement, it should be collected by the system. A process engineer never knows in advance just what data are going to be needed to solve a process problem. If needed data are missing, the time for problem solution climbs steeply and profitability drops steeply. The process information system, when first installed, should be implemented with considerable spare capacity, about 50 percent, to allow for future growth and to be easily expandable. An integration project or a new process optimization is quite likely to require additional data points, especially analytical data, in order to allow tuning of process models or to perform data reconciliation. When a complex process model is used for planning but not for control, then analytical data are commonly required only on a periodic basis, not continuously. When data from samples taken by hand are needed to tune a process model, it will also be necessary for the process to be close to steady state when the samples are taken. In this case, the process information system must include means for detecting steady-state conditions and call for sample taking during such periods.

Data Communications Networks for Easy, Standardized Transfer of Information between Elements

Referring again to Fig. 11.1, we see clearly that all the arrows on this figure represent an information transfer. Each process with its accompanying advanced control system will have a *local control network* (LCN) and will be attached to a *local-area network* (LAN) that serves the entire plant. This network is very likely attached to a *wide-area network* (WAN) that enables data transfer with other plant networks or a central office system.

Each of the network levels should use a common architecture so that the methods and protocols for transfer are standardized. If this is not done, both hardware and software become uniquely associated with particular data transfers. Not only will maintenance of such a system be much more expensive, but also the ability to change or migrate to a new system will be restricted.

A Central Database for Storage and Dissemination of All Inputs and Results

Each part of the system should get its shared input from, and put its results into, a central database. The physical storage of the database could be centralized or distributed over several devices. The database should appear to users as a single entity. Using this principle as a design basis has numerous advantages. First, this results in a standardized interface to be used by all applications. Users have to learn only one database access method.

Second, this makes it easy for various elements to use computer programs developed by different groups or vendors, at different times. All vendors or internal software developers must be able to interface with your database, but this is usually a simple task compared to interfacing three or four different products together directly. New applications are easier to develop if the input questions relate to just which data, rather than to how to obtain the data.

Third, this will make it easier for the continuous improvement and updating that will be required in each element. If you want to completely change the computer program used for an element, you can put the new program in parallel with the old and verify that the new version is satisfactory without jeopardizing the production version or having to touch one of the other applications. Seldom are things done absolutely right the first time. You have to plan for continuous improvement.

Fourth, the central database makes it easier to have only one copy of each data item available for use. All users accessing a particular data item would get the same value. Many systems have their own unique databases that are probably mutually incompatible. However, procedures can always be put together to move data into the central database, so access outside the particular element becomes standardized.

The central database system is a critical resource, requiring very high reliability. The database has to be available all the time. System or communications failures cannot be tolerated. Consequently, the database system must use redundant or fault-tolerant hardware and must be protected from misuse. The physical equipment should be at the plant site and should not be used for any other purpose. Operational procedures for both hardware and software upgrades need to be especially well thought out, to minimize the risk of downtime.

Model-Based Data Reconciliation for Overall Plant and for Individual Process

Raw process data are always subject to measurement error, even if the instruments are in perfect condition. In addition to random measurement error, instrument drift and failure can occur. The latter are gross errors, and their presence precludes realistic data reconciliation. Techniques of data reconciliation depend upon known standard errors of measurement for each data value. These errors are assumed to be random. A nonrandom error, such as drift, cannot be adjusted correctly. Consequently, a procedure for gross error detection will always be needed as a first screen for data. The measurement that has stuck or drifted off calibration needs to be found quickly. It may not be possible to do any process optimization while gross errors exist.

Gross error detection can sometimes be done one data point at a time. Data reconciliation is then done after the gross errors are corrected. Alternatively, the same model as that used for data reconciliation can be used to find gross errors. For example, a gross error is suspected if any data value adjustment is larger than two or three standard errors from the measurement.

Data reconciliation requires redundant information. *Redundant* in this context means that it must be possible to calculate the value of a measurement to compare with the measurement itself, e.g., a flow that can be either determined directly by a flowmeter or calculated from a combination of other flows and tank-level changes. Without redundancy, one must either accept all measurements as measured or, worse, guess values for missing data. Predictions based on either of the latter alternatives cannot help but be misleading.

A pair of simple distillation columns separating a mixture of known components was described in Ham et al. (1979). The data reconciliation model is composed of component balances and an overall balance. The component balances are nonlinear equations so that a nonlinear quadratic programming formulation needs to be used, as described in Chap. 4.

Mehta (1991) describes an application of an equation-based process simulator to model an oil-producing area gas plant. The model is used in an on-line optimization of the operating conditions of the several distillation columns and flash drums. After gross error detection, the model is tuned so that model predictions match the plant values exactly. In this application, the data reconciliation is not separated from model tuning.

Since each process in a plant will have a model and control system of different structure, the data reconciliation procedures will also be different. It is not realistic to think in terms of using a single reconciliation methodology for all applications. If a commercial process model is purchased from an outside vendor, data reconciliation and tuning procedures will probably be part of the model.

For some specific applications, data reconciliation may not be necessary. A paper by Braden et al. (1992) describes a model-based control application in which a dynamic model is developed by neural network technology. As the paper describes, useful models can be developed with this technology by using unreconciled data. Since the model is being used only to predict steady-state values based on current as-measured dynamic values, the range of prediction is small and the effect of error correspondingly small. However, gross errors still have to be found and corrected before a process optimization can be meaningful. A change in the process error characteristics will also result in misleading predictions until the neural network is retrained. Consequently, a gross error detection scheme and periodic retraining will be needed, even though the training can be done with unreconciled data.

It is also possible to develop a steady-state model for planning by using neural network techniques (Chitra, 1993). Reconciled data should be used to develop these models, so that predictions will be weight-balanced. It is easy to see that the base part of a base-delta model must be weight-balanced, or volume-balanced if that is appropriate. The delta correctors must not disturb the balance when they are used to modify the operation. A planning optimization will try to take advantage of a change that produces extra amounts of products and will try to avoid a change that reduces the amounts. The optimization will be affected by the prediction errors rather than by realistic changes in the process.

Keep in mind that many items of analytical data are not subject to adjustment by data reconciliation. There is no substitute for care and diligence in analytical measurements, either in the laboratory or with a process analyzer.

Advanced Process Control Including Process Optimization

Many advanced control projects have been implemented over the years that perform single-process optimization. These systems are at a high level of sophistication and are likely to continue to improve. They are already adequate to the job of process optimization. When they do not achieve their potential, the cause is primarily an inadequate means of determining the proper targets, specifications, and economic values (Cutler and Ayala, 1993).

At the optimum operating point, a process can be in one of three categories:

1. Constrained by physical limits

2. Constrained by physical limits, targets, and specifications

3. Unconstrained by physical limits or targets in total, so the operating point depends on economic values

Where the optimum can be predefined in terms of physical limits on the operating conditions, the optimization consists of driving the process to these limits. A gas-fired electric generating plant usually fits this criterion. The plant is run at maximum capacity and efficiency, observing only its own limitations. These processes can be optimized as individuals. A control system that drives to constraints is all that is needed.

If a process operation can be defined in terms of physical limits combined with targets or specifications, then the optimization consists of driving to the physical limits and the targets, while not violating any of the specifications. Many petroleum and chemical processes fit into this category. The targets and specifications embody the interaction with other processes. For example (Kennedy, 1980), a catalytic reformer is run to meet a specified octane number in the reformate product. The value for octane desired is obtained from a gasoline planning program that determines the optimum value by planning production over a 1-week or 1-month horizon. Let us suppose that separate studies of the reformer have shown that it is always most profitable to make as much reformate at the specified octane as possible (this is actually the case in most circumstances). This can be done by attempting to maximize the feed rate to the reformer, while meeting the octane target and not violating any physical constraints such as maximum temperatures in furnaces, reactors, etc.

The process optimization will consist of increasing the feed rate until one or more constraints are reached and a further increase is not possible, all the while holding the octane at its target value.

The result of the constrained optimization does not depend on economic drivers. The octane target supplied by the planning program provides the economic coordination between the overall plant and the reformer. The process optimization does not need to have the dollar values of reformate, utility costs, catalyst costs, etc. Changes in these values would not affect the optimum. The optimum depends upon only physical limits and targets that are known in advance. For this case of a constrained optimum, the optimization succeeds and the expected benefits of the advanced control system are achieved, *as long as the octane target is correct.*

Of course, if the volume of reformate is changed, the required octane number for the gasoline pool may also change. That is, if the volume is increased over what the plan expected, the required octane probably drops slightly.

This effect could be calculated in advance by varying the reformate volume in the gasoline planning system. The result could then be sent to the reformer optimization in terms of a variable octane specification that depends upon the reformate volume. However, second-order effects such as this are usually not worth the cost of their determination. The required extra calculations would increase the complexity of both gasoline planning and reformer optimization. If the reformer calculation is done with a reasonable frequency, such as whenever demand patterns change, then the expected benefit will be obtained anyway when the change in reformate production is considered on the next planning cycle.

Some processes, such as crude distillation, fluid catalytic cracking, and ethylene cracking, have great flexibility in their ability to make different yields and qualities of products and/or to change their operation depending upon the dollar values of products, alternative feedstocks, and utilities and energy costs. The flexibility can always be removed by setting a sufficient number of targets. However, an economic optimization can be performed to take advantage of any remaining flexibility and to allow moves away from targets on the basis of economics. In this case, the planning and scheduling functions have to provide both targets or specifications in terms of either volumes or qualities, and dollar values for the various feeds and products. The generation and use of these economic values in process optimization are complex enough that Chap. 12 is devoted entirely to this subject.

Note that in the above three categories, a process control model is not necessarily required for the optimization. However, a model may be required by the control system in order to achieve stable and reliable operation at the targets, etc., determined by the optimization.

Determining the category into which a process fits is an important step. The complexity of the control scheme and of the optimization increases markedly from category 1 to 3. A formal procedure for establishing the purpose of each individual control loop and the process control system taken as a whole, known as *control objectives analysis* (Hadley, 1977), should be helpful here. As presented, the procedure attempts to find "concise, precise, true-all-the-time statements which define the operating objectives of a process." The objectives are to be defined by a group of people representing operations, process, and control engineering. Expanding the group to include planning and scheduling would enable overall plant optimization considerations to be included in the analysis. This should result in a formal statement of information requirements on the part of the planning, scheduling, and control functions, and it should permit proper placement of the process in the above optimization categories.

A Formal Computerized Scheduling System to Interpret Planning Results into a Form Useful to the Advanced Process Control Systems

Scheduling is the specification of inputs to and the outputs from each process and inventory as well as the timing and sequencing of production operations over some short time horizon, such as 1 week or 10 days. Formal scheduling systems are justifiable on their own merits because of their ability to improve management of processes and inventories and thereby to improve customer satisfaction. Variability in operations is reduced, and problems are anticipated. Every scheduling application implemented has reduced average inventory, reduced operating costs, and reduced "crisis management" problems. Implementation of scheduling systems is now one of the fastest-growing areas in the process industries.

The scheduling system has to interpret the results of the planning system and combine them with known timings of inputs and demands to generate a schedule. Part of the schedule results is the targets, specifications, and dollar values needed by the advanced control systems. Thus, the scheduling system acts as the interface and interpreter between planning and control. Even though the targets and economic values are based on as accurate a prediction as possible, the optimization system on a process may be able to improve profitability over the plan case. The schedule needs to be rerun, usually at least daily, as the processes are changing to keep the processes and schedule in synchronization. Many other events can arise to make current operation different from what the schedule expects. The processes can have equipment failures, fouling beyond that anticipated, etc.

Circumstances will arise such that the plan from the planning system cannot be actually implemented in a schedule. The average operation calculated by the planning system may fail when the exact timings of supplies and/or demands are imposed (ships drawing over 30 ft routinely traverse San Francisco Bay, which has an average depth of only 2 ft). In these cases it is necessary to add constraints or change existing ones in the planning model and to rerun until an implementable plan is generated.

It is important that these iterations between the plan and the schedule be accomplished quickly. If rerunning the plan is slow or awkward, the scheduler will be tempted or forced to implement a suboptimal schedule that is not in harmony with any actual plan. Some existing applications (Howard, 1993) make use of an expert system application to modify the plan model as a result of changes made by the scheduler to try to achieve feasibility. The reoptimized plan results are then brought back to the schedule, and scheduling calculations are resumed.

A Responsive Tactical Planning System with Real-Time Updates to Process Representations in Model; a Plan Redeveloped as Often as Necessary to Maintain Coordination between Customer Requirements and Processes

Most planning systems today use mathematical programming optimization tools. *Linear programming* (LP) is the most popular, especially with its extensions such as distributive recursion and *successive linear programming* (SLP). *Successive quadratic programming* (SQP) is seeing greater use where very complex process models are employed directly in a nonlinear optimization (Bodington and Baker, 1990).

Successive linear programming and several gradient techniques have been used for years for small problems such as gasoline blend or single-process optimization (Stadnicki and Lawler, 1983; or Houghton et al., 1969).

The actual process representation in the matrix that is presented to the optimization technique is predominantly of the base-delta form described in Chaps. 7 and 9. The *base* corresponds to current operation yields and qualities or is a prediction based on the tuned complex model. The *deltas* are the first derivatives of product rates and qualities with respect to the independent operating variables of the process. The state-of-the-art applications now in operation use complex process models to develop the base and delta values. These complex process models are tuned to their processes in real time. Even though the papers describe applications that are not fully integrated at this time, see Stramwasser and Davis (1993) or Bannayan and Treat (1993). In a nonlinear optimization, such as used by McKelvie (1993), the base and delta values are redetermined in each step. Thus the final result is not an extrapolation of the base-delta model, but is a base value developed from the tuned complex model directly. This has resulted in an improvement in the credibility and acceptance of the planning model predictions.

Obtaining the accuracy of predictions necessary to match the process performance probably requires this direct use of a complex process model. Consequently, the planning system for the future must also be capable of nonlinear optimization if the complex model is nonlinear. In most petroleum applications, nonlinear modeling will be necessary for processes such as fluid catalytic cracking, hydrocracking, reforming, and crude distillation. In many petrochemical applications, a linear model can be devised and the use of nonlinear optimization avoided to some extent.

The technique of distributive recursion used to solve the pooling problem in linear programming is actually a nonlinear technique (see Chap. 7 for a detailed explanation). In fact, solution of pooling problems by an SLP approach is more robust than distributive recursion since it avoids many of the occasional problems with recursion, such as endless cycling or getting stuck at a poorly selected set of starting values (Lasdon and Joffe, 1990). It is preferable, therefore, to move to a nonlinear optimization for tactical planning unless your problem is truly linear in all aspects.

Most of the planning tools and applications in the petrochemical and refining industries have been in use for a long time. The technology and user community are well established. The fact that so much is already in place may actually be a disadvantage if the presently installed system is not flexible enough to integrate with scheduling and control and is not easily interfaced with the central database.

What was acceptable in the old use environment may not be adequate in the new integrated environment. If the present planning tools do not fit in easily, they will have to be replaced, however expensive this might appear to be. In the long run, staying with a familiar but inadequate system will be very expensive, since it will limit the performance of the integrated system.

Another major change to be considered in the planning area is a change in philosophy from top-down to bottom-up thinking. The top-down approach imposes the plan on the schedule and the processes. If the processes deviate from the plan, the process supervisors are required to explain why. The top-down attitude is in large part responsible for the setting of poorly defined targets for advanced control systems, as described by Cutler and Ayala (1993).

In the bottom-up approach, the plan is tuned to the processes. The processes are still subject to targets and specifications set by the plan. Processes may indeed be more tightly controlled than in a nonintegrated system. However, the plan is rerun as often as necessary to keep it in harmony with how the processes are actually operating. Everyone realizes that conditions change. The reaction to change should not be excuses, but action to take advantage of ever-present change.

Behavior modification to bottom-up thinking causes a deemphasis in the importance of an artificial fixed plan cycle, such as a monthly tactical plan. We focus instead on a moving horizon of, say, 30 days from now. We focus on the attitude: Given what I know about the foreseeable future, what is the best, most profitable thing for me to do today? This new focus might require a plan revision every week, or even every day. Even though the plan may be for 1 week or 1 month, it is executed day by day. Note that with closer coordination between plan and operations, the view of operations is actually extended to a longer time horizon. The view of operations becomes more long-range than was possible before the integration project was implemented.

What is happening at the process level will drive the frequency of plan revisions just as much as what is happening on the supply side and with customer demands. The fundamental idea in *supply chain optimization* is to improve the coupling among supply, demand, and production to achieve improved responsiveness to change. Bottom-up thinking is part of this process.

The strategic planning model may be a different version of the tactical planning model or a separate model, perhaps even used by different people within the company. Especially when the strategic model is multiplant, multiperiod, the emphasis in the model is supply and demand balancing over the long term. The details of process operations within each plant are usually less important than the distribution of feedstocks to plants and the allocation of demands. In this case it is possible to generate a simplified model by using the technique of extreme-point modeling, as described in Chap. 7.

An extreme-point model is a base-delta model generated for the plant as a whole. The plant is represented by only 10 or 15 columns in the matrix instead of the thousands that are in a complete plant model. The extreme-point model also is linear and therefore can be solved much more quickly. Some modeling systems can develop extreme-point models automatically through the use of run instructions, usually called *macros*. Expert system applications are also used to automatically run cases on the tactical plan system and to generate the extreme-point plant model.

There will be cases for which the simplified model is not adequate. For example, if interplant transfers of intermediate streams are to be studied, then there is little choice but to combine the several entire-plant models into a very large overall model. The planning and modeling system you use should allow you to do this combination quickly and easily. Through the use of macros and expert systems rules, it should be possible to automate the process.

In this discussion of planning systems, we have concentrated on those using mathematical programming techniques. Although these techniques are the most heavily used, they are not necessarily used everywhere. Many alternatives exist, such as process simulators and spreadsheet programs used on personal computers. Regardless of what is used, the important points are that the prediction of process performance should be based on current actual performance and that the plan should be easily regenerated when necessary due to either changes in process performance or infeasibilities in the schedule.

The plant planning level is the lowest level at which realistic plant optimization can be performed. At any lower level, the viewpoint is either too short-range or too localized to a single process for anything but a suboptimization to be possible, unless it is coordinated with information from the plant planning level. It is very rare for a single process to be at an optimum point when that point was determined on the merits of the process alone, without regard to effects on the entire plant. It is, of course, possible if the plant is composed of only one process, but this is a limiting case.

Optimization only at a higher level than the individual plant implies that there are no alternatives that have any economic impact at the tactical planning level—a highly unlikely situation. This could be the case if the higher-level strategic plan included or were the same as the plant tactical plan. Where this is not the case, optimization at too high a level will actually represent a suboptimization.

Strategic planning is not directly part of the tactical planning/scheduling/control loop. However, it is necessary for the strategic planning system to be integrated with the database and communications network so that strategic process models and other process information can be easily updated. The elements of risk and uncertainty are being considered to a much greater extent in recent strategic planning applications than in the traditionally simple deterministic approaches of the past.

Chance-constrained programming (Roush et al., 1994) is an extension of linear programming that accounts for variability in input data, assuming that the standard deviation of the input is known. While the particular example described by Roush et al. is for animal feed formulation, the technique itself, which is described in the article, has broad applicability. The constraints are augmented with a nonlinear function of the variance of the individual variables. Consequently, the problem becomes nonlinear even if the underlying deterministic problem is linear. The technique is shown to be more accurate in achieving a certain level of performance than the very common procedure of changing the constraint limits by the amount of a safety factor equal to some fraction or multiple of the dependent-variable standard deviation.

Robust optimization (Masch and Baker, 1991) is a technique that simultaneously compares a set of scenarios to generate a strategy that is very near optimum under favorable conditions, good under a wide range of circumstances, and acceptable under the most adverse conditions. An example of the use of robust optimization for facility planning under uncertainty is given by Lindner-Dutton et al. (1994).

Use of *mixed-integer programming* (MIP) for facility planning and scenario development is also being made more efficient and less compute-time-intensive by the use of an embedded expert system application, to reduce the number of branches that must be searched when a branch-and-bound algorithm is used.

Expert System Applications Embedded in All Other Elements to Interpret Data and Results and Improve Efficiency of Data Analysis

Although expert systems may be used as the primary technology for one of the elements, the use of concern here is that of an adjunct or assistant to another procedure. For example, an expert system application may be used for a preliminary gross error detection, before data reconciliation. There will always be situations or exceptions that cannot be directly handled by the primary algorithm used in an application. Consequently, the availability of an embedded expert system is essential to the implementation. Chapter 8 gives examples of the use of expert systems in setting up business planning cases using mathematical programming, direct inclusion in the mathematical solution process, interpretation of results, marginal cost analysis, infeasibility analysis, and translation of planning results to a starting point for a schedule. These and other uses are indicated in this chapter in the descriptions of the other elements.

Process Models Tuned in Real Time so that at No Time Is a Planning Prediction in Error Relative to Actual Current Operation

Tuned process models for either planning or control optimization are a product of model-based data reconciliation. In this section we describe other aspects of model tuning that are in addition to those brought up under the topic of data reconciliation.

If the same process model can be used for planning and control, agreement between the two functions is ensured. In addition, the data used for control, which are being collected in real time, are all that is necessary. No additional data need be taken and reconciled for the planning model. However, use of the same model for both functions implies a steady-state model. In many reported applications, such as Stramwasser (1993), steady-state models are used for both planning updates and process optimization. The process must be close to steady state before model-tuning data can be taken.

In some techniques for advanced process control, the process itself is used to develop a dynamic model. Small step changes are made in variables, and the dynamic response is measured. The dynamic model is then used to predict the steady-state process conditions. The control system will move the process set points if the predicted steady state is not going to be at a desired target or will go beyond a limit or specification. Some attempts have been made to use the predicted steady state as input to the planning or optimization model reconciliation and tuning. If these approaches can be made to work in your environment, the need to achieve steady state for model tuning can be avoided. However, error in the prediction of the equivalent steady state will increase the variability in the tuning parameters.

If any additional data are required, such as special analytical data on feeds and products, these values would have to be measured in real time and included in the steady-state prediction procedure. A large amount of data would be collected to be used only on infrequent planning model updates. Suppose the planning model only needs to be tuned once a week. Analytical costs would be very high if we put in a process analyzer to continuously measure a value needed only weekly.

Consequently, we conclude that predicted steady-state procedures for model tuning should be used only if it is very difficult or impractical to achieve steady state. The examples discussed in Part 3 of this book and most applications reported in the literature use steady-state operation as the basis for model tuning.

An Organizational Structure that Rewards Cooperation and Teamwork

If the plant that is the object of an integration project now has the gap between planning and control discussed in Chap. 1, there is probably an organizational or people "gap" as well as an information gap. If the computer systems are put in place without changing the people structure, the information gap can be ready to be closed, but the people gap can still be there. The stage is set for an expensive failure, because the people gap may prevent the closure of the information gap.

The existing organizational structure probably should not be computerized intact. The roles of planners, schedulers, and controllers will be changed by the integrated system. Bottom-up thinking instead of top-down thinking will change the way that people work with each other. The existing staff in one function may never have thought about their counterparts in another function with an "us" view. The view may have been adversarial, a "them versus us" attitude. Since this attitude will subvert the integration, it will probably be necessary to change people's responsibilities, supervision, and job objectives. A new mission statement will be needed, if you will. Many integration projects are preceded by or accompanied by a major organizational change, a "reengineering" or cultural change.

If the organizational structure fosters the proper cooperation and teamwork, the next management problem is to ensure the new users buy into the project. The history of computer applications is littered with examples of technical successes but financial and political failures because the users would not use the system. In most cases, this resulted from the application being "stuffed down the throats" of potential users. Two situations exist: (1) The users were right to reject the application, and (2) the users should have found the application useful.

Many failures were caused, and are still being caused, by the developers going into seclusion and, without outside contact, coming out with a finished application to be implemented. Applications that are developed in the absence of contact with the ultimate users are likely to miss many important points. Users are right to reject such applications. Development without user involvement is an unforgivable error.

On the other hand, it is possible for applications of proven utility to be rejected by a particular group. Perhaps some people in the group use the application, and others do not. Rejection by users in this case is a management failure. Avoiding failure due to this cause is one of the reasons for major organizational changes to accompany an integration project. It is essential to work with the long-term ultimate user when you try to enlist user support. The user must be convinced that the application will be personally useful, not only to "other people." A user group that is unconvinced will try to assign someone to the project who is low-ranked, is about to be transferred, or even is about to be fired. In any case, the group has not really bought into the project. If the people in the development group do not have a personal, financial, and career interest in a successful project, do not bother trying to do it.

The last subject in the category of management is *training*. It is not possible to overemphasize the importance of training new users to handle the new operational environment. Formal procedures for training replacements for the people in functional groups are also very important. When an integrated system is implemented, the people involved become knowledge workers. That is, they acquire special knowledge about the new system and how it works and how they must work with their counterparts in other functions. As described more fully in Chap. 10, this knowledge must be preserved over personnel changes, retirements, etc. Only by careful training of replacements can the knowledge be preserved. Otherwise, every personnel change will be accompanied by a fall-back and relearning period. It is possible for operation to never return to its former efficiency.

Formal procedures need to be established and followed. No one would consider putting an operator in charge of a process plant without adequate training. With systems for planning and scheduling integrated with control, the impact on profitability of poor or nonexistent training of planners and schedulers is financially just as important as the quality of training of operators in actually running the processes. Excellent training is essential to the success of the integration project and to long-term continuous improvement.

References

Bannayan, M. A., and M. G. Treat (1993): "Decision Making Based upon Integrated Information Systems," paper CC-93-121, National Petroleum Refiners Association Computer Conference, New Orleans, LA, November 15–17.

Braden, W. B., T. Graettinger, A. Federowicz, and N. V. Bhat (1992): "A Neural Network Based Control and Optimization Program," ORSA/TIMS national meeting, San Francisco, November.

Chitra, S. P. (1993): "Use Neural Networks for Problem Solving," *Chem. Eng. Prog.*, vol. 89, no. 4, April, pp. 44–52.

Cutler, C. R., and J. S. Ayala (1993): "Integrating Off-Line Schedulers with Real Time Optimizers," paper 40a, presented at the American Institute of Chemical Engineers national meeting, Houston, TX, March 28–April 1.

Hadley, K. L. (1977): "Control Objectives Analysis," paper CC-77-88, presented at the National Petroleum Refiners Association Computer Conference, New Orleans, LA, October 31–November 2.

Ham, P. G., G. W. Cleaves, and J. K. Lawlor (1979): "Operation Data Reconciliation: An Aid to Improved Plant Performance," Tenth World Petroleum Congress Conference, Bucharest, Romania; Preprints, Heyden & Son, Inc., Philadelphia, PA, no. PD23.

Houghton, W. T., L. Iscol, and W. J. Ruspino (1969): "In-Line Blending with an Off-Line Computer," paper CC-69-90, National Petroleum Refiners Association Computer Conference, New Orleans, LA, November 17–19.

Howard, J. B. (1993): Chesapeake decision sciences, private communication, Houston, TX.

Kennedy, J. P. (1980): "Multivariable Control System for Regulating Process Conditions and Process Optimizing," U. S. Patent 4,228,509, October 14.

Lasdon, L., and B. Joffe (1990): "The Relationship between Distributive Recursion and Successive Linear Programming in Refining Production Planning Models," paper CC-90-135, National Petroleum Refiners Association Computer Conference, Seattle, WA, October 29–31.

Lindner-Dutton, L., M. Jordan, and M. Karwan (1994): "Beyond Mean Time to Failure," *OR/MS Today*, April.

Masch, V. A., and T. E. Baker (1991): "Robust Optimization," presented at the American Institute of Chemical Engineers spring national meeting, Houston, TX, April.

McKelvie, J. (1993): "Process Model/LP Interface—BP Oil, Kwinana Refinery," private communication, June 4.

Mehta, C. (1991): "A Distributed CIM System for Process Plants," American Institute of Chemical Engineers spring national meeting, Houston, TX, April 7–11..

Roush, W. B., R. H. Stock, T. L. Cravener, and T. H. D'Alfonso (1994): "Using Chance Constrained Programming for Animal Feed Formulation at Agway," *Interfaces*, vol. 24, no. 2, March-April, pp. 53–58.

Stadnicki, S. J., and M. B. Lawler (1983): "An Integrated Planning and Control Package for Product Blending," *Proceedings of the Second Annual Control Engineering Conference*, Control Engineering, Des Plaines, IL, pp. 315–321.

Stramwasser, R., and J. Davis (1993): "On-Line Optimization at El Palito Refinery," paper CC-93-139, National Petroleum Refiners Association Computer Conference, New Orleans, LA, November 15–17.

12

Marginal Economics

Generating and Using Marginal Economic Values in Optimization

C. Edward Bodington
Consultant

Introduction

If we were able to simultaneously optimize the plan, the schedule, and the operation of all processes in a plant by means of a single very large computer application, we would not have very much concern about marginal economic values. The economic values needed would be based on the marketplace for our feeds and products. Attempts to accomplish this in a single computer application have usually been complete failures. The huge, monolithic computer application is too time-consuming to run, to keep current, and to keep correct. In fairness, a few applications have been successfully made to relatively simple plants. One example for a producing area gas plant (Mehta, 1991) uses a process simulation system to model an entire plant. This model is then used in a planning optimization after the model is carefully tuned to the actual processes. Note that scheduling is not a factor in this particular situation, which significantly simplifies the situation. The simulation model involves about 25,000 nonlinear equations, solved for the plan case by using *successive quadratic programming* (SQP).

Although there is no logical limit to the size of plant that could be handled with this procedure, the practical reality is that the model for a complex plant would be enormous, and time-consuming, even for the computers of the foreseeable future. Since scheduling also must be considered in most situations, the combinatorial nature of the scheduling problem further increases problem size by orders of magnitude. We also expect that the interpretation of the answers from such an application would be beyond human capabilities.

The problem must be segmented into a set of cooperating, hierarchically related subproblems of manageable size. Many of the subproblems, particularly those for individual processes, will need marginal economic values for their feeds and products that cannot be obtained directly from a marketplace.

As was described in Chap. 11, many process optimizations can be accomplished by defining a sufficient number of physical constraints and targets to specify the operation of the process. However, for many other processes, constraint and target setting alone is not sufficient to specify process operation completely. In these cases, economic values for feeds, products, and various aspects of operation are needed in the process optimization, which is then expected to achieve an optimum point independently (see Fig. 12.1). These cases are the subject of this chapter.

Marginal economic values are sometimes called *incremental values.* It is the economic value of a change in some operating variable from its current level, or the value of an increment of production. Fixed costs that are not affected by changes in operation are usually not considered. Marginal values of feeds and products are equal to the sale or purchase price at the appropriate level of production or consumption.

The marginal values of primary feeds and final products are determined by the marketplace. Although the price at the plant may be somewhat different due to transportation, storage, and marketing costs, for instance, the value is definable within close limits. This is

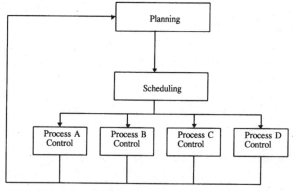

Figure 12.1   Integrated system optimization loop.

not the case for myriad intermediate streams within the plant. A process that uses an intermediate and produces other intermediates that are not sold directly needs some way to evaluate its feeds and products and thereby evaluate its own operation. The objective of this chapter is twofold: to describe the conventional techniques used to determine marginal values for intermediate streams and to describe a methodology whereby the individual processes can optimize more or less independently, by using shared information in such a way that the final result approaches an overall global optimization. The theoretical background for such an optimization involves the decomposition principle of linear programming and another concept known as *duality*.

The Decomposition Principle

This procedure was originally developed, in the 1950s, to allow large problems in linear programming to be segmented into a group of small problems that were easier to solve on the limited-capacity computers available at the time. Dantzig and Wolfe (1960) called the partitioning a decomposition of the original problem. Hence, the procedure is known as the *decomposition principle of linear programming*. For a relatively recent detailed description of the decomposition principle algorithm, see the article by Ho and Loute (1981). Although the original development was based on linear programming, the principles have been extended to nonlinear problems.

For the purposes of integrating planning, scheduling, and control, the principle is not important today for its ability to reduce problem sizes. Computer capacity today is sufficient to solve global plant optimizations in their entirety. The principle is important because it justifies the use of transfer prices for flows between subunits to gauge economic performance of the subunits independently.

The basic idea is as follows: The master problem (see Fig. 12.2) is

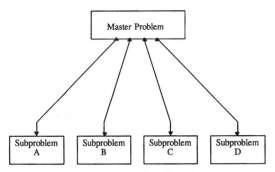

Figure 12.2   Optimization of distributed systems.

solved, and trial values of the prices of all the inputs and outputs to the subproblems are generated. Given the prices, the subproblems are solved; and the solutions give the amounts of inputs consumed, products produced, and net profits made. This cycle continues, with the master problem generating prices and the subproblems reporting their optimum situation for the particular set of prices.

This cycling procedure will converge and give results identical to an overall optimization of the original, undecomposed problem. At the overall optimum, the subproblems are each at an optimum point and are all in balance with each other regarding production and consumption. The dollar values that effectively cause this balance are termed the *transfer prices,* since they assign value to the transfers between subproblems via the master.

Duality

When given the final optimum prices, each subproblem will find the optimum productions and consumptions independently. And vice versa. If the subproblems are given the optimum productions and consumptions, they will compute the same values for the transfer prices. The same optimum solution can be achieved by giving a subproblem either prices or required production and consumption. This property is called *duality* or the *duality principle.*

The decomposition principle and duality together form a theoretical justification for the use of transfer prices between subunits to achieve an overall optimum for an entity while allowing subunits to optimize independently. The use of transfer prices is popular and has been institutionalized by common practice. Many corporations use them for valuing transfers between domestic and international branches, between production and marketing, etc.

Application to Operating Processes

Application of the decomposition principle to a situation involving actual operating processes requires making the planning model equivalent to the master problem and the individual process optimizations the subproblems. The planning model would generate trial values of the transfer prices to be used by the subproblems. Each process would then optimize and return results to the planning model. Finding the transfer prices by this procedure poses several difficulties:

First, it can take a large number of iterations for a decomposition problem to converge. Doing many iterations when the subproblem is an actual operating process is impractical. The transfer prices are changed for each iteration, and the process must achieve optimum operation for each new set of trial transfer prices. It is quite common and necessary for the transfer prices to vary widely above and below the final optimum values. No operator would be willing to move and reoptimize the process many times in succession as this procedure might dictate. The size of moves required would be potentially very large compared to the usually small changes used in process experiments or the step changes made to determine response models.

Second, the planning model is not really the decomposition principle master problem from which the process optimizations have been removed. The process optimizations are still embedded in the tactical planning model. The tactical plan performs the process optimizations in parallel with the processes themselves. The transfer prices can therefore be developed directly from the tuned process models in the tactical planning system, or by use of tactical plan results. Interaction with the processes is not necessary to develop the transfer prices; it is only necessary to validate them by performance feedback. Therefore, the planning tool needs to be designed to produce the correct transfer prices. This is one of the major reasons why the predictions of the planning model must be accurate. Otherwise, the transfer prices will not be accurate enough to be usable at the process level.

Finally, bulk transfer prices for the input and output streams are not sufficient at the process level. The transfer price is valid only for a certain quality of the stream. If operational changes affect the quality, then additional information is needed to evaluate the effect on economic value.

Formulation of the Tactical Plan Model

In order to use the planning model to determine transfer prices, the formulation must be developed so that the economic effect of parameters important at the process level can be evaluated. To fit this purpose, most planning models will need redesign or enhancement with more attention to economic and process details. In a nonintegrated environment, shortcuts are common, so the tactical model does not truly reflect important details in process operation. For example, some feed and product qualities may be essential at the process level, but are not included in the planning model. Unless the important qualities are considered, it is not possible for the planning tool to develop the economic effects of changes. Each parameter in the process optimization that needs an economic valuation must be included in the planning model.

The objective function must be directly related to changes in plant profit. Fixed costs can be neglected, but all variable items must be included. The values needed are the economic effect on profit of changes in operation. These values are the first derivatives of plant profit with respect to changes in process operation variables. These derivatives are the marginal values or marginal costs.

The derivatives of plant profit are needed with respect to both rate and quality. A stream has the value of its rate derivative only at some specific quality. The economic impact of changing the rate at constant quality can be calculated from the rate derivative alone. If the quality changes, then the stream is now different and both the rate derivative and one or more quality derivatives must be used to account for the fact that the value is not a function of just rate alone (Fig. 12.3). Note that many sales contracts for products contain a provision for price adjustment based on quality. For example, wine grapes in California's Napa Valley normally demand a premium on the price per pound for sugar content over 22 percent.

In the formulation of the plan model, it is clearly important that current operation be explicitly modeled as well as future operation. The plan result must be directly applicable to current operation so that the schedule can relate an operation in the plan to a real operation of the process. Otherwise, economic values do not apply to current actual operation. This means that blocked operations or various modes of operation must not be averaged in the plan, unless an unequivocal technique is available to develop the economic values for individual operations.

Although most process industry plants use a linear programming model for tactical planning, any modeling approach can be used as

---

Change in Profit, \$/day = Delta Rate*$d\$/dR$ + Delta QR*$d\$/dQR$ + ...

Alternatively, depending upon formulation:

Change in Profit, \$/day = Delta Rate*$(V + dV/dQ$*Delta Q + ...)$

Where:

        Delta Rate = product or feed rate change.

        $d\$/dR$ = V = partial derivative of profit with respect to rate. This is commonly available as an LP shadow price.

        $d\$/dQR$ = partial derivative of profit with respect to the quality-rate product. This is the form most commonly available as an LP shadow price.

        Delta QR = change in stream quality-rate product.

        dV/dQ = change in rate value with quality.

        Delta Q = change in stream quality.

(Consistent units assumed throughout)

Figure 12.3 Accounting for effects of rate and quality changes on profit.

long as it is quality-sensitive. By *quality-sensitive* we mean that effects of changes in the quality of feed streams or operations are represented in the model and will affect operations and stream qualities in model results. A "barrel balancer" that considers only rates will not be satisfactory unless qualities are truly not important.

Determination of the Planning Horizon

Another aspect of model formulation for correct determination of marginal values is the planning horizon, which is the time period into the future that the plan considers.

In general, the horizon should be long enough that plan results are essentially independent of what will happen after the horizon period. The profit we are trying to maximize is that over the long haul, assuming that the company is to stay in business. A short-range viewpoint will compromise the future. We do not want to make a high profit this week or this quarter and go broke the next. The main considerations that establish the needed horizon are inventories of intermediates and finished products, variability and seasonality of demands, and variability of production capacity.

A conventional approach in short-range tactical planning is to use a two-time-period model. The first period is the time over which the demand and supply schedule is accurately known. A second period is then added, which is long enough so that one can make a good forecast of average operation during the period. The purpose of the second period is primarily to control the volume and quality of final inventory left from the first period. This approach is frequently used for planning product blending (Bodington, 1992). For blending applications, a 1-week first period followed by an average 30-day period is typical. Plant tactical plans usually consider a longer period of 1 month or more.

As the horizon is made longer, the effect of inventories diminishes. Long-range strategic plans usually can ignore inventory considerations. A rule of thumb is that if the throughput is more than 20 times the inventory, then the inventory can be neglected in planning.

Determination of the Plan Revision Frequency

Most process industry plants recalculate the tactical plan on at least a monthly cycle, or more frequently as a function of how dynamic their demand pattern is. For example, some refineries with integrated planning and control systems need to revise their gasoline blending plan daily. This frequency is dictated by uncertainty and difficulty in forecasting demands. Every day, the demand pattern is revised to reflect current information. Other refineries, with planning and control just as integrated, can run their gasoline plan once per month, because demands and operations are stable and accurately known over a 1-month time frame.

Most planners arrive at a comfortable tactical planning cycle by experience. However, if the experience is gained in a nonintegrated environment, then the subject needs to be reexamined when the move is made to an integrated system. As the system becomes more integrated, the frequency of plan revisions is very likely to increase. In some reported applications, such as some of those described in Part 3, where the plan and the process optimization are combined, the plan is revised every few hours.

Calculation of Marginal Values

Once the formulation of the planning model is adequate to generate the needed marginal values, two general approaches can be used: *linear programming* (LP) and the *delta method.*

The LP approach is probably faster, since most of the derivatives needed are available from the results of one run. The derivatives are called *shadow prices* in LP terminology. Figure 12.4 gives the definition and derivation of shadow prices and their interpretation as derivatives. The shadow price values are a strict function of the final optimum solution, or the *optimal basis,* as it is called. Without using a sensitivity analysis, which determines how much a constraint may be changed without causing a change in the optimal basis, it is not known over what range constraint values may be changed without the shadow prices changing. Changing the basis usually changes many, if not all, of the values of the shadow prices. In nonlinear optimization using *successive linear programming* (SLP), move limits are imposed on the variables during each LP optimization so that the amount of change from one step to the next will not be larger than the amount that corresponds to a reasonably good linear approximation to the nonlinear functions. An optimum solution can be obtained that is constrained by some of the move limits rather than by the actual constraints of the problem. In these cases, the shadow prices obtained may not be usable as the profit derivatives we need. A result constrained by move limits is actually not a result of the original problem, and therefore the shadow prices are not really correct. It is preferable to continue steps of the SLP algorithm until all constraints are those of the actual problem. Some procedures for nonlinear optimization by SLP do not consider a problem converged unless constrained by limits of the original problem, and they therefore give reliable results directly.

The Linear Programming Problem:

Constraints: $AX = B$
Objective: $CX = Z$

Where:

A = the matrix of coefficients m rows by n columns
X = the column vector of n variable values
B = the column vector of m constraint values
C = the row vector of n cost coefficients
Z = the value of the objective function

At the Optimum Solution:

$Xb = (A$ inverse$) B$
Where Xb is the basic portion of X
and $(A$ inverse$)$ is the optimal basis inverse
m rows and columns

$Z = CbXb$
Where Cb is the basic portion of the cost row.
(All nonbasic X values are zero.)

Some Algebra:

$Z = Cb (A$ inverse$) B$

The Definition of the Shadow Price:

$P = Cb (A$ inverse$)$

so that:

$Z = P B$

From the above, it follows that P can be interpreted as:

$P = dZ / dB$, or the derivative of the objective with respect to the constraints for any member i of P and B.

Figure 12.4 Shadow prices in linear programming.

If the process optimization requires costs for being above or below a target, the shadow price approach will give only half of the required values. For a quality or rate constraint, the shadow price is usually the economic value for an increase above the constraint (the sense depends upon the model formulation). The effect of a decrease below the constraint, which could be a different value, needs to be determined by the delta method. The delta method can be used with any modeling technique. The method involves making runs with parameters changed from their base-case values by small increments and subtracting the two profit results to obtain a delta. The incremental value is then simply the delta profit divided by the amount of parametric change. The values are numerical derivatives of the profit. If the delta method for evaluating the economic values is required, many runs will be needed to obtain the derivatives. One additional run for each derivative is needed, which for a complex plant could run into the thousands.

If the planning method is one that converges to a solution, the convergence tolerance must be very small relative to the magnitude of the delta between cases. If the convergence tolerance is large relative to the delta, then variation in the convergence point will be counted as part of the delta and will make the delta values essentially meaningless. Delta values of the same order of magnitude as the convergence tolerance are best set to zero, under the principle that no effect is better than the wrong effect.

The marginal economic values are used by simply combining them with values of the process variables in the optimization objective function. Figure 12.3 illustrates the use of rate and quality value information to evaluate a stream. The units of measurement must be determined. Linear programs, e.g., may not carry along explicit units for the column or row values. Only the model developer knows what the units are.

Once defined, the units of the economic values determine how they will be used. Specification giveaway costs are usually measured in dollars per unit specification per unit volume or weight. Quality target deviation values have the same units as specification giveaway. A major difference is that there are two values, one for positive deviations and one for negative. Economic values for rates are measured in dollars per volume or weight unit.

The effect of stream quality is usually measured in dollars per unit quality per unit volume or weight. The units of quality may be different in the economic plan and the process optimization. In this case, unit conversion will be needed before use. For example, the process may use the actual pour point, while the economic plan model uses a pour point blending index.

A Simple Example Using Linear Programming

The following example is included to demonstrate that a subproblem can be optimized independently of the global problem as long as correct transfer prices are used. The global problem will be defined in a small linear program and solved for the optimum solution. Then the global problem will be divided into two subproblems, which will be assigned transfer prices from the global solution. We will show that the same answers are obtained for the processes as subproblems or as part of the global problem. We will also show that small errors in the transfer prices will cause a significant change in the optimum solution found for a subproblem.

The global problem is defined in Fig. 12.5, which shows a flow diagram of a plant with a single distillation column and a cracking plant. Together these processes produce two products, A and B. The basic

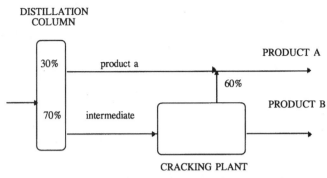

DISTILLATION
COLUMN

Figure 12.5   Example of decomposition principle.

yield for the column is 30 percent product *A* and 70 percent of an intermediate that is fed to the cracking process. The yield of *A* can be increased at a cost and at some loss of overall yield. The base yield of product *A* from the cracking process is 60 percent, and that of product *B* is 40 percent. In this process also, the yield of *A* can be increased at a cost and at some loss of overall yield. The linear program matrix and the optimum solution are shown in Fig. 12.6. The column labeled *RHS* is the value of the equations, and the row labeled *VALUES* is the solution value at optimum.

The transfer price of the intermediate stream is found to be 26. This value can be obtained from the shadow price on the INTERM row or by the delta method. If the delta method is used, an additional optimization is run with the constraint on row INTERM set to 1.0 instead of 0. The objective will be found to have increased from the original value of 326 to 352, or 26 units higher. The transfer prices for products *A* and *B* are equal to their sales prices of 40 and 38, respectively.

According to the decomposition principle, we should be able to separate plant 1 and plant 2 into two problems and by using the transfer prices achieve the same operation and the same overall profit as in the combined problem. Figures 12.7 and 12.8 show that this is indeed the case. The two profit values of 242 and 84 sum to the correct value of 326, and the production and consumption totals are identical.

The solution for plant 1, shown in Fig. 12.7, agrees exactly with the global solution because we left the plant 2 feed constraint of 70 units active. If we eliminate this constraint, the amount of intermediate produced rises to about 71 at the optimum solution. An exact match is no longer obtained because the transfer price of 26 used for the intermediate was very close but not exact. The solution is very sensitive to small errors in this value.

This demonstrates an important point: If only economic information is given to a subproblem, the productions and consumptions

	PLANT NO. 1		PLANT NO. 2		SALES		RHS	OBJECTIVE
	COLUMN	DELTA	REACTOR	DELTA	PROD A	PROD B		
PROFIT	-28	-10	-12	-7	40	38	326	OBJECTIVE
INPUT	1						110	120
CAPY-1	1						110	110
PROD A	0.3	0.9	0.6	0.9	-1		5.71E-07	0
INTERM	0.7	-1	-1				1.19E-07	0
PROD B			0.4	-1		-1	2.98E-07	0
CAPY-2			1				70	70
RATIO C	1	-10					40	0
RATIO R			1	-10			70	0
VALUES	110	7	70	0	81.3	28	326	

Figure 12.6 Complete problem matrix and optimum solution.

	PLANT NO. 1 COLUMN	DELTA	TRANSFER INTERM	SALES PROD A	RHS	
PROFIT	− 28	− 10	26	40	242	OBJECTIVE
INPUT	1				110	120
CAPY-1	1				110	110
PROD A	0.3	0.9	0	− 1	1E-06	0
INTERM	0.7	− 1	− 1		0	0
PROD B		0			0	0
CAPY-2			1		70	70
RATIO C	1	− 10			40	0
RATIO R			0		0	0
VALUES	110	7	70	39.3	242	− 84

Figure 12.7   Plant 1 decomposition matrix and solution.

found to be optimum will not match the global optimum solution unless the transfer prices are exactly correct. However, adding some operational information, in this case the rate constraint, makes it possible to easily achieve the same answer.

Optimization in the Presence of Errors

Even with performance feedback, data reconciliation, and model tuning, the process optimizations done with the tactical planning tool will not be exact. If the scheduler communicates only the inexact transfer prices, the process subproblems will not get the same answer for rates and qualities as the planning model does. If the scheduler communicates only the inexact rate and quality targets and specifications, then the transfer prices from the standpoint of the processes will not match the planning model prices. Thus, in the presence of error, transferring only one kind of information, economic or operational, will not produce agreement on the best way to operate the processes.

A Close Approach to the Optimum

Since error cannot be eliminated, present practice is to assume that a close approach to the optimum can be achieved by using a combination of both price and operational information in the process optimizations. This method has actually been used for a long time. Published experience covering many years is particularly available for gasoline blending systems (Lasher, 1967; Houghton et al., 1969; Stadnicki and

	TRANSFER INTERM	PLANT NO. 2 REACTOR	DELTA	SALES PROD A	PROD B	RHS	OBJECTIVE
PROFIT	-26	-12	-7	40	38	84.00002	
INPUT	1					70	70
CAPY-1	1					70	105
PROD A	0	0.6	0.9	-1		-4.5E-07	0
INTERM	1	-1				0	0
PROD B		0.4	-1		-1	-1.1E-07	0
CAPY-2		1				70	75
RATIO R		1	-10			70	0
VALUES	70	70	0	42	28	84.00002	-1886

Figure 12.8 Plant 2 decomposition matrix and solution.

Lawler, 1983) and more recently for other processes as described in Part 3, Chaps. 14 through 18.

For example, in the integrated planning and control system described by Stadnicki and Lawler, a planning program predicts recipes or compositions for gasoline blends. The recipes are the operational information, and the economic values of the components are the transfer price information. Both are communicated to the blending process. When the predicted composition is used on the actual process, the qualities achieved differ, more or less, from those expected. The process optimization therefore moves away from the recipe targets to reduce or eliminate giveaway costs on specifications, using the component prices to minimize the cost of the recipe change. To use this approach for any process, the control system must have all the following:

- Specifications to be met exactly

- Specifications allowing giveaway and the cost for giveaway

- Targets on rates or qualities and the cost or benefit for missing the targets, both for above and below the targets

- Transfer prices on inputs and products as well as the cost or benefit of quality changes

- Costs for utilities and supplies

As described above, the costs or benefits are the marginal values equal to the first derivatives of plant profit with respect to the operating parameters. It is now up to the advanced control system to improve performance by using the above data.

A Gasoline Reformer Example

A tactical plan is often used to determine the proper octane number for the reformate from a reformer process that will optimize the reformer operation and the subsequent blending of gasolines. This octane level becomes a target for the reformer optimization.

If the octane is higher than the target at the same rate, the gasoline blended will come out higher in octane than is needed or expected, resulting in giveaway. Therefore, the quality cost associated with an octane increase is negative. If the octane is lower than the target at the same rate, the production of gasoline will be reduced. A low-octane component will have to be removed from the pool to compensate for the lower reformate octane. Therefore, the quality cost associated with a reduced octane is also negative. This has to be the case if we have an optimum solution. Any change that does not involve changing a constraint will cause a reduction in profit. A change that involves changing a binding constraint can be positive or negative depending on the direction of the constraint change. For example, if the rate can be increased at constant octane, then production of gasoline can be increased at a small cost in giveaway. Therefore, the value of increasing the rate is positive. By using the equation in Fig. 12.3, the profit could be further increased if more reformate could be produced at slightly lower octane to keep the giveaway at zero. The net effect would be an increase in total gasoline production at constant octane. These effects give the reformer advanced control system an incentive to maximize reformate production while keeping octane at a proper level for the blending pool.

Crude Unit Example

The application of a very accurate model and an optimization procedure to a crude unit is described in Chap. 17. The application shows the use of the combination of targets, upper and lower limits, specifications, and marginal economics in the optimization phase. The quality of most of the streams is set by placing specifications on several distillation points. On the heavy vacuum gas oil, rather than trying to specify product quality, the price is made a function of quality. Values for the other streams are set by a base value up to a breakpoint and then an incremental value for production above the breakpoint. The breakpoint rate would correspond to the demand or desired rate from planning. All the ideas presented above in the section on a close approach to the optimum are used in this application.

References

Bodington, C. E. (1992): "Inventory Management in Blending Optimization," ORSA/TIMS national meeting, San Francisco, November 1–4.

Dantzig, G. B., and P. Wolfe (1960): "Decomposition Principle for Linear Programs," *Oper. Res.*, vol. 8, pp. 101–111.

Ho, J. K., and E. Loute (1981): "An Advanced Implementation of the Dantzig-Wolfe Decomposition Algorithm for Linear Programming," *Math. Prog.*, vol. 20, pp. 303–326.

Houghton, W. T., L. Iscol, and W. J. Ruspino (1969): "In-Line Blending with an Off-Line Computer," paper CC-69-90, National Petroleum Refiners Association Computer Conference, New Orleans, LA, November 17–19.

Lasher, R. J. (1967): "Computer Control of Motor Gasoline Blending," paper CC-67-84, presented at the National Petroleum Refiners Association Computer Conference, St. Louis, MO, November 7–9.

Mehta, C. (1991): "A Distribution CIM (Computer Integrated Manufacturing) System for Process Plants," Preprint 236, AIChE National Meeting, Houston, TX, April 7, 1991.

Stadnicki, S., and M. B. Lawler (1983): "An Integrated Planning and Control Package for Product Blending," *Proceedings of the Second Annual Control Engineering Conference*, Control Engineering, Des Plaines, IL, pp. 315–321.

Financial Justification

Why Should We Integrate Planning, Scheduling, and Control?

C. Edward Bodington
Consultant

Where is the money? What improvements will be made in the financial performance of a plant to justify the expenditures in time and equipment? How rapidly will the project pay back its costs? Can we just do part of the project and get a large portion of the benefits? Is there a best order in which to implement the stages of the project for maximum benefit? These are appropriate questions that deserve thorough answers. We begin by reviewing a survey whose purpose was to determine company managements' opinion about the most profitable areas for integration. Then we describe the benefits reported for several projects that represent several approaches to an integrated system. The projects described in Part 3 of this book also report benefits achieved. Next, we review articles that represent forecasts of benefits made to justify eventual implementation of an integrated system. Finally, we describe several benefit categories and suggest ways to forecast benefits. This chapter should give you a good idea of where to look for justification and how to obtain an order-of-magnitude estimate of the actual benefits to be expected.

Important Areas for Integration

A recent survey of many hydrocarbon processing industry companies (Yoshimura, 1993) asked what the company management thought were the major areas or functions that should be integrated in the future. The results, based on over 100 responses, for the top four combinations were

1. Sales and planning
2. Planning and operations management
3. Operations management and control
4. Planning and distribution

Taken together, these show that company management supports supply chain optimization: sales, planning, operations management (scheduling), control, and distribution. The integration of planning, scheduling, and control is a central component of the complete system.

Supply chain optimization can be considered to fall under the umbrella of *computer-integrated manufacturing* (CIM), applied to the process industry. A paper by Amos et al. (1993) reported that many CIM projects are now under way for 13 refineries in Europe, 14 refineries in Asia and Australia, and 15 refineries in the United States and Canada. These numbers represent only a small fraction of the total number of plants that could mount CIM projects. If we combine the indications of the survey with the actual activity going on at present, it would appear that we are at the beginning of a surge of new projects to implement CIM in the process industry. Certainly, the integration of planning, scheduling, and control will be an important part of these projects.

Reported Results

Mehta (1991) reported 4.7 percent profit improvement by optimum feed selection for an ethylene cracker at Idemitsu Petrochemical. The profit improvement was revised upward to 5 percent in a 1993 paper by Watano et al. (reprinted and discussed in Chap. 16). An *Oil and Gas Journal* special supplement in 1991 reported a $1.3 million per year profit improvement on a 100,000 bbl/day crude unit due to an improvement in yield structure ("Computer Report," 1991).

Heller (1989) reported a 50 percent productivity improvement since 1985 with partial implementation of a CIM system for nylon fibers production. A 5-year payback period was estimated. Wilmsen and Densman (1992) report payback periods in a petroleum refining application of 18 months to 7 years. They point out the sensitivity of payback time to changes in parameters not under the plant's direct control, such as energy unit costs and changes in feedstock and product prices. Most of the benefits in their partially completed series of projects were from advanced control, process optimization, and labor savings.

Benefit Forecasts

Amos et al. (1993) break down a benefits estimate for a refinery by process and then by function, e.g., planning and scheduling. They forecast a potential benefit total of $0.80 to $1.80 per barrel of crude oil feedstock. This substantial total represents a significant increase in the average refining margin.

Grein (1990) analyzed the benefits in a different fashion and estimated them for categories such as a reduction in manufacturing lead time for new products, reductions in average inventory, reduced labor cost, improvement in capacity, reduced cost for producing first-quality products, etc. This paper applied percentages to each of the above improvements, which could be evaluated in economic terms for a specific site.

Summary of Benefit Categories

Advanced control and unit optimization

This area encompasses many benefit subcategories. Advanced control reduces the variability of process operation, allowing processes to operate closer to physical limits and to product specifications. Unit optimization adds the movement of the process to a maximum profit point based on economic values for feeds, products, and operation cost.

Benefits are typically evaluated by analyzing past performance, process by process, and comparing periods of very good operation with average and poor periods. The assumption is made that operation will improve from the past average up close to the level of the best performance. A dollar value can be assigned both for improvements in capacity and yields and for reductions in specification giveaway, energy consumption, and inventory. In some cases, value can be assigned for higher quality at the same or lower cost, leading to improved market share. The value of an increase in market share is very high, but difficult to predict (Edwards Deming, 1982). Producers can gain market share and increase customer loyalty by making higher quality at the same or lower cost than other producers [anyone who doubts this should read *The Reckoning* by Halverstam (1986)].

Planning and scheduling

Benefits estimates for planning are usually made by comparing a forecast with actual operations over a reasonable period such as a month. Since it is necessary to prove that the predicted operation is achievable in practice, the planning tool has to be validated for the operation of each process in advance. This is not a trivial task before planning and operations have been integrated. After integration, these comparisons are made almost in real time. Realistic tuning of the process models in the planning tool is very difficult unless a process information system and data reconciliation procedures are already in place. Benefit studies for gasoline blending are possible if one can prove that the predicted blend compositions are correct and usable by making hand blends in the laboratory. A clear understanding of normal statistical variation is important in determining the acceptability of the results. Doing pilot or laboratory studies for other processes may be possible, depending on how closely the laboratory results agree with commercial process results. If pilot or laboratory results are not in good agreement with the full-scale process, or if none of this equipment is available to you, the justification for planning integration becomes a major, difficult project. Many do not bother and push ahead with the concept: How else can you coordinate the operation of the processes? If you do not plan ahead with the best tool possible, you cannot make any progress. Without a definite plan to enforce, the operation of the plant can become politicized and dependent for guidance on the questionable insights of the person best at argumentation. Benefits analysis for the scheduling function is quite different from planning. In the scheduling case, the major direct benefits are inventory reduction and production cost reduction. Many secondary benefits include the interpretation of the plan to control strategies, anticipation rather than reaction to problems, and therefore smoother operation, leading to enhanced customer support and satisfaction.

With a formal, computerized scheduling system, it is easy to determine when a new customer order can be filled. A new sales request can be scheduled and the entire impact on the plant understood in minutes to hours instead of hours to days. Although this may be more critical to the specialty producer than the commodity producer, the scheduling system can mean the difference between getting a customer or not, accepting the order or not, making an expensive mistake or not. Consequently, these secondary benefits may actually be worth more than the primary direct benefits, in the long run.

Benefits in Areas Ancillary to Planning, Scheduling, and Control

An integrated system for planning, scheduling, and control must have all the other functional elements described in this book present. That is, the process information system, communications networks, database management, data reconciliation, accurate and tunable process models, and a conducive personnel organization are all required. A consensus is developing that it is not possible to get a majority of the benefits with a small fraction of the expenditures. While many elements can be combined physically in hardware or software, all the elements need to be logically present.

The ancillary functional elements have their own justifications in their own right.

Process information systems have been easily justified in the past on the basis of better operation, better process engineering, and better quality control. Their use can also reduce maintenance costs due to better information about process condition and the focusing of maintenance effort on priority items that affect profit.

Communications networks are justifiable on the basis of labor savings in rapidly transferring and transcribing data and in avoiding duplication of effort.

Database managers are already important for record keeping and process history information retrieval. Storage of process operating data, diagrams, maintenance history, inspection records, and other data is needed for many engineering and management purposes. There is also an increasing record-keeping requirement due to government regulations imposed by the Occupational Safety and Health Act or by the Environmental Protection Agency and other agencies. The requirements of the Occupational Safety and Health Act regarding process diagrams and the history and control of process changes are enough to justify a *database management system* (DBMS) by themselves (e.g., see Hoskins and Worm, 1993; and Nimmo, 1993). Companies desiring to achieve ISO 9000 registration should not even think about it without a commitment to a DBMS. Consequently, these systems are probably a necessity, with the added benefit that they are the least expensive way to keep records in the long run.

Data reconciliation procedures improve the reliability of forecasts based on the data. Gross error detection helps focus maintenance on measurements needing work. Data reconciliation procedures are justified on the basis that without them, forecasts and decisions will be misleading and will have increased variability. Most process information systems and commercial process models have a data reconciliation procedure built in. Process models that are accurate and tunable are an essential part of modern process design and engineering. They are such an important part of most process optimizations that they are readily available from numerous vendors both for models alone and in conjunction with advanced control systems. The cost is usually reasonable and much less by at least an order of magnitude than the cost of internal development, unless you already possess a large, complete, and high-quality data bank of process information.

Justifying the changes in the organization is usually easy in a superficial way. This is because most full integration projects will be accompanied by or even follow a major change in the company's organization. Reductions in overall staff are usually part of a reengineering or reinvention of the production process. However, the reduction may be partly illusory. Training and basic staff quality requirements will be considerably increased. Putting more responsibility for operations and decisions affecting profit lower down in the organization sharply increases training, backup, and transition personnel needs.

While much attention has been paid to operator training, almost no formal training has ever been given to schedulers or planners. This has been fine in the nonintegrated environment of most plants where the plan is actually not directly implemented. Mistakes and misuse of the planning tools were not serious since the operators could simply ignore the plan if they did not understand it. In the future integrated environment, the plan is the profit optimization of the plant and is directly implemented at the processes as targets and specifications. Mistakes and misuse in the new environment cannot be tolerated. Consequently, training of planners and schedulers must be brought to as high a degree of sophistication as that used for process operators.

Will We Be Able to Find the Benefits in the Bottom Line?

The answer to this question is a definite maybe. The problem of finding the economic benefits in the plant's or company's bottom line for any particular project stage completion is a difficult one for many reasons.

The plant profit or margin is subject to extreme variation in the short term, mainly due to changes in costs and product prices, which are not under the control of the company. For example, the refining margin for typical U.S. plants can vary from −$2 per barrel to +$4 per barrel over the course of a few months. In December 1990, average margins were a loss of $0.56 per barrel. By the end of January 1991, they were back up to +$2.00 per barrel. With this kind of variation, finding a benefit due to the improvement in a single process of, say, $0.04 to $0.10 per barrel of feed to the process is going to be almost impossible. Therefore, as we implement more and more stages of the entire integration or CIM project, the profit improvement overall will be difficult to find except as a long-term trend as we are able to average out the variations due to external factors.

As an example of the situation, suppose you buy a new car that gets better gas mileage than your previous car. If you try to determine how much money you are saving in gasoline cost by looking at your total monthly expenses, you will probably not notice a thing. Your monthly totals will vary so much that the gas cost savings will be unrecognizable. The only way you can tell that you are indeed saving money is by a detailed measurement of gasoline consumption on the car itself. Looking at the details will show you the benefits, even though you cannot find them at the overall total-expenses level. Such it is with trying to find the benefit from a single process by looking at the overall profit margin. Indeed, there may actually not be any net profit improvement. The effect of the CIM project may have been to maintain margins, where they would have gone down if the CIM project had not been done. Consequently, comparisons with the past are likely to be misleading since so much changes in addition to those items caused by the CIM project.

Corporate downsizing and restructuring also play havoc with any attempts to check present performance with the past. Downsizing certainly reduces the staffing levels and therefore gives a boost to apparent productivity. The workload of the remaining staff has clearly gone up, so the benefit of the CIM project may be to keep performance at the same level as in the past, but with a smaller staff.

The full implementation of a CIM or an integration project may require 5 to 10 years. During such a long time, the economic environment of the company, the products made, the processes used, and the quality demanded will change dramatically. Consequently, for all the above reasons, it is probably naive to expect to be able to find a direct cause-and-effect relationship between the CIM project and the company profit margin. We are left with using the same techniques for auditing our improvements as we have used for years: Compare each process with its own performance in the past, isolating it from the rest of the plant. If the process has been improved according to what was anticipated from a process standpoint, then the project is a success. No matter what the economic performance is on an absolute basis, the performance is better than it would have been if the project had not been undertaken.

The cost of any project is the economists' sunk cost; the money has been spent. Arguments about what could have been done with the money are specious. The only decision we really have to make concerns what to do now and in the future. For example, the oil price shocks of the 1970s and 1980s caused an extensive conservation effort. Many companies planned projects in this period that were justified based on energy savings. Many of these projects were subsequently canceled when the price of energy dropped back to a much lower level. Those projects that were implemented saw their payback periods double, even though they successfully reduced energy consumption. Those companies that implemented the projects enjoy a slightly higher margin than those companies that did nothing, even though the improvement is not as great as anticipated.

Do We Have to Do the Whole Project?

Many times one hears that one can obtain 80 percent of the benefits by spending only 20 percent of the money on a project. The implication is that the last 20 percent of the benefits will require the expenditure of more money than it is going to be worth. While the percentages may be wrong, it is true that all projects have stages or segments that can be prioritized and perhaps justified individually. The danger in this kind of view, if taken too narrowly, is that each segment will be required to be justified on the merits pertaining to only the process or function of the project itself.

For example, if the project is a process information system, the data collected could be limited to those items that are of immediate use to operating the process. This view would result in a smaller computer and storage requirement, fewer sensors, a lower load on communications systems, and, therefore, a generally cheaper project.

However, the effect on other functions is devastating. The data are likely to be inadequate for process engineering since even a material balance or energy balance may be impossible without extra work. The data are likely to be inadequate to planning because needed data values are absent. The advanced control optimization is weakened since the targets and economic values from planning are based on inadequate information and could be wrong. Thus, the narrowly defined, minimum process information system essentially precludes an integration of planning, scheduling, and control. An integration project will be much more expensive because the process information system must be expanded in data collection and storage capacity as an addition to the project. Fortunately for those companies which have them, process information systems installed in the last 5 years or so have taken a broader view and have included data sufficient for process engineering and planning model updating. Older installations, done when the narrow view was more common, will find the integration project a much more expensive proposition. Each of the elements described in this book must be present in the integrated system, and each must be adequate to the job. Within each element, the 80/20 rule still applies. The element does not have to be gold-plated, with every feature and bell and whistle that anyone can envision. However, every element must be adequate to the integration purpose and not narrowly defined. Certainly some elements may be combined in a single software/hardware entity. For example, data reconciliation may be part of the process information system. The database manager may be included in this same system or may be an expansion of an existing plant system for sales, supply, and distribution information. Scheduling for some plants can be so simple that it is included in the planning system as a short-range application. Regardless of how the elements are physically implemented, they will all be present. Leaving out an element subverts the integration and any possibility of valid optimization. Without advanced control, the close control of the process to targets or constraints and the reduction of process variability cannot be achieved. Without planning, the determination of proper targets and economic drivers for process optimization can only be a crude approximation. Without data reconciliation, the model tuning is based on errors instead of true process performance.

Is There a Best Order of Implementation of Project Segments?

The logical order of implementation can be developed from a standpoint of providing information when it is needed. That is, a segment is not implemented before all data required are available. Assuming that a plant starts from scratch, this makes the order of project *completion* as follows:

Process information system

Advanced control

Data reconciliation

Data communications network

Database management system

Process models and tuning

Planning

Scheduling

Process optimization

It may seem strange to have process optimization last on the list. This is because of the need for valid targets and economic information from planning and scheduling as input. In actual fact, many companies have implemented process optimization projects right after or simultaneously with an advanced control system. While doing these projects early may result in lower benefit than their true potential (see, e.g., Cutler and Ayala, 1993), the economic benefit can still be substantial. One cannot argue with a success that everyone likes, even if the benefits will jump after better target-setting information becomes available.

Process optimization systems have a longer lead time than the others and represent a series of projects, one for each process in the plant. Establishing the best order of project *initiation* pushes the process optimization projects toward the top of the list. This is especially true since profit improvement only comes from actually changing something in the processes.

References

Amos, J. D., P. B. Truesdale, and R. Tucci (1993): "Planning for Refinery Computer Applications for the Nineties," *Hydroc. Tech. Int.*, pp. 137–138, 140–142.

"Computer Report: Special OGJ [*Oil & Gas Journal*] Supplement/Data Integration Key to Improved Process Operations," *Oil & Gas J.*, vol. 89, no. 12, March 25, 1991, pp. 40-14–40-16, 40-18–40-20.

Cutler, C. R., and J. S. Ayala (1993): "Integrating Off-line Schedulers with Real-Time Optimizers," Paper 40a, AIChE National Meeting, March 28–April 1, Houston, TX.

Edwards Deming, W. (1982): *Out of the Crisis,* Massachusetts Institute of Technology, Center for Advanced Engineering Studies, Cambridge.

Grein, L. J. (1990): "CIM—A Processing and Manufacturing Plant Strategy," paper CC-90-128, National Petroleum Refiners Association Computer Conference, Seattle, WA, October 29–31.

Halverstam, D. (1986): *The Reckoning,* Avon Books, New York.

Heller, K. (1989): "Integrated Management Gets It All Together," *Chem. Week,* vol. 145, no. 17, pp. 36–37.

Hoskins, R. K., and G. H. Worm (1993): "Develop an Effective Management of Change System," *Chem. Eng. Prog.,* vol. 89, no. 11, November, pp. 77–80.

Mehta, C. (1991): "A Distributed CIM System for Process Plants," American Institute of Chemical Engineers spring national meeting, Houston, TX, April 7–11, Preprint N.23b 20P.

Nimmo, I. (1993): "Start Up Plants Safely," *Chem. Eng. Prog.,* vol. 89, no. 12, December, pp. 66–69.

Watano, T., K. Tamura, T. Sumiyoshi and P. Nair (1993): "Integration of Production Planning, Operations, and Engineering at Idemitsu Petrochemical Company," paper 40f, American Institute of Chemical Engineers spring national meeting, Houston, TX, March 28–April 3.

Wilmsen, W. F., and B. Densman (1992): "Computer Integrated Manufacturing in a Petroleum Refinery," paper CC-92-123, National Petroleum Refiners Association Computer Conference, Washington, November 16–18.

Yoshimura, J. S. (1993): "Computer Integrated Manufacturing/Processing in the HPI," *Hydroc. Proc.,* vol. 72, no. 5, May, pp. 65–68.

Examples of Integrated Systems

This part of the book, Chaps. 14 through 18, republishes several recent papers that exemplify important steps on the path toward complete integration of planning, scheduling, and control. A short analysis precedes each chapter, noting the important elements that are integrated and some of the salient characteristics of the application. These chapters have been selected because the editor has personal knowledge of the people involved and the application. Consequently, the analysis may describe aspects that are actually not readily apparent from the chapter itself. All the chapters describe a real application that has been implemented and is in everyday use to the extent stated.

Although each of the applications uses particular software and hardware from certain vendors, no endorsement of these vendors is meant or implied. Nothing in the analysis is meant to be vendor-specific. Similarly, since the integration of the subject functions is one given highest priority by refinery and petrochemical management (Chap. 14: Yoshimura, 1993), numerous applications could have been chosen for these chapters. If you are doing better than the applications described, we applaud your efforts. If you are not doing better, then we urge you to use the information in this book to improve your situation. Several references are given at the end of Chap. 14. Recent articles that discuss various aspects of integration and others that are good examples of partially integrated systems are included.

14

Gasoline Blending with an Integrated On-Line Optimization, Scheduling, and Control System

Michael L. Bain
Kent W. Mansfield
Jimmy G. Maphet
Robert W. Szoke
Ashland Petroleum Company
Ashland, KY

William H. Bosler
Texas Consultants, Inc.
Houston, TX

Dr. J. Patrick Kennedy
Oil Systems, Inc.
San Leandro, CA

Analysis

In-line blenders for gasoline have been installed for years. However, only a small number of installations have integrated upper-level planning with blending. In an integrated system, the recipes generated

Presented at the National Petroleum Refiners Association Computer Conference, November 15–17, 1993, New Orleans, LA.

in planning are directly used in blending with only minor adjustments to account for changes since the recipe was generated. A still smaller number of installations have included batch scheduling by computer. The following material by Bain et al. is about a project that incorporates all the elements of an integrated system. The major justification for the system is the difficulty anticipated in making reformulated gasoline with minimum loss of production capacity and at lowest cost. Blend scheduling is also anticipated to be more difficult in the future due to the more complex blends.

The planning optimization generates blend recipes based on volumes and qualities from an on-line process information system. The recipes are transferred, and a blend schedule is set up by a formal scheduling system. The recipe is adapted to the current real situation, and then the modified recipe is used on the blender. Quality analyzers monitor the blend and provide high-accuracy feedback for short-term adjustments. The difference between predicted and actual quality is fed back to the planning system in the form of biases to improve prediction accuracy. This use of biases is equivalent to a model-based data reconciliation. The system also features a multivariate property controller that is model-based. Analyzer time lag is compensated, and inferential control is used for several calculated properties. The importance of accurate component analyses and predictive models is also stressed. The database system will be expanded to handle reporting and certification functions in the future.

Several blender applications that integrate at least the planning and control functions have been reported (Houghton et al., 1969; Stadnicki and Lawler, 1983). At least one, developed many years ago (Lasher, 1967), was a completely integrated system very similar in concept to our most recent example. Perhaps the most surprising aspect of these applications is that there are not more completely integrated systems already installed. The paper is a progress report representing the status as of September 1993. By April 1994, the planning system was being used for recipe generation, but the scheduler was not in regular use. Bain et al. estimate that the entire system will be operational by the fall of 1994.

Abstract

Advanced control projects are designed to maintain a target; if the environment for setting that target is not changed at the same time, the benefits are unpredictable at best. This chapter presents the preliminary results of an integrated blending system designed to handle the demands of reformulated fuels, where the advanced control target contains component limits, properties, and the output of a model supplied by the Environmental Protection Agency. The EPA model is not currently embedded into the system, but the underlying controls are designed to be able to control both predicted and measured properties. The unique feature is that the planning and scheduling functions are integrated tightly into the advanced control, including sharing of the same property prediction models at all levels. The unit is operational with the exception of the integrated planning and scheduling functionality. Actual results will be presented in a later paper. This paper provides the background and the basic structure of the system.

Introduction

Reformulated fuels legislation will present extremely difficult technical challenges for gasoline blenders—almost to the point that blending without good models will be impossible or impractical. Balancing the component use against the plan will require that both the gasoline blenders and the planners use the same models with a practical update strategy. In addition, there will be increased paperwork, higher accuracy requirements, and difficult adjustments to meet the legal restrictions simultaneously on components, properties, and the imputed effect on an average engine. Finally, if the refinery margins are not considered at the design stage, any strategy will fail. If the proper yield of salable products cannot be achieved, the refinery cannot sustain profitability—an elusive set of targets.

Blending and Scheduling Hierarchy

The main driving force for better control of the blender comes from the requirements for reformulated fuels that lower emissions in areas with high levels of carbon monoxide or ozone. There are several good summaries of these rules, but the net result is that the procedures (e.g., how to certify), properties (e.g., must run a vehicle), predicted effect on an average vehicle engine (EPA complex model), and other complications (e.g., no longer fungible) are all drastically changed by the law. Each would make blending difficult; and, together they make it extraordinarily complex and hard to manage gasoline blending. With reformulated fuels, component management will become critical to the success of a refiner's blending program.

Some analysts have estimated that component tankage will need to double in order to blend the smaller batches with "tolerable" quality giveaway. Others believe that we will have to simulate component tankage quality over time and schedule the refinery to blend gasoline. Scheduling the refinery to blend gasoline will be a very different refinery production focus. The driving force will have to be very clear before most refiners will make such a drastic change.

The optimal solution to this problem is to use advanced information techniques to help the operator and planner guide the refinery down this narrow path that remains; this is the strategy taken by Ashland. The goal was not to simply do advanced control of the blender; it was to change to whole environment used to set these targets as well. The project was to automate the gasoline blender at Catlettsburg with a system which has integrated elements that address three phases of gasoline production:

- Blender control
- Model-based property control
- Integrated planning and scheduling

There are additional elements that should be considered in the future such as enhanced reporting and certification paperwork, quality control, and performance monitoring; but the three elements above formed the basis of the original project. The function of the blender control was to provide state-of-the-art blending utilizing advances in *distributed control system* (DCS) equipment. The model-based property control is an essential element that allows the operator to set properties and component limits instead of ratios. The third element—the planning and scheduling system—is critical to effect a good environment for setting the targets in the first place. Figure 14.1 shows a schematic of how these are done. This chapter describes each of these elements and reviews the current status of the project. The system is currently being used to ratio-blend the gasoline with planning and scheduling done off-line. The planning and scheduling function is currently being commissioned, and results will be reported in a subsequent paper. The basic regulatory control functions are accomplished by using standard BRC (Blend Ratio Control, a Honeywell product) plus some additions required for the specific needs of Ashland and the demands of the integrated system. The blend functions are programmed into the PM (process manager) and AM (applications module)—the programmable elements of the TDC3000. Figure 14.2 shows how these pieces fit together. SDM (storage data management) was used to provide graphics of the gasoline tanks and strapping. SDM is also a product of Honeywell.

The BRC/SDM software was a useful starting point and included prebuilt displays and algorithms covering ratio control, pacing, and

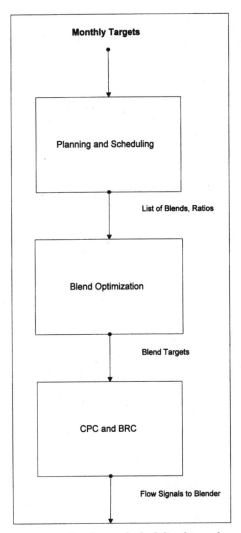

Figure 14.1 Blending and scheduling hierarchy.

- Verify Lineup
- Enter Recipe
- Start Blend
  - ⇒ Start Blender
  - ⇒ Monitor Blend
  - ⇒ Two Tank Blend
- Stop Blend/Report

Figure 14.2 Blend ratio control.

trim control. These run completely within the TDC, which makes operator interfacing very easy. Several additions were required by Ashland—these were straightforward to add in the same modules as the control. The major additions were

- Analyzer lag estimators
- Predicted properties
- Critical property control
- Two-tank blending

These are typical of the special accommodations to a blender that must be made in a large refinery. The older fixed-function blenders (as opposed to software-programmable blenders) could not be changed to reflect the special needs of a particular site. These elements are defined below:

Lag estimators. Blender control is a steady-state control, and lags in the analyzers can be very destabilizing to the controls. Estimators allow the control system to manipulate the predicted steady state of the blender and let the system catch up at its own pace. The analyzers ensure that the final target is met by resetting this estimate to match the prediction when the sample time has passed. BRC uses a lag time in its trim control, but does not estimate the property change; it makes a move and waits for it to be sensed.

Predicted properties. The original property control blenders required that a controlled property be measured, but this is not always possible (e.g., sulfur, oxygen). This added the capability to be able to control a computed property and reset with laboratory data, if available. Clearly, good component properties are critical when there is no analyzer to correct the error.

Critical property control (CPC). This is a multivariable control algorithm useful for controlling nondeterministic situations (i.e., the number of controlled variables does not have to equal the number of manipulated variables); see Fig. 14.3. The method was developed by Oil Systems, Inc., and programmed into the BRC by Honeywell/ICOTRON. This controller translates analyzer readings and current percentage of components into control moves to move the blender toward a blend header quality target. Note that although CPC regulates the blend header quality, the prediction of the final tank properties is done in the blend optimizer, MGBLEND. All information from models is downloaded to the TDC so that this control can run with the computer down.

- Accept/Validate Analyzer Readings
- Eliminate Analyzer Lag
- Model Based Ratio Adjustment
- Output Ratios

Figure 14.3 Critical property control.

Two-tank blending. Programmable systems are much more flexible than the fixed-ratio blenders. A good example of the need for this flexibility is two-tank blending which took extension to BRC plus careful integration with the blend optimization (see Figs. 14.4 and 14.5). At Catlettsburg, the blender can blend 8000 bbl/h to a barge loading tank or 3000 bbl/h to a truck loading tank. If the blender is throttled to 3000 bbl/h when Ashland's tanks are filled for truck loading, this is a loss of capacity that is unacceptable. Since there could be different heels in these tanks, this is a difficult problem.

- Line Out Blend to barge loading tank and truck loading tank
- Slip Stream to truck loading tank
- End truck loading tank
- Correct barge loading tank
- End barge loading tank

Figure 14.4 Two-tank blending.

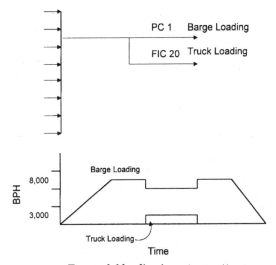

Figure 14.5 Two-tank blending inventory pattern.

The problem was solved by integrating the two blenders in the blend optimizer (MGBLEND) with separate calculations for truck loading and barge loading. The blender would be used to blend to truck loading and allow the remainder of blender throughput to go to a barge loading tank. When the truck loading tank blend was completed, the heel in barge loading tank and all that had been blended to that time would be turned into a new heel, and a second blend optimization would be done to ensure that both tanks were "on spec."

Early blenders with high- and/or low-octane blending components could implement a simple *trim* control, where a high-octane component is increased or decreased to increase or decrease the measured octane. When other properties (e.g., volatility) are added, the algorithm becomes much more complex and the actual interaction coefficients become quite small and environment-dependent; e.g., the effect of reformate on octane in an unleaded superpremium is quite different from the same component in an unleaded regular.

In addition, the analyzers are on the blend header, not the tank, and representative samples are difficult to obtain. Modern equipment uses flow-ratio samplers to try to get a more representative sample, but these still do not accommodate a heel. The prediction of octane and the *Reid vapor pressure* (RVP) was estimated by the octane analyzers by using a volume-weighted average of the streams as they were blended. With modern blending, it is necessary to predict more accurately and match these models with the planning system. These models were based on the regression of many blends. This had the disadvantage of being very difficult to update and sometimes even rendered useless because of the changing components one gets from different crudes. In addition, it would sometimes be required to use a component that was not a standard component (e.g., when an off-specification tank needed to be blended into the products over time).

Chevron successfully solved this problem by implementing transformed octane (developed and published by Mobil) in the blend optimizer. Chevron also converted the remaining properties to blend indices, which would blend linearly, and then fit one set of constants to equations based on the physical properties of the components. The equations used on blenders were then this expression plus a bias per product (since the correction required was quite environment-dependent). The resultant bias matrix (number of properties times number of products) plus a single set of equations could then be used for all components and blends. These correlations were also made in terms of the properties of the component streams. This allowed new components to be added by testing their properties.

The program they developed was called *GINO* (gasoline *in*-line optimization) which Ashland licensed from Chevron. To the base package,

Oil Systems added an *applications program interface* (API), which would allow other programs to access these property methods. This was critical because the planning and scheduling modules must use the same models as the on-line system for two reasons:

1. If there are no constraints, they get the same initial answer.
2. When updates (in the form of new biases) to the model are sensed, they can be uploaded to the planner.

It is only in this way that the accuracy required for integrated scheduling can be achieved.

The full-screen implementation of GINO was done by Oil Systems and is called MGBLEND (motor gasoline blender). It has three modes: initial, midcourse, and final. An important feature of MGBLEND is that it makes adjustments to the ratios with minimum deviation from the ratios used by the planner. This was another of the methods pioneered by Chevron (once the blend is started, the opportunity for optimization is lost); the blend optimizer is actually an inventory management program, and optimization is done at the planning and scheduling level. MGBLEND also has an on-line monitor function that was not present in GINO, which continuously displays the progress of the blend and the predicted tank properties. This was important because the integrated tank properties at both the barge loading and truck loading tanks could be monitored, not just the overall blend properties.

The initial program is used to profile the blender and set up the initial blend, check availability of the components based upon the initial volume and the run down rate during the estimated time of the blend, and compute the proper blend header target given the volume and composition of the heel. The program will then download the recipe and the model coefficients (slopes). Operators will usually run the blender for 30 min until everything lines out before going to critical property control.

The midcourse correction can be run as often as desired. At the Catlettsburg blender, there are analyzers for most everything, but manual tests can be run if desired. To run a midcourse correction, the laboratory values or calculated integrated tank qualities based upon analyzer values and stream flows and the volume blended when the sample was taken are input to MGBLEND either manually or by uploading the data from the data historian. By using the offset between the predicted property and the actual property, new blend targets and recipes are computed. These targets are calculated so that the tank will be "on test" when the tank is full or nearly full. This type of midcourse operation is very important when there are active volatility constraints because the control "handles" are extremely small (e.g., how do you lower the T50 and raise RON while holding MON?). The new recipe or both the new recipe and new model interaction coefficients can be downloaded after the midcourse calculation. New biases can be saved, if desired, at the midcourse correction.

The final program is based on the actual composition after the tank is mixed and a composite sample is taken. The final program will get the tank on specification, using the minimum amount of correction components, and, if pump-out is required, will compute how much to pump out and how to replace it. Staying close to the recipe is not a consideration with the final program. In addition, the system has a goal of minimal manual data manipulation. The quality of the final blends is analyzed via the on-line process data management system (PI from Oil Systems). A complete reporting function is included for the necessary blend reports.

After finishing a blend, the operator can add the new bias numbers to the correlation if desired; in this way, the drift in the model parameters is computed with each blend. Plotting these bias numbers shows a remarkable variation in the accuracy of even rigorous nonlinear models, which explains why many recipes sent down from the planners are not used. It is clear from these results that the most critical factor in valid predictions is good properties (the drifts indicate only the problem, not the solution) which included frequency of component tank testing, sampling methods, and the stability of the process units producing the components.

Planning and Scheduling

Advanced controls are not very useful if they hold the process reliably at the wrong target; thus, it is important to upgrade the environment for setting the targets when we install advanced controls to hold the targets. In this project, we were determined to follow the lead of Chevron and provide an integrated planning system that uses the same models as the blend optimizer. We have taken it a step further and have installed an integrated scheduling module. This has alleviated a lot of the time staging. Time staging is still important, however, since the recipe for a product can change only between time stages.

We selected the Chesapeake MIMI/E, MIMI/S, MIMI/LP suite of programs for this function. MIMI begins by reading an initial data set from MGBLEND. The rules vary depending on the type of data; substitution of missing data and different data treatment (e.g., instantaneous values for the inventories, average values for component flows) were the obvious problems. MIMI/LP is used to develop a time-staged optimization which results in the proper recipes. MIMI/S is used to match the pools with truck and barge schedules.

Computing Environment

Ashland had an Oil Systems PI system, called ARTIS (Ashland real-time information system), installed in 1985. The blender project added a separate PI system and used a PI-to-PI link to get laboratory and process data to the blender VAX and provide its data to ARTIS. The MIMI software runs on a VAXstation 3100 and gets data from the blender VAX via PI-API, a special client that allows transparent, high-speed data access. See Fig. 14.6.

Another feature of this blender is the use of modern analyzers. The near-infrared (NIR) octane analyzer was developed and integrated directly into the TDC, providing accurate and nearly continuous read-

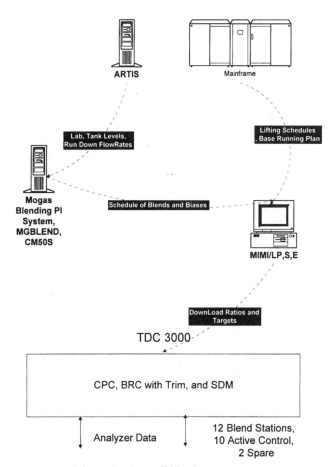

Figure 14.6 Schematic of overall blender.

- MIMI — 28 Components, 40 Products/time, Many time periods
- MGBLEND — 12 of 28 Components
- BRC — 12 Components, 2 dyes & 1 additive of 40 possible. (Each component location can have up to 3 Component tanks/streams feeding it.)
- Blender — (barge loading tank) + (truck loading tank) = 8000 BPH; (truck loading tank) = 3000 BPH
- SDM — All Gasoline Tanks

Figure 14.7 System limits.

ings. There is also an on-line D3710C 'D86GC' analyzer. The system limits are summarized in Fig. 14.7.

Commissioning and Current Status

Operator training on the TDC3000 control system was complete in May 1992. The simulator developed by Oil Systems for staging and testing was used as a training aid to give operators hands-on experience. The TDC3000 control system was installed in June 1992, and the system was checked out in July and August of 1992. The first blend using the TDC3000 control system was made on August 31, 1992, successfully replacing the functions of the old Waugh blender. BRC trim control was commissioned for octane and RVP in September 1992. Initially the knock engine analyzer was used for the measured octanes. In February 1993, BRC trim control was added for the NIR octane analyzer octane signals. Trim control did not prove to be adequate to control the blend header at the target octane and vapor pressure and was eventually abandoned. Since the plans were to go to multivariable trim control, there was only a limited effort to make trim control work.

Commissioning of an ABB D-86 GC (D3710 method correlated to D86) is still in progress. No provision has been made to use signals from this analyzer for trim control with BRC. CPC is designed to use signals from this analyzer in its multivariable trim control calculations. MGBLEND and CPC (critical property control) were commissioned on June 17, 1993. CPC has proved to work very well in holding the blend at the proper octane and vapor pressure targets. The ABB D-86 analyzer is still in the commissioning process, so CPC has not been used to control distillation points. One concern with MGBLEND was the complexity of the software and operator training. Each blend operator was given 40 h of instruction in the use of MGBLEND, which was sufficient except for the operators who worked the gasoline blender only occasionally. While there have been some minor problems, the blend operators at the Catlettsburg refinery have become proficient in operating the program. Deficiencies in the operation of MGBLEND will be addressed in refresher training to be held this winter.

The quality of the input component data to the GINO models at the core of MGBLEND determines the accuracy of the model. The bias corrects each product defined in MGBLEND for prediction error; but it is inadequate to correct for measurement error in the components.

Bad laboratory data on components can result in a meaningless calculation. An exception-checking routine checks all laboratory data before they are input to MGBLEND to flag suspect data. The PI alarm package was used for this function. Another function of MGBLEND is inventory management. MGBLEND can calculate the component availability based on the inventory in the tanks plus the anticipated rundown to the tanks during the blend. The rundown to the tanks is based on a rolling hourly average rundown rate. If the amount of component calculated for a blend exceeds the amount that will be available during the course of a blend, then a warning is issued by the MGBLEND program.

A problem that had to be overcome in the commissioning of MGBLEND was octane analysis of very high- and very low-octane components. Several of the components in the Catlettsburg refinery gasoline pool have octanes which are out of the stable range of operation for ASTM knock engines. These components were typically mixed with a suitable component to bring the octane of the mixture into the proper operating range for ASTM knock engines. The blended octane values that resulted were not suitable for use with MGBLEND.

The GINO model that is at the heart of MGBLEND uses the Mobil transformation method to determine a transformed octane which blends linearly. The transformation method determines the compositional effect of aromatics, olefins, and paraffins of the components on the octane of the blend. The blended octane value includes a contribution due to the interaction of the component and the material for which it is blended. It was found that even though the octane values for these components are outside the stable range of normal knock engine operation, the octane value which resulted when it was run straight was adequate.

GINO does not handle oxygenates in the same way as hydrocarbons. These are handled as chemicals and have built-in properties in the GINO model. Poor prediction of the octane for premium blends containing MTBE has made the built-in properties for MTBE in GINO suspect. Refinery-grade MTBE may have enough variation in composition to make a fixed set of properties inadequate. A suitable alternate for the built-in MTBE properties in GINO is being studied. Published values for the octanes of aromatic chemicals such as toluene appear to work well with GINO.

Near-infrared (NIR) determination of the component octanes using NIR correlation based on knock engine data has been successfully implemented at the Catlettsburg refinery. The NIR analyzer also determines the olefin and aromatic concentrations of the component, using correlations based on PIANO (paraffins, isoparaffins, aromatics, naphthenes, olefins) analysis. The sample set for the calibration of the analyzer is currently being increased to make the correlation more robust. There is the possibility that the RVP of the components can also be determined by NIR determination.

An Infratane on-stream NIR analyzer at the blend header has been in service since September 1992. The Infratane technology was developed by Ashland R&D and is available for purchase from Fluid Data. The Infratane analyzer is calibrated with samples analyzed by a single "best" operator on the laboratory knock engines. Recently the NIR analyzer's calibration was expanded to three sets to reduce the standard error of the octane measurement. Three different calibrations will be maintained: blends prepared for off-site blending with ethanol, blends that include MTBE, and finished-product blends without MTBE. An automated prototype fuel calibration system that further improves the octane measurement is also being added to this analyzer. Commissioning is underway and should be completed during October.

The MIMI planning and scheduling software was commissioned in mid-1994. Engineering support personnel worked with Chesapeake Decision Sciences to improve solution times and implement expert rules and macros to simplify operation.

Trademarks

VAX and VAXstation are trademarks of Digital Equipment Corporation.

PI, CPC, and MGBLEND are trademarks of Oil Systems, Inc.

BRC, PM, AM, SDM, and TDC3000 are trademarks of Honeywell, Inc.

MIMI, MIMI/E, MIMI/LP and MIMI/S are trademarks of Chesapeake Decision Sciences, Inc.

ABB D-86GC is a product of Asea-Brown-Boveri.

Infratane analyzers are a product of Fluid Data Corporation.

References

Amos, J. D., P. B. Truesdale, and R. Tucci (1993): "Planning for Refinery Computer Applications for the Nineties," *Hydroc. Tech. Int.,* pp. 137–138, 140–142.

Atkinson, N. (1987): "Taking Automation beyond Process Control," *Process Eng. (Lond.)* (ISSN 0370-1859), vol. 68, no. 12, December, pp. 29, 31.

Ayres, R. U., and D. C. Butcher (1993): "The Flexible Factory Revisited," *Am. Sci.,* vol. 81, September-October.

Baker, T. H. (1988): "CIM that Works...Managing Inventory and Product Quality while Controlling a Distillation Operation," American Institute of Chemical Engineers Annual Meeting, Washington, November 27–December 2.

Barsamian, J. A. (1986): "Justifying Plantwide Computer Control," *Chem. Eng.,* vol. 93, no. 9, May 12, pp. 105–108.

Boston, J. F., H. I. Britt, and M. T. Tayyabkhan (1993): "Software, Tackling Tougher Tasks," *Chem. Eng. Prog.,* vol. 89, no. 11, November, pp. 38–49.

"Computer Report: Special OGJ [*Oil and Gas Journal*] Supplement/Data Integration Key to Improved Process Operations," *Oil & Gas J.,* vol. 89, no. 12, March 25, 1991, pp. 40-14–40-16, 40-18–40-20.

Conley, R. C., and A. T. Clerrico (1992): "Select and Implement a Plant-wide Information System," *Hydroc. Proc. Int..* vol. 71, no. 5, May, pp. 47–50, 54–55.

Gidwani, K. K., R. S. Bhullar, and S. Sandler (1991): "Computer Integrated Manufacturing for a Refinery Complex," *Adv. Instrum. Control,* vol. 46, no. 1, pp. 607–616.

Heller, K. (1989): "Integrated Management Gets It All Together," *Chem. Week,* vol. 145, no. 17, October 25, pp. 36–37.

Houghton, W. T., L. Iscol, and W. J. Ruspino (1969): "In-Line Blending with an Off-Line Computer," paper CC-69-90, presented at the National Petroleum Refiners Association Computer Conference, New Orleans, LA, November 17–19.

King, M. J., and H. N. Evans (1993): "Process Control/Assessing Your Competitors' Application of CIM/CIP," *Hydroc. Proc.,* vol. 72, no. 7, July, pp. 57–60, 62.

Lasher, R. J. (1967): "Computer Control of Motor Gasoline Blending," paper CC-67-84, presented at the National Petroleum Refiners Association Computer Conference, St. Louis, MO, November 7–9.

Mather, T. W., and H. E. Garner (1989): "Implementing CIM in an Existing Facility," *Hydroc. Proc.,* vol. 68, no. 1, pp. 43–49.

Mehta, C. (1991): "A Distributed CIM System for Process Plants," American Institute of Chemical Engineers spring national meeting, Houston, TX, April 7–11.

Savage, P. (1988): "CPI [chemical process industries] Likes CIM," *Chem. Eng., (N.Y.)* vol. 95, no. 4, March 28, pp. 20–21.

Stadnicki, S. J., and M. B. Lawler (1983): "An Integrated Planning and Control Package for Refinery Product Blending," presented at the *Second Annual Control Engineering Conference,* Control Engineering, Rosemont, IL, May 24–26, pp. 315–322.

Wanato, T., P. Nair, T. Sumiyoshi, and K. Tamura (1992): "Reaping the Benefits of CIM in the Petrochemical Industry," paper CC-92-121, National Petroleum Refiners Association Computer Conference, Washington, November 16–18.

Wilmsen, W. F., and B. Densman (1992): "Computer Integrated Manufacturing in a Petroleum Refinery," paper CC-92-123, National Petroleum Refiners Association Computer Conference, Washington, November 16–18.

Yoshimura, J. S. (1993): "Computer Integrated Manufacturing/Processing in the HPI," *Hydroc. Proc.,* vol. 72, no. 5, May, pp. 65–68.

Gasoline and Fuel Oil Production with an Integrated Planning, Scheduling, and Control System

John Critchley
Osvaldo Salas
Peter Smit
ENGEN
Durban, Republic of South Africa

Jeffrey Howard
Chesapeake Decision Sciences
Houston, Texas

Analysis

This chapter is important because it illustrates the point that an accurate model prediction by planning leads easily to integration with and acceptance by control. The project is very similar in most respects to that described in Chap. 14 by Ashland Petroleum. There are two major differences:

1. There are no analyzers on the blender at present.

2. The components are available in still tanks, measured for quality just before use.

Presented at the National Petroleum Refiners Association Computer Conference, November 15–17, 1993, New Orleans, LA.

In the present operation, the optimum recipe from planning is adjusted for the quality of the actual components and then is used on the blender, which, since there are no analyzers installed as yet, is just used as a ratio controller. The final tank qualities as blended by ratio are so close to those predicted by the optimum recipe that two out of three blends do not require any further adjustment to be ready for shipment. Before the new accurate prediction capability was available, each blend required an average of three adjustments to get to an acceptable level of giveaway or to get on specification. This demonstrates the validity of our contention that accurate input data and accurate prediction models allow the optimum operation predicted by planning to be directly implementable at the control level, thereby integrating the functions.

In this application, the integration includes heavy fuel oil production, and it will be extended to middle distillates in future. The fuel oil system does include automatic control of properties based on on-line analyzers. Adding analyzers to the gasoline blender is also planned as a future project.

Abstract

This chapter discusses the experience of ENGEN's Durban refinery while upgrading its planning and scheduling functions related to gasoline and fuel oil production. The chapter describes the planning and scheduling model's functionality including the interactions with the refinery laboratory and oil movement and storage modules. The operational benefits and future goals are also presented.

Introduction

In 1992, ENGEN embarked on a major expansion and modernization project at its Durban refinery (Fig. 15.1). To facilitate the anticipated increased throughputs, it was determined that the fuel oil and gasoline blending areas would also be upgraded to modern in-line blending facilities.

In addition to the physical modifications required for the new blend facilities, it was decided that a state-of-the-art *blend control system* (BCS) would be installed to support the new blending areas. The overall goals of the system were as follows:

Integration of information flows

Data elements such as tank properties would be entered only once and would be made electronically available to any system requiring the information. This was seen as a key requirement since it would

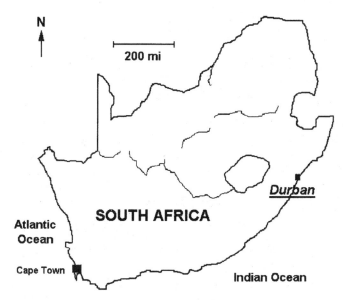

N

200 mi

SOUTH AFRICA

Atlantic
Ocean

Cape Town

Durban

Indian Ocean

Figure 15.1   ENGEN Refinery in Durban, South Africa.

ensure that consistent, up-to-date information was used in each application and would reduce the amount of manual input required by the users of each application module.

Tools for planning and scheduling of the blends

A set of software tools would be provided to assist the planners in long-range planning, short-term scheduling, including tank movements, and single-blend optimization. Only tools meeting the integration objective would be considered.

Advanced control software for the execution of blends

A set of software tools would be installed to blend the volume of product to the stated recipe and would have the capability to dynamically modify the recipe to meet product specifications while minimizing property giveaway.

A task force was formed under the supervision of Fluor, SA, the engineering management contractor, to evaluate the vendors who could potentially supply systems that would meet the stated goals. Honeywell/ICOTRON was selected to provide the blender control hardware and software and to manage the overall project integration.

Chesapeake Decision Sciences was selected to provide the blend planning and scheduling tools.

Even though a great deal of effort was expended on the plant equipment and advanced control portion of the project, the primary focus of this chapter is on the planning and scheduling tools.

System Design

Tools for blend planning and scheduling

The system was built by using a planning and scheduling tool kit, Chesapeake's Manager for Interactive Modeling Interfaces (MIMI). The system is generic and has been used in a variety of application settings ranging from enterprise planning to detailed plant operations scheduling and for gasoline blending applications. The key features of the system are

- Database

- Expert system

- Linear and nonlinear optimization

- Graphical user interface (GUI)

- Interactive planning/scheduling board

- Scheduling algorithms

The software application was built based on the requirements specified by the refinery *planning and economics* (P&E) department, which is responsible for the overall coordination of plant operations. Based on discussions with the end users and management of the P&E department, a decision was made to build three distinct models (long-range planning, short-range scheduling, and a single-blend optimization model) for each of the blending areas. Simplified schematics of the blending areas are shown in Figs. 15.2 and 15.3.

Long-range planning

The goal of the long-range models is to allow the user to balance the product demand requirements against the projected refinery component volume and property pools. The models for both blend areas are classical multiblend, multiperiod models. The models were initially formulated with two time periods spanning 4 weeks. This appeared to cover a long enough horizon, and the two periods allowed sufficient level of detail given that a short-range scheduling model would also

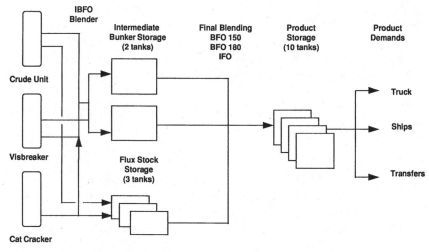

Figure 15.2 Fuel oil blending facility.

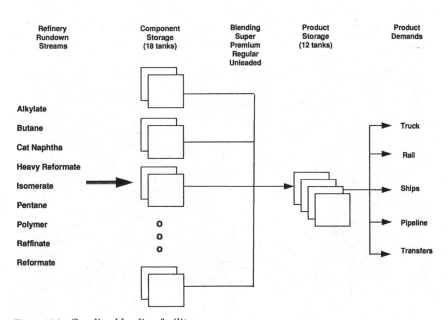

Figure 15.3 Gasoline blending facility.

be in use. The gasoline model was also formulated to give direction on the required severity of the reformer unit.

All user data are accessed by the user through the use of pull-down menus. The menu items are logically grouped in submenus and, where applicable, are the same in each of the blending models. The results of the optimization routine are captured both in custom reports and on the planning board. An example of the planning board is shown in Fig. 15.4.

Short-range scheduling

The scheduling models are used to coordinate the component and product tank movements with the blending of product. In addition, the fuel oil model is used to determine and electronically transfer the refinery rundown streams and property goals to be used by the intermediate bunker fuel oil advanced control system. Each model has a horizon of 7 days but can easily be modified to any user-desired duration. The primary interface to these models is the planning board, examples of which are given in Figs. 15.5 and 15.6. The planning board is used to manage refinery rundowns, blending operations,

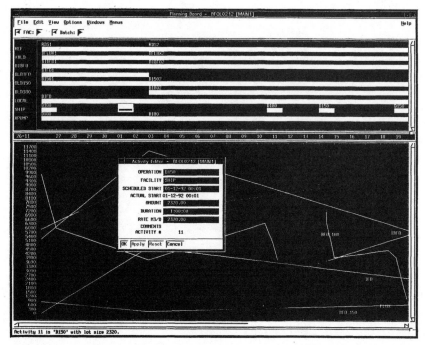

Figure 15.4   Fuel oil long-range planning model.

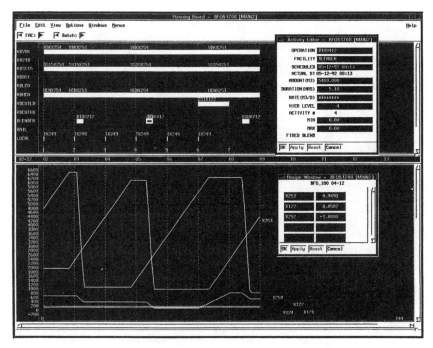

Figure 15.5   Fuel oil scheduling model.

tank-to-tank movements, and product demands. The top portion of the planning board represents operations taking place over time. The bottom portion displays the tank positions over time based on current operations. The user can modify or move operations (e.g., a ship arrival date), and the system will automatically rerun the background simulator to instantaneously update the tank inventory profiles.

The user may invoke a nonlinear optimization routine to determine the most economical blend recipes based on the current scenario specified on the planning board. Upon completion of the optimization routine, the user can elect to move the results of the optimization back to the planning board and use the tools provided to analyze and make any required changes to arrive at a satisfactory schedule.

Figure 15.7 presents an example report of tank and blend properties that are calculated based on the current contents of the planning board. The user can make any modifications to tank or blend operations (e.g., modify a blend recipe) on the planning board and request that the report be recalculated and displayed.

Once a satisfactory schedule is achieved, the user can select any blend on the schedule, using the mouse, and elect to download the

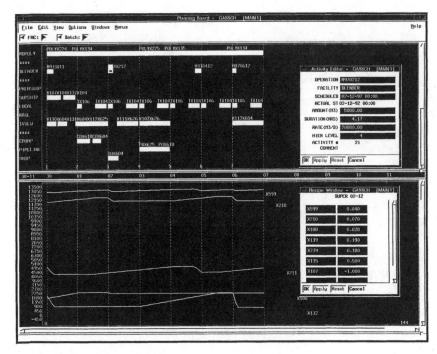

Figure 15.6 Gasoline scheduling model.

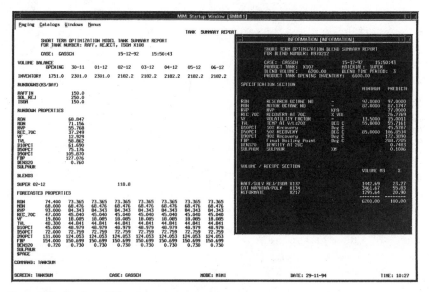

Figure 15.7 Tank and blend summary reports.

parameters (i.e., date and time of the blend, recipe, and recipe percentage limits) to the single-blend optimization models.

Single-blend optimization

The models are used to generate the blend start-up recipes. The models are multigoal formulations that balance the relative cost of components against product specification (e.g., research octane number) giveaway. A recipe produced and stored on the system by the scheduling models can be reoptimized based on the latest available tank data, including the product heel volume and properties. The electronic transfer of the recipe to the recipe management system is done on demand by the planner. Plant operators can then access the produced recipe by requesting a download of the recipe to the *distributed control system* (DCS).

The models can also be used to correct or doctor blends which violate specifications or which fall outside corporate guidelines for property giveaway. If the system determines that no feasible solution exists based on the product tank's current product level, then the models will advise the user of the amount of product that must be pumped out before components can be added to bring the blend to the required specifications.

System Integration

Data

As previously stated, a main overall objective of the system is to ensure that each of the individual components of the system uses the most up-to-date information. The information includes

- Component and product tank properties
- Component and product tank volumes and working capacities
- Current property bias, used for property prediction

Figures 15.8, 15.9, and 15.10 give an overview of the system interfaces for the gasoline and the intermediate and the final fuel oil blending systems. The data are retrieved from the plant *storage data management* (SDM) system, a subsystem of the Honeywell Oil Movement & Storage package, and stored in a relational database. Users of the blend planning tools can request an upload of this information from a pull-down menu option which is available in each of the blending models. The menu option requests a report from the

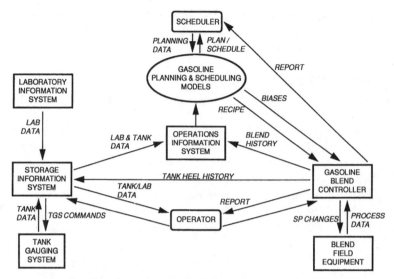

Figure 15.8 Gasoline planning and scheduling system interfaces.

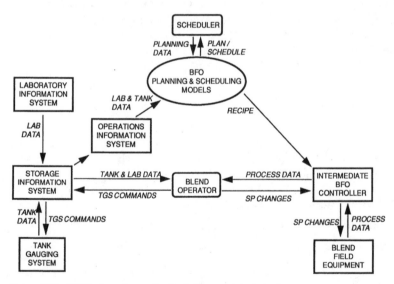

Figure 15.9 IBFO planning and scheduling system interfaces.

relational database and subsequently reads it into the blend planning database. The Chesapeake programs have the ability to make direct SQL calls to the database, but the flat file transfer procedure used has proved adequate for this application environment. An example of a tank report is given in Fig. 15.11.

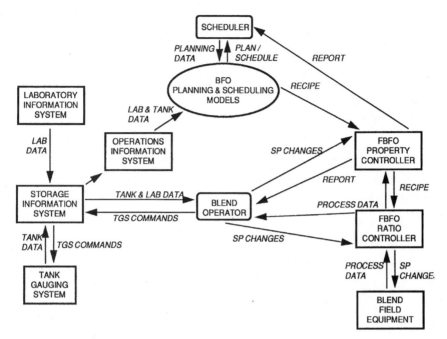

Figure 15.10   FBFO planning and scheduling system interfaces.

```
┌─┐                            INFORMATION [INFORMATION]                          ┌·┌─┐
│                                                                                          │
│                                                                                          │
│                                                                                          │
│         TANK REPORT TANK: X253  IBFO            24-11-92  10:35:33                        │
│         CERTSTAT:  NOT CERT SCANSTAT:  SLOW     ACTSTAT:  INACTIVE                        │
│ PROPERTY  VALUE      NEW VALUE      DATE      TIME        STATUS    NEW STATUS            │
│                                                                                          │
│ VOL        1971.000                23-11-92  10:28:59  GOOD                               │
│ VOL_MIN     880.000                23-11-92  10:28:59  GOOD                               │
│ VOL_MAX    8000.000                23-11-92  10:28:59  GOOD                               │
│ VISC50_A    288.300                18-11-92  13:00:00  GOOD                               │
│ DENS20_A      0.992                18-11-92  13:00:00  GOOD                               │
│ FLASH_PH     76.000                18-11-92  13:00:00  GOOD                               │
│ SULPHUR       3.340                15-11-92  08:00:00  GOOD                               │
│ CCR          21.360                15-11-92  08:00:00  GOOD                               │
│ POUR_PT       5.000                15-04-92  10:00:00  GOOD                               │
│                                                                                          │
└──────────────────────────────────────────────────────────────────────────────────────┘
```

Figure 15.11   Tank summary report.

Property prediction

The same property calculation procedures, supplied by Chesapeake, are used in all the blend planning and scheduling tools including the *blend property controller* (BPC) supplied by Honeywell. The following is a list of properties tracked:

Gasoline:

Research octane number (RON)

Motor octane number (MON)

Reid vapor pressure (RVP)

ASTM D-86

IBP, 10%, 30%, 50%, 70%, 90%, FBP

Volatility factor (VF)

Vapor/liquid ratio (VL)

Density

Sulfur

Lead

Fuel oil:

Viscosity

Density

Flash point

Conradson carbon (CCR)

Pour point

Sulfur

The property calculation procedures for RON, MON, and ASTM D86 are nonlinear and thus require that nonlinear optimization be employed in each of the application modules. The remaining properties blend linearly on a volume or weight basis by using either the raw property values or the blending indices.

Implementation effort

The implementation of the six models was a joint customer-contractor effort conducted over 6 months. A stepwise implementation approach was used to allow end users to become familiar with the new hardware and software technologies presented to them.

The implementation followed a two-phase process. The first phase was a *factory acceptance test* (FAT) performed at the contractor's premises, followed by on-site commissioning. The FAT spanned 2 weeks, during which time the planning and economics (P&E) representative was involved in the final design stages of the model's functionality and the initial testing.

Due to the complex nature of the model's interfacing with the plant information system and blending control packages, the main thrust of the implementation effort was focused on the on-site commissioning phase. This last phase was broken down into three separate periods.

During the first period, all interfaces were tested for functionality and robustness. At the same time, the single-blend optimization models were handed over to the refinery's P&E department. The remaining models were tested, debugged, and transferred to ENGEN during the second commissioning period. After the users had executed the models using real-time data, several of their suggestions were incorporated during the final commissioning period. One such request was to add a modem dial-in facility which allowed the planners to execute the system during after-hours duty.

The implementation period came to an end with the delivery of the systems documentation together with a comprehensive user's manual.

Hardware Requirements

Figure 15.12 displays the overall hardware configuration for the blend control system (BCS). The blend system hardware essentially is comprised of three DEC VAX computers and a number of modules on an existing Honeywell TDC 3000 platform.

One DEC VAX 4000-300 computer and two VAX 3100 workstations are configured as a *local-area VAX cluster* (LAVC), which enables optimum resource sharing between the three machines.

Communications are ensured by an existing Ethernet network. The planning and scheduling model manager resides on both workstations, while data files are stored in the VAX 4000-300 computer. One of the VAX 3100 workstations is located in the P&E scheduler's desk while the other is assigned to the refinery planner.

To support the Honeywell Oil Movement & Storage packages on blend history, recipe management, and property control, a relational database manager is installed in the VAX 4000-300 computer, which is connected to the TDC 3000 via a computer gateway. Remaining hardware equipment in the blending area supports other Honeywell packages related to tankage and blend data, blend ratio control, and product transfers.

The existing laboratory information system resides in an HP 1000 computer linked to the Ethernet network.

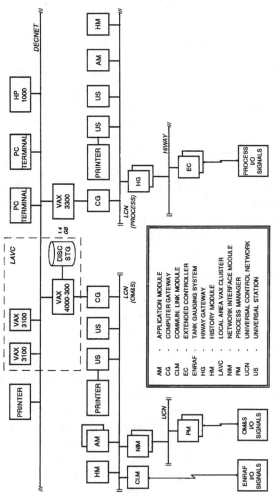

Figure 15.12 OM&S planning and control system installed hardware.

The tank farm gauging system was interfaced with the TDC 3000 computer via a 19,200-baud communications link module.

System Benefits

A comprehensive audit was undertaken in July 1993, approximately a year after the project was commissioned. Although data were collected from January 1989, a period of 1 year (July 1991 to June 1992) was chosen as the time basis prior to the installation and a comparison of 6 months (January 1993 to June 1993) as the postinstallation period.

The major justification for the revamp was based on the increase in refinery throughput. The BCS has a number of additional benefits of which the following can be quantified: The blend properties moved closer to the specifications. The three properties which are used for gasoline giveaway reporting are RON, the volatility factor (VF), and lead. These properties have been used to determine the benefits of moving closer to the specifications.

Research octane number

Average gasoline RON showed a small improvement of only 0.01 octane. This is due to the fact that batches are mostly reblended when outside the RON giveaway limits. A better indication of the improvement is thus the reduction, from 2.5 to 0.3, in the number of reblends per batch.

Volatility factor

Previously, VF used to account for 98 percent of the reported giveaway. The improvement in VF is 0.3 unit.

Lead

The maximum lead specification at present is 0.4 g/L. The amount of lead added has decreased due to initial hardware problems experienced and an octane-rich component pool forced by the refinery hydrogen-balance requirements. The decrease in lead use amounts to a penalty of 0.02 unit.

The data in Table 15.1 give an overview of the reduction in giveaway of the three gasoline properties in property units and U.S. cents per barrel. Inventory holding is reduced.

The benefit calculated for reduced component inventory holding is approximately $0.005 per barrel based on local interest rates.

TABLE 15.1   Project Benefits

Property	Giveaway	Giveaway before	Delta variation after	Benefit, U.S. cents per barrel
RON	0.134	0.124	− 0.010	0.3
VF	0.57	0.27	− 0.300	6.6
Lead	0.017	0.036	0.019	− 2.8

Laboratory workload reduced

A 26 percent reduction in the number of gasoline laboratory tests and a 38 percent reduction in the number of bunker fuel oil laboratory tests have been realized. This is equivalent to approximately $50,000 per year.

Intangible benefits of this project are as follows:

1. Reduction in the average turnaround time for a gasoline product tank from 6 to 2 days. This is largely due to the reduced number of reblends per batch.

2. Stabilization of gasoline production, which reduced the dependence on other refineries for product accommodations, creating additional business opportunities and improved reliability with respect to marketing partners and customers.

3. Improved productivity of the operations staff as well as the production and scheduling staff.

4. The basis for integration of *oil movement and shipping* (OM&S) operations database with current and future refinery information systems.

It is estimated that the OM&S automation project payback period is 4 years. The production planning and scheduling portion of it, which accounted for 12 percent of the project cost and contributes to approximately 25 percent of the benefits, shows a payback on the order of 2 years.

Future Goals

ENGEN's Durban refinery is currently aiming for the integration of the gasoline and fuel oil long-range planning tools with its plantwide linear programming (LP) planning model. The refinery is considering, as well, extending the use of the same scheduling tools to other areas such as crude oil movements, lube oil manufacture, and diesel oil blending.

Finally, with the advent of commercially reliable near-infrared gasoline property analyzers and their real-time integration with the gasoline blending property control application, the refinery plans to use the single-blend optimizer only as a backup recipe generator.

Acknowledgments

The authors wish to thank ENGEN Management for granting us permission to publish this paper. We are grateful for the support provided by the Durban refinery personnel during the implementation and commissioning of the BCS, particularly Michael B. McDonnell as the overall project manager. Finally, we would like to acknowledge the outstanding contribution of all the vendors involved.

Trademarks

DEC, VAX, and VAX Cluster are trademarks of Digital Equipment Corporation.

HP 1000 is a trademark of Hewlett-Packard Corporation.

TDC 3000 is a trademark of Honeywell, Inc.

MIMI is a trademark of Chesapeake Decision Sciences, Inc.

Integration of Production Planning, Operations, and Engineering at Idemitsu Petrochemical Company

Takahiko Watano
Keiji Tamura
Tatsunori Sumiyoshi
Idemitsu Petrochemical Company

Pratap Nair
ChemShare Corporation

Analysis

This application actually goes beyond the integration of planning, scheduling, and control, to include the rest of the supply chain from customer orders to product delivery. All the elements described in Part 1 of this book are present and integrated:

- *A process information system*

- *Model-based data reconciliation*

- *The use of the same very accurate process simulation model for all three functions of planning, advanced control, and engineering*

Presented at the American Institute of Chemical Engineers Spring National Meeting, Houston, TX, April 1993.

- *Use of an integrated database*
- *Scheduling, although not mentioned explicitly, associated with order processing*
- *Use of AI (expert system) technologies*

Note especially the emphasis on making fundamental changes in the organization. The chapter refers to "restructuring the production department and its integration with other business functions." Their experience supports our contention that an existing organizational structure should not be computerized intact.

Abstract

Computer-integrated manufacturing (CIM) is the path chosen at Idemitsu Petrochemical to pursue our goal of becoming an "integrated chemical company." The first step, completed in 1990, entailed the reconstruction of information systems in management, sales, distribution, and accounting. The next step, described in this chapter, was to reconstruct the production system and to integrate it with other business functions.

The production system consists of two parts: production control and planning, and operation control. The brains for these kinds of systems are mathematical models. Traditionally, several different levels of modeling sophistication ranging from linear programs to rigorous simulators have been used as production system brains. In reconstructing our production system, our goal was to use a single, rigorous on-line model for all purposes with the objective of providing consistent and more profitable information for making decisions.

Better decisions resulted in a 5 percent increase in profits due to improved feed slate selection and an additional 5 percent increase in profits due to improved operations. In both cases, the comparison is with respect to our previous traditional production system.

Introduction

Idemitsu Petrochemical Company is committed to becoming an integrated chemical company. Computer-integrated manufacturing is regarded as the pathway toward this goal. A large part of this effort entails developing the information system. A first step was the reconstruction of systems in management, sales, distribution, and accounting departments. Most of this work was completed in 1990. The effort since then is to reconstruct the production system and integrate the various systems. The CIM process requires an up-front plan and management commitment. During this process, Idemitsu

Petrochemical Company has incorporated several new technologies and has seen paradigm shifts in the way it conducts its business. The key step in the CIM process is the restructuring of the production department and its integration with the other business functions. This integration and restructuring of the production department is extremely important in achieving any significant benefit from CIM. Due to the significance of this step, it is itself often referred to as CIM. To differentiate, Idemitsu Petrochemical Company refers to the production system revamp as *CIM in the narrow sense* and to the comprehensive CIM system as *whole-company CIM.*

In this chapter, we outline the key elements of CIM and focus on its most crucial step—the production control system—its significance, and the concepts involved. Concepts and activities in other areas of CIM at Idemitsu are described in several earlier papers (see Watano, 1991a, 1991b; Yamamura, 1990). We conclude with an enumeration of some of the benefits we gleaned and some of the general lessons we learned in the implementing process.

Motivation

The factors motivating the CIM effort at Idemitsu Petrochemical Company are

- Increasing international competition
- Potential increased demand due to new markets in eastern Europe
- Changes in consumer values
- Increased quality expectations
- Need to produce a wider variety of products in varying quantities
- Workforce shortage in manufacturing

Idemitsu Petrochemical Company believes it requires CIM to remain competitive and to be able to survive in the long run. With the better-quality and timely information flow enabled by CIM, Idemitsu Petrochemical Company is able to better respond to the rapidly changing business conditions. With CIM, Idemitsu Petrochemical Company is better able to address changing consumer values and increased quality expectations and to manufacture a wider variety of products more efficiently.

CIM enables faster business operations, reducing time to market and minimizing lost opportunities. CIM improves managerial efficiency severalfold, helping cope with the workforce shortage.

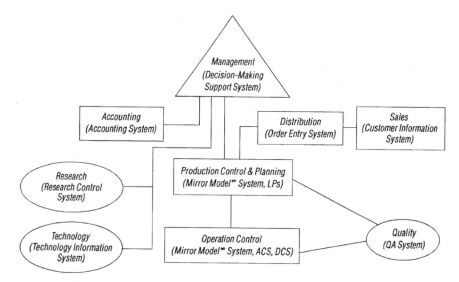

Figure 16.1   Elements of the CIM system.

Components of CIM

The major system elements comprising CIM are shown in Fig. 16.1. The decision-making support system provides management with easy access to decision quality information. This includes office automation and software tools to analyze the data made available to management. It is considered as the summit of the CIM system. Idemitsu Petrochemical Company's decision support system is known as *IDEA* (*I*demitsu *de*cision support *a*ssociation), shown in Fig. 16.2. Good decision making requires a mix of quantitative data and information based on perception. IDEA provides the quantitative information as well as picturized information to stimulate the creativeness of the manager.

The customer information system is considered the front end of the CIM system. At Idemitsu, the customer information gathered by salespeople is very highly valued. The customer information in the form of figures, character, and images is combined and analyzed by ACUA (*a*dvanced *cu*stomer *a*nalyzer), as shown in Fig. 16.3. This integrated information is used to guide sales. The order entry system is considered the pipeline connecting sales and production. Configuration of Idemitsu's order entry system is shown in Fig. 16.4. This system processes orders and coordinates shipment and supply of several thousands of products. It ties in order acceptance to real-time processing.

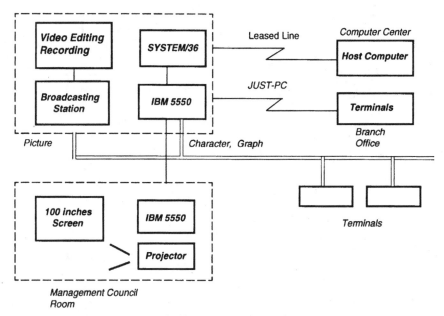

Figure 16.2   IDEA (*I*demitsu *de*cision support *a*ssociation).

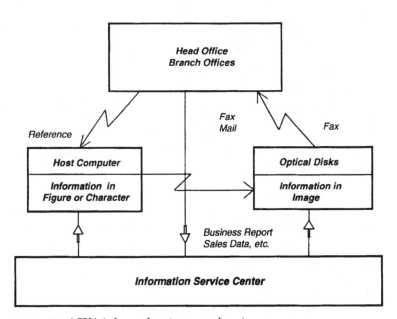

Figure 16.3   ACUA (*a*dvanced *cu*stomer *a*nalyzer).

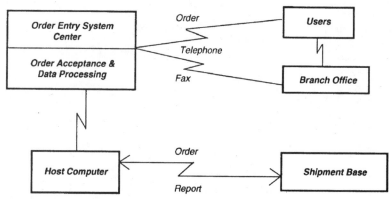

Figure 16.4   Order entry system.

The production control and planning system is the brain of the CIM system. Operating strategies have a direct impact on margins. Selecting the best strategy to run operations so as to maximize profit while satisfying regulations and constraints is the function of the production control and planning system. This system helps select the best feed from the available feedstocks. It provides operations with the best way to run the plant. It helps engineers design changes to the existing process to meet new requirements and conditions optimally. This system links plant operations to business.

The operation control system forms the base of the CIM system. It enables stable operation of the plant for a given plan provided by the production control system. It makes sure the plant produces the specified quality and quantity of products, in spite of constant disturbances. The operation control system includes systems that control the plant as well as systems that provide the operator with raw data (process measurements) that tell her or him the state of the process.

The accounting system, quality assurance system, research control system, and technical information system are other supporting components of CIM, further details of which are discussed elsewhere (Tamura, 1990).

Several technologies go into supporting the CIM system. These technologies are summarized in Table 16.1.

Common Difficulties in Current Operating Practice Affecting the CIM Implementation

The individual business and engineering functions have remained the same for decades. These functions are based on a flow of information from the process floor to the business office (Mehta, 1992). Decisions

TABLE 16.1   System Technologies Supporting CIM

System technology	Application	Significance/effect
AI technology	Anomaly diagnosis	Standardization of technologies and know-how
	Operation support	Improvement of safety
	Production plan/scheduling	Flexible response to environmental change
	Decision-making support	Stabilization of quality
		Labor-saving
MirrorModel system	Optimal planning	Maximization of profit
	Optimal operation	Flexible response to environmental changes
	Optimal engineering	Improve quality and maintenance management
	Management of operations	Improved understanding of process behavior and its connection to business by all employees (employee empowerment)
Controlling technology	Operation control	Improvement of safety
		Quality stabilization
		Continuation of optimal operation
Automation technology	Automatic start-up	Labor-saving
	Automatic shutdown	Improvement of safety
	On-site operation	Mechanization of dangerous operations
Factory automation technology	Brand switchover	Flexible response to environmental change
	Processing process	
Sensor technology	Anomaly diagnosis	Labor-saving
	Operation control	Stabilization of operation
		Stabilization of quality
Information communication technology	LAN	Improvement of operational handling
	Integrated database	Improvement of analytical technology
	Network	Cost reduction

are made based on the information received. Final implementation occurs at the process level. CIM enables faster and more accurate decisions by enhancing the flow of decision quality information.

Communication between engineering and business has always been a weak link in the decision-making process. Business functions require information not readily available in a directly usable form from the process. On the other hand, targets set by business groups are not always achievable by operations, due to lack of timely information and assumptions not consistent with reality.

The inherent complexity of the processing step necessitates retrieving data from several parts of the process before making decisions. In the past, lack of sufficient process information resulted in a separation of the business decisions from actual operational feasibility and operational efficiency decisions. The operational aspect required in making a business decision was often filled in by "gut feeling" and experience.

Newer digital control systems make large quantities of process data easily available. However, inherent errors in raw plant data make them difficult to use for decisions. Hence, even with process data easily available, the traditional gut-feeling technique continues. This separation of business from operational decisions results in lost opportunities due to delayed or inaccurate decisions.

Addressing the weak link that causes this separation between business and operations is required for CIM to be successful. Traditionally, models describing process behavior are used to plan in advance. These models represent the complex process behavior. Models are the next best thing to running experiments on the plant (an undesirable option) and deciding what can be done. The flip side to models is that they may not represent reality, making the decisions made by using them suspect. Operations typically use simulators to do their modeling.

Planners use linear programs. A common difficulty with these models is that they are extremely cumbersome to keep updated to reflect reality. Another problem is keeping the planning and operations models consistent. Inconsistency between models is one of the reasons for the traditional discrepancy between what the planners intend to make versus what operations thinks it can produce. Linear programs require large amounts of accurate data, generally unavailable, to be able to accurately represent reality. Simulation models never match process data. The difficulty arises from the inherent errors in plant data. This may be due to instruments requiring recalibration, stuck values, leaks, and fouling not known to the operator. The measurements are the only source of knowing what is occurring within the pipes in process. The model may consistently match some of the measurements. The same model could be adjusted to fit the data in several ways, by assuming errors to lie at different locations.

This brings to light another use of models: to determine process data consistency. However, substantial work is required to determine the consistency by using traditional simulators. Moreover, things are constantly changing in the plant so that it is similar to hitting a moving target.

The CIM implementation needs to address these difficulties in order to obtain significant benefits. These difficulties must be overcome at the production control level.

Requirements

To achieve the CIM goals for current operations, you need to know

- How economic conditions affect current plant profitability
- The state of present operations
- The optimal state of current operations
- How to achieve optimal operations
- That it has been achieved

To achieve the CIM goals for future planning, you need to know

- Possible economic conditions and how they would affect plant profitability (scenarios)
- Plant operations for future options
- Constraints limiting higher operating profits
- How to modify operations and/or remove constraints at minimal cost

Idemitsu Petrochemical Company uses the mirrorlike modeling technology from ChemShare Corporation to meet these requirements (Yang and Canfield, 1991). This is new technology (Nair and Canfield, 1992) that addresses the common difficulties encountered while using traditional techniques, described in the previous section.

Mirrorlike modeling—The key to CIM

The mirrorlike modeling concept (Fig. 16.5) entails the automatic and continuous on-line maintenance of rigorous models that reflect plant operations. This is made possible by *complete and rigorous model reconciliation* (CRMR) (see Nair and Iordache, 1991). The functions of CRMR are

- Identification of bad measurements
- Calculation of time values for bad measurements consistent with the laws of nature
- Calculation of fouling factors and other equipment efficiency factors continuously
- Prediction of values for unmeasured process variables
- Automatic maintenance of a model that mirrors the entire plant operation, without sacrificing on the individual equipment details

As depicted in Fig. 16.6, the mirrorlike model is a consistent system

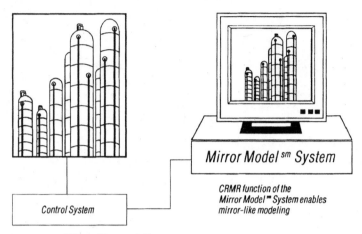

Figure 16.5   Mirrorlike modeling.

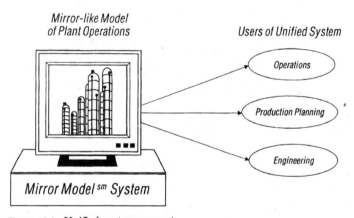

Figure 16.6   Unified system concept.

used by operations, production planning, and engineering groups. The use of a common model by all three groups minimizes the discrepancy arising from multiple bases for models.

Figure 16.7 displays the new production control system and its connection to other systems at Idemitsu Petrochemical Company. The unified mirrorlike model is connected to the planning linear programs. The same model used for feedstock selection in the planning arena is used for on-line plantwide optimization of all equipment. This provides set points to the operations control system. Results from the automatic model analysis are stored together with sales and distribution information in an integrated database (Fig. 16.8).

The integrated database is a source of information for the mirrorlike model. The model provides consistent information to the data-

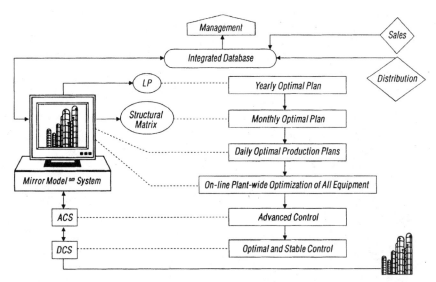

Figure 16.7 CIM application at Idemitsu Petrochemical Company at the production level.

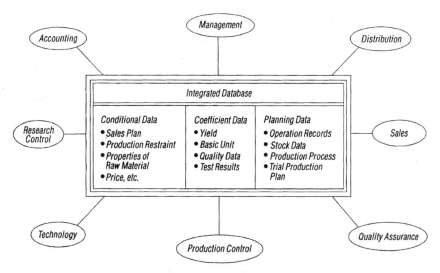

Figure 16.8 Integrated database at Idemitsu Petrochemical Company.

base, forming usable input to management. The decision-making support systems convert the information to reports as required by management. The decision-making support system provides the "pretty pictures" and presentation. The mirrorlike model makes certain that the numbers entered in these reports are correct.

The MirrorModel* system provides the correct information and also serves as a tool for what-if studies for various users. The main deviation from traditional practice is that these studies are now based on current reality.

Benefits Gleaned So Far

The reconstruction of systems in the management, sales, distribution, and accounting departments is almost complete. Idemitsu has observed increased efficiency in all sections. These systems have made administration more flexible and have accelerated the speed of doing business. The improved systems that went into the CIM construction resulted in a 7 percent improvement in gross sales.

Improved operations from the new production control system alone resulted in an improvement in operating profit of 5 percent. Better feedstock selection improved profits by 5 percent due to recognition of the opportunities lost by choosing suboptimal feeds, using traditional tools.

The new system has promoted maintenance by exception because of proactive identification of problem areas. Better understanding of the process made possible by the new system has already proved to be valuable in preventing incorrect decisions. In one such case, reconciliation identified operation close to a constraint that was limiting throughput. Optimization via the reconciled mirrorlike model solved this problem, by offering an alternate operational strategy which involved operating away from the constraint and at the same time increased operating profits, a solution that was not possible with traditional tools. This prevented a decision in the wrong direction, which otherwise would have been made.

The system has helped to accurately predict the value of going to a higher level of automation. For example, it predicts exactly where it would be worthwhile to add advanced control and the value added to the plant as a whole. It predicts regions where better instrumentation is warranted and the exact value that its addition would provide.

Both planners and operations can now quickly react to changes in business and supply conditions and be sure they have made the optimal decision. The CRMR feature helps track implementation of optimal decisions and verifies whether the predictions are consistent with what actually happens.

---

*MirrorModel is a service mark of ChemShare Corporation.

General Lessons We Learned

These are some of the lessons we learned in going through with the CIM implementation:

- Do not design projects to minimize conflict within the organization.
- Do not rely on interviewing users of new systems alone. This does not reveal what we need from the system.
- Postpone small improvements if a fundamental change is what is required.
- Redesign process before hurrying to automate.
- Divide the CIM activity into projects, and structure projects so that there are visible payoffs along the way.
- Try out prototypes or perform quick up-front studies wherever possible, to get early feedback on the possible use and benefits of the system.
- CIM applications require a change in paradigm. Very few complete CIM applications exist in the process industry today. The fact that a couple of other manufacturers are going down a particular path or using certain systems does not make it the norm to be followed. The model that works for your company is always unique.
- We have found that the speed of implementation of CIM is limited more by people and by the organization than by technology. So in any implementation, organizational issues must be given equal consideration. Select respected managers and train them in new technologies. This turns them from "bashers" into "boosters."

References

Mehta, Chetan D. (1992): "Process Control. The Business Connection," *Chem. Eng.,* vol. 99, no. 5, May, p. 90.

Nair, Pratap, and Frank B. Canfield (1992): "Consider Computer Integrated Manufacturing for Continuous Process Plants," *Chem. Eng. Prog.,* November, pp. 71–81.

Nair, Pratap, and Cornelius D. Iordache (1991): "Rigorous Data Reconciliation Is Key to Optimal Operations; Complete and Rigorous Model-Based Reconciliation Facilitates Operations, Planning and Engineering," *Control,* vol. 4, no. 10, October, p. 118.

Tamura, Keiji (1990): "Development of CIM in the Petrochemical Industry," presented at ISI Dentsu User's Conference, July, Chiba, Japan.

Watano, T. (1991a): "Factory Automation in the Petrochemical Industry," *Chem. Apparatus,* September, p. 32.

Watano, T. (1991b): "CIM in the Petrochemical Industry," presented at the American Institute of Chemical Engineers annual meeting, *Integrated Approaches to Computer Aided Process Operations,* Los Angeles, November.

Yamamura, Toshiyuki (1990): "Approach to CIM with ACS in Petrochemical Plant," *IBM Rev.*, p. 108.

Yang, Sun Fu, and Frank B. Canfield (1991): "A Process Computer Integrated Manufacturing System Using Complete and Rigorous Models," presented at International Conference and Exhibition on Petroleum Refining and Petrochemical Processing, September 15, Beijing, China.

17

Rigorous On-Line Model for Crude Unit Planning, Scheduling, Engineering, and Optimization

Sanjeev Mullick
Simulation Sciences Inc.
Houston, TX

Analysis

This chapter describes an application to a single unit in a refinery. Consequently, the application does not represent a complete integration of planning, scheduling, and control for an entire plant, but a step along the way to that goal. All the elements necessary for a complete integration are present, given that only one process is involved:

- *A process information system*

- *Model-based data reconciliation*

- *A very accurate process simulation system model, used with advanced control, planning, and engineering*

- *AI (expert system) technology*

- *Database and networking technologies*

Prepared for presentation at the American Institute of Chemical Engineers Spring National Meeting, Houston, TX, April 1993, updated March 1994.

Note especially that the reconciled operating point and derivatives for changes in operation are made available to the planning system. Use of this information would integrate planning and control for this one unit.

Introduction

The refining, petrochemical, chemical, and gas processing industries all over the world are faced with a challenge to effectively respond to market and regulatory changes. These pressures are becoming more demanding as the 1990s unfold. Stricter environmental rules, product specifications, and narrow profit margins are forcing many companies to seek better ways to run their operations to remain competitive. With almost no new facilities being planned, existing units are being revamped for capacity enhancements and operating flexibility. Therefore, a need exists for improved process analysis and optimization of not only individual units but also the entire complex, to take advantage of the interactions between units. Applications range from planning, scheduling, operations, monitoring, and maintenance to design engineering.

Furthermore, this analysis requires high speed and minimum engineering effort and user input. The proliferation of data acquisition systems and of computers in processing plants makes this possible; reduced staffing levels make it a necessity. This has been successfully accomplished now in several installations by the application of a *rigorous on-line model* (ROM)* to the unit(s). This chapter describes in detail one refinery application of a ROM to a crude distillation unit and provides summaries of some additional ROM projects.

This specific application was for a refinery in the United States. The ROM has been in regular on-line use since the fourth quarter of 1992. In this chapter we look at several aspects of this project in particular and ROM technology in general.

- Crude unit overview
- Project scope
- Software and hardware configuration
- ROM structure and data flow
- Applications experience

---

*Note that in this chapter ROM is a trademarked name; it does *not* mean read-only memory.

- Software enhancements
- Future developments
- Additional ROM projects

Crude Unit Overview

Besides crude units, the refinery complex has fluid catalytic cracker (FCC), coker, hydrotreating, reforming, sulfur recovery, and gas processing units. The selected crude unit has a modern supervisory control system fully integrated with an advanced regulatory control system and networked with the plant database computer.

The unit comprises atmospheric and vacuum distillation towers, a preflash tower, and desalters. More than 50 heat exchangers exist including 38 in the crude preheat train. In all, four pump-arounds are tightly integrated with the preheat train. The unit produces up to 10 liquid products which are feeds to several downstream units. Figure 17.1 shows a schematic of the flow sheet.

The unit possesses many lineup options. These options provide flexibility to place groups of exchangers in series or in parallel, to use certain exchangers before or after the desalters, and to take one of the three atmospheric heaters out of service at low throughputs. Other options allow exchangers to be completely or partially bypassed for cleaning or pressure-drop considerations. More than 35 lineup options

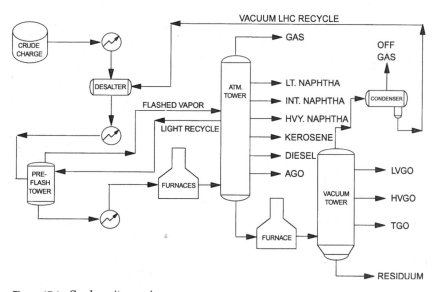

Figure 17.1 Crude unit overview.

have been included in the model. These options are user-configurable through scrollable menus with preprogrammed options.

Project Scope

The ROM project was preceded by a scoping study to identify the potential benefits of an on-line system. Project justification was based on the following potential benefits:

- Increase yields of higher-value products.
- Minimize energy consumption through improved heat recovery.
- Optimize without violation of constraints.

The project scope included most of the operating equipment on the unit to account for all heat-exchange and fractionation effects. All utilities and economics were included for profit calculations and for a rigorous energy balance. The project objectives were to provide a system for on-line optimization and case studies. The planning component of the project required the model to be easily configurable for crude blend evaluation including tracking of over 25 special refining properties, such as the freeze point, flash point, and so on. A detailed list of these properties is presented later in the chapter. Finally, the ROM was required to generate a predictive model that could be used off-line for engineering design studies.

Software and Hardware Configuration

The main engines of the ROM are the Simulation Sciences PRO/II and DATACON software packages. PRO/II is a flow sheet simulator providing process models that are a blend of equation-based and sequential modular solution techniques. The model representations of plant equipment are based on first principles with minimal use of empirical correlations except where commonly used in engineering design practice. An advantage of the models is that they are predictive over a wide range of operating conditions. Besides automatically adjusting to variations in charge rates and setpoints, they can be effectively used in evaluating new operating scenarios without loss of accuracy. PRO/II's well-documented and multifeature keyword input language provides the means to quickly create rigorous models of complex flow sheets with no programming or compilation. This also provides modularity for rapid development and diagnosis and the ability to enhance models in phases.

Data reconciliation is the most important part of the ROM's initial information handling. DATACON data reconciliation software turns real-time process data, which are subject to bias and random error, into statistically sound reconciled data. Both material and heat balances are considered in the reconciliation process, compared to material-only methods. Consideration of heat balances provides much more redundancy, resulting in a more extensive reduction in measurement error than with material balances alone. DATACON also detects instrumentation error and then statistically isolates it to specific instruments. This allows the suspect instruments' measured values and the resulting bias to be eliminated from the final calculations. This function provides essential data for instrument maintenance. DATACON creates a report that lists suspect instruments and provides estimated values which are consistent with heat and material balances. DATACON uses a keyword input language that is similar to PRO/II and offers the same advantages.

Each ROM system comes preconfigured with the necessary models and various options. The user selects options through a menu-driven interface which includes both lineups and run modes (reconciliation, case study, optimization, etc). The ROM and its auxiliary software reside on a dedicated IBM RS/6000 UNIX workstation. This ROM computer is networked with other refinery computers, allowing automated data transfer from the plant database computer (DCS and laboratory data) as well as convenient access to several users. Figure 17.2 illustrates the hardware setup.

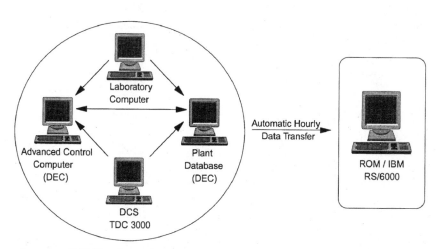

Figure 17.2   ROM hardware design.

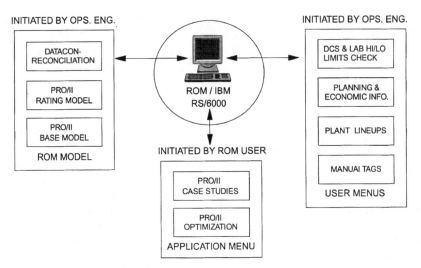

Figure 17.3 ROM data flow diagram.

ROM Structure and Data Flow

Figure 17.3 shows the main elements of the ROM system's data flow.

Input data

The ROM accesses over 250 *distributed control system* (DCS) measurements (flow, temperature, pressure, and valve positions) and over 200 laboratory measurements. The DCS hourly averaged data values are automatically transferred once per hour. The latest laboratory data are also transferred similarly. In addition, users can synchronize the DCS data with laboratory sample collection times. This option uses the database of historicized values stored on the refinery database computer (DEC).

Hourly calculations

Hourly computations include automated data checking and updating for high/low limit violations, data reconciliation, and calculation of an hourly gross profit index (dollars per hour and per barrel). This index is historicized for trending the unit's economic performance.

Data screening

In the on-demand mode, the user obtains a synchronized set of data using utilities that automate the process. These data are screened for

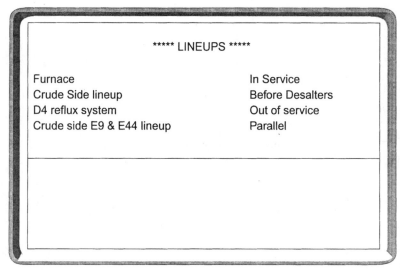

Figure 17.4   Equipment lineup overview.

high/low limit violations and laboratory data consistency. A function-key-based menu system initiates various actions—manual override of a measured value, reset current value to default, change high limit, change low limit, reset to high limit, or reset to low limit.

Lineup configuration and economic data

Once the input data have been screened, the user is presented with menus to update the lineup configuration and pricing data (Figs. 17.4 and 17.5). A two-tier pricing structure has been implemented. This requires entry of a base price, a breakpoint, and an incremental price for products, feed, and utilities. Additional pricing tiers exist for products with a value based on a measurable property. For example, the value of HVGO is a function of its TBP 90 percent point. The price is lower if the TBP 90 percent value is higher than the breakpoint.

Model update

Once data screening and updating are complete, the ROM initiates reconciliation calculations using DATACON. As discussed earlier, this step generates a consistent set of flow and temperature data and reports the duties of various heat exchangers and heaters. A separate list of suspect instrumentation is also created. Results may be viewed through a menu-driven utility. Figure 17.6 shows a portion of the report generated.

STREAM/UTILITY	BASE PRICE	BREAKPOINT	INCREMENTAL
Fuel gas	3.50 $/MMBTU	0.00 MMBTUH	3.50 $MMBTU
Steam 100#	4.00 $/MLB	0.00 MLB/HR	4.00 $/MLB
Electricity	15.00 $/MMBTU	0.00 MMBTUH	15.00 $/MMBTU
Crude	50.00 C/GAL	0.00 MBPD	50.00 C/GAL
Lt. Naphtha	55.00 C/GAL	0.00 BPH	55.00 C/GAL
Hvy. Naphtha	60.00 C/GAL	0.00 BPH	60.00 C/GAL
KERO	65.00 C/GAL	0.00 BPH	65.00 C/GAL
Diesel	60.00 C/GAL	0.00 BPH	60.00 C/GAL

Figure 17.5   Feed, product, and utility pricing.

***** OVERALL VOLUME BALANCE *****

TAG	UNIT	DESCRIPTION	DCS	DATACON	MODEL	BIAS
		FEEDS				
F301	MBPD	CRUDE CHARGE	188.9	191.7	191.7	0.0
TOTAL	BPH		8014.6	8131.6	8131.5	- 0.1
		PRODUCTS				
F403	BPH	Lt. Naphtha	183.9	183.8	183.9	0.1
F411	BPH	Hvy. Naphtha	1745.0	1748.0	1748.0	0.0
F431	BPH	Kerosene	1176.0	1169.8	1169.8	0.0
F461	BPH	Diesel	836.9	835.8	835.7	- 0.1
F755 to F751		Resid	494.1	496.1	505.5	9.3
TOTAL	BPH		8176.2	8131.7	8135.5	3.8
		IMBALANCE				
IMBAL	BPH		-161.7	-0.1	-3.9	

Figure 17.6   Plant, reconciled data, and rating model.

The reconciled set of data is used in the rating (or parameter update) mode. This mode calculates parameters such as heat-transfer coefficients and biases which now reflect equipment performance in near real time. In addition, a report summarizing the results of a rigorous energy balance of the unit is created. Rigorous heat-exchanger calculations are also done which provide fouling factors and heat-transfer coefficients for trending. This trend information is useful in monitoring antifoulant programs and determining when exchangers need to be cleaned.

A base model that reflects current plant performance is generated by using unit parameters from the rating mode. This fully predictive model is configured to honor various operating and equipment constraints and mimics the existing advanced control schemes. This model, like the rating model, uses an updated crude composition by back-blending the product flows and assays. The base-case model is used in all subsequent optimization and what-if case studies.

Optimization and case studies

The ROM system facilitates case studies which allow process engineers to make multiple changes to operating setpoints and to generate reports on the predicted process changes and the economic impact. Case studies are reviewed for feasibility and constraint violation before process changes are implemented. Sample case study reports are described later in the chapter.

Over 75 independent parameters have been provided for case study through a menu-driven interface (Fig. 17.7). These include the crude charge rate, furnace outlet temperatures, key unit temperatures, column pressures, product qualities such as cut points and freeze points (which have advanced control loops), and heat-transfer coefficients. The heat-transfer coefficients allow users to look at the economic impact of cleaning exchangers.

A variation of the case study mode is the assay or feedstock case study feature. The assay case study feature allows the user to evaluate the performance of the plant if a different crude blend is charged

```
                **** ROM CASE STUDY MAIN MENU ****
        -------------- Parameter ----------------- Current (Rec)    New
        Total Crude Charge Rate (MBPD)     191.7            0.0
        Atm. Furnace - (F)                 675              0.0
        Vacuum Furnace Temp (F)            737              0.0
        Atm Twr TPA Duty (MBTU/bbl)        7                0.0
        Atm Twr BPA Duty (MBTU/bbl)        18               0.0
        Atm Twr Str. Steam (Lb/bbl)        2                0.0
        Kerosene Str. Steam (Lb/Hr)        4490             0.0
        Diesel Str. Steam (Lb/Hr)          1000             0.0

        **** [Esc] to proceed    -    [PgDn] for more parameters ****
        **** [Enter] to select / de-select    -    [F2] to edit value ****
```

Figure 17.7 Variable menu of case study.

ROM OPTIMIZATION PARAMETER SELECTION MENU
On-Demand Case

---------- Parameter ----------	Mini	Current (Rec)	Maxi
Crude Charge Rate (MBPD)	100	189	200
Atm. Heater - Outlet Temp, (F)	650	675	715
Atm Twr TPA Duty (MBTU/bbl)	5	7	10
Atm Twr BPA Duty (MBTU/bbl)	15	18	23
Atm Twr Str. Steam (Lb/bbl)	1	2	3
Kerosene Str. Steam (Lb/Hr)	500	4490	5000
Diesel Str. Steam (Lb/Hr)	100	1000	2000

**** [PgDn] for more parameters ****

Figure 17.8   Optimization parameter menu.

to the unit. This feature is best implemented in conjunction with an assay database manager. The user selects the crude blend and chooses either the current conditions or a number of case study parameters. The optional parameters allow the user to change operating setpoints or product qualities which may be more compatible with the crude blend being studied.

A variety of menu-driven optimization options are available (Fig. 17.8). Optimizations are similar to case studies in that users select an unlimited number of setpoints that they want to change. But unlike case studies, the ROM determines the optimum setpoints that meet the optimization objective while honoring all independent- and dependent-variable constraints. Examples of dependent-variable constraints are equipment and product quality limits (Fig. 17.9). The objective may be to maximize profit, or to maximize charge rate, or to maximize some other function that the customer identifies and which has been built into the ROM. Optimizations are constrained in the following ways.

- Model responses are forced to duplicate the advanced control system strategy. Loops, like stripping steam ratio controls, product cut point controls, and minimum/maximum heat removal in pumparounds, are accounted for.

- Optimizations may be limited by production minimum/maximum settings. These are entered to keep product yields in conformance with refinerywide demands or limitations.

- Optimizations are bounded by equipment limitations. Some parameters, such as heat-transfer coefficients or tray flooding, are

```
***** OPTIMIZATION CONSTRAINT MENU *****
            On-Demand Case

-------- Constraint --------   Current (Rec.)   Mini   Maxi
Hvy. Naphtha D86 EP (F)        357.0            0.0    375.0
Hvy. Naphtha D86 95% (F)       329.0            0.0    355.0
Kero D86 EP (F)                528.0            0.0    550.0
Kero D86 95% (F)               493.0            462.0  0.0
Atm. Htr. Duty (MMBTU/Hr)      377.6            0.0    650.0
Vac. Htr. Duty (MMBTU/Hr)      111.4            0.0    160.0


*** [PgUp] for parameters  -  [PgDn] for more constraints ***
```

Figure 17.9 Optimization constraint menu.

accounted for automatically. However, other constraints, such as the pump, control valve, compressor, or heater capacities, are determined and tuned during use of the model. Users may implement the model-calculated values for these constraint variables as guides for setting the minimum/maximum limit values.

The ROM requires regular user input to maintain a system that conforms to existing operating conditions, unit lineups, planning targets, and pricing or market conditions. In most sites, the planning, scheduling, and economic functions are not yet fully integrated with operations. Thus, economic information is manually entered through convenient input screens. All this data input may be automated if available via plant network. Therefore, while the ROM does not require the user to know DATACON, PRO/II, or UNIX, knowledge of the crude complex and the current refinery planning strategy is often needed.

The ROM provides a host of information when it is used for any type of application. For example, the overall volume balance or balance around individual columns is available; an assortment of data on unit performance such as furnace duties, product yields and quality, column loadings, exchanger fouling, instrument maintenance recommendations, economics, and energy use is also provided. Extensive data are also available on the shifts in the dependent variables (derivatives) that result from ROM manipulations, including economics, preheat temperature, product yields and qualities, and column pressures and pump-arounds. This is especially true when the model is used in the planning mode.

Applications Experience

ROM applications were implemented both during project execution and on a postproject basis by the client. These include

- Maintenance
- Operations
- Planning
- Scheduling
- Engineering

Maintenance: Heat-exchanger monitoring

The ROM is currently rigorously modeling and tracking 40 of the 55 exchangers in the crude unit. Of these, 38 are preheat exchangers. Data on fouling factors and heat-transfer coefficients have been trended since January 1992, when project execution began. By doing case studies, engineers on the unit were able to prioritize the exchanger cleaning sequence. They have since cleaned eleven exchangers based on fuel savings projected by ROM. The ROM has also been used to evaluate and monitor preheat-exchanger antifoulant performance. This application is particularly significant since unit lineups at this facility change quite frequently and tracking exchanger performance through a fixed model would not be possible. The ROM lineup flexibility makes it possible. Figure 17.10 shows

***** FOULING SUMMARY *****

Heat Exchanger	Heat transfer. MMBTU/HR	Heat Tr. Coeff. BTU/HR/FT2/F	Fouling Factor
E1	39.638	78.68	0.0018
E2	22.686	51.52	0.00689
E3	23.209	49.42	0.00898
E4	23.104	33.01	0.01845
E5	32.730	25.80	0.02823
E6	20.737	43.66	0.01029

**** [PgDn] for more exchangers ****

Figure 17.10   Heat-exchanger analysis screen.

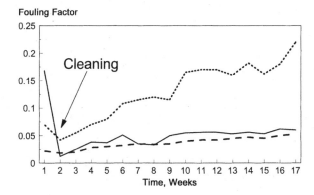

Figure 17.11 Heat-exchanger fouling trends.

a portion of the heat-exchanger analysis report. Figure 17.11 shows fouling factor trends of some of the cleaned exchangers.

Operations: Vacuum residual reduction

The ROM optimizer was used to recommend optimum conditions for maximum vacuum residual reduction. The optimizer varied the crude and vacuum furnace outlet temperatures and the crude and vacuum tower stripping steam rates within equipment and operational constraints. It recommended decreasing the crude furnace outlet temperature, decreasing crude tower stripping steam, increasing vacuum tower stripping steam, and increasing vacuum heater outlet temperature. The net result was an increased amount of lights in the reduced crude from the bottom of the atmospheric tower. These lights produced a stripping action in the bottom of the vacuum tower that resulted in more product recovery as LVGO and HVGO.

The changes were implemented on the unit. The result: the vacuum residual yield decreased by 5 percent. This was achieved with no net increase in energy consumption. Figure 17.12 is a typical economic summary report available from the ROM optimizer.

Operations: Maximize heat recovery from pump-arounds

The ROM optimizer was used to maximize heat recovery in the atmospheric and vacuum tower pump-arounds. A total of four such pump-arounds exist—two in each column. The advanced controls on the unit allow operators to set heat recovery setpoints in terms of Btu's per barrel of feed. The constraints are based on either the maxi-

Product	BaseCase	Case/Opt	Change
		Product Values	
Lt. Naphtha	4157.6	4067.9	-18.3
Hvy. Naphtha	35991.0	35704.0	-53.9
Kerosene	31290.0	31721.0	63.5
Diesel	16432.0	16191.0	-29.2
AGO	15481.0	15505.0	-61.9
LVGO	14234.0	15532.0	1245.7
HVGO	22668.0	21896.0	-361.5
Resid	4190.3	4069.1	-128.3
		Crude Costs	
Crude	100000.0	100000.0	0.0
		Utility Costs	
Fuel Gas	973.5	979.9	[5.2]
Steam (100 PSIG)	238.2	241.3	[3.1]
Steam (400 PSIG)	30.9	31.6	0.7
Preheat to PS	264.0	261.3	-0.5
		Profit Summary ($/Hr.)	
Total Feed Cost	155450	154960	0.0
Total Prod. Value	164680	164630	334
Net Utility Cost	1069	1102	6.1
Gross Profit	8163	8562	328.2
		Improvement ($/Yr.)	
Improvement	0.0	1,000,000	1,000,000

Note: Numbers have been changed and may not be consistent in this figure.

Figure 17.12 Economic summary.

mum pump capacity or minimum internal liquid flow on the tray above the pump-around. Other constraints that can also influence the pump-around are the kerosene freeze point specification or the diesel D86 90 percent point specification.

The optimizer recommended the limits to which heat recovery could be increased within constraints. The result was an increase in heat recovery of 8 percent without a noticeable sacrifice in fractionation. On a separate occasion, a similar move resulted in 4°F of additional preheat, resulting in substantial furnace fuel savings.

Operations: Hourly monitoring tool

The unattended hourly economic calculations have been used to monitor unit performance. The operations engineers have used this information to adjust unit conditions to maximize and maintain economic performance. For example, when a downturn in the hourly economic trend was observed, they looked into the possible reasons for this change. As a result, they adjusted the advanced control setpoints on product distillation specifications to maximize distillate yields within specifications set by the economics and scheduling group.

Operations: Rigorous energy balance

A common problem in many plants is the lack of complete and accurate accounting of energy consumption. Prior to the ROM, it was typical for as much as 20 percent of the energy input to be unaccounted for. After the ROM was implemented, the unaccounted balance usually has been less than 5 percent. This improvement is due to the rigorous models accounting for all energy flows including those associated with products leaving the unit, cooling water flows, waste heat recovery, and tower heat losses calculated by the rating case. An energy-balance report is generated every time a rating case is run (Fig. 17.13). This feature results in saving several worker-hours of effort over the previous practice.

Planning: Crude evaluation and linear program derivatives

The predictive model in the ROM has been used in the assay case study mode to evaluate the performance of different crudes and crude blends. Over 50 such runs have been made. Applications include evaluating the economics of operation, identifying bottlenecks, and tracking over 25 refining properties, such as those listed below.

Energy In	MMBTU/HR
Crude	-42.158
Fuel / Pilots	460.440
Steam (100)	112.460
Electric	29.930
Other	-8.55
Total In	552.110

Energy Out	MMBTU/HR
Recovered:	
Steam (400)	12.830
Preheat	192.740
Product Credit	78.826
Total Recovered	284.390
Lost:	
Products Coolers	87.081
Heaters	102.410
Brine	20.327
Steam Vent	7.529
Unacc. Steam	7.549
Power Gen. Loss	19.754
Tower Losses	7.137
Other	2.309
	254.090
Unaccounted Balance - 2.649%	14.623
Total Lost	268.713
Total Out	552.110

Net Energy Use -   268.720 MMBTU/HR

Gross Energy Use -   552.110 MMBTU/HR

Figure 17.13   Energy balance.

Reid vapor pressure (RVP)   Research octane number (RON)
Motor octane number (MON)   Nitrogen (wt%)
Naphthene content (vol%)   Aromatic content (vol%)
Benzene content (%)   Sulfur (wt%)
Mercaptans (wt%)   Refractive index
Aniline point   Viscosity and viscosity index
Freeze point   Cloud point
Pour point   Flash points
Neutralization number   Naphthalene content (vol%)
FIA aromatics   Ramsbottom carbon (wt%)
Iron (ppmw)   Nickel (ppmw)
Vanadium (ppmw)

The model was also perturbed to study the effect of setpoint changes. The derivatives or vectors so generated are written to a separate file in a form that can be fed directly to the refinery linear program.

Scheduling: Improve FCC feed quality

The economics and scheduling group identified an opportunity to improve the combined performance of the crude unit and the FCC unit. They instituted case studies to evaluate the best recovery of distillates from the FCC feed. This was done by determining the effect of changes in the D86 90 percent point of diesel. The recommended adjustment in the cut point resulted in increased diesel recovery by 12 to 15 percent while providing a more appropriate quality feed to the FCC unit. A typical case study report is shown in Fig. 17.14.

Engineering: Unit revamp

ROM's predictive model has been used off-line by process design engineers to study the changes required to convert the crude unit to run heavier, high-sulfur crudes. They used it as the design basis to determine operational effects on product specifications and equipment performance and to identify bottlenecks.

This application is possible because of the rigorous and truly predictive nature of the models used in the ROM. Although the models are complex, incorporating 150 to 200 unit operations, they are essentially PRO/II input files. Therefore, such models may be run off-line on any hardware from personal computers to mainframes that have a version of PRO/II available. This allows the ROM to provide "the model" for all applications, rather than having users maintain several smaller and perhaps conflicting models of small sections of the unit.

***** ATMOSPHERIC TOWER VOLUME BALANCE *****

TAG	UNIT	DESCRIPTION	DCS	BASECASE	CASE/OPT	CHANGE
F34	BPH	Lt. Naphtha	195.9	195.8	198.3	2.4
P35	BPH	Hvy. Naphtha	1743.0	1746.0	1752.8	8.8
F37	BPH	Kerosene	1176.0	1169.8	1163.9	- 5.8
F38	BPH	Diesel	838.9	837.8	845.3	7.5
F41	BPH	AGO	670.7	692.5	697.1	4.6
F91	BPH	Reduced Crude	2454.2	2553.5	2543.3	-10.2
TOTAL	BPH		8141.0	8368.9	8368.2	- 0.7

————————————— IMBALANCE —————————————

| IMBAL | BPH | | -755.6 | -10.0 | -10.0 | |

| TOTAL FURNACE FIRED DUTY | (MMBTU/HR) | 372.1 | 371.5 | - 0.6 |
| TOTAL FURNACE ABSORBED DUTY | (MMBTH/HR) | 305.2 | 304.7 | - 0.5 |

Figure 17.14   Case study before-and-after comparison.

System Enhancements

The installed ROM discussed in this chapter is planned to be upgraded in the future. Features such as assay case studies, scheduled (or automatic) optimizations, and links to the planning system are likely enhancements. These features have already been successfully implemented in several other ROM installations.

SimSci offers ROM users the choice between menu-driven and graphic interfaces. The ROM can be upgraded to a graphics interface based on Gensym's G2 product. G2 is an object-oriented real-time expert system. Figure 17.15 shows a typical screen used in a G2-based ROM. The graphical interface provides a convenient mechanism for identifying alarm conditions that violate any constraints. It also allows the ROM to be used by a much broader community of users, including unit operators.

Future Developments

Models similar to the ROM discussed in this chapter have been implemented for other refinery units. The goal is to link individual unit ROMs into a refinerywide, on-line model that is coupled with the planning system. This will enable better operating plans to be generated and will improve operations by taking advantage of the complex integration of the units, through the setting of consistent and feasible

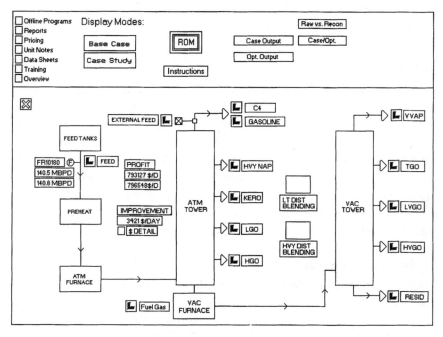

Figure 17.15 Example of graphics interface display.

targets, by better evaluation of crude blends for purchasing, processing of opportune feedstocks, optimization around constraints, and quicker evaluation of bottlenecks.

Additional ROM Projects

As additional ROM projects are launched, our clients have enjoyed a variety of benefits. Postaudits or performance assessments are a key part of the project. It is interesting to note the expected benefits that were estimated to justify the original project versus the actual benefits that were quantified after the ROM was installed:

Crude distillation unit project:	Profit impact (cents/bbl)	
	Project justification (estimated)	Actual
Crude unit A	2.19	6.03
Crude unit B	1.83	2.92
Crude unit C	1.08	2.35
Crude unit D	1.37	6.58

The actual numbers provided above were determined by client and ROM engineers.

Ethylene project

An ethylene client utilized a ROM to modify feed and operating conditions to realize a $1.1 million per year profit increase at an ethylene production rate of 450 Tlb/yr.

Gas plant

A 100 MMSCFD gas plant with a ROM installation wanted to improve profitability while maintaining its steam balance. ROM allowed this client to optimize fuel composition while reducing steam consumption by 15 percent.

Operator empowerment

Operators use ROM to run what-if analyses. A well-respected operator with 20 years' crude distillation unit experience credits ROM with teaching him more about the unit than he ever thought possible. Based on product pricing data and hourly DCS data, the operator was able to make operating changes on the ROM to run a what-if scenario that provided an average increase in unit profitability of $13,000 per day.

Improved decisions

Other clients have informed us of instances in which ROMs allowed them to run cases to support accepted common wisdom, only to determine that both operating conditions and common wisdom could be adjusted to improve profitability.

Refinery reactor units

A ROM has also been implemented on a multiunit hydrotreating catalytic reforming complex. Commercially available third-party reactor models for hydrotreating and reforming reactors have been integrated with PRO/II for this project. Besides its other advantages, this ROM allows the refinery to optimize around hydrogen availability and provides a much better understanding of its hydrogen balance.

Summary

In summary, we have successfully applied the ROM to a crude distillation unit. We now have extensive experience in developing, implementing, and delivering systems that open many opportunities for the users. The following conclusions can be drawn based on this ROM's performance.

- ROM provides a rapid and robust model of current plant operations.

- Users are able to improve profitability and operations through case studies and optimization around hard and soft constraints.

- ROM is an effective heat-exchanger and plant instrumentation monitoring tool.

- ROM is easily configured and updated as lineups, planning targets, and economics change.

The technology discussed in this chapter is by no means limited to crude units. ROMs are being successfully applied to a wide variety of refining, petrochemical, chemical, and gas processes. In more than one instance, plans are in place to implement ROMs to several units in the refinery complex including those requiring integration of rigorous reactor models. For example, ROMs on hydrotreating, reforming, and FCC units have been implemented or are in various stages of completion. This will ultimately lead to refinerywide or complexwide models.

ROMs are being installed in a closed-loop optimization (CLO) mode. Expanding use of ROMs in daily operations has led many clients with existing ROMs to consider upgrading them to CLO mode. The availability of a common on-line model that may be used by all groups in an organization is rapidly becoming a competitive necessity. ROMs provide

- Better and faster operations analysis, quality control, and optimization

- Effective coordination with operations planning and scheduling systems to ensure that top-level goals are incorporated in unit-level optimization

- Timely analysis of alternative feedstocks and changing market conditions

- A consistent basis for design changes and future plant operations

The technology to deliver on these goals is now available. The results are well proved. The ROM is a low-cost tool for achieving broad and often unforeseen benefits leading to project payouts ranging from 2 weeks to 6 months.

Trademarks

PRO/II, DATACON, and ROM are trademarks, and SimSci is a service mark of Simulation Sciences, Inc.

IBM and RS/6000 are trademarks of International Business Machines, Inc.

DEC is a trademark of Digital Equipment Corporation.

G2 is a trademark of GENSYM, Inc.

18

Computer-Integrated Manufacturing at the Monsanto Pensacola Plant

Jorge L. del Toro

Analysis

This chapter by Jorge del Toro describes a major computer-integrated manufacturing *(CIM) project that has been in progress for several years. The project is especially significant because it represents almost a reinvention of the company. Organizational changes preceded and have also paralleled the implementation of the various systems that make up the CIM system. Particular features to be noted are as follows: Top management initiated the drive for the CIM project and has vigorously supported it. A plantwide communications network was installed as almost the first phase of the project. This network had impressive dimensions and was sized to handle the long-term future requirements. The network was justified on the basis of the expected benefits of future phases of the project that would be installed even many years later. The project has emphasized training at every stage. Almost every employee has been trained in* total quality management *(TQM) concepts, and many were trained in team leadership. According to an article in* The

---

Prepared for presentation at the American Institute of Chemical Engineers spring national meeting, Houston, TX, April 10, 1991, revised June 1, 1994.

Economist *(March 19, 1994)*, *Monsanto gets back $33 for every $1 spent on training. The TQM system described goes beyond a planning, scheduling, and control integration. All the elements needed are present in this project, with an emphasis on the management and organizational aspects.*

Abstract

The integrated manufacturing strategy of the Monsanto Pensacola plant—called the *plant of the 1990s*—emerged within a climate of change precipitated by world competition. It integrates three elements: the total quality process, employee participation, and improved technology (Fig. 18.1). Computer-integrated manufacturing (CIM) is an improved technology thrust aimed at improving quality, productivity, and employee involvement by facilitating the integration of manufacturing functions through information sharing and processing. The process that the Monsanto Pensacola plant followed in developing the CIM strategy arose from the Pensacola plant's experiences and situation in the mid-1980s. It is a process that continues to evolve and adapt as plant and business conditions change. During the last 4 years, several building block CIM projects have been completed that demonstrate the contributions of CIM to the overall integrated manufacturing strategy. The challenges for the next 5 years are (1) how to maintain the momentum necessary to continue with functional integration while undergoing changes in management, organiza-

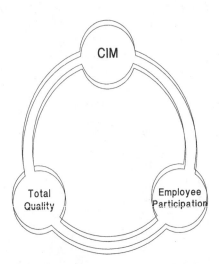

Figure 18.1   Manufacturing strategy: Plant of the 1990s.

tional style, and economic conditions and (2) how to extend manufacturing integration to the business enterprise.

Background

The Monsanto Pensacola plant, built in 1953, is Monsanto's largest manufacturing facility. Its primary products are nylon chemical intermediates (such as adipic acid, hexamethylene diamine, and nitric acid) and nylon fiber for both the carpet staple and tire yarn markets. In addition to these products, the Pensacola facility hosts a number of other Monsanto businesses including the world's largest maleic anhydride plant, Monsanto's Vydyne nylon resin plant, and the Santoprene plant of Advanced Elastomers Systems, L. P. (jointly owned by Monsanto and Exxon). In 1985 the Monsanto Pensacola plant faced a number of challenges that would impact its future. The pressure for change was evident from many fronts. The loss of one of its key product lines to foreign competition was imminent. Dislocations and reorganization in manufacturing were anticipated as the Fibers Division of Monsanto (to which Pensacola belongs) consolidated the manufacturing operation of several products. This would result in some product lines leaving Pensacola while others would be added. The R&D facility faced a major staff reduction, and there was anticipation of companywide early-retirement programs. Survival was the name of the game in the early to mid-1980s. In 1985–1986, change did come and breakthroughs were made. A major cost management program laid the foundation for survival by reducing waste and cost throughout the site. Monsanto withdrew or sold part of the businesses at Pensacola. The downsizing of research and development and early-retirement programs became a reality with a significant reduction in staff and hourly jobs. Total head-count reduction across the site was about 33 percent with a 50 percent reduction in supervisory ranks (mostly due to the early-retirement programs). On the positive side, the Pensacola site was chosen as the site for the first full-scale manufacturing of a major new product for Monsanto—Santoprene.

The above story was being repeated in all the Fibers Division plants. They had survived the turmoil, but Don Bell, the Fibers Division general manager of manufacturing at the time, knew that major productivity improvements were necessary to ensure long-term survival. He challenged plant managers to improve productivity by 50 percent and to achieve a 65 percent cost reduction in quality control. This was the catalyst for the integrated manufacturing strategy known as the *plant of the 1990s*. Each of the three components of the plant of the 1990s—improved technology, employee participation, and total quality—had a separate origin, but as they came into being, their integration became essential.

Total Quality

The *total quality* process was initiated by Robert Potter, president of the Monsanto Chemical Group. He challenged Monsanto to become "the best of the best." Pensacola, like the other plants within the company, started the process with a renewed initiative to educate all employees in the philosophy, concepts, and tools of total quality. The cornerstone of the total quality process is a commitment to continuous improvement. A broad-based total quality education instilled this concept while providing employees in all functions with the necessary tools: problem-solving methods, statistical process control, experimental design, and a 10-step process for project-by-project quality improvement. In time over 100 quality improvement teams in manufacturing, accounting, purchasing, shipping, and engineering contributed in excess of $5 million in productivity and quality benefits.

Employee Participation

The Pensacola plant has always had a positive employee relations program in terms of job conditions, safety, pay, and benefits. However, in the mid-1980s the plant still relied more on the hourly employees' physical contributions than on their ideas. To effectively compete in today's markets, total employee participation was necessary. In 1985, Pensacola began to adopt a new approach to employee involvement that included work design teams to address the reorganization needed after the reduction of first-line supervision. These teams were given information on various aspects of the business such as maintenance, sampling, and manufacturing costs. They were trained in interpersonal interaction, supported with engineering and other services, and assisted by dedicated and trained team leaders. The work design teams together with plant management transformed the plant organization and management style. Today, many of the manufacturing units operate with self-managed work teams. For example, the chemical laboratory prior to 1985 operated four shifts with a supervisor per shift. Today this laboratory operates the same four shifts with self-managed work teams. Likewise, entire manufacturing units operate the evening and weekend shifts with no direct supervision. Self-managed work teams conduct new employee interviews, determine shift assignments, and are beginning to deal with peer reviews. In 1992 an important step was reached in employee involvement when all hourly employees became salary nonexempt. The plant is moving from the very traditional management hierarchy with multiple classes of employees toward a team-based management style.

Supporting the total quality process and employee participation thrusts is the third element of the plant of the 1990s—computer-integrated manufacturing.

Background on the CIM Planning Process

In 1985 management established the Fibers Division CIM task force composed of plant and division staff representatives with the mission to develop a generic model of the plant of the 1990s. This generic model became the guide for each plant's own specific plans. The task force developed a vision for each plant organization, addressing both technological and organizational issues. Figure 18.2 illustrates the generic model for the production or manufacturing function.

From the very beginning, the need to integrate technology and employee participation was evident. On the technology front, the model outlined the types of technologies that the organization would be employing in the 1990s and beyond, while on the organizational front, the model outlined the elements that would constitute the organizational structure. Several consistent themes emerged from the model. Technology would emphasize networking, real-time information access, and ease of use. The organizational themes were to align service and support groups with product line manufacturing and to establish central groups for specialized skills. Once the generic model was developed, each plant organized its own task force to tailor the model to its own cultural and technological circumstances. The

Figure 18.2   Plant of the 1990s.

TECHNOLOGY

Plant-wide, Fully Integrated Data Base
Plant Production Models (e.g., Utilities)
Closed Loop Process Control
Real-Time Cost Control

ORGANIZATION

Integration of Service Functions into Production
Consolidated Control Rooms

Figure 18.3   Production, typical generic model.

Pensacola plant organized its CIM task force within the larger framework of the plant of the 1990s, and so it became one of four operating committees under the auspices of the plant of the 1990s steering committee (Fig. 18.3).

The plant of the 1990s steering committee consisted of the plant manager's staff and the R&D manager. It provided overall direction to each of the four operating committees; namely, CIM, improved technology, total quality, and employee participation. The CIM committee was headed by the superintendent of information and systems technology. The membership of the committee was representative of all plant functions, namely, engineering, process technology, manufacturing, accounting, and quality assurance. This representation ensured wide acceptance and support of the committee's plans as well as a broad source of ideas.

The CIM Committee Work

The mission of the CIM committee was

- To develop a single consolidated plan for all automation projects
- To identify the top automation projects and the critical path for implementation
- To identify capital requirements that should be incorporated in the business long-range plan
- To support and "champion" key CIM projects

The CIM committee conducted a survey of the state of automation and information services on the site. The results of the survey were mapped into the typical CIM pyramid (Fig. 18.4):

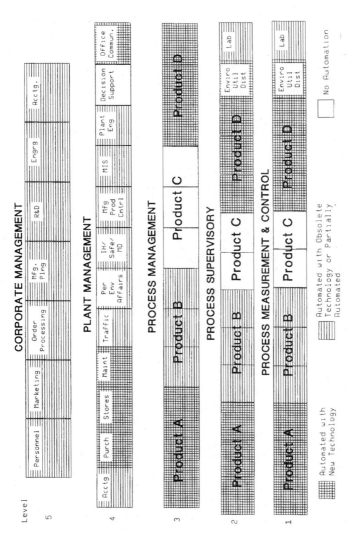

Figure 18.4 Automation opportunities.

Level 1:   Process measurement and control

Level 2:   Process supervisory

Level 3:   Process management

Level 4:   Plant management

Level 5:   Corporate management

Systems were categorized according to their level of automation and the age of the technology employed:

1. Automated with new technology 3 years or less—limited opportunity for improvement

2. Automated or partially automated with outdated technology—high potential opportunity for improvement

3. Not automated—substantial opportunities for improvement

The committee examined the state of available technologies and outlined emerging technologies that deserved to be investigated such as expert systems, distributed databases, robotics, bar coding, etc. It became evident that if integration were to be a reality, certain guidelines or standards had to be established for computer platforms, software, and vendors. As a result, primary vendors and software were selected as "preferred" for the Pensacola plant.

With all this preparatory work accomplished, the CIM committee began to identify projects and strategies. It met with additional plant organization representatives to identify areas of opportunities and needs for integration. A series of brainstorming meetings yielded over 800 automation ideas that were eventually consolidated to 80 key integration programs or initiatives (Fig. 18.5). These were prioritized according to need. Many of CIM building block projects have been

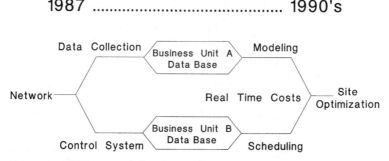

Figure 18.5 CIM proposed planning guide.

implemented while some are currently under way. Some of these are highlighted below.

Plant Network

At the top of the CIM project list was the plant network. In 1985 the Pensacola plant had about 30 Digital Equipment Corp. minicomputers and over 300 terminals. Communication between computers was point-to-point, and for the most part terminals were directly connected to them. This environment limited access to computers and limited data sharing between applications on different computers. If the integration of information were to take place, it was essential that any application be able to share data with any other application that needed them, regardless of the platform on which they resided. In 1986 a $1 million project was approved to install a sitewide local-area network. Management recognized that the local-area network was a key element in achieving CIM and consequently provided funding based on the potential benefits of future CIM projects. After bids from several vendors were reviewed, Digital Equipment Corporation was chosen to install an Ethernet-based network with both broadband and baseband components. Seven miles of broadband cable and thirteen miles of baseband cable were installed. Today every computer on the site is connected to the network, and any person with appropriate authorization can access any or all systems on the network by using a terminal or personal computer (Fig. 18.6). Presently with over 500 personal computers and another equal number of terminals and more

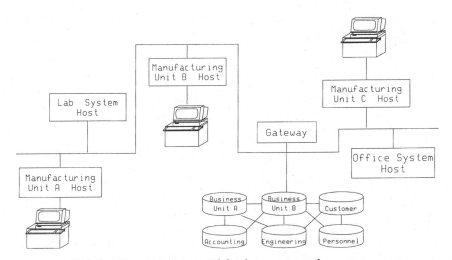

Figure 18.6 Distributed control system and database on network.

than 50 minicomputers, the plant network is approaching its capacity limits. Plans are under way to increase capacity and to enhance its connectivity to the overall enterprise network.

Process Automation

The second major effort of the CIM committee was to support process automation. Like many other process industry plants, Pensacola has employed process automation to ensure a safe and reliable operation. However, in the 1980s and 1990s, the market demanded significant quality and productivity improvements for which the pneumatic control devices of the previous decades were no longer adequate. In 1983 Pensacola had entered the distributed control system (DCS) era with the installation of Fisher's distributed control system ProVOX. In 1986 the CIM committee reaffirmed this commitment to distributed control systems, and over the next 4 years several projects were submitted and approved to automate the process of each major operating area. Individual projects were championed by manufacturing unit management and supported by the CIM committee. Projects were submitted on the basis of quality and yield improvements, energy cost reduction, and labor savings. Savings from these projects exceeded $10 million annually. Significantly more benefits were gained in improved productivity. The distributed control systems started with process automation, but in time advisory and supervisory control systems have been added. More recently the plant has been addressing the functional integration of process supervisory control and laboratory systems, and advanced control strategies. While process automation was under way, other CIM initiatives began in the area of improved factory data collection, office automation, product distribution, and manufacturing databases.

Office Automation

In 1984 the Pensacola plant had implemented an office automation system that included a mainframe computer-based electronic mail system and 50 personal computers for secretarial and professional use. By 1985, the plant had learned a great deal about electronic mail and personal computers. The system needed to be part of the existing plant computer architecture in order to provide broad access to its functions. Word processing was a success, but the uses of personal computers had been underestimated. If the CIM vision of providing wide access to information were to become a reality, the scope of office automation had to be broadened. The tools of office automation had to be made available to all professionals as well as to the clerical employees. With the new plant network installed, it became possible to install a more versatile electronic mail system and to expand the personal-computer base.

The new office automation strategy combined the use of Digital Equipment's All-In-One system with personal computers. Access to office systems functions was provided to anyone with a need. Today over 60 percent of plant personnel have access to electronic mail and the other systems available under All-In-One. More importantly, the system has grown from its "office automation" boundaries to a plantwide communication and information integration tool. For example, today one application developed under All-In-One integrates the customer services functions located in the Atlanta office with the plant quality assurance functions providing electronic feedback on product performance from field operation to manufacturing. The complete cycle of customer service is supported by tracking customer problems, test production, and corrective action. In manufacturing, another All-In-One application provides electronic notification of production scheduling changes throughout manufacturing and in the future will be integrating product specifications with production recording and laboratory applications.

Manufacturing Databases

Since the Pensacola site hosts several Monsanto businesses with their own distinct processes, product configurations, and business priorities, it was decided that manufacturing databases would be aligned around product or business units. Experience had taught us that change was inevitable and so systems had to be designed for ease of change. From a systems viewpoint, this called for a flexible relational database platform.

The first manufacturing database effort encountered a number of challenges from which much was learned. The relational technology curve is quite steep; time must be allowed to educate technical personnel on tools and concepts. Sufficient effort must be expended to obtain adequate support from manufacturing. The successful database projects have customer support, as evidenced by the high client participation in prototyping and testing of the systems. Indeed, the project leader is generally a client representative. To overcome the learning curve, Pensacola has employed outside consultants and extensive training.

Finally, the first project must be a manageable size. After paying its dues, Pensacola has been able to develop and implement several manufacturing database projects. Every major product line has its own database integrating information and functions from the production floor, inventory, quality assurance, and shipping.

The Future of CIM at Pensacola

In 1990 the CIM committee commissioned Digital Equipment Corporation to review the state of the CIM plan and to make recommendations for the future. Over a 3-month period, all the plant's functions, departments, and groups were interviewed in the context of a workshop environment.

Information from these workshops, together with interviews with the management staff and CIM committee, was used to understand the business mission and objectives. The current state of integration was determined by reviewing the existing plant information architecture including hardware and software. The study recognized the progress that CIM has made at Pensacola at the same time that it pointed out deficiencies and the need for further work. The study highlighted several systems that still existed as loosely connected "islands of automation" with limited integration. It recommended the use of industry standards that go beyond the original CIM standards for common user interfaces, software, and decision support tools. An investment portfolio (Fig. 18.7) for the next 5 years outlined key CIM efforts, and an economic model identified the cost and benefits to be achieved from each investment. A conceptual model of the integrated manufacturing environment was proposed along with top-level models for the integration of each manufacturing function (Fig. 18.8). One such model, the total quality management system (TQMS), is discussed below.

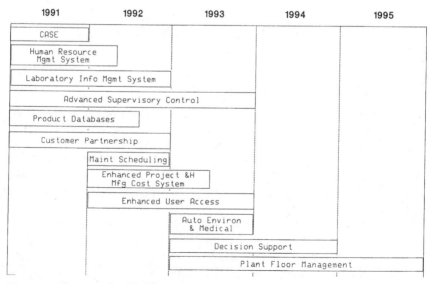

Figure 18.7 Integrated manufacturing system, proposed implementation plan.

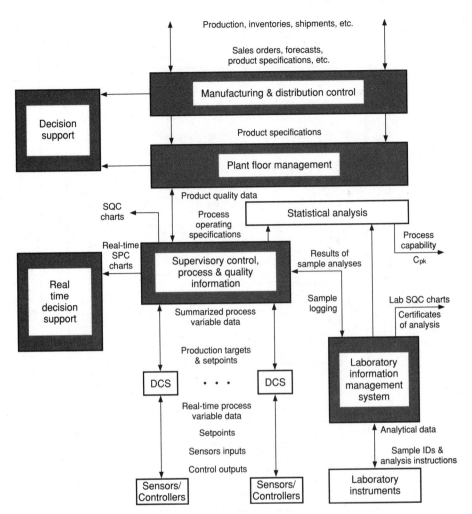

Figure 18.8 Integrated TQM system.

Total Quality Management System

The *total quality management system* (TQMS) brings together the manufacturing and support functions through the integration of process control, laboratory, and decision support (Fig. 18.9). TQMS consists of a *supervisory control system* (SCS) receiving real-time data from the *distributed control system* (DCS). It uses an expert system to determine when samples need to be pulled based on schedule, batch completion, or exception conditions that may result. The supervisory system electronically notifies or logs in samples to the *laboratory*

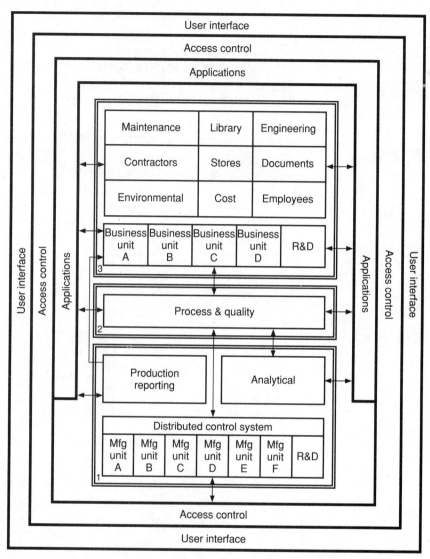

Figure 18.9 Integrated manufacturing system, proposed conceptual data model.

information management system (LIMS), which in turn prints sample labels in the appropriate location and, when necessary, notifies laboratory personnel that there has been a change in the sample schedule. LIMS also notifies the supervisory control system upon receipt of the sample in the laboratory. The SCS notifies the chemical control room operator that the sample is "in progress" and provides the operator with the ability to continue to monitor the sample status throughout the laboratory without leaving the SCS.

When the appropriate analyses are completed, LIMS sends the result to the SCS and to the appropriate manufacturing and decision support databases to produce certificates of analysis and production histories. Process engineers and supervision are alerted by the supervisory control system or LIMS via the office system when results indicate that the process is not in statistical control. As required, the engineer can access the SCS, the decision and analysis support systems, or any other system through the engineer's workstation, which provides a common user interface. In the meantime, the real-time decision support expert system continues to monitor the numerous process and quality parameters. When it detects that the process is back in statistical control, the expert system notifies the operator, engineers, and LIMS that sampling should be returned to normal schedule. This integrated TQMS will provide more timely feedback of information to enable a proactive approach to operations management; a consistent means to use tools and information for process troubleshooting and deviation analysis; accurately identify samples associated with process conditions; and keep accurate records of all production parameters for subsequent customer support.

The benefits of this integrated system were identified to be $550,000 to $6,800,000 annually in yield, quality, and professional productivity. In 1990, the first steps toward the realization of TQMS were taken with the approval of a project to install a LIMS and the adoption and acquisition of SAS for one of the analysis tools; and work was started on the selection of a supervisory control system and a real-time decision support system. Several components of this TQMS have been implemented since 1991.

Challenges for the Future

The Monsanto Pensacola plant has come a long way in its CIM efforts. As the CIM effort continues to unfold, it continues to encounter many challenges. One challenge is how to maintain the momentum of CIM and the support needed in an ever-changing team-based organization. Thus far the impact on the CIM effort has been favorable, but as the key players change roles, particularly as new personnel are brought into the decision-making process, there is a need to enroll these people in the CIM vision. The CIM vision is currently being maintained by the individual project teams. For example, the LIMS project from its early stage has had a high degree of involvement from the user and owner community. User design teams are called upon to contribute to systems design, validation, and implementation. These user design teams are most important for dealing with the sociotechnical issues that undoubtedly arise (see

Mumford, 1983). We have already learned that the productivity benefits of CIM are enhanced when work redesign and organizational issues are incorporated into the CIM projects.

As the employee participation process develops, operators will broaden their job responsibilities; and as additional information technologies are implemented, new challenges will be faced in the area of human factors. Information and decision support tools must be integrated within the operator's job structure and must employ appropriate human-interface elements that integrate distributed control, supervisory control, laboratory information, and decision support systems, as well as radio and telephone communication.

It is now becoming clearer that CIM does not stop at the plant boundaries. The potential for improved market response time, customer relations, and product quality cannot be achieved without the integration of the plant with the business enterprise. Daily decisions in marketing, production scheduling, inventory management, and material resource planning are made at the business level. Many of today's enterprise systems that support these functions are loosely interfaced with plant systems. Integrating plant systems with the enterprise is the next challenge of CIM. This effort will require broad cross-functional cooperation and consequently the need for enterprisewide teams. Once again we are seeing that CIM must be integrated with organizational changes.

Trademarks

Vydyne is a trademark of Monsanto Company.

Santoprene is a trademark of Advanced Elastomers Systems, L.P.

ProVOX is a trademark of Fisher Controls International.

All-In-One is a trademark of Digital Equipment Corporation.

References

Monsanto Company (1987): *Computer Integrated Manufacturing Plan,* June 9.
Monsanto Company and Digital Equipment Corporation (1990): *Integrated Manufacturing Systems Strategy,* July.
Mumford, Enid (1983): *Designing Human Systems,* Manchester Business School, England.

Glossary

Advanced Control   The simultaneous regulation of more than one process variable at a time either to meet a set point, which may be a limit or a target, or to maximize or minimize some process function. Economic optimization of a process can be included. Numerous complex control techniques are also covered by the term, such as multivariable predictive model control, inferential control, constraint control, and adaptive control.

Available to Promise (ATP)   In customer order handling, the determination of date when product sufficient to fill the order will be available.

Cascade   In process control, a configuration in which a controller output is used as the set point of another controller.

Constraint   A limit, such as a maximum tank volume, a maximum furnace wall temperature, or a minimum road octane number in a blend of gasoline. Constraints can be physical equipment limits, quality specifications, or even market limits set by product price or demand.

Control   The second-by-second regulation of a process variable to a predefined set point. But the term also can include the economic optimization of a process within the context of an optimum plan and schedule.

Correlation   An equation or relationship, linear or nonlinear, that predicts the value of a dependent variable from the values of one or more independent variables.

Data Communications   The transfer of data between computers or between computers and terminals attached to computers. Data are usually in the form of 8-bit bytes, or groups of bytes called *packets*. Data transfer speeds can range from 1200 bits/s to over 1.5 million bits/s. The data are physically transferred over electrical conductors such as telephone lines and coaxial cable or by fiber-optic cable. Data communications also takes place over microwave and lower-frequency radio transmissions.

Deadtime   The elapsed time between a change in an operating parameter and the response of the process to the change.

Empirical Relying on practical experience, observations, or experiments, without regard to theory or fundamental knowledge.

Expert System A computer program that is able to perform within a limited domain, field, or application area at the level of a human expert in that domain. Rule-based expert systems are made up of a knowledge base and an inference engine. The knowledge base consists of facts and rules, which are "If...and...or...then...else" structures. The inference engine provides the reasoning function that works through the rules and facts of the knowledge base to arrive at conclusions.

Feedforward Modification of a process controller set point in anticipation of an imminent change in process characteristics measured by an independent sensor.

Fourth-Generation Language The fourth generation of programming languages used to create computer programs, e.g., the SQL language for accessing database systems. The first three generations were machine language, assembly language, and compiled languages, such as FORTRAN or C.

Horizon The total time period over which a planning or scheduling study is concerned. For example, if a planning model run is made for the next month, it is said that the planning horizon is 1 month.

Integration Automation of the transfer of information between functions so that they may be effectively coordinated.

Knowledge Worker Person whose job requires special knowledge pertaining to the specific job performed.

Linear Equation An equation such as $AX + BY = Z$, where A and B are constants and X, Y, and Z are variables. A plot of Z versus X will be a straight line (i.e., a linear relationship) with a slope equal to A.

Linear Programming A method for finding the values for a set of independent variables that maximize or minimize a linear objective equation involving the variables, subject to an additional set of equations that must be satisfied, known as *constraints*. The number of variables exceeds the number of equations, so the set is not determined. The original solution technique was known as the *simplex method* and was invented by George B. Dantzig in 1947.

Mathematical Model Generally, a computer program that responds to input data and operating conditions in the same way as the real process and predicts the outputs and behavior of the process.

Mathematical Programming The general subject matter of optimization of an arbitrary objective subject to arbitrary constraints.

Nonlinear Equations As opposed to linear, *nonlinear* means that a plot of one variable against another results in a curve rather than a straight line.

Nonlinear Optimization The nonlinear counterpart of linear programming wherein the objective or the constraints or both are nonlinear equations. Many methods exist, such as successive linear programming, successive quadratic programming, and various gradient techniques.

Object Orientation   Data grouped as an object, rather than data as individual items. For example, a complete set of data from a process taken at a given time is an object. A complete description of an activity on a facility is an object. The entire contents of a pull-down menu on a video terminal are an object. Object-oriented software development incorporates the concepts of data encapsulation, inheritance, and object identity. This approach has been implemented in languages and extensions to languages, such as C++.

Open Systems   Systems that either use standard procedures for access or data transmission or use clearly documented procedures so that unrelated systems can gain access. This is opposed to closed systems in which access and data transmission protocols are unpublished and proprietary.

Paradigm   The way some activity is performed. For example, the way customer orders are handled and production of the order is scheduled is the paradigm for the order handling and scheduling process.

Planning   The forecasting of the average performance of a plant (a collection of interconnected processes) over some specified time, such as a month or year. The act of planning results in a plan which specifies, again on the average, what inputs are needed and how plant inputs are going to be used to produce the plant outputs. The plan usually includes forecasts of the values of individual process performance parameters such as yields, product qualities, flow rates, temperatures, and pressures.

Plant   Also called a *refinery,* or *petrochemical plant,* a plant is a collection of interconnected processes designed to produce commodity or consumer products from crude oil or crude chemical feedstocks.

Process   Sometimes called a *process plant,* a process is composed of equipment designed to perform one or more chemical engineering unit operations. These are the distillation columns, heat exchangers, reactors, pumps, and other operations required to produce certain products from certain input feedstocks. A group of processes is called a *plant, refinery,* or *petrochemical plant.*

Propagation   In neural networks, the application of an object to the network (the calculation of the network for one set of data).

Proportional, Integral, Derivative (PID)   The fundamental output law for a process controller. The output signal is proportional to the error between measurement and set point, to the integral of the error over time, and to the derivative of the error value.

Protocol   In data communications, the specific structure of blocks or packets of data sent on the communications network. TCP/IP and X.25 are common protocols in use.

Punch List   In project implementation, a list of problems discovered during the implementation process.

Recursion   In linear programming applications, the repeated resolving of the optimization after modifying the matrix on the basis of an examination of the intermediate optimum solutions.

Regulatory Control   The adjustment of a single manipulated variable to meet a set point. The objective of the adjustment is usually steady, stable operation and safety. The manipulated variable usually corresponds to a control value.

Scheduling The specification of the inputs to and outputs from each process and inventory, and the timing and sequencing of each production operation over some short scheduling period, such as 1 week or 10 days. Although the horizon is 1 week or 10 days, today's operation is the most important. Operations are not averaged over the scheduling period; rather time and operations move continuously from the beginning of the period to the end. Ideally, the schedule is revised each day as needed so that it always starts from what is actually happening.

Simulation (or Process Simulation) Representation of a process with a mathematical model or a group of connected mathematical models. A sequential modular simulation calculates through the models one at a time, following the process flow for the most part. An equation-based simulator solves all models simultaneously. A *Monte Carlo* simulation is the repeated calculation of a simulation by using input values randomly selected from a distribution of values, for the purpose of determining expected levels of performance over the long term.

Supply Chain The chain of functions and operations from customer order to delivery of the ordered product.

Transformation Method In physical property blending, component properties are transformed by some calculation procedure, based on the component property alone, to an index which can be a volume fraction or weight fraction averaged. The blend property is then calculated from the index by an exact reverse calculation procedure.

Transmission Control Protocol/Internet Protocol (TCP/IP) One of the most widely used data communications protocols.

UNIX The name of a multiuser operating system for computers developed by AT&T. UNIX is a trademark of AT&T.

Windup In process control, the continual change in the output signal of a controller due to the controller integral action when the error is not responding to controller output.

X-Windows A graphical user interface (GUI) developed by the Massachusetts Institute of Technology (MIT). X-Window Systems is a trademark of MIT.

Index